Over the past two centuries, Japan has undergone Westernization not only in the external realm of material culture and sociopolitical organization, but also in the inner realm of thought and morals. *Modern Japanese Thought* brings together four chapters from Volumes 5 and 6 of the *Cambridge History of Japan*, plus a new Introduction and a chapter on postwar intellectual history. This comprehensive intellectual history describes the forces that made Japanese thinkers both receptive of and hostile to Western ideas and values from the 1770s to the 1990s. The important themes reflected throughout the book are: the potential of Western knowledge to discredit as well as bolster the existing order; and the perennial tension between indigenous and alien, traditional and modern, and rulers and ruled in Tokugawa, imperial and postwar Japan. More specific topics include: Japan's turn to the West from the medium of books in late Tokugawa to that of direct contact in Meiji; the Meiji Enlightenment and enthusiasm for Westernization; the mid-Meiji conservative reaction; socialism and nationalism in the prewar years; the shock of defeat and the growth of democracy since 1945.

Modern Japanese thought

MODERN JAPANESE THOUGHT

Edited by

BOB TADASHI WAKABAYASHI

York University, Toronto

CAMBRIDGE
UNIVERSITY PRESS

PUBLISHED BY THE PRESS SYNDICATE OF THE UNIVERSITY OF CAMBRIDGE
The Pitt Building, Trumpington Street, Cambridge CB2 1RP, United Kingdom

CAMBRIDGE UNIVERSITY PRESS
The Edinburgh Building, Cambridge CB2 2RU, United Kingdom
40 West 20th Street, New York, NY 10011-4211, USA
10 Stamford Road, Oakleigh, Melbourne 3166, Australia

First published 1998

Printed in the United States of America

Typeset in Plantin

Library of Congress Cataloging-in-Publication Data
Modern Japanese thought / edited by Bob Tadashi Wakabayashi.
p.   cm.
Includes bibliographical references and index.
ISBN 0-521-58810-3 (pbk.). – ISBN 0-521-58218-0 (bound)
1. Japan – Intellectual life – 1868–   . I. Wakabayashi, Bob Tadashi.
DS822.25.M63   1997
953.02'3 – dc21   96-40358
                                                         CIP

*A catalog record for this book is available from
the British Library.*

ISBN 0 521 58218 0 hardback
ISBN 0 521 58810 3 paperback

CONTENTS

ACKNOWLEDGMENTS

I am responsible for all shortcomings in this book, but I wish to thank the following persons for their kind help in producing it. Professor Marius Jansen first approached me with the idea of editing this volume, and he warmly encouraged me to overcome deep-seated inhibitions about taking on the task. Throughout this project, he displayed his legendary graciousness and tolerance for differences of opinion. I thank the authors of Chapters 2 through 6 for their patience in the face of production delays, and beg their pardon if any untoward editorial changes were made to their work. As many readers will discern, I owe huge scholarly debts to Professors Ienaga Saburō and Matsumoto Sannosuke for much of Chapter 1. The following colleagues and friends – and I hope no one is overlooked – kindly sent me needed source materials from Japan: Watanabe Hiroshi, Eizawa Kōji, Awaya Kentarō, Igarashi Akio, Honda Itsuo, Yoshida Toshizumi, Suzuki Masayuki, Hirayama Kazuhiko, Kitaoka Shin'ichi, Janice Matsumura, Clark Taber, Liu Pik-Chun, and Motohara Akiko. Barry Shikatani and Morisada Kazuhiro provided technical assistance with the computer. Finally, due credit should go to Elizabeth Neal of Cambridge University Press as well as to Eric Newman and Rosalie Herion Freese for their painstaking efforts in bringing a difficult manuscript to print.

B.T.W.

CHAPTER 1
INTRODUCTION
BOB TADASHI WAKABAYASHI

Perhaps all developing societies since the Industrial Revolution are fated to undergo Westernization. Japan certainly did. After opening their land under pressure from Perry and Harris in the 1850s, the Japanese adopted Western ways not only in the outer realm of material culture and political forms but also in the inner realm of thought, spirit, and values. Today, Western sociopolitical ideals are so compelling that most Japanese would refuse to live by the pre-1945 imperial ethos. Thus democracy, individual freedom, egalitarianism, pacifism, and the rule of law to uphold basic human rights can be violated only by devious means and over public protest. Yet none of those ideals derived from Japanese or East Asian tradition; all originated in the modern West. Very few present-day Japanese would applaud an act of disembowelment. Fewer still would approve of police torture used to extract confessions. And virtually no one would tolerate a form of slavery whereby a father may sell his daughters into legalized prostitution – while filial piety enjoins them to submit meekly if not cheerfully. However, the Japanese would not have disowned these former folkways without the benefit of Western example, influence, or compulsion. Today, Japanese leftists condemn, and government leaders are obliged to deplore, war crimes and atrocities committed before 1945. But here too, most of those deeds can be deemed "criminal" or "atrocious" only when judged against the ethical standards that Western societies developed. This drastic refashioning of thought and values has not been an easy or straightforward process – many Japanese, often in positions of political authority, have obstructed it. It is this clash between native and alien, traditional and modern, rulers and ruled, that serves as the unifying theme for this book. We have taken the following four chapters from volumes 5 and 6 of the *Cambridge History of Japan*, and we commissioned the sixth chapter on postwar intellectual trends especially for this project.

PRAGMATIC RECEPTIVITY, 1774–1889

Japan received its higher culture from China for most of the past two millennia; and from the West, only in the last two centuries. To embrace this new Western culture as advanced, the Japanese first had to reject time-honored Eastern learning as backward, and the 1774 translation of *Ontleedkundige tafelen* (also known as *Tafel Anatomia*) symbolizes this changed attitude. Sugita Genpaku and his colleagues checked organs from an exhumed corpse against the diagrams in this Western text, found these to be more accurate than those in medical classics reputedly written by the ancient sages, and began a tradition of translation and lexicography that continues to this day. As Hirakawa Sukehiro notes in Chapter 2, these fields of study presumed a keen desire to learn from the West and made that endeavor easier for later generations. Sugita's "practical learning," based on a spirit of skepticism and empiricism, spread to more sensitive areas where an accurate grasp of world conditions discredited key ideas and institutions that upheld the old order. For example, in 1838, Mito daimyo Tokugawa Nariaki argued that to engage in foreign trade would squander precious resources on worthless luxury goods. He believed that "Japan is a small island country, but it brims with rice, gold, and silver; so of course other lands envy our wealth."[1] Such economic views were "common sense" in that day. People presumed that foreigners sought trade because they coveted Japan's abundant riches. Since Japan enjoyed these in a "natural" state of seclusion, or *sakoku*, there was no need to seek more through trade or conquest overseas. As Confucian moralists such as Kaibara Ekken had always preached, all would be fine if each of the four classes would be content with its status and share of wealth as allotted by Heaven (*chisoku anbun*).[2] Feudal leaders suppressed the people's desires for higher living standards at home and rejected expansion abroad through fatalistic precepts of resignation and providential plenitude. But Western

1 Yoshikawa Keizō, ed., *Mitohan shiryō: bekki jō* (Tokyo: Yoshikawa kōbunkan 1970), pp. 93–7.
2 See, for example, *Rakkun* in Ekken kai, ed., *Ekken zenshū* (Tokyo: Kokusho kankōkai, 1973), vol. 3, pp. 612–14. Kano Masanao stresses this *chisoku anbun* idea in *Shihonshugi keiseiki no chitsujo ishiki* (Tokyo: Chikuma shobō, 1969), pp. 50–1 and 55–64.

learning impugned the worth of these precepts and policies by exposing Japan's true position in the world. As a result, *sakoku* lost cogency and Western doctrines of imperialism and colonialism gained sway. Common sense by Meiji times told the Japanese that their land was small and dirt-poor. So they, like the British, would have to seek wealth and resources overseas – either through trade or conquest.

This practical Western learning subverted established authority in political and military affairs too. The Japanese daimyo and samurai gloried in martial prowess, esteemed victory over culture, and viewed their land as "the divine realm" whose emperor was descended from Sun Goddess Amaterasu. Such sentiments might quickly evolve into nationalism. Even before the Opium War of 1840–2, Tokugawa Nariaki asserted: "All previous wars took place in Japan between Japanese, so victory or defeat did not matter. But if one inch of soil or one person in Japan ever fell subject to a foreign state, the national disgrace would be huge."[3] To prevent that, he called for adopting Western ways to a surprising if limited extent. He introduced milk drinking and smallpox vaccinations, and he demanded that a battlefleet be built according to Western techniques because "flimsy Japanese boats make poor warships."[4] After hearing of British victories in the Opium War, bakufu advisor Sakuma Shōzan declared that Western power – not Eastern moral culture – determined world affairs. Foreigners threatened Japan's imperial line "unbroken for a hundred reigns." Here was a menace "to the entire divine realm and everyone born in it not just the Tokugawa house."[5] After Satsuma and Chōshū lost to Western armed forces in 1863 and 1864, the slogan "revere the emperor, expel the barbarians" became "revere the emperor, emulate Western civilization." Thereafter, reformers overthrew the Tokugawa bakufu and launched a crash program of cultural borrowing under imperial court aegis. Indeed, the Meiji emperor decreed that Japan should "seek knowledge throughout the world" and "abolish evil practices from the past." Sugita's private endeavor had become official state policy.

Unlike contemporary Ch'ing self-strengtheners, Meiji Japanese reformers did not just buy the outward products of Western civiliza-

---

3 Yoshikawa Keizō, ed., *Mitohan shiryō: bekki jō*, p. 97.
4 Ibid., *Bekki ge*, pp. 226 and 231.
5 Shinano kyōikukai, ed., *Shōzan zenshū* (Tokyo: Meiji bunken, 1975), vol. 2, p. 31. See also Matsumoto Sannosuke, *Tennōsei kokka to seiji shisō* (Tokyo: Miraisha, 1969), pp. 84–94.

tion, such as guns, trains, and ships, in ready-made form. Their real goal was to master the inner "spirit" of that civilization – the principles that Westerners used to invent those products. Indeed, Fukuzawa Yukichi often glossed the old term "practical learning" (*jitsugaku*) as "science." This civilization and its spirit were valid and applicable everywhere. Westerners may have discovered these first, but any people could catch up. Moreover, the Meiji state fostered capitalistic development to launch a Japanese industrial revolution. Japan amassed capital and technical expertise to build guns, trains, and ships in the *Self-Help* manner of Samuel Smiles. Unorthodox ideas abounded. On paper if not totally in fact, the new regime tolerated Christianity, ended polygamy, prohibited discrimination based on class or occupation, and abolished cruel punishments.[6] Mori Arinori suggested adopting English as the nation's official language. Many thinkers ate meat, and a few sought to marry Westerners, in order to "improve the Japanese race."[7] In the main, Enlightenment (*bummei kaika*) thinkers called for upholding freedom of speech, assembly, and belief, and they affirmed the open clash of ideas as bringing progress. In 1875, Katō Hiroyuki declared that "the emperor is human and the people (*jinmin*) too are human";[8] and Nishimura Shigeki contended that "it is just as bigoted to label someone who 'opposes the imperial court' a 'traitor' as it is to call foreign states 'barbarian.' "[9] Thus deviation from the imperial will did not constitute treason.

Actually, Enlightenment figures acted from nationalism as much as from a genuine respect for Western civilization. In an age when a future prime minister might kill his wife in a drunken rage,[10] Fukuzawa confessed: "As you know, I've always been a heavy drinker. But lately I've been reading Western books and thinking

6 For example, actual prison conditions showed no improvement over Tokugawa times. See Yoshida Shōin's description of an Edo jail and his proposals for reform in Yamaguchi-ken kyōikukai, ed., *Yoshida Shōin zenshū* (Tokyo: Iwanami shoten, 1939), vol. 2, pp. 268–308. Compare this with Baba Tatsui's 1887 exposé of Meiji prison conditions published in an American newspaper, "In a Japanese Cage," in Meiji bunka kenkyūkai, ed., *Meiji bunka zenshū: Jiyū minken hen (zoku) bessatsu* (Tokyo: Nihon hyōronsha, 1968), pp. 29–33.

7 In March 1883, a certain Takahashi Yoshio advocated intermarriage with Westerners, and Katō Hiroyuki immediately rebutted that view. See Meiji bunka kenkyūkai, ed., *Meiji bunka zenshū bekkan: Meiji jibutsu kigen* (Tokyo: Nihon hyōronsha, 1969), pp. 109–10.

8 Katō Hiroyuki, "Kokutai shinron," in Yoshino Sakuzō, ed., *Meiji bunka zenshū: Jiyū minken hen* (Tokyo: Nihon hyōronsha, 1927), p. 112.

9 Quoted in Matsumoto Sannosuke, *Meiji shisōshi* (Tokyo: Shin'yōsha, 1996), p. 52.

10 In 1878, Kuroda Kiyotaka committed this act but escaped criminal prosecution due to his government position. See Irokawa Daikichi, *Nihon no rekishi 21: Kindai kokka no shuppatsu* (Tokyo: Chūōkōronsha, 1966), pp. 12–14.

about the meaning of life and work. . . . I now see how shameful drinking is, and limit myself to one or two bottles a night."[11] Yet he might also fume: "Who said whites are civilized? They're beastly white devils. . . . Big-shot ministers and consuls of the civilized British state don't just ignore countrymen who rape [wives of our officials], they aid and protect those criminals, and so oppress our land, Japan."[12] Meiji leaders reformed Japan along Western lines in part from anti-Westernism. Legislation to "abolish evil practices from the past" stemmed from a desire to revise unequal treaties and recover sovereignty. Both the Enlightenment reformers and People's Rights activists linked personal freedom and rights with national autonomy. Without a sense of self-respect, rights, and duties, Japanese commoners would grovel before foreign colonial masters just as they had grovelled before Tokugawa feudal lords. Enlightenment reformers and government leaders, however, saw personal freedom and rights largely as an effective means to achieve and expand state power. By contrast, radical People's Rights thinkers held that individual rights and freedom took precedence over state authority, and that Japan should remain a small-scale power who eschewed empire building in favor of prosperity at home.[13]

As part of the new Westernized view of society, Fukuzawa Yukichi taught that "Heaven does not create some people above or below others." This was not a formula for socioeconomic leveling. He believed that inequalities of wealth and status did and should exist, but Heaven had not created these. So, no one need resign himself to penury and base status fatalistically – as Tokugawa Confucians had preached. Anyone could achieve personal wealth and eminence by diligently pursuing practical Western studies and would thereby further national strength and advancement as well. For the individual in Japan, as for the state of Japan, "rising in the world" (*risshin shusse*) now meant "progress."[14] Later Meiji aggression followed logically, if not inevitably, from this affirmation of "self-help." Enlightenment reformers espoused liberalism in its nineteenth-century laissez-faire sense – coupled with big doses of Social Darwinism.

11 Letter dated 1869, in Keiō gijuku ed., *Fukuzawa Yukichi zenshū* (Tokyo: Iwanami shoten, 1966) vol. 17, pp. 69–70.
12 Letter dated 1875, in ibid., pp. 183–4.
13 See Matsunaga Shōzō, "Jiyūminken-ha ni mirareru shōkokushugi shisō," *Shichō*, no. 89 (October 1964), pp. 56–65.
14 The idea of progress was not wholly lacking in Edo times. See Watanabe Hiroshi, "'Shinpo' to 'Chūka': Nihon no bawai," in Mizoguchi Yūzō et al., eds., *Ajia kara kangaeru 5: Kindaika zō* (Tokyo: Tokyo daigaku shuppankai, 1994), pp. 133–76.

They cast off the shackles of inherited status and demanded freedom for themselves and for Japan to demonstrate ability and to pursue material gain in open competition. Yet the flip side of this demand was that the losers deserved whatever lot befell them. Fukuzawa despised the Chinese and Koreans as poor and backward.[15] In 1883, he argued that "the strong devour the weak," so "we should side with the civilized nations . . . in search of choice morsels."[16] Likewise, he despised destitute Japanese women and suggested that they work in brothels overseas to earn money and benefit Japan.[17] Enlightenment thinkers were tolerant and progressive compared with Tokugawa Confucians and Shōwa fascists. In 1871, Fukuzawa idealistically declared, "We defer to the black slaves of Africa when reason is on their side; we defy the warships of Britain and America when principle is on our side." As Maruyama Masao poignantly noted, "for a beautiful fleeting moment he balanced individual freedom with national autonomy and national autonomy with the equality of nations."[18] But by the 1880s, Fukuzawa would have Japan fortify Korea as a defense bulwark. And, citing Ch'ing self-strengthening efforts after the 1884 Sino-French War, he argued that losing the war actually helped China because it sparked a sense of independence and a desire for self-help.[19] Lost wars provoked backward peoples into accepting civilization and enlightenment – as the 1863 Satsuma and 1864 Chōshū defeats had done for Japan. Thus Fukuzawa justified aggression against the Ch'ing in 1894–5.

Almost all of the Meiji Enlightenment figures were high state officials who bequeathed a mixed legacy. They saw "reform" as embracing universal "world trends" emanating from the West; indeed, they said Japan should "dissociate from Asia" for that reason. And they presumed themselves best able to guide Japan toward

15 One indication is found in his *Autobiography* subheading, "I was as contemptible as a Korean toward my domain." There, he confessed that in his youth he borrowed money with no thought of repaying it: "Just like a Korean, I grubbed after money with no sense of honor or shame." Keiō gijuku ed., *Fukuzawa Yukichi zenshū* (Tokyo: Iwanami shoten, 1966), vol. 7, pp. 210–11. These ethnic references do not appear in Eiichi Kiyooka, trans., *The Autobiography of Yukichi Fukuzawa* (New York: Columbia University Press, 1960), pp. 273–4.
16 *Jiji shinpō* (October 1, 1883). Keiō gijuku ed., *Fukuzawa Yukichi zenshū* (Tokyo: Iwanami shoten, 1966), vol. 9, pp. 195–6.
17 *Jiji shinpō* (January 8, 1896), ibid., vol. 15, pp. 362–4.
18 Maruyama Masao, "Kaidai," in Fukuazawa Yukichi chosaku hensankai, ed., *Fukuzawa Yukichi senshū* (Tokyo: Iwanami shoten, 1952), pp. 414–15.
19 *Jiji shinpō* (January 6, 1887). Keiō gijuku ed., *Fukuzawa Yukichi zenshū* (Tokyo: Iwanami shoten, 1966), vol. 11, p. 177; and *Jiji shinpō* (January 7, 1887), ibid., pp. 178–80.

"civilization." Soon, however, elitism and privileged status blunted their critical spirit. From about 1875, they closed ranks with fellow state officials, muzzled dissidents, retracted their former radical views, and supported the government after it nullified or reversed earlier progressive reforms. For example, despite legislating equality of all classes in 1871, the government ignored persisting discrimination against outcastes and reestablished social inequality by creating a peerage based on imperial ranks in 1884. Moreover, the Enlightenment thinkers' high-handed imposition of Western ways in defiance of native traditions provoked a sharp right-wing reaction by the mid-Meiji period. On the other hand, their nineteenth-century "liberal" form of unbridled capitalism – which told poverty-stricken girls to abandon chastity and homeland – aroused left-wing indignation by the late Meiji period. Yet in their heyday from the 1860s to early 1870s, Enlightenment thinkers carried on the Tokugawa tradition of seeking practical knowledge from the West. They repudiated "blind adherence to [invalidated] old ways" (koshū no wakudeki) and stressed the advanced nature of Western ideas and institutions.[20] In this way, they unwittingly inspired radical People's Rights advocates and socialists whom they later suppressed.[21]

The radical People's Rights leaders Ueki Emori and Nakae Chōmin produced few original ideas. Instead, their significance lay in advancing a radical alternative vision for Meiji Japan that the government promptly quashed. All Japanese, they argued, had been born free and equal but now lived in an unfree and unequal condition because the Meiji state had arbitrarily deprived the people of their original freedom and inalienable rights. Hence the Japanese people had to "reclaim" these actively from below, not wait for the emperor to "bestow" these from on high. Nor should the existing state impose a constitution on the people. They should elect a Diet based on universal suffrage – without restrictions on sex, education, or wealth. The Diet would draft a constitution that defined the form

20 For this positive appraisal, especially of Fukuzawa, see Matsumoto Sannosuke, *Kindai Nihon no chiteki jōkyō* (Tokyo: Chūōkōronsha, 1974), pp. 48–83; and Matsumoto, *Nihon seiji shisōshi gairon* (Tokyo: Keisō shobō, 1975), pp. 56–63. Also Maruyama Masao, "Fukuzawa Yukichi ni okeru 'jitsugaku' no tenkai," in Ishida Takeshi, ed., *Kindai Nihon shisō taikei 2: Fukuzawa Yukichi shū* (Tokyo: Chikuma shobō, 1975), pp. 563–78; Maruyama, "Fukuzawa ni okeru chitsujo to ningen," and "Fukuzawa Yukichi no tetsugaku," both of which are in Hidaka Rokurō, ed., *Gendai Nihon shisō taikei 34: Kindaishugi* (Tokyo: Chikuma shobō, 1964), pp. 55–92; and Maruyama, *Senchū to sengo no aida* (Tokyo: Misuzu shobō, 1976), pp. 93–115.
21 On this "tradition of republicanism," see the classic 1958 study by Ienaga Saburō, "Nihon ni okeru kyōwashugi no dentō," reprinted in Kuno Osamu and Kamishima Jirō, eds., *Tennōsei ronshū* (Tokyo: San'ichi shobō, 1974), pp. 328–42.

of government for a new state and ensured the people's rights and freedom. Then the people would ratify and present this constitution to the government, thereby signifying their consent to live under that state. In sum, Ueki and Nakae advanced theories of popular sovereignty and the social contract so that the Japanese people could create a state designed to serve their own interests.

People's Rights leaders all over Japan were producing draft constitutions for the new state.[22] In 1881, Ueki Emori completed his own draft, Article 1 of which reads: "the nation of Japan is founded on, and shall function in accordance with, this Constitution."[23] Ueki wanted the people to create a constitution that would bind the government to democratic provisions. His draft called for seventy American-style equal, independent "states" (shū) to form a federal government that would observe the division of legislative, executive, and judicial powers. Armed forces would exist solely to defend the Constitution, not to wage foreign wars. Section Four of his draft was a thirty-five-article bill of rights. It provided for protection against torture and capital punishment; for the rights to free speech, assembly, and religious belief; and for the right to disobey and to offer armed resistance to unlawful or unjust state actions. Thus Ueki would empower the Japanese people to overthrow their emperor and government if need be in order to recover their original rights and freedom.[24] Section Five of Ueki's draft listed the functions of an emperor (kōtei, not tennō) whose position as a salaried civil servant with no pretense of divinity derived solely from the constitution. This section came after the people's bill of rights – in contrast to the constitutions of 1889 and 1947 – where the emperor comes first. Taking a line from Fukuzawa, Ueki wrote the lyrics to a popular ballad in 1879: "When Heaven created people, it made them all the same, with none above or below others, and all with equal rights."[25] Yet Ueki took the ideal far further, by crusading for the rights of

22 About forty of these are extant. For a summary of their contents, see Ienaga Saburō, *Rekishi no naka no kenpō, jō* (Tokyo: Tokyo daigaku shuppankai, 1977), pp. 33–51; and Irokawa Daikichi, Ei Hideo, and Arai Katsuhiro, eds., *Minshū kenpō no sōzō* (Tokyo: Hyōronsha, 1970).

23 For a text of this Ueki draft constitution, see Ienaga Saburō, ed., *Ueki Emori senshū* (Tokyo: Iwanami shoten, 1974), pp. 85–111. Most of the following material on Ueki derives from Ienaga, *Kakumei shisō no senkusha* (Tokyo: Iwanami shoten, 1955); and Ienaga, *Ueki Emori kenkyū* (Tokyo: Iwanami shoten, 1960). For a revisionist work from a psychohistorical perspective that also stresses Ueki's debts to traditional Confucian thought, see Yonehara Ken, *Ueki Emori* (Tokyo: Chūōkōronsha, 1992).

24 Ienaga, *Ueki Emori kenkyū*, pp. 279–93; also Ienaga, *Kakumei shisō no senkusha*, p. 105.

25 "Minken inaka uta," in Ienaga, ed., *Ueki Emori senshū*, p. 44.

women and the poor. Although society relegated these groups to its lowest rungs, he said, neither was responsible for its current plight. Ueki turned the existing socioeconomic hierarchy upside-down by arguing that women and the poor, who worked for their daily keep, were more valuable to society than the rich, who idly consumed wealth. He was one of the few non-Christian Meiji Japanese to work actively for abolishing the patriarchal rights that fathers enjoyed over their daughters' labor under legalized prostitution. Finally we should note that, unlike the Enlightenment thinkers, Ueki never traveled abroad and could read no Western languages. He derived his knowledge of Western political thought and institutions solely from Japanese sources. Thus the Tokugawa tradition of lexicography and translation might subvert, as well as bolster, state authority well into Meiji times.

Nakae Chōmin was even more radical than Ueki on many issues excepting women's rights.[26] Nakae eschewed honors and high state office and instead chose to live among the dregs of Meiji society. He dressed as a day laborer. He visited Ainu settlements and denounced exploitive Meiji colonization policies in Hokkaidō. He took up residence in an Ōsaka outcaste slum and represented its constituents in the Diet. Nakae excoriated Tokutomi Sohō and his *heiminishugi* colleagues for refusing to support *full* equality for *all* Japanese commoners. Instead, they reinforced the very class- and culture-bound discrimination that they claimed to be attacking. Following Rousseau's "noble savage" idea, Nakae trumpeted "the nobility of despised persons." He claimed that fringe groups in Japan Okinawans, Ainu, outcastes, and the working poor – displayed a pristine form of liberty, equality, and goodness. As such, they were just as entitled to equal treatment as Tokutomi's upstart "new generation." Nakae supported a "rich state" but claimed that this goal precluded "strong arms." A pacifist, he opposed conscripting a national army and instead favored creating voluntary militia to protect purely local interests. Nakae believed that the universal spirit of civilization lay in liberty, popular sovereignty, and human rights, and he denounced Western practices that violated those ideals. Thus he rejected empire building and argued that Japan should remain a small-scale power who helped neighboring Asian states resist Western colonial takeover. Nakae came to admit the temporary infeasibility of "popularly reclaimed" rights and freedom after the

26 My discussion of Nakae follows Matsunaga Shōzō, *Nakae Chōmin* (Tokyo: Kashiwa shobō, 1967); and Matsunaga, *Nakae Chōmin no shisō* (Tokyo: Aoki shoten, 1970).

government in 1881 pledged to bestow these by granting an imperial constitution from above. Until his death in 1901, he strove to raise the Japanese people's political consciousness so that someday they would revise this "downright stupid" Meiji Constitution into a truly democratic document that enshrined popular sovereignty and protected human rights.

Meiji socialists such as Abe Isō, Kōtoku Shūsui, and Kinoshita Naoe carried on ideas that Enlightenment thinkers first espoused and People's Rights activists later developed. The socialists argued that the vast inequalities in wealth and status that had emerged in Japan were *not* a proper reflection of individual merit and effort as proven under fair, free market conditions. Instead, as Peter Duus and Irwin Scheiner discuss in Chapter 4, Meiji socialists insisted that huge government-linked monopolies perpetuated and exacerbated those inequalities, and they believed that this situation was unhealthy for both individuals and the nation as a whole. They proposed limiting private ownership and employing it for the public good.[27] By contrast, men like Fukuzawa Yukichi insisted that the ever-widening schism between haves and have-nots reflected progress and civilization. His main concern late in life was to keep the have-nots from destroying these goals that he had devoted his life to furthering. To that end, he argued for Meiji state leaders to exploit the opiate of religion, he urged the rich to aid charities, and he proposed ridding Japan of paupers through emigration. Above all, he argued against educating the illiterate poor for fear of what a little bit of learning would do to hungry rabble-rousers.[28] As Kenneth Pyle shows in Chapter 3, government officials and capitalist leaders chose to defuse malcontent at home by implementing Bismarckian social reform policies. And the Meiji state itself launched foreign wars of aggression on the road to great-power status – thereby whipping up patriotic sentiment to neutralize criticism and forestall social upheaval.

INTELLECTUAL RETROGRESSION, 1889–1945

A pragmatic receptivity to Western thought and values grew up from Tokugawa to mid-Meiji times. But then the Japanese seemed to

---

27 Matsumoto Sannosuke, *Meiji seishin no kōzō* (Tokyo: Nihon hōsō kyōkai shuppankai, 1981), pp. 170–6.
28 For one of the earliest and best discussions of Fukuzawa's later thought, see Ienaga Saburō, *Kindai seishin to sono genkai* (Tokyo: Kadokawa shoten, 1950), pp. 171–205.

withdraw inward, just when opportunities for learning from abroad were greatest. For one thing, treaty revision was largely over by 1899, so external pressure for Westernization fell off. Equally important, the imperial court lost its former Westernizing zeal and began to inhibit cultural and intellectual change. To be sure, there had always been taboos. Ueki Emori spent two months in jail for publishing "A Monkey Monarch" in 1876,[29] and lese majesty came into being with the penal code of 1882. But despite such government suppression, the air was still relatively free. In that sense, the 1889 Meiji Constitution and 1890 Imperial Rescript on Education do indeed mark a great divide. These sacred texts enshrined the *kokutai*, or "national essence and polity," that placed limits on legal and moral permissibility in Japan. Before 1889–90, Japanese thinkers enjoyed remarkable freedom to debate many sensitive issues. They might dispute what form of government the new Meiji state should adopt, where its locus of sovereignty should lie, what role the emperor should play, how far individual rights and freedoms should extend, whether Japan should remain a small state or build a great empire, how society should create a more just division of wealth, and so on. After 1889–90, however, the number and scope of such disputable issues diminished. To be sure, learning from the West continued apace; translation and lexicography flourished as never before. The complete works of Marx and Engels, for example, appeared in Japanese before any other language. As Chapters 4 and 5 of our present work relate in detail, Japanese thinkers continued to produce their share of unorthodox ideas. But their ability to enunciate and implement those ideas in society decreased steadily. Thus, between 1889 and 1896, the government shut down Kuga Katsunan's newspaper *Nihon* thirty times for a total of 230 days.[30] In 1902, Kōtoku Shūsui claimed, "socialism does not violate the *kokutai*; those who oppose socialism do."[31] But in 1911, the state executed him and eleven others, ostensibly for wanting to kill the emperor. This violent suppression intensified – until a revised Peace Preservation Law in 1928 stipulated death for anyone who would alter Japan's *kokutai* or system of

29 The title as Ueki actually wrote it was "Monkey Government." The editor who made this mistake (?) in print spent a year and a half in jail and paid a ¥300 fine.
30 Matsumoto Sannosuke, *Meiji shisō ni okeru kindai to dentō* (Tokyo: Tokyo daigaku shuppankai, 1996), p. 174. For an excellent recent study of Kuga's thought, see Honda Itsuo, *Kokumin, jiyū, kensei* (Tokyo: Bokutakusha, 1994).
31 In *Rikugō zasshi* (November 15, 1902), included in Kōtoku Shūsui, *Shakaishugi shinzui* (Tokyo: Iwanami shoten, 1953), pp. 70–4. See also Kano Masanao, *Meiji no shisō* (Tokyo: Chikuma shobō, 1964), pp. 125–6; and F. G. Notehelfer, *Kōtoku Shūsui: Portrait of a Japanese Radical* (Cambridge: Cambridge University Press, 1971), p. 86.

private ownership. This law precluded any revival of the short-lived political and social activism that erupted in the 1910s and early 1920s which some historians label *"Taishō demokurashii."* When Japan invaded Manchuria in September 1931, the mass media applauded armed expansion.[32] In February 1932, the influencial financial daily, the *Tōyō keizai shinpō,* reversed its stand on the advisability of liquidating unprofitable colonial holdings such as Manchuria and began to support imperialist aggression.[33] Another watershed came in 1935–7, when the government "clarified" the *kokutai.* Finally, in November 1944, the Koiso cabinet declared that "defending the *kokutai"* was Japan's foremost war aim – ahead of "self-preservation" and "liberating Asian peoples."[34] Eventually, it took a nuclear holocaust and a foreign army of occupation to restore the degree of freedom for thought and expression that Japan had enjoyed before 1889.

The Meiji constitutional system placed strict limits on Japanese political action. Ueki's draft constitution had spoken of a Japanese "people" or *jinmin* (as used in "people's republics") under an emperor called *kōtei* (used for dynastic heads worldwide). By contrast, the 1889 Meiji Constitution prescribed the people's status as "subjects" of a uniquely Japanese emperor *(tennō)* – not as "citizens" entitled to inalienable rights in civil society. This Constitution bestowed limited rights to subjects, but it also imposed theocratic imperial sovereignty. That is, it based the emperor's "sacred and inviolable" position as sovereign head of state on a decree issued by Sun Goddess Amateraus. In essence, this was a modernized version of the divine right of kings. The Meiji Constitution stipulated "imperial assistance" above parliamentary control. The emperor chose cabinet members, chiefs of staff, and other officials to "assist" his rule, and they in turn bore responsibility to him, not to the people. Aspiring democratic thinkers such as Yoshino Sakuzō and Minobe Tatsukichi waged uphill battles to curb the power of imperial assistants – elder statesmen, general staff officers, the House of Peers,

32 Eguchi Keiichi, "Manshū jihen to daishinbun," *Shisō* no. 583 (January 1973), pp. 98–113.
33 Until February 6, 1932, the *Tōyō keizai shinpō* had argued that Japan should abandon colonies because their cost was prohibitive. See Eguchi Keiichi, "Santō shuppei, 'Manshū jihen' o megutte," in Inoue Kiyoshi and Watanabe Tōru, eds., *Taishō-ki no kyūshinteki jiyūshugi* (Tokyo: Tōyō keizai shinpōsha, 1972), pp. 353–92; see also Inoue Kiyoshi, "Nihon teikokushugi hihanron," in ibid., pp. 115–86.
34 Tanaka Nobumasa, *Dokyumento Shōwa tennō 4: Haisen, jō* (Tokyo: Rokufū shoten, 1987), pp. 344–5.

Privy Councillors, and former prime ministers – who were generally averse to parliamentary rule. No Japanese could openly advocate revising articles in the Constitution dealing with the emperor because that would violate the *kokutai*. So Yoshino resorted to a tactic that, in the postwar period, would become known as *kaishaku kaiken* with respect to Article 9 of the 1947 Constitution. *Kaishaku kaiken*, or "de facto revision through contrived interpretation," somewhat resembles what American gun lobbies do to Article 2 of the U.S. Constitution. Democracy in the literal sense of "the doctrine of the people as sovereign," or *minshushugi*, violated the *kokutai* and imperial sovereignty under the Meiji Constitution. Therefore, Yoshino substituted the principle of *minponshugi*, or "government based on the people," for that of genuine popular sovereignty. Unlike in a Western democracy, he argued, the locus of sovereignty did not matter in Japan as long as imperial assistants exercised it for the people's welfare. If they stopped doing so, however, his sophistry was at an end. Moreover, the imperially bestowed Meiji Constitution gave antidemocratic forces far more leeway to contrive interpretations. Article Eleven precluded civilian interference with the emperor's supreme command over imperial armed force. But military officers could broaden its scope far more easily than bureaucrats or party politicians could narrow it. The supreme command at first pertained only to wartime tactics and field strategy. Over time, however, the Diet lost control over all matters related to the armed forces. Moreover, like Kōtoku Shūsui before him, Yoshino had no choice but to declare that his ideas conformed with the *kokutai*.[35] Thus it is not surprising that he gave himself low marks for political theory and instead declared his greatest achievements to lie in the field of Sino-Japanese relations.[36] Constitutional monarchy took eight centuries to develop in Britain. Given more time, liberal democrats in Japan might have overcome built-in obstructions, gone on to establish parliamentary controls and lasting party cabinets, and so create a functioning constitutional monarchy. But to do all of that, they needed to be far more open to Western currents of thought and value.

The Imperial Rescript on Education and narrow patriotism that it

35 Matsumoto Sannosuke, *Kindai Nihon no chiteki jōkyō* (Tokyo: Chūōkōronsha, 1974), pp. 145–58.
36 Quoted in Mitani Ta'ichi, "Shisōka toshite no Yoshino Sakuzō," in *Nihon no meicho 48: Yoshino Sakuzō* (Tokyo: Chūōkōronsha, 1972), p. 43. See also Matsuo Takayoshi, *Taishō demokushii no kenkyū* (Tokyo: Aoki shoten, 1966), pp. 286–306.

spawned over time made for less, not more, openness. The rescript prescribed national morality based on state shinto, the imperial family state, and the *kokutai*. In the 1870s, Fukuzawa Yukichi and Katō Hiroyuki had used this term to denote "nationality" or "a nation's sovereignty." Likewise, Shiga Shigetaka coined *kokusui* to translate "nationality." Thus some key Meiji thinkers spoke of *kokutai* and *kokusui* in a general sense. The Japanese had *a* national polity and essence worth preserving, as did other peoples. But after the 1889–90 watershed, *kokutai* became *the* national polity and essence that made Japan not only different from but also better than other lands – and defense of Amaterasu's divine imperial line became its categorical imperative. Rather than try to share more in common with the world, the Japanese began to exalt peculiarities that set themselves apart. Above all, they came to embrace the myth that their families were an extension of the imperial line; so all of them partook of divinity. As children of the father-sovereign, they owed him the same unquestioning filial submission that they owed their real parents.[37] Popular and scholarly works on the Japanese national character written between 1925 and 1945 show a fixation with traits like "the Yamato spirit" and *bushidō*.[38] Morality textbooks as revised in 1941 held up 102 paragons for youthful emulation, but only two were Western.[39] As the Education Ministry's "Way of the Imperial Subject" exhorted, all Japanese owed their "every bowl of rice and piece of dress" to the emperor. In repaying these august blessings, they "must not forget devotion to His Majesty and service to the state . . . even in their sleep."[40] This total merging of private and public selves demanded unlimited sacrifice. In response, the army invented a suitable Japanese "tradition." The daimyo and samurai who lost at Sekigahara in 1600 did not prefer death to dishonor; they heeled before a new master – the Tokugawa shogun. The same held for Tokugawa retainers who joined the Meiji regime after 1868. During the Russo-Japanese War and Siberian Intervention, Japanese prisoners of war who returned home could and did receive the Order of the Golden Kite, the emperor's highest military

37 Ishida Takeshi, *Meiji seiji shisōshi kenkyū* (Tokyo: Miraisha, 1954), pp. 6–215; and Karasawa Tomitarō, *Kyōkasho no rekishi* (Tokyo: Sōbunsha, 1956), pp. 270–329.
38 Minami Hiroshi, *Nihonjinron: Meiji kara konnichi made* (Tokyo: Iwanami shoten, 1994), pp. 137–83.
39 They were Benjamin Franklin and Edward Jenner. See Karasawa Tomitarō, *Kyōkasho no rekishi: bessatsu dai ni hyō*.
40 "Shinmin no michi," quoted in Eguchi Keiichi, *Taikei Nihon no rekishi 14: Futatsu no taisen* (Tokyo: Shōgakukan, 1993), pp. 362–3.

decoration.[41] But by the 1940s, *gyokusai* – or annihilation before surrender – became expected of soldier and civilian alike in defense of the *kokutai*.[42]

Thus the Meiji Constitution and Rescript on Education neutralized dissidence at home – and Japan's openness to the outside world diminished accordingly. Enlightenment thinkers, People's Rights advocates, and socialists in Meiji times all had resented Western imperialism. But they still agreed that the West was "advanced" in matters of culture and morals and that catching up would help more than harm Japan. This willingness to admit Japan's backwardness lessened after Versailles, and Konoe Fumimaro's travel accounts of Europe and America in 1919 reveal this changed attitude. The Great War had tremendous worldwide implications. Of the great powers who began it, only France had been a republic. But by the war's end, only Britain remained a monarchy. Revolution had destroyed three great dynasties, and this bode ill for the *kokutai*. Furthermore, as Konoe carefully noted, open covenants shaped by "public opinion" had replaced old-style secret diplomacy. The right of national self-determination, another Wilsonian ideal, won avid support from weak peoples whom imperial powers such as Japan had colonized. Finally, America had displaced Europe as the center of world power. As a result of all these changes, Konoe stressed, oppressed nationalities such as the Irish and Koreans strove to win U.S. public support in their struggles for independence. Chinese propagandists also played on American idealism by labeling Japan an aggressor in Shantung. Japan must counter these smear tactics with reasoned polemics to convince Americans that Japanese imperialism was just. Wilsonian idealism did not truly embody humanity and justice; power politics still prevailed. On the one hand, Westerners vetoed Japan's bid to insert a racial equality clause in the League Charter.

41 Fujiwara Akira notes that none of the 2,088 soldiers captured in the Russo-Japanese War ever received a court martial on returning home, and some received the Golden Kite; Fujiwara, *Taiheiyō sensō ron* (Tokyo: Aoki shoten 1982), p. 156. On the Siberian Intervention, see testimony by Tsuchiya Yoshio in Asahi shinbun Yamagata shikyoku, ed., *Kikigaki: Aru kenpei no kiroku* (Tokyo: Asahi shinbunsha, 1991), pp. 20–1.

42 Eguchi Keiichi dates the start of this change in March 1932 with the suicide of Major Kuga Noboru, who had been captured while wounded at Shanghai and was later released to the Japanese. See Eguchi, *Shōwa no rekishi 4: Jūgonen sensō no kaimaku* (Tokyo: Shōgakukan, 1988), pp. 157–9. The change was complete in 1941 with the issuance of *Precepts for the Front* (Senjinkun), which explicitly forbade the disgrace of capture. In a popular edition of this work, Lieutenant-General Okamura Yasuji cites Kuga's suicide as exemplifying this precept. See Tokyo nichinichi shinbunsha and Osaka mainichi shinbunsha, eds., *Kaisetsu: Senjinkun* (Tokyo: Tokyo nichinichi shinbunsha, 1941), pp. 108–9.

On the other hand, America flaunted its century-old Monroe Doctrine to block League intervention in its colonial sphere, whereas Britain promoted "equality" of voting rights in the League for its colonial dependents (e.g., two votes for Hejaz).[43] Established Western powers advanced narrow national interests behind reputedly universal ideals such as peace, equality, democracy, and self-determination. If this was the case, then Japan had to pursue legitimate expansion by "rejecting a pacifism rigged to favor Britain and America."[44]

There is much insight and some validity in Konoe's contentions. He exposed the racially motivated double standard in Western civilization and urged Japan to exercise critical judgment in accepting or rejecting world trends. But Japanese tradition gave him little with which to "overcome" modern Western ideals. For example, the *kokutai* perforce thwarted any determined pursuit of peace. Thus the 1928 Kellogg-Briand Pact, which outlawed wars of aggression, violated the emperor's sovereignty because his delegates signed "in the name of their respective peoples [*jinmin*]." So, bowing to right-wing threats of violence, the government amended this clause to conform with the *kokutai*.[45] In order to uphold peace, states must agree reciprocally to limit or reduce armaments. But imperial navy leaders tried to block ratification of the 1930 London Naval Treaty by arguing that only the emperor could determine Japan's fleet size; diplomats and cabinet ministers could not do so in league with foreigners. This navy tactic failed, but later cabinets stopped challenging the military on money issues, and by 1937, 50 percent of Japan's budget was going to armaments. Finally, any desire for peace presumed some willingness to submit disputes for international arbitration. This principle violated the *kokutai* and imperial sovereignty too, but military leaders did not have to argue the point. Foreign Minister Shidehara Kijūrō himself spurned League arbitration over Manchuria in a move that foreshadowed Japan's Asian Monroe Doctrine and withdrawal from the League.[46] Such examples show that in Japanese eyes the Shōwa emperor's "sacred and inviolable" authority stood above and beyond diplomatic covenants. Thus it

43 Konoe Fumimaro, *Sengo Ō-Bei kenbunroku* (Tokyo: Chūōkōronsha, 1981), pp. 34–49, 68–72, 116, 122–3, and 136–49.
44 Konoe, "Ei-Bei hon'i no heiwashugi o haisu," in Kitaoka Shin'ichi, ed., *Sengo Nihon gaikō ronshū* (Tokyo: Chūōkōronsha, 1995), pp. 47–52. There is an English translation, "Against a Pacifism Centered on England and America," in *Japan Echo*, vol. 22 (1995), pp. 12–14.
45 Nezu Masashi, *Tennō to Shōwashi, jō* (Tokyo: San'ichi shobō, 1976), pp. 72–4.
46 Ōsugi Kazuo, *Nit-Chū jūgonen sensōshi* (Tokyo: Chūōkōronsha, 1996), pp. 73–9.

follows that the imperial rescript declaring war in 1941 – unlike those issued for all previous wars – omitted the stipulation that Japan should respect international law.[47]

Konoe pointed to national self-determination as another example of Western deceit, and as the years passed, he became more forceful in rejecting what he saw as a rigged Anglo-American world order. But here again, Japanese tradition proved unable to overcome modern ideals emanating from the West – even when these were deceitful. Indeed, Konoe himself used a modern Western argument to justify imperialism. In 1937, he asserted that "the Chinese are incapable of exploiting the god-given natural resources in their land, so Japan is doing this for them out of friendship."[48] And in 1938, his repudiation of Anglo-American universalism moved him to proclaim Japan's historic mission of erecting a "new order for East Asia." Like Kyoto Faction thinkers described by Tetsuo Najita and Harry Harootunian in Chapter 5, Konoe declared that Japan sought to liberate Asians from Western exploitation. Japan's "new order" would bring "the eight corners of the world under one roof" (hakkō ichiu), and each Asian people would "find its proper place" on a hierarchy headed by the emperor. This ideal derived from the mythical Jimmu emperor circa 660 B.C. But in August 1940, Konoe became the first Japanese leader to make it official state policy, and one month later, the Shōwa emperor cited it in a rescript to sanction the Axis Pact.[49]

Thus Westerners propagated universal ideals such as equality, national self-determination, and the illegality of territorial aggrandizement through aggressive war. As Konoe had noted in 1919, there was much self-serving hypocrisy in those principles. The right of national self-determination, for instance, did not gain "universal" affirmation until well past 1945, when third-world nations won independence from Western colonial rule – often by violent means. Yet even so, the British did accede to Sinn Féin demands for an Irish Free State in 1920. By contrast, the Japanese annexed Korea in 1910, brutally quashed demands for independence in 1919, and tried to stamp out the Koreans' culture and ethnicity by transforming them

47 Imperial rescripts for war in 1894, 1904, and 1914 include this stipulation. See Kisaka Jun'ichirō, Shōwa no rekishi 7: Taiheiyō sensō (Tokyo: Shōgakukan, 1989), p. 27; and Eguchi Keiichi, Taikei Nihon no rekishi 14: Futatsu no taisen (Tokyo: Shōgakukan, 1993), pp. 21–2.
48 Quoted in Eguchi Keiichi, Shinpan: Jūgonen sensō shōshi (Tokyo: Aoki shoten, 1991), p. 113.
49 Eizawa Kōji, "Daitō-A kyōeiken" no shisō (Tokyo: Kōdansha, 1995), pp. 102–7.

into "imperial subjects" until 1945. After tasting equal measures of hypocrisy under Western and Japanese domination, Asian colonial peoples chose modern ideals of equality and self-determination over antiquarian notions of submission "under one roof." The Japanese themselves were not as perceptive. The aforementioned Western ideals presented themselves in the 1928 Kellogg-Briand Pact, the 1930 London Naval Treaty, the 1933 Lytton Report, the 1941 Atlantic Charter, the 1943 Cairo Declaration (which first mentioned Korean independence), and the 1945 Potsdam Declaration. The Shōwa emperor and his government accepted only the last document – and only after verifying that "We have been able to preserve the *kokutai*."[50] During the three weeks while they frantically sought that verification, two atomic bombs fell on Japan, and Soviet troops entered Korea – whose liberation would come under a divided state.[51]

LIBERATION IN DEPENDENCE, POST-1945

The Potsdam Declaration stipulated that the "Japanese government shall remove all obstacles to the revival and strengthening of democratic tendencies among the Japanese people." But as Matsumoto Sannosuke bitingly observes, "there were no democratic forces around to be 'revived'."[52] They were either in prison, some for eighteen years, or underground where they could do little but scrawl antiwar graffiti on lavatory walls. By accepting the declaration, Japan pledged that "freedom of speech, of religion, and of thought, as well as respect for fundamental human rights shall be established." In fact, imperial authorities were redoubling efforts to suppress those freedoms and rights. Key elements in the Higashikuni cabinet were bent on defending the *kokutai* by continuing to prosecute dissidents – and they hoped for Allied support. Then on September 26, Reuters correspondent Robert Reuben learned of Miki Kiyoshi's death in prison from unnatural causes. He questioned Interior Minister Yamazaki Iwao, and on hearing the authorities would continue to enforce the Peace Preservation Law, Reuben published a scathing

---

50 So reads the imperial rescript of August 14, 1945. See Senda Kakō, ed., *Tennō to chokugo no shōwashi* (Tokyo: Sekibunsha, 1983), p. 392.
51 On Japanese culpability for the eventual division of Korea owing to this delayed acceptance of the Potsdam Declaration, see, for example, Tokyo University Professor Wada Haruki in *Asahi shinbun*, February 3, 1995.
52 Matsumoto, *Kindai Nihon no chiteki jōkyō*, p. 195.

exposé in *The Pacific Stars and Stripes*.[53] According to Hidaka Rokurō, this incident forced MacArthur to dissolve the Higashikuni cabinet and to order sweeping reforms – such as abolishing thought control laws and the military police – which amounted to a faithful execution of the Potsdam peace terms. As Hidaka painfully relates, no Japanese journalist broached the issue of Miki's death with Yamazaki or tried to secure MacArthur's intervention on behalf of other detainees. For seven weeks after the surrender, no Japanese cared enough about human rights to notice that prisoners of conscience were still dying because of the *kokutai*. It took an erstwhile enemy national to gain their release and to force the dismissal of a regime dead set against democratic reform.[54] About that time, author Takami Jun sardonically mused: "When you lose a war and a foreign army takes over your country, you expect it to curtail your freedoms; but here it is upholding these. What a humiliating disgrace!"[55] A later generation would call such meddling foreign pressure "Japan bashing" in a positive sense – as being needed to ram through progressive measures that Japanese cannot implement on their own. In all, some 3,000 political prisoners in Japan, many of them Communists and Koreans, gained freedom in October 1945 – not August 1945.

This *Stars and Stripes* episode speaks volumes about the "democratic enlightenment" that Andrew Barshay describes in Chapter 6. When Japan sought to confirm that "the said [Potsdam] Declaration does not comprise any demand which prejudices the prerogatives of His Majesty as a sovereign ruler," the Americans replied that "the ultimate form of the government of Japan shall . . . be established by the freely expressed will of the Japanese people." Ueki Emori had hoped for as much in the 1880s. But it was the U.S. war machine that first destroyed Japan's capacity to reject the Potsdam demands and later exacted compliance with these. Unlike in Italy and Germany, there was no resistance movement out to kill the emperor and overthrow the wartime government because the right to revolt had never taken root among the Japanese people. Nakae Chōmin had wanted his countrymen to revise the Meiji Constitution along democratic lines. That never happened. "Old liberals" such as Minobe

---

53 For a detailed account, see Takemae Eiji, *Senryō sengoshi* (Tokyo: Iwanami shoten, 1992), pp. 94–169.
54 Hidaka Rokurō, *Sengoshi o kangaeru* (Tokyo: Iwanami shoten, 1980), pp. 1–12.
55 Takami Jun, *Haisen nikki* (Tokyo: Bungeishunjūsha, 1991), p. 296.

Tatsukichi, Shidehara Kijūrō, and Matsumoto Jōji denied any need to rewrite the text in a major way. It was U.S. Navy Commander Alfred Hussey who wrote the new Constitution's Preamble, which enshrines the "universal principle" that "sovereign power resides with the people" and "Government is a sacred trust of the people." And, it was the Occupation's GHQ that forced a recalcitrant Japanese government to include this Preamble in the final document.[56] Likewise, Education Minister Maeda Tamon insisted that the 1890 Imperial Rescript on Education provided just the kind of inspiration and moral guidance needed to rebuild the nation. Clearly, then, Japanese in positions of authority near the emperor would go only so far if left to their own devices.

Many historians call the Occupation a "second opening of Japan" – after that by Perry and Harris in the 1850s. The analogy is imperfect, for the scale of Japanese death and misery made this second opening decisively different. Perry and Harris did exploit the threat of military action to get their way, but it was nothing like that applied by MacArthur. The Satsuma and Chōshū wars in 1863–4 against Westerners had ended in a few days. The Restoration civil war from Toba-Fushimi to Hakodate ended in thirteen months with 8,263 dead, very few of whom were nonsamurai.[57] By contrast, the Asia-Pacific War from 1931 to 1945 killed 3.1 million Japanese, including 873,000 civilians.[58] Over half the area in Japan's cities lay in rubble. Individual caloric intake fell to 1,325 per day. Living within the law became literally impossible. Teachers or judges of high principle – such as Kameo Eishirō in October 1945 and Yamaguchi Yoshitada as late as October 1947 – who refused to buy illegal black-market food starved to death. Such conditions discredited most traditional pillars of authority and made the Japanese far more willing to accept radical change than in Meiji times. However, they still lacked what postwar thinkers called *shutaisei*. As lawyer-activist Masaki Hiroshi railed, the emperor state's education system and propaganda had turned the Japanese people into domesticated "barnyard animals."[59] The task now was to make them politically conscious, morally au-

56 *Yomiuri shinbun*, August 15, 1996. This revelation is based on documents declassifed in 1995.
57 Inoue Kiyoshi, *Nihon no rekishi 20: Meiji ishin* (Tokyo: Chūōkōronsha, 1966), p. 131.
58 There is some discrepancy about the number of civilian dead. I used Fujiwara Akira, Awaya Kentarō, and Yoshida Yutaka, eds., *Shōwa 20-nen, 1945-nen* (Tokyo: Shōgakukan, 1995), p. 122.
59 Masaki Hiroshi, *Chikaki yori 5: Teikoku Nihon hōkai* (Tokyo: Shakai shisō sha, 1991), pp. 288–309. For a study of Masaki's life and thought, see Ienaga Saburō, *Kenryokuaku to no tatakai* (Tokyo: Kōbundō, 1964).

tonomous agents who actively and responsibly implemented radical change to suit their own needs as determined by themselves. Here, Americans provided the key catalyst by violently destroying most of the old imperial order. Tragic though it was, defeat in the war promoted *shutaisei* and sparked a desire for enlightened reform in the Japanese people – much as Fukuzawa Yukichi had hoped would happen to the Chinese in 1894–5.

The desire for another round of Enlightenment did arise in the Japanese, as can be seen in social studies texts such as *Minshushugi* used in secondary schools from April 1948 to March 1954. Authors Ōkōchi Kazuo, Odaka Asao, Tsuchiya Kiyoshi, and Miyazawa Toshiyoshi[60] noted that Japan fell into military dictatorship and totalitarianism due to a defective Meiji value system. The people "just borrowed things from the West" and "did not make the democratic spirit their own." They clung to a narrow-minded, unscientific, feudal ethos of chauvinism, loyalty to the emperor, and submission to hierarchy, which "produced torture, inhumane judicial procedures, and slave-like bondage." Postwar Japan possessed true democratic institutions and political processes not because the people struggled and sacrificed to create these; instead, they received these gifts from "advanced Western nations" only because of losing the war. Now the Japanese had to internalize the "basic spirit of democracy" and practice it in their daily lives, for this inner spirit was far more vital than outward institutions and processes. As the textbook *Minshushugi* repeatedly quotes Samuel Smiles, "Heaven helps those who help themselves." In this regard, the authors devote a full chapter to women's rights. They stress that the inferior status of women in Japan had not derived from nature but rather from male "tyranny." Women gained legal equality thanks to Potsdam; now they had to exercise their rights and duties in an informed, responsible manner. Above all, they had to repudiate what Meiji Enlightenment thinkers had called "blind adherence to [invalidated] old ways." Thus the text asserts, "No civilized nation in the world today has eating habits that force women to boil rice three times a day." This robbed them of their right and duty to take part in sociopolitical affairs. Rice eating, and the whole socioeconomic structure that supported it, obstructed democratization. Likewise, the system of sole inheritance by eldest sons, the duty of their wives to live with and care for parents-in-law, as well as other forms of female servi-

---

60 Katagami Shūji has identified them as the authors. See *Asahi shinbun*, August 21, 1995.

tude must end. Postwar Japanese had to root out these and similar "atavistic" "feudal remnants" in order to build a "cultured state" (*bunka kokka*) founded on democracy, science, and peace. These ideals were informed by "modernity," which must be perfected, not "overcome." "Science" in this postwar Japanese context assumed normative connotations that were often but not always Marxist. "Science" mocked all of the absurdities that Japanese humanists or social scientists had been forced to avow under "emperor state fascism": unquestioned obedience to imperial orders, a crude belief in archaic myths, and the irrational affirmation of *bushidō* and a mystical "Yamato spirit." According to *Minshushugi*, "science" meant "to think like a scientist" by being skeptical and critical. One must uphold freedom of inquiry and expression, question received wisdom and established authority, and thereby debunk myths and expose demagoguery. Above all, to be "scientific" required one to respect deviant or opposing views the way a scientist heeds data that invalidate his hypothesis.[61]

Postwar thinkers believed pacifism to be an offshoot of modern democracy. Japan went to war because its imperial government and armed forces deemed themselves responsible only to the emperor. The basic spirit of democracy lay in accountability to the people, plus respect for individuals, equality of rights and opportunity, and toleration of differences. If all states adhered to this democratic spirit, wars could not occur. Based on this logic and on sad experience, the authors of *Minshushugi* argued that democracies did not wage wars of aggression; only authoritarian or dictatorial states did.[62] Above all, democratic societies observed the rule of law, and, as Yokota Kisaburō argued, aggressive warfare between states had lost all basis in legality. In January 1946, he wrote that sovereign states had affirmed war as a last resort in settling disputes before 1914, but mediation replaced war as the only legal means to that end after the 1928 Kellogg-Briand Pact. This constituted a revolution in international law that created a new type of war crimes: those "against peace and humanity." Japan's actions since 1931 were clearly aggressive, not taken in self-defense. Hence it was legitimate to indict wartime leaders for Class-A war crimes. The Japanese people, Yokota claimed, could never hope to establish a healthy, functioning democ-

---

61 See the reprint edition, Monbushō, *Monbusho chosaku kyōkasho: Minshushugi* (Tokyo: Komichi shobō, 1995), pp. 15–32, 66, 88–91, 127–8, 146–9, 286–7, 291–4, 311–34, and 350–7.
62 Ibid., pp. 335–9.

racy unless they recognized this principle of the illegality of war.[63] The next logical step was to write it into the new Constitution as Article 9: "The Japanese people renounce war as a sovereign right of the nation and the threat or use of force as means of settling international disputes." Hence "land, sea, and air forces, as well as other war potential, will never be maintained. The rights of belligerency of the state will not be recognized."

In addition to such ethical, legal, and logical grounds for Article 9, Shimizu Ikutarō in 1950 noted some practical ones. In a best-selling paperback entitled *Aikokushin* [Patriotism], Shimizu argued that gangster-led, *shishi*-style Japanese patriotism remained at the primitive tribal level, unrefined by the democratic ethical principles that had "modernized and rationalized" patriotism in advanced Western peoples. The task for true Japanese patriots now was to democratize, "not demand rearmament." And in any case, recent world trends precluded all but nonbelligerent forms of patriotism in Japan. The mass destructiveness of nuclear arms had made warfare unacceptable; only militarists, politicians, and capitalists could hope to benefit. Most importantly, sovereign states who enjoyed rights of belligerency were a thing of the past. Only two countries in the world now had the real capacity to wage war – the U.S.A. and U.S.S.R. All other nations were American or Soviet "substates" whose armed forces were just "ornamental and symbolic" of their former sovereign status. Patriotism as the Japanese had known it was anachronistic. So Japan did not need armed forces. Moreover, a unified world government would emerge sometime in the future.[64]

Thus postwar Japanese democracy and pacifism as manifested in the 1947 Constitution, and especially Article 9, owed much to American coercion. Yet large segments of the Japanese people – those who felt revulsion for anything that smacked of nationalism and war – welcomed that coercion. Leftist teachers' unions went even further. They charged that postwar Japanese should abolish their wartime national anthem and flag – *Kimigayo* and the Rising Sun – just as postwar Germans had abolished *Deutschland über alles* and the Swastika. Some even likened the emperor to Hitler.

The Cold War, however, drastically altered the path that postwar Japan would follow. The "reverse course," an article of faith among

---

63 Yokota Kisaburō, "Sensō hanzai to kokusaihō no kakumei," *Chūōkōron* (January 1946), pp. 31–40. For a more detailed account, see Yokota, *Sensō hanzai ron* (Tokyo: Yuhikaku, 1947).

64 Shimizu Ikutarō, *Aikokushin* (Tokyo: Iwanami shoten, 1950), pp. 137–59.

Japanese scholars, reputedly began with NSC document 14/2 in October 1948, if not the quashed general strike of February 1947. The Occupation retracted its original plans to demilitarize, democratize, and perforce weaken Japan through punitive indemnities. Japan was now a key ally in the crusade against Peking and Moscow – not a defeated enemy to be punished or pinned down – so it was imperative to rebuild Japanese military and economic power. Radical change was now undesirable; too much democracy in the form of political agitation or labor unrest might bring a Red takeover. Americans regretted their earlier reformist zeal, especially after the Korean War broke out in June 1950. For many Japanese, too, this event invalidated any rationale for Article 9. But in December, Shimizu Ikutarō, Maruyama Masao, and other influential thinkers published a "Third Statement on Peace" wherein they reaffirmed unilateral pacifism. Wholesale slaughter would accompany a third world war. Japan might foster conciliation between the two camps and would best avoid being dragged into any such war by staying unarmed and nonaligned. Such views represent left-wing thinking on world affairs and the Constitution. First, leftists demanded a "comprehensive peace," that is, one concluded with all nations, not just those whom Americans deemed acceptable. No just or meaningful postwar settlements could result if the Chinese and other Asian peoples whom Japan victimized were barred from the peace table, and the Soviet absence was grievous for other reasons. Second, leftists insisted on adhering to the letter of Article 9 by rejecting not only Japan's own rearmament but also any foreign military presence in Japan. This meant unarmed neutrality.

By contrast, "old liberals" such as Yoshida Shigeru believed that imperial Japan had grown rich and strong as a junior partner of Britain and America. But in an act of hubris, Konoe Fumimaro and the army "rejected" that patronage, sought an alliance with Nazi Germany, and began an unwinnable war that predictably led to ruin. Japan must not pick the wrong side again. Future prosperity depended on U.S. largesse in the form of economic aid, cheap technology transfers, and full access to markets and raw materials. Thus Japan must rely on America's nuclear umbrella and bases for defense needs. Japan would rearm as slowly and minimally as the Americans would tolerate, while claiming to uphold Article 9 in order to parry fierce antiwar criticism from the Japanese public.[65] This "Yoshida

65 Watanabe Osamu, *Nihonkoku kenpō "kaisei" shi* (Tokyo: Nihon hyōronsha, 1987), pp. 72–
    85. According to Watanabe's analysis, Yoshida resorted to this ploy of *kaishaku kaiken*.

Line" entailed a close adherence to U.S. military and foreign policy dictates. Thus over 140 Japanese merchantmen as well as Coast Guard minesweeping units secretly aided American troop landings at Inchon and Wonson in the Korean War.[66] This "Line" also forced Yoshida and his government to engage in a postwar version of the constitutional sophistry known as *kaishaku kaiken* – de facto revision through contrived interpretation. This time it was not to institute *minponshugi* but to accommodate U.S. demands first for rearmament and later for permanent military bases. As this shell game went, Japan's new artillery corps were "special units," infantry corps were "regular units," and they brandished "special vehicles" that looked like tanks. "Police Reserves," "Peace Preservation Units," and "Self-Defense Forces" – as these were successively renamed – amounted to four divisions and took up 3 percent of the GNP in the early 1950s. But they were not an army, navy, and air force with "war potential," so their existence did not violate Article 9. As the satirical lyrics of a popular 1952 student song put it, "A tadpole isn't a frog."[67]

By signing the San Francisco Peace Treaty and U.S.–Japan Security Pact, Japan became an American dependency. To be sure, there was ample room for conservatives to dispute the nature and degree of Japanese subservience or to debate the meaning of "state sovereignty" in the Cold War bipolar world. (As Shimizu Ikutarō himself admitted in 1950, all nations were U.S. or Soviet "substates.") Even so, awkward political and economic facts remained. The two treaties forced Japan to "dissociate from Asia" and snuggle into the U.S. orbit. Japan had to follow America's pro-Taiwan policy of not recognizing and not granting U.N. membership to Peking – until Nixon's *volte-face* in 1972, which humiliated Japanese leaders. Moreover, Japan's survival and prosperity depended on U.S. war making in Asia. Postwar recovery did not begin until the United States spent some $8 billion on Korean War "special procurements" that accounted for 60 percent of all Japanese exports in 1952. Japan's trade balance with the United States still remained unfavorable until the Vietnam War. Then, more special procurements of war materiel plus

---

66 Based on declassified U.S. documents, Takemae Eiji reports that 140 Japanese merchantmen participated in these operations; see *Asahi shinbun*, November 1, 1996. For the Coast Guard minesweeping units, see Fujiwara Akira, *Taikei Nihon no rekishi 15: Sekai no naka no Nihon* (Tokyo: Shōgakukan, 1993), p. 140; and Kanda Fuhito, *Shōwa no rekishi 8: Senryō to minshushugi* (Tokyo: Shōgakukan, 1989), pp. 412–13.

67 Shibagaki Kazuo, *Shōwa no rekishi 9: Kōwa kara kōdo seichō e* (Tokyo: Shōgakukan, 1989), pp. 43–4.

related exports put the account in the black, where it has been ever since. As leftists stress, Japan produced 92 percent of the napalm that U.S. forces used in Vietnam.[68] The northern part of Vietnam suffered 2 million starvation deaths due to Japanese rice levies in World War II, but the U.S. forced Japan to recognize and pay an indemnity only to South Vietnam.[69] According to this left-wing view, America robbed the Japanese of the freedom to make just settlements to those peoples whom they had despoiled most during the war, and Japan as a U.S. client continued to victimize those Asian peoples after the war. Indeed, the Japanese media and general public did not come to recognize this war guilt toward fellow Asians until the late 1970s, and the process is still only beginning.[70]

Ever since the Meiji Enlightenment, Japanese thinkers have deemed their personal moral autonomy to be linked with national autonomy. Could they as individuals maintain their *shutaisei*, self-respect, and integrity now that they were beholden to a tainted foreign power for their increasingly comfortable standard of living? The Kameo-Yamaguchi mode of principled free choice held little appeal. Sensitive souls felt this dilemma all the more keenly because the foreign power in question had done so much to foster democracy in postwar Japan compared with their own non-efforts before 1945. The Japanese made two attempts to resolve this dilemma of dependence. One came from the left – the Japan Communist Party during the 1950s. After the Occupation rescued Party stalwarts from eighteen years of imprisonment in October 1945, the JCP idealized Americans as "liberators." This view turned into enmity after the reverse course and the Security Pact, when the Party applied Leninist theories to define the Japan–U.S. nexus as colonial servitude. Liberation required a Maoist-style, rural-based revolutionary guerilla struggle to drive out U.S. imperialism.[71] An intense and disastrously counterproductive anti-Americanism has debilitated the far left ever since, especially since American liberals would have assisted many left-wing causes. A similarly radical attempt to reestablish national autonomy came from the right – under Prime Minister Kishi Nobusuke from 1957 to 1960. His ultimate aims were: (1) to remove all U.S. forces from Japan in return for implementing

68 Yoshizawa Minami, *Betonamu sensō to Nihon* (Tokyo: Iwanami shoten, 1988), pp. 36–44.
69 Ienaga Saburō, *Sensō sekinin* (Tokyo: Iwanami shoten, 1985), pp. 101–2 and 375.
70 See Ōnuma Yasuaki, *Saharin kimin* (Tokyo: Chūōkōronsha, 1992), pp. 72–3, 149. One pioneering effort in this respect was Senda Kakō, *Jūgun ianfu* (Tokyo: Futabasha, 1973).
71 Shibagaki, *Kōwa kara kōdo seichō e*, pp. 274–5.

full-scale Japanese rearmament, (2) to replace the U.S.–Japan Security Pact with a full-fledged military alliance between equals, (3) to restore the emperor as Japan's sovereign head of state, and (4) to revise the Constitution formally – not through contrived interpretation – in order to achieve all these goals. Kishi's attempts failed because of left-wing opposition in the Diet, and his forced revision of the Security Pact in 1960 triggered massive protests by labor, student, and citizens' groups. This violence toppled Kishi's regime and ended conservative hopes of reviving elements of the pre-1945 imperial order and ethos.[72]

The Japanese intellectuals' dilemma of dependence would resolve itself through economic growth, democratization, and internationalization. After the thaw in – and eventual end of – the Cold War, military might gave way to economic development as the chief index of national strength. The gap between America and Japan along with other industrialized nations has vastly diminished. In 1955, the U.S. economy was 26 times that of Japan's; in 1995, it was barely twice that of Japan's. The United States today is but one of the Big Seven and seeks cooperation from the other six to achieve policies beneficial to all. Likewise, as shown in the Gulf War, the United States must work through the U.N. far more than before in the military field as well. Thus U.S.–Japanese dependence is no longer one-sided. Meanwhile, the benefits of economic development have spread through Japanese society quite evenly, so that schisms along class, gender, and regional lines have shrunk immensely compared with prewar days. Having survived oil crises, dollar shocks, and a burst economic bubble, the Japanese people have developed confidence and pride in their nation. They now embrace a rather benign form of nationalism and a consumer-oriented culture that more or less affirms the status quo – minus corruption. A nativist resurgence has taken place, especially since the tenure of Nakasone Yasuhiro as Prime Minister from 1982 to 1987. But this new conservatism and nationalism pose little danger, for they are based on a general contentment with prosperity – not on a dissatisfaction with Japan's position in the world or a glorification of putatively unique Japanese qualities. And present-day conservatism and nationalism carry almost no threat of a militarist resurgence. Today, *kokutai* denotes a high-school "national athletic meet," not divinely ordained imperial rule.

72 Watanabe Osamu, *Nihonkoku kenpō "kaisei" shi*, pp. 234–331.

One seemingly trivial postwar reform – the writing or translating of laws, official documents, and above all the Constitution in colloquial Japanese – has had far-reaching democratic effects. The Meiji Constitution's antiquarian language served its purpose of enhancing the imperial mystique. But it also kept ordinary Japanese from understanding their rights and challenging state actions that violated these. Due to modernized legal language and a vastly expanded education system, the highest law of the land is now intelligible to every high-school student, so the gap between, say, legal norm and armed reality is apparent to all. This constitutional reform, in a little-noticed way, did much to further the mass protests by citizens' groups that erupted from the 1950s through the 1970s. Those often-violent protests – against U.S. bases in Japan and Okinawa, against discrimination in society, against environmental pollution, against official corruption, against the unequal status of women, and above all against war and nuclear arms – have made democracy a part of the people's everyday lives in a way that was inconceivable before 1945. Ordinary Japanese now take democracy for granted as being their own – much as they perceive curry rice to be a Japanese dish despite its foreign origins.

This gradual maturing of the postwar Japanese people into citizens, aware of their rights and willing to assert these, has been matched by similar democratic groundswells around the world. These developments have been mutually reinforcing and work decisively against a recrudescence of prewar-style Japanese thought and values. Ienaga Saburō has suggested that the 1947 "revolutionary Constitution" and the early Occupation policies of demilitarization and democratization were forced on Japan not so much from above as "from the sides," that is, by world opinion among ordinary people in support of peace over war and freedom over fascism.[73] Ienaga's analysis can be extended to many postwar popular movements that cut across state boundaries. For example, in 1946, MacArthur ordered the abolition of Japanese "comfort women" recruited by the imperial government for GI use. This was a move from above. But as Duus Masayo shows, MacArthur was of two minds on the issue. What really persuaded him to act was sideward pressure from largely female public opinion at home opposed to legalized prostitution on principle everywhere.[74] And the substantial end to unregulated pros-

---

73 Ienaga, *Rekishi no naka no kenpō, jō* (Tokyo: Tokyo daigaku shuppankai, 1977), p. 283.
74 However, fear of venereal disease among U.S. troops was another motive. Duus Masayo, *Haisha no okurimono* (Tokyo: Kōdansha, 1995), pp. 129–78.

titution in Japan came in 1956 due to mass protests "from below" by Japanese womens' and mothers' groups.[75] Human rights organizations throughout the world today support Japanese antiwar, antinuclear, antipollution, women's rights, and childrens' rights movements, and Japanese organizers in turn seek out such "foreign pressure" for its political-use value against conservative interests. Conversely, as Japanese leftists fondly note, Article 9 has inspired and encouraged pacifists all over the globe.

In sum, there is little or no significant "Japanese thought" untouched by world opinion today, and this internationalization will continue in the new century. Two key issues await resolution in this regard. First, world opinion in support of human rights will aid Japanese leftists who seek to atone for – or at least disclose the true nature and extent of – Japan's war crimes. The most egregious victims are Asian "comfort women" and other wartime slave laborers, as well as Korean and Taiwanese former colonial subjects – including imperial army veterans maimed in the war. These Koreans and Taiwanese and their offspring live in Japan but were stripped of Japanese citizenship in 1952 and are cruelly deprived of civil rights and social welfare benefits.[76] The related issue of discrimination, especially against former outcaste groups, must be addressed also. Second, Western pressure will help conservatives convince the Japanese public to lance the boil of Article 9. In fact, Japan's military forces – for that is what these are – have taken part in U.N. peacekeeping operations in the Persian Gulf, Southeast Asia, Africa, and the Golan Heights. Before too long, the Japanese will formally rewrite Article 9 in keeping with these realities but will probably expressly prohibit conscription and the possession of nuclear weapons.[77] In its own devious way, such a defeat for the Japanese left wing may actually further the cause of democracy in Japan because no society that claims to respect the rule of law and democratic process can tolerate forever this gross a violation of its Constitution.

75 Shibagaki Kazuo, Kōwa kara kōdo seichō e, pp. 193–5.
76 Three examples from a rapidly growing body of scholarship on these issues are: Yoshimi Yoshiaki, Jūgun ianfu (Tokyo: Iwanami shoten, 1995); Nozoe Kenji, Kikigaki: Hanaoka jiken (Tokyo: Ochanomizu shobō, 1992); and Utsumi Aiko, Chōsenjin B-C kyū senpan no kiroku (Tokyo: Keisō shobō, 1982).
77 These are among the proposals for constitutional revision submitted by the Yomiuri shinbun on November 3, 1994.

CHAPTER 2
JAPAN'S TURN TO THE WEST

HIRAKAWA SUKEHIRO
TRANSLATED BY BOB TADASHI WAKABAYASHI

Although Japan was never a "closed country" in the sense that *sakoku* literally implies, it did awaken from two hundred years of substantial "national isolation" in the last half of the nineteenth century to devote its full energy toward the realization of one goal – the establishment of a modern nation-state. This effort itself is better evidence of Japan's turn to the West than anything else, for the concept of a modern nation-state had yet to manifest itself in any non-Western country. In economic terms, a modern nation-state is a state that has experienced an industrial revolution; in social terms, it is a state with a centralized political system under which popular participation is structured through the parliamentary institutions of a constitutional order. By any measure, such characteristics of a state are thoroughly Western in nature and origin.

These distinguishing characteristics were not to be found in the Tokugawa *bakuhan* state. Nineteenth-century Japanese society was preindustrial, and its economy was based on forms of production that depended on animate rather than mechanical sources of power. A large bourgeoisie did exist to carry on commercial and financial enterprise, but it was excluded from participating in political decisions. The Tokugawa political structure was composed of a bureaucracy, representing feudally privileged classes that operated within a system that reconciled theoretically incompatible elements of feudalism and absolute shogunal "monarchy." Despite Japan's high level of cultural homogeneity – or perhaps because of it – the concept of a people as a "nation" that participated actively in the affairs of a "state" was unknown.

Confronted by an apparently superior "civilization" represented by the states of Europe, the Japanese confronted tasks of achieving modernity – making themselves into a "nation" and a "state" –

30

following the opening of their country (*kaikoku*). To that end, they had to create a central government, train bureaucrats to run the state, institute an army and a navy based on universal conscription, organize a legal system, foster capitalism, abolish feudal privilege, implement the "equality of the four status groups," consolidate a system of education, and reform their customs.

The individual who was perhaps most responsible for formulating these goals and was central to their execution in early Meiji years was Ōkubo Toshimichi (1830–78), a Satsuma leader who held real political power during the first decade of Meiji rule. Compared with his Chōshū colleague Kido Takayoshi (Kōin, 1833–77), Ōkubo was more conservative and less willing to sacrifice tradition in the quest for modernization. At the seashore near Osaka one day, Ōkubo gazed despondently at a clump of tree stumps – all that remained of a pine grove famous for its beauty – that had been leveled as a consequence of the policy of "foster industry and promote enterprise" (*shokusan kōgyō*), of which he himself was the leading proponent. Feeling the need to admonish the prefectural governor responsible for this insensitive act, Ōkubo composed the following poem:

> The pines at Takashi beach
> in spite of their renown,
> could not escape the ravage of
> historic tidal waves.[1]

Even for Ōkubo, however, the policy of "civilization and enlightenment" (*bummei kaika*) that Japan had adopted remained synonymous with Westernization. In an apparent belief that the Western powers were pure and simple embodiments of civilization, he wrote that "at present all the countries in the world are directing all their efforts toward propagating teachings of 'civilization and enlightenment,' and they lack for nothing. Hence we must imitate them in these respects."[2]

A revealing anecdote about the process by which the Meiji constitution was formulated points by extension to the larger question of preconditions within Japanese society that affected, assisted, and channeled the process of appropriating the Western example. In 1883, Itō Hirobumi, the chief architect of the future constitution, led

---

[1] Nihon shiseki kyōkai, ed., *Ōkubo Toshimichi monjo*, vol. 9 (*Nihon shiseki kyōkai sōsho*, vol. 36) (Tokyo: Tokyo daigaku shuppankai, 1969), p. 347.

[2] Ōkubo Toshimichi, "Seifu no teisai ni kansuru kengensho," in *Ōkubo Toshimichi monjo*, vol. 3, p. 11.

a delegation to Europe to study its various national constitutions. Because the Meiji government had already more or less decided to model its new constitution on that of Prussia, Itō and his delegates first visited the jurist Rudolf von Gneist (1816–95) in Berlin to seek his advice. Gneist's advice was cool and discouraging. He told them that several years earlier Bulgaria, one of several newly independent and semiindependent countries that developed in the Balkans after the Russo-Turkish War, had asked for assistance in framing a constitution. Though all of Gneist's colleagues were hampered by a lack of knowledge about conditions in that country, one legal scholar had volunteered to go there to produce a constitution within six months' time, an offer that brought scornful amusement. True to his word, however, the man made good his boast. But upon his return to Berlin, he had provoked loud laughter among his colleagues with the quip, "After all, how long does it take to gloss over a bronze vessel with gold paint?"

Gneist went on to advise his Japanese guests as follows:

I am most grateful that you have chosen to come all the way to Germany on your mission. Unfortunately I know nothing of Japan, and have never studied it. Let me first ask you about Japan, about the relationship between ruler and ruled, its manners and customs, about the sentiments of its people, and about its history, etc. Clarify all these things for me first, and then I will think about them and provide you with an answer that might be of some assistance to you.[3]

In short, Gneist began by bluntly admonishing Itō that only those nations possessing a minimum degree of latent potential, that is, a certain level of cultural advancement, were capable of creating a truly meaningful constitution. To undertake such a task before acquiring the requisite capacity would merely result in an elaborately embellished piece of paper. Gneist then insinuated that in Japan's case the drafting of a constitution might very well be meaningless.

This brusque reply was thoroughly disheartening to Itō, the representative of a small, backward, East Asian country who stood face to face with a European civilization that was at the zenith of its power and glory and that was convinced of its own superiority as none other in recorded history had been. How could the words of a famous Berlin jurist fail to ring true in both East Asian and European ears?

Yet if as Gneist asserted, a constitution, the framework of a

3 Yoshida Masaharu, "Kempō happu made," in Oka Yoshitake, ed., *Kindai Nihon seiji-shi* (Tokyo: Sōbunsha, 1962), vol. 1, pp. 286–7.

modern nation-state, "is more a legal document," if indeed it is "the manifestation of a people's spirit and the measure of a nation's capacities," then the fact that a modern nation-state did emerge in nineteenth-century Japan indicates that something in the "relationship between ruler and ruled," the "manners and customs," the "sentiments of its people," and its "history, etc." facilitated the creation of a new form of state based on the Meiji Constitution. To put it differently, this process, and indeed the rapidity, of Japan's Westernization indicates that the gap between Japan and the West at that time was entirely bridgeable.

Japan's turn to the West had to be carried out in two separate dimensions: (1) the importation and assimilation of modern ideas and institutions on a technical, formal level, such as Gneist's constitutional "legal document"; and (2) the adaptation of an indigenous, traditional culture and institutions to bring out their latent potential, in Gneist's terms, "the national spirit and capacities."

THE MEDIUM OF BOOKS: FIRST AWARENESS OF MODERN WESTERN CIVILIZATION

Dutch studies

Tokugawa society was culturally creative and produced much that we now consider "traditionally Japanese," but Japan was not by any means intellectually secluded during its period of national isolation. Intellectual activity during the Edo period can be broadly classified into three categories: (1) Confucianism, which had a distinguished pedigree and possessed great prestige; (2) Japanese learning (*kokugaku*), which arose in mid-Tokugawa times as a reaction to the sinocentrism that then prevailed in scholarly circles; and (3) Dutch studies (*rangaku*), whose emergence was signaled by the translation into Japanese of a Dutch translation of a work on anatomy by the German doctor Kulmus called *Ontleedkundige tafelen*, and also referred to as *Tafel Anatomia*, which was completed in 1774 by Sugita Gempaku and his colleagues. Dutch studies sprang up as an adjunct to medicine and gradually spread to other areas, such as language study, astronomy, geography, physics, chemistry, and military science. Although they appeared on the academic scene relatively late, Dutch studies had wide currency by late Tokugawa times, and the awareness of some Dutch studies specialists of the need to reconsider the system of national seclusion played an important role in bridging the intellectual gap between the West and Japan in the mid-nineteenth century.

It is significant that two of these three principal fields of Tokugawa learning derived from China and the West and were alien in origin. Japan remained in contact with China and Holland, the cultural homelands of Confucianism and Dutch studies, throughout the Edo period, although to be sure the degrees of contact differed greatly. Nevertheless, conventional generalizations about the period of "national isolation" (*sakoku*) prepare one poorly for understanding the amount and quality of information about the outside world that was accessible to Tokugawa thinkers. Chinese books, including Chinese translations of Western works, were imported every year from Ch'ing China. The Dutch East India Company maintained a Nagasaki outpost whose superintendent was required to submit reports on foreign affairs (*Oranda fūsetsugaki*) to the bakufu via the Nagasaki magistrate whenever Dutch ships made visits to that port. The same superintendent was obliged to travel to Edo at regular intervals for a formal shogunal audience, at first annually, then every other year, and finally every four years. On these trips, he and his associates were able to convey information to doctors and astronomers there who were thirsting for knowledge about the West. There was thus direct, though limited, contact with representatives of European civilization. Just as Tokugawa Confucians reaped the benefits of Ch'ing philological and historical scholarship, Japanese students of Dutch studies profited from many of the modern scientific advances in contemporary Europe and America. Consequently, despite the restrictions imposed by national isolation, there was a considerable degree of openness and receptivity to East and West in the intellectual milieu of Tokugawa Japan.

Even so, one cannot fail to be struck by the extraordinary speed with which Dutch studies spread. That speed reflects both the intense curiosity of those Japanese who pledged themselves to this new exotic discipline and the enthusiasm with which they pursued it. Moreover, the seemingly unsystematic activities of the Dutch studies specialists belie a certain underlying regularity. All these elements – speed of diffusion, curiosity, enthusiasm, and selective approach – anticipate Japan's more ambitious, post-Restoration attempts to assimilate modern Western civilization.

In 1815, the eighty-two-year-old Sugita Gempaku (1733–1817) published *Rangaku kotohajime* (The beginnings of Dutch studies), in which he recalled the circumstances under which he, Maeno

Ryōtaku, and their associates had begun the formidable task of translating a volume of anatomical tables, *Tafel Anatomia* (*Ontleedkundige Tafelen*), forty-three years earlier in 1771. It can be said that with that endeavor they initiated modern Japan's independent and eclectic assimilation of advanced Western civilization through the medium of books. Sugita decribed the speed with which Dutch studies subsequently spread and the strength of will displayed by its early proponents:

At present, Dutch studies are in great fashion throughout Japan. Those who have decided to pursue them do so avidly, although the ignorant among the populace praise and admire these studies in greatly exaggerated terms.

Reflecting upon the beginnings of Dutch studies, I realize that in those days, two or three friends and I decided to take them up almost on the spur of the moment. Yet close to fifty years have since elapsed, and how strange it is! When we began, I never in my wildest dreams thought that Dutch studies would achieve the popularity they enjoy today.

It was only natural for Chinese studies to develop and prosper gradually here in Japan. After all, in ancient times the government dispatched scholarly missions to China; later, learned clerics were also sent to the continent where they studied under Chinese masters. In either case, after their return to Japan, such persons were placed in positions to teach high and low, nobility and commoners, alike. But that was not the case with Dutch studies. . . .[4]

Sugita, probably like other Japanese intellectuals with a similar historical consciousness, saw his own efforts at assimilating Western culture as sharply at variance with Japan's established methods of assimilating Chinese culture, which had been followed for over a millennium. He posited three principal methods through which a foreign civilization could be assimilated: (1) experience, observation, and study abroad; (2) instruction by foreign or Japanese teachers; and (3) books. Between A.D. 607 and 894, the Japanese court had sponsored over a dozen scholarly missions to China for the direct observation of and instruction in Sui and T'ang culture. The contrast between these subsidized enterprises and Sugita's own humble efforts loomed large in his mind, for the sole medium of cultural assimilation accessible to him and his colleagues was books written in a language they could not read.

But despite these handicaps – the lack of official support and awesome linguistic difficulties – toward the end of his life Sugita remarked that Dutch studies had developed like "a drop of oil,

4 Odaka Toshio and Matsumura Akira, eds., *Nihon koten bungaku taikei*, vol. 95: *Taionki, Oritakushiba no ki, Rantō kotohajime* (Tokyo: Iwanami shoten, 1964), p. 473.

which, when cast upon a wide pond, disperses to cover its entire surface," a process that "brings me nothing but jubilation." The advances made by Dutch studies had now reached a point at which, as Sugita noted, "every year new translations appear." With historical hindsight, we can add that the tide of translations from the Dutch in early nineteenth-century Japan may have been roughly comparable to the amount of translation from Japanese into Western languages a century or so later.

Sugita's jubilation was well founded, for unlike the days when Japan had imported Chinese civilization, study in the West was out of the question, and devotees of Dutch studies could not even get instruction from fellow Japanese, much less from foreign teachers, except for the bits and pieces of information they could cull from Japanese interpreters who accompanied the Dutch East India Company representatives during their stays in Edo. Deprived of even the most elementary language training, Sugita and his associates had to begin their translation of *Tafel Anatomia* by substituting Japanese equivalents of foreign names for parts of the body that appeared on anatomical diagrams.

For example, we spent a long spring day puzzling over such simple lines as "An 'eyebrow' is hair growing above the eye." We sometimes stared at each other blankly from morning to dusk, unable to decipher a single line from a one- to two-inch passage of text.

Nevertheless, they gradually overcame these difficulties by application and enthusiasm:

Yet we believed that "Man proposes, Heaven disposes" and persevered. We would meet six or seven times a month and devoted ourselves body and soul to the project. No one ever begged off on the scheduled meeting days; we all assembled without being prevailed upon to do so, and we would read and discuss the text together. "Perseverance will prevail," we would reassure ourselves and pressed on.

After a year or so, our command of vocabulary gradually increased, and we naturally discovered a great deal about conditions in Holland. Later on, we became capable of reading as much as ten or more lines of text per day if the particular passage was not too difficult.[5]

Sugita's satisfaction in recollecting these experiences lay in the fact that the cultural legacy of Dutch studies to subsequent generations of Japanese owed its existence to the determination and zeal displayed by this small group of pioneers.

5   Ibid., pp. 515, 493, 495.

In the 1860s, Dutch studies and the Dutch language were abandoned in favor of English, which soon became the primary Western language for Japanese intellectuals. This transition from Dutch studies to Western learning was depicted by Fukuzawa Yukichi in his autobiography in which he described his experiences in the foreign sector of Yokohama after the ports had been opened in 1859. Fukuzawa tried to speak Dutch with foreigners only to find to his dismay that communication was impossible. Undaunted, he made up his mind to "devote himself to English." Fukuzawa was a pioneer in the study of English and became an Enlightenment thinker who explained the development of Japanese history in Western terms. By emphasizing the importance of fundamental changes needed in Meiji Japan, he tended to slight Tokugawa achievements. Yet even Fukuzawa expressed his indebtedness to men like Sugita in the Dutch studies tradition. Having obtained a copy of Sugita's *Rangaku kotahajime*, Fukuzawa and Mitsukuri Shūhei sat opposite each other and read and reread it. When they reached the portion that compared the way that those pioneers had set out on the translation of *Tafel Anatomia* to sailors "drifting about in a boat without rudder or oar, helpless and baffled on a vast expanse of ocean," he wrote that they "sobbed wordlessly until they came to the end." Fukuzawa wrote: "Each time we read this book we realize how great their toil must have been; we are amazed at their courage; we feel their sincerity and singleness of purpose; and we try to hold back the tears."[6] Fukuzawa republished Sugita's book at his own expense in 1868, and in the foreword he related his feelings after having first read the work: "It was like encountering an old friend, someone I thought was dead, reborn and well." He wrote that the source of energy propelling Meiji Japan toward modernization could be traced to forerunners like Sugita and argued that "the beginnings of knowledge of Western civilization existed" a century before his time among scholars on this small island in East Asia, that "today's progress . . . is not a product of blind chance."[7]

The deciphering of *Tafel Anatomia* by Sugita and his associates illustrates Japan's positive response toward Western civilization. There are two explanations of this enthusiastic response. First, it reveals the Japanese intellectuals' unusually strong curiosity toward the outside world, and it shows that the value system to which they

6 Quoted in "Rangaku kotohajime saihan no jo," in *Fukuzawa Yukichi zenshū* (Tokyo: Iwanami shoten, 1962), vol. 19, p. 770.   7 Ibid.

were committed did not emphasize intellectual self-sufficiency: To a large extent, alien doctrines and learning could be absorbed and accommodated. Second, the personal motivation that sustained the pioneers demonstrates both their intellectual curiosity and their pragmatism. Maeno Ryōtaku "desired to make Dutch studies his life's work, to learn all there is to know about that language and thus to find out all there is to know about conditions in the West and to read numerous books,"[8] whereas Nakagawa Jun'an "had long been interested in what things were made of and wanted by this means to learn about Western products."[9] On the one hand, we discover an orientation of almost purely intellectual curiosity, and on the other, one of practicability, both driving people toward Dutch studies. In Sugita's own case, the motivation for translating *Tafel Anatomia* lay in his professional consciousness of being a physician. As he put it:

First and foremost, I wanted to make manifest the fact that actual dissections performed on human bodies confirmed the accuracy of Dutch anatomical diagrams and disproved Chinese and Japanese theories. Then I wanted to apply the Dutch theories in clinical treatment and to make these available to other physicians in order to encourage the development of new techniques.

Sugita's sense of mission had first been sparked by witnessing an autopsy performed at Kotsugahara in Edo in 1771. On the way home, he wrote, he discussed its results with Maeno and Nakagawa:

What a revelation that day's demonstration had been! We were truly embarrassed to discover our ignorance. Each of us, who was responsible for serving our lord as a physician, proved to be totally ignorant of the basic anatomical structure of man, which is fundamental to medical science. It was a disgrace that we had been carrying on our duties all along in this state of ignorance.

Some writers have tended to associate Dutch studies with a critical attitude toward feudal authority, but here we find one of its most devoted proponents troubled by the sense of "disgrace" stemming from his unworthiness to "serve his lord" properly. Such an ethos, emphasizing as Sugita did the responsibilities of a physician's hereditary status, easily transforms itself into an occupational ethic. The intensity of this spirit – related also to *bushidō* – and the ease with which it could be translated into an occupational ethic can be

8 *Nihon koten bungaku taikei*, vol. 95, p. 499. 9 Ibid., pp. 491–2.

considered two key factors that made Japan's turn to the West possible at an early stage, thereby distinguishing the Japanese experience from that of other non-Western countries.

The significance of Tokugawa lexicography

In the initial phase of contact between Western and non-Western peoples, most lexicography was a product of the burgeoning, expansive West. This is seen, for instance, in the *Vocabulario da Lingoa de Iapan* containing over thirty thousand entries compiled by the Jesuit Joao Rodriguez Tcuzzu in 1603. Later, however, non-Western peoples who perceived Europe to be "advanced" and strove to "catch up" with Western civilization seized this lexicographic initiative. The Japanese provide a good example. The growth of Dutch studies in Japan was ensured after 1796, when Inamura Sampaku published a Dutch-Japanese dictionary, the *Edo Halma*. This was an adaptation of François Halma's eighty-thousand-word Dutch-French dictionary in which Inamura substituted Japanese translations for the French equivalents. In the era of early encounters with English-speaking peoples that followed, Dutch-English conversation books, English-Dutch dictionaries, and then English-language dictionaries were used. Webster's dictionary first reached Japan via the Perry squadron; and later, in 1860, Fukuzawa Yukichi and Nakahama Manjirō each brought back a copy from San Francisco. The first English-Japanese dictionary, the six-thousand-word *Angeria gorin taisei*, was compiled at the bakufu's direction by the Nagasaki Dutch interpreter, Motoki Shōzaemon, in 1814; but Hori Tatsunosuke's *Ei-Wa taiyaku shūchin jisho*,[10] containing over thirty thousand entries and published in 1862, received far greater use. Hori used entries and sample phrases and sentences from the English-Dutch portion of H. Picard's *A New Pocket Dictionary of the English-Dutch and Dutch-English Languages*, eliminated the Dutch definitions, and supplied Japanese equivalents from the *Nagasaki Halma*, a Nagasaki version of the *Edo Halma* that had more colloquial expressions. Thus the study of English developed from that of Dutch, and knowledge accumulated rapidly. Among the dictionaries compiled by Americans in Japan is the *Wa-Ei gorin shūsei*, a work containing over twenty thousand words, published in 1867 by James Hepburn (1815–1911), a Presbyterian medical missionary who came to Japan in 1859.

10 Hori changed the "pocket" of Picard's pocket dictionary to a kimono sleeve; hence the character *shū*, as in *sode*.

But thereafter, almost all the best dictionaries, whether English-Japanese, Japanese-English, German-Japanese, Japanese-German, French-Japanese, Japanese-French, or Russian-Japanese, were compiled by Japanese.[11]

A nineteenth-century figure who perceived the significance of Tokugawa lexicography was Sakuma Shōzan (1811–64), a scholar of both Confucian and Western learning. Sakuma planned to publish a revised and enlarged edition of the *Edo Halma*, and to cover the expenses he borrowed twelve hundred *ryō* from his domain by pledging his own stipend of one hundred *koku* rice as collateral. Although this plan came to naught because the bakufu refused to grant permission, Sakuma's petition shows his perception of the importance and meaning of the enterprise he proposed:

If only you would see this project as a way of laying the foundation for access to and mastery of proficiency in the arts and sciences, as a step toward adopting the strong points of countries on every continent in order to create a Japan forever able to maintain its autonomy in the world, then whatever criticism it might draw would be as inconsequential as the flapping of a mosquito's wings.[12]

The "science" referred to in Sakuma's famous slogan "Eastern morality, Western science" is often taken to mean only "technology," but in fact, his term has broader implications, including the arts and sciences that form the basis of that technology. This can be seen in comments he made to a correspondent:

At present the learning of China and Japan is not sufficient; it must be supplemented and made complete by inclusion of the learning of the entire world. Columbus discovered a new world by "investigating principle"; Copernicus worked out the theory of heliocentricity; and Newton recognized the truth of gravitational laws. Since these three great discoveries were made, all arts and sciences have been based on them – each is true, not one is false.[13]

---

11   Professor N. I. Konrad's *Japanese-Russian Dictionary*, a possible exception, remains unsurpassed by Japanese efforts, a fact that probably indicates Japanese priorities in foreign-language study. What has been said about Western-language dictionaries applies equally to Chinese. Morohashi Tetsuji's reference dictionary of classical Chinese, *Dai Kan-Wa jiten*, published in 1960 by a publishing house that had to set the work a second time after its plant was destroyed in 1945, is recognized as standard in all countries where Chinese characters serve as the written medium. Like the Western-language dictionaries, this work represents an attempt to assimilate a superior foreign culture by a less developed civilization, but it nevertheless surpasses all similar lexicographical achievements in China itself.

12   "Haruma wo hangyō nite kaihan sen koto wo chinzu," in *Shōzan zenshū* (Tokyo: Shōbunkan, 1913), vol. 1, p. 128.

13   "Letter to Yanagawa Seigan," dated 3/6/Ansei 5 (1858), in ibid., vol. 2, pp. 845–6.

Sakuma believed that Confucianism was fully compatible with Western military technology and hence that Chinese and Western doctrines were ultimately identical. To him, dictionary compilation was an indispensable means to acquire this fundamentally identical knowledge. In the petition cited earlier, he also stated:

Nothing is more important to the conduct of war, nor is there anything more pressing in present-day coastal defense, than Sun Tzu's adage "Know the enemy." Hence, I would like to see all persons in the realm thoroughly familiar with the enemy's conditions, something that can best be achieved by allowing them to read barbarian books as they read their own language. There is no better way to enable them to do this than publishing this dictionary.

The compilation and publication of this dictionary thus symbolized Sakuma's desire to understand foreign civilization in a fundamental and comprehensive manner. He was also eager to disseminate such understanding among his countrymen. The assimilation of Western culture through such a process of enlightenment was pursued on a national scale by the Meiji government a few years later, but to Sakuma, it still seemed as though the task hinged entirely on the bakufu's approval for publishing his laboriously brush-copied dictionary manuscript. Such was this Tokugawa intellectual's intensity on the eve of the Meiji Restoration.

The cultural and intellectual milieu of Dutch studies

Consideration of the setting within which Dutch studies was able to develop in Tokugawa times must include attention to general cultural traditions as well as an awareness of the specific trends of eighteenth-century intellectual life. Tokugawa intellectuals began with an awareness of their ancestors' ability to adopt and adapt Chinese civilization; a millennium earlier, the Japanese had also thought of their land as existing on the outer fringes of a world cultural sphere. In a sense, nineteenth-century Japanese intellectuals needed only to transfer that center from China to the West. In this regard, the Japanese consciousness and problems differed strikingly from those of China, and consequently Japanese thinkers were probably better equipped psychologically for assimilating Western culture than were their Chinese counterparts. Just as they had earlier studied Chinese civilization under the slogan "Japanese spirit, Chinese skills," now they spoke of "Japanese spirit, Western skills."

The eighteenth-century pioneers in Dutch studies were fully aware of this parallel. Sugita Gempaku concluded his recollections of the growth of Dutch studies by asking: "Was it not because our minds had already been trained through Chinese learning that Dutch studies were able to develop this rapidly?"[14] Moreover, the "training" he had in mind had linguistic as well as attitudinal aspects. Unlike other East Asian peoples on the fringe of the Chinese cultural sphere, the Japanese early developed a method for adapting texts in classical Chinese to the syntactical rules of their own language, instead of reading classical Chinese as a foreign language. The result, known as *kambun* reading, was a complex and cumbersome procedure, but it involved rigorous intellectual training in translation that had as one consequence the nationalization of a foreign language.

Partly because of this and partly because of its relative isolation, Japan was never overwhelmed by Chinese – or Western – learning but retained a substantial cultural autonomy from which assimilation could be managed. Just enough could be learned about the outside world to whet the curiosity of men seeking knowledge and instill in them admiration for the West without totally absorbing them into the "superior" culture. Given the physical isolation in which Tokugawa scholars of Dutch studies labored, there was never any possibility of their identifying themselves completely with the alien culture; their admiration for the West was fated to be pursued along purely intellectual lines. This geographical limitation contributed to the emphasis on retaining and strengthening the "Japanese spirit" while pursuing "Western skills." Hashimoto Sanai (1831–59) wrote that Japan should "adopt mechanical devices and techniques from the West but retain the benevolence, righteousness, loyalty, and filial piety of Japan."[15] Yokoi Shōnan (1809–69) agreed and urged his countrymen to "make manifest the Way of Yao, Shun, and Confucius and to obtain a thorough knowledge of mechanical techniques from the West."[16] Sakuma Shōzan also spoke of "Eastern morality and Western techniques." The future Meiji government accepted these goals under the slogan "Adopt what is best

14 "Rantō kotohajime," in *Nihon koten bungaku taikei*, vol. 95, p. 505.
15 "Letter to Murata Ujihisa," dated 10/21/Ansei 4, in Nihon shiseki kyōkai, ed., *Hashimoto Keigaku zenshū*, vol. 2 (*Nihon shiseki kyōkai sōsho*, vol. 47) (Tokyo: Tokyo daigaku shuppankai, 1977), pp. 471–2.
16 "Letter to Nephews Studying in the West," in Nihon shiseki kyōkai, ed., *Yokoi Shōnan kankei shiryō*, vol. 2 (*Zoku Nihon shiseki kyōkai sōsho*, vol. 40) (Tokyo: Tokyo daigaku shuppankai, 1977), p. 726.

in the culture of Europe to compensate for shortcomings in that of Japan."

It is also useful to examine eighteenth-century intellectual trends that helped give rise to Dutch studies. For the most part, the era was characterized by empiricism, a development that arose also within Ch'eng-Chu Confucianism, the grand system of speculative philosophy that provided the principal current of orthodox learning during the Edo period. This discussion is limited to the development of empirical trends in relation to Tokugawa medicine, the womb from which Dutch studies emerged. Japan first encountered Western civilization in the late sixteenth century, before the national isolation of Tokugawa times. In that warring era, survival of the fittest was the rule, and political leaders were keenly aware of the need to appropriate any new device that would increase their chances of achieving victory. They were utterly indifferent as to whether cultural accretions like firearms or surgery were of foreign or native origin. At that time, the Japanese learned early Western-style surgery through direct observation of Iberian practice rather than through written accounts, and a distinct school of "southern barbarian" surgery developed. This school of surgery was dominant until it was superseded by techniques developed by students of Dutch studies, but it contributed almost nothing to the latter's emergence. The impetus behind Dutch studies lay elsewhere, in Tokugawa Confucianism.

Toward the end of the seventeenth century, a number of private scholars challenged the Ch'eng-Chu Confucian school that then dominated the Tokugawa scholarly world. One of the foremost was Itō Jinsai (1627–1705) of Kyoto, who propounded the so-called Ancient Learning (also known as the School of Ancient Meanings), which rejected medieval commentaries and sought the "Way of the sages" by going directly back to the *Analects*, the *Mencius*, and other Confucian classics. Thus Jinsai's school may be considered a form of antiquarian revivalism. Slightly later, Ogyū Sorai (1666–1728), also an advocate of Ancient Learning, had an even greater impact on the contemporary intellectual scene. The influence of these teachings was felt beyond the field of Confucian scholarship. For example, Japanese learning (*kokugaku*) held that the pristine "true Japanese heart" could be discovered only by rejecting the "spirit of China" that had come to muddy it in later ages and that this could best be done through studying the *Kojiki*, the *Manyōshū*, and other ancient Japanese classics.

Until the middle of the Edo period, Tokugawa medical thought was dominated by the Li-Chu school of Chinese medicine that had developed under Li Tung-yuan and Chu Tan-ch'i during the Chin and Yuan periods. It was a form of speculative philosophy that discussed human pathology in terms of *yin–yang*, the Five Elements, the Five Circulations, and the Six *ch'i*. But under the influence of mid-Tokugawa Ancient Learning, a movement arose among nongovernment scholar-physicians to reject such speculative ideas as latter-day inventions and to return to the "Way" that medicine had supposedly been practiced in ancient China, as depicted in works such as *Shanghan lun*.[17] This movement was related to the School of Ancient Learning in its emphasis on the empirical. Gotō Konzan (1683–1755), who was an admirer of Itō Jinsai, sent one of his own disciples, Kagawa Shūan (1683–1755), to study at Jinsai's private academy. Under Kagawa there evolved a form of Confucian-medical thought that viewed Confucius' "Way of the sages" as being basically identical with a "Way of medicine." According to Kagawa, the sages and worthies of antiquity were staunch in their reverence for empirical fact, and latter-day speculative philosophers had obfuscated that emphasis. The School of Ancient Method, as it came to be known, repudiated such latter-day accretions in favor of a return to the direct study of ancient Chinese medical texts.

The critical basis for this antiquarian revivalism was a positivism that insisted that hypotheses be verified. In time, this emphasis made its proponents skeptical of the validity of ancient as well as medieval medical texts. For example, one scholar, Nagatomi Dokushōan (1734–66), related the story of a T'ang palace painter, Han Kan, who, when ordered by the emperor to paint a horse, was offered pictures done by former palace artists for reference. He replied, "I have no desire to look at such pictures, for the horses kept in Your Majesty's stables will provide far better reference." The physician too, Nagatomi concluded, must work in this manner. The mere reading of texts was insufficient; the physician had to be free of preconceived notions, tend a real patient, conduct a close and direct examination, and use his own ingenuity to devise a cure. This process was known as *shinshi jikken* (personal examination and actual experience). Yoshimasu Tōdō (1702–73), who stressed this method of *shinshi jikken*, devoted himself to what is now called the

17   A medical text written by Chang Chung-ching of the later Han dynasty. The oldest extent edition was compiled by Wang Shu-ho of the Western Chin. Centuries later in the Sung, Lin I published a newly edited edition.

"symptomatic treatment" of diseases. In his book *Medical Diagnoses*, he wrote that "principles" (*li*), or a priori speculative theories, are subjective, vary with the people who hold them, and lack established standards by which they can be confirmed or disproved. Diseases, on the other hand, have specific symptoms. In short, a doctor should not employ subjective theories without careful and accurate diagnoses of the diseases. Yamawaki Tōyō (1705–62) was long skeptical of the traditional anatomical diagrams used by Tokugawa specialists of Chinese medicine. With encouragement from his teacher, Gotō Konzan, he dissected an otter. Next, after obtaining official permission, he performed an autopsy on an executed criminal in 1754 and recorded his observations in a work entitled *Account of an Autopsy*. This work shocked the Tokugawa medical world. Yamawaki became the object of much censure and attack, but he steadfastly maintained his views. In his *Account*, he wrote: "Theories [*li*] may be overturned, but how can real material things deceive? When theories are esteemed over reality, even a man of great wisdom cannot fail to err. When material things are investigated and theories are based on that, even a man of common intelligence can perform well."

Yamawaki and his colleagues brought to the autopsy a Dutch translation of a textbook on anatomy written by a professor at Padua University. They were astonished to discover how closely the book's diagrams matched the corpse's organs. Yamawaki had originally viewed Vesling's diagrams with some disbelief because of their great discrepancy with prevailing Chinese medical theories, but when he compared these Western diagrams with actual human anatomy and verified their accuracy, he realized how outlandish the Chinese versions were. As he put it: "He who treads the Way of fact reaches the same end though living ten thousand miles away. How can I suppress my admiration?" This reveals the idea that differences of nation or race are irrelevant to the quest for objective fact and the realization that the road to truth, which had been obscured in China since medieval times, paradoxically existed among those very Westerners normally considered barbarians.

There was thus a clear relationship between the textual rigor of the School of Ancient Learning and the practical and empirical emphases of Dutch studies. The connection can also be traced in personal as well as intellectual terms. Kosugi Genteki, a student of Yamawaki Tōyō who witnessed the autopsy, was a domain physician in Obama and thus a colleague of Sugita Gempaku. Another Yamawaki disciple, Kuriyama Kōan, himself performed two autopsies in Hagi, the castle town of Chōshū, and Sugita in 1771 managed to arrange and be present at an autopsy in Edo, which he described as the starting point of his dedication to truth through experiment. The accuracy of the anatomical tables of the Kulmus volume he had with him that day so impressed him that he and his colleagues resolved to translate the entire work.

Sugita's memoirs no doubt risk exaggerating the role of this event in a tradition already being transformed, but it should at the least be considered symbolic if not pivotal. There is a sense, moveover, in which Sugita and his contemporaries followed Ancient Learning to go a step beyond the promising beginning made earlier by Yamawaki. Despite the rhetoric of practicality and observation found in Yamawaki and his contemporaries, they tended in practice to restrict themselves to the wisdom of antiquity and refrained from pushing their ideas to their logical conclusions.[18] Sugita, however, in his *Nocturnal Dialogues with My Silhouette*, described how his reading of Ogyū Sorai's treatise on military science, *Kenroku gaisho*, motivated him to try to formulate a systematic study of medicine based on empirical methods:

Sorai writes that true warfare is very different from what so-called masters of the art of war teach us. Topography may be hilly or flat, and armies may be strong or weak. One cannot make identical cut-and-dried preparations that will be right for all times and all places; one cannot discourse on victory and defeat in unvarying, stereotyped fashion prior to the commencement of an engagement. . . . Victory or defeat are determined on a case-by-case basis by constant study of strategic principles and by the capacities of great generals.[19]

In this way, military strategy discussed by the leading proponent of Ancient Learning was transferred to the realm of medicine, combined with systematic observation (*shinshi jikken*), and applied to the appropriation and utilization of Dutch medical and scientific lore by the pioneers of Dutch studies in late eighteenth-century Japan. A half-century later, the crisis in foreign relations found the emphasis shifting back to military concerns; ultimately it flowered in the Meiji government's policies of selective Westernization. These develop-

18 For developments in medicine and thought on the eve of the rise of *rangaku*, see Fujikawa Hideo, "Kohōka to rangaku," in Fujikawa Hideo, *Seitō shiwa* (Tokyo: Tamagawa daigaku shuppanbu, 1974), pp. 9–20. For a general treatment of *rangaku* and Western learning, see Satō Shōsuke, *Yōgakushi kenkyū josetsu* (Tokyo: Iwanami shoten, 1964).

19 Sugita Gempaku, "Keiei yawa," in Fujikawa Yū et al., eds., *Kyōrin sōsho* (Kyoto: Shibunkaku reprint edition, 1971), vol. 1, p. 106. This passage is also quoted in Satō, *Yōgakū-shi kenkyū josetsu*, p. 60.

ments were thus of momentous significance for Japanese thought and Japan's assimilation of Western culture.

FROM BOOKS TO EXPERIENCE: LATE TOKUGAWA AND EARLY MEIJI TRAVELERS

Japan's longing to see the outside world

One of the striking phenomena of mid-nineteenth-century Japan is the strong desire of educated Japanese to see the outside world. With an eighty-year history of Dutch studies behind them, many Japanese grew dissatisfied with relying solely on books to learn about the West. Presented with the evidence of Perry's "Black Ships" that Japan had fallen behind during its two-century absence from the stage of world history, many young men resolved to meet the challenge posed by technological superiority of Western civilization by investigating Western civilization at its source. Yamaji Aizan described the late Tokugawa zeitgeist as a "desire to speed to foreign shores and take up the great task of observing far-off lands."[20] Miyake Setsurei, in his *History of Our Times*, wrote: "Only the ignorant and indolent among the samurai were surprised upon learning of [Yoshida] Shōin's plan to visit America, for not a few likeminded men were making similar preparations. Ultimately his plan was implemented in the form of sending a bakufu warship to San Francisco in 1860."[21] Thus the steam engines of Perry's Black Ships, considered symbolic of the West's superior technology, convinced Japanese of their country's inferiority; their "consciousness of crisis" dictated that "there is no more pressing need in our defense against the barbarians at present than 'knowing the enemy.'" This realistic, empirical outlook made it a prime task to "investigate enemy conditions," a goal mirrored in the title of Fukuzawa Yukichi's best-seller, *Conditions in the West*.

That this determination was shared by different sorts of men can be shown by comparing the cases of Yoshida Shōin and Niijima Jō. At first glance, they seem an unlikely pair. Yoshida (1830–59) is known to history as a fiery nationalist and exponent of total, unquestioning loyalty to the emperor. His fury at the bakufu's agreement to sign the humiliating unequal treaties led him into

---

20 Yamaji Aizan, "Niijima Jō ron," in Yamaji Aizan, *Kirisutokyō hyōron, Nihon jimminshi* (Tokyo: Iwanami shoten, 1966), p. 44.
21 Miyake Setsurei, *Dōjidaishi* (Tokyo: Iwanami shoten, 1949), vol. 1, pp. 2–3.

teaching and plotting so extreme that he was executed in the Ansei purge carried out by Ii Naosuke. His unwavering espousal of the imperial cause as the highest duty made him a rallying point and martyr for later nationalism and nationalists. As early as 1867 the Chōshū loyalist Takasugi Shinsaku, and as recently as 1970 the novelist Mishima Yukio, invoked his words in justifying ritual suicide in the national cause. Niijima (1843–90), on the other hand, is known to his countrymen as an ardent Christian and Westernizer, a runaway from feudal jurisdiction who found protection, kindness, and Christianity in America, was educated at Amherst College and Andover Seminary, and returned to Japan to found its first Christian university (Dōshisha) in Kyoto, the ancient capital and heartland of Japanese Buddhism. Nevertheless, Yoshida and Niijima shared a basic receptivity and curiosity regarding the West and a great desire to learn in the hope of preparing themselves and their country to accept the challenge posed by that West.

The case of Yoshida Shōin

Yoshida Shōin's encounter with the West came at the dawn of Japan's opening by the squadron of Commodore Perry's Black Ships. Perry arrived in 1853, left President Millard Fillmore's letter requesting formal diplomatic relations, and sailed away with a warning that he would return for a reply in the spring of 1854. In the interim, Sakuma Shōzan counseled his young student Shōin that it would be worthwhile to try to leave Japan with the squadron when it returned in order to equip himself with direct knowledge of the West.

While Perry's ships were inspecting the harbor of Shimoda in April 1854, J. W. Spaulding, captain's clerk of the *Mississippi*, was ashore for a stroll one afternoon when two young men dressed as samurai approached him, ostensibly to examine his watch chain. Once within reach, one of them thrust a letter into the vest of the startled clerk. Flawlessly written in classical Chinese, which S. W. Williams, the American interpreter, could read, it stated: "We have ... read in books, and learned a little by hearsay, what the customs and education in Europe and America are, and we have been for many years desirous of going over the 'five great continents'." The exaggerated metaphors of the *kambun* document reveal the intensity of Yoshida's desire to learn about the world outside Japan:

When a lame man sees others walking, he wishes to walk too; but how shall the pedestrian gratify his desires when he sees another one riding? We have all our lives been going hither to you, unable to get more than thirty degrees east and west, or twenty-five degrees north and south; but now when we see how you sail on the tempests and cleave the huge billows, going lightning speed thousands and myriads of miles, scurrying along the five great continents, can it not be likened to the lame finding a plan for walking, and the pedestrian seeking a mode by which he can ride?[22]

The abortive effort of the two young men to secure passage on the *Mississippi* in the dead of night, before an answer could be given to this document, is well known. Perry felt it poor policy to help them break the laws of their government against travel overseas so soon after securing the treaty he had come to negotiate, and he reluctantly denied their request after discussing it with them through the interpreter on board. What should be noted, however, is the recklessness of the attempt and the intensity and, no doubt, naïveté, of their behavior. This disregard for personal danger and single-mindedness of purpose earned the warmhearted understanding of S. Wells Williams, the interpreter, which can be inferred from Yoshida's *Account of a Spring Night*, Spaulding's *Japan Expedition*, and F. L. Hawks's *Narrative*.

Spaulding's account described the consequences for the two:

A few days afterward, some of our officers in their strolls ashore ascertained that there were two Japanese confined in a cage at a little barrack back of the town, and on going there they were found to be the persons who had paid the midnight visit to our ships, and they also proved to be my unfortunate friends of the letter. They did not appear greatly down-cast by their situation, and one of them wrote in his native character on a piece of board, and passed [it] through the bars of his cage, to one of our surgeons present....[23]

The officers of the American fleet discussed the possibility of intervening to save the men's lives, but the next time they went ashore, the two were nowhere to be seen. Rumor had it that they had been transferred to an Edo prison, and when an official they questioned gestured ominously with hand to throat, the Americans realized that the two had or would soon be executed. Spaulding, recalling that the writing on the letter that had been thrust into his vest appeared "neat

---

22 Yamaguchi-ken kyōikukai, ed., *Yoshida Shōin zenshū* (Tokyo: Iwanami shoten, 1936), vol. 10, p. 876. Also in Francis L. Hawks, *Narrative of the Expedition of an American Squadron to the China Seas and Japan: Performed in the Years 1852, 1853, and 1854, Under the Command of Commodore M. C. Perry, United States Navy, the Official Account* (Washington, D.C.: Beverley Tucker, Senate Printer, 1856), p. 420.
23 Hawks, *Narrative*, pp. 884–5.

and sharply defined," concluded that the writer was surely "a man of intelligence and taste," and Hawks's *Narrative* account of the initial encounter concurs that "the Japanese were observed to be men of position and rank, as each wore the two swords characteristic of distinction, and were dressed in the wide but short trousers of rich silk brocade. Their manners showed the usual courtly refinement of the better classes. . . ."[24] Clearly, the Americans were impressed by the courageous sense of purpose shown by Shōin, convinced of his qualities, and sympathetic toward his fate. The affair no doubt served to convince them all the more strongly of the justness of their mission to open Japan.

The message written on a small piece of wood that Yoshida was able to hand to the American naval surgeon who happened to pass by his cage was described by Hawks as a "remarkable specimen of philosophical resignation under circumstances which would have tried the stoicism of Cato." It read in part:

When a hero fails in his purpose, his acts are then regarded as those of a villain and robber . . . while yet we have nothing wherewith to reproach ourselves, it must now be seen whether a hero will prove himself to be one indeed. Regarding the liberty of going through the sixty States [Japanese provinces] as not enough for our desires, we wished to make the circuit of the five great continents. This was our hearts' wish for a long time. Suddenly our plans are defeated. . . . Weeping, we seem as fools; laughing, as rogues. Alas! for us; silent we can only be.[25]

Yoshida lived another five years, during which he inspired a generation of Chōshū disciples in the academy that the domain authorities permitted him to direct during his confinement. As he explained to one such student, Shinagawa Yajirō:

If one is loath to die at seventeen or eighteen, he will be equally reluctant at thirty, and will no doubt find a life of eighty or ninety too short. Insects of the field and stream live but half a year, yet do not regard this as short. The pine and oak live hundreds of years, yet do not regard this as long. Compared to the eternity of Heaven and Earth, both are ephemeral insects. Man's life span is fifty years; to live seventy is a rarity. Unless one performs some deed that brings a sense of gratification before dying, his soul will never rest in peace.[26]

This was not to be; further plotting brought Yoshida's extradition to Edo and his execution in 1859. Yoshida described himself as one

---

24 Ibid.   25 *Yoshida Shōin zenshū*, pp. 874–5; and Hawks, *Narrative*, pp. 422–3.
26 "Letter to Shinagawa Yajirō," dated circa 4/Ansei 6, in *Yoshida Shōin zenshū*, vol. 6, p. 318.

"who fails in every enterprise undertaken, who bungles every chance for power and fortune." All the schemes he concocted, not only his trip to America, seemed to go awry. Yet his determination to know the West and his fervent loyalism lived on in his students and caught the eye of a sympathetic writer as early as 1882. Robert Louis Stevenson learned of Yoshida Shōin through a student of his Chōshū school, Masaki Taizō, who was studying at Edinburgh, and the stories that Masaki told about his teacher became a chapter in Stevenson's *Familiar Studies of Men and Books*. Stevenson quoted Thoreau to the effect that "if you can 'make your failure tragical by courage, it will not differ from success'" and concluded that "this is as much the story of a heroic people as that of a heroic man." Stevenson's other heroes in this volume possessed characteristics similar to those with which Japanese admirers have associated Yoshida Shōin: bravery, self-reliance, tenacity of will, a high sense of honor, and fervent aspiration. They were qualities required by Japanese who resolved to travel to the West in late Tokugawa days, and they were surprisingly common.

The case of Niijima Jō

Yoshida Shōin and Niijima Jō were part of the same late Tokugawa phenomenon, an urge to experience the West directly. Yoshida's attempt was abortive partly because it was made too early, in 1854, and partly because he chose the official channels of Perry's fleet on its initial diplomatic mission. By contrast, Niijima's attempt came a decade later, in 1864, and through the private auspices of an American merchant ship. Moreover, during the ten intervening years, there had been much exchange and travel. The Tokugawa warship *Kanrin maru* had sailed to the California coast to accompany the shogunal mission to Washington in 1860, the first of a series of ever-larger and evermore observant official missions to the West as treaty relations intensified. In 1862, the shogunate had sent Nishi Amane, Enomoto Takeaki, and Tsuda Mamichi to Holland to study. In 1863, the domain of Chōshū violated shogunal law by sending Itō Hirobumi and Inoue Kaoru, students of Yoshida's, to study in England; and the southern domain of Satsuma was preparing a large mission of fourteen students to go to England in 1865. Knowledge of such travel usually spread to at least the families of those involved. When the Chōshū samurai (and later foreign minister) Aoki Shūzō visited the castle town of Nakatsu in Kyūshū while Fukuzawa

Yukichi was abroad as interpreter for one such official mission, Fukuzawa's mother was able to show him letters and photographs – the first Aoki had ever seen – from her distant son.

Nevertheless, individual travel was still quite different, and very dangerous. Niijima later described in English still far from perfect his eagerness to travel: "Some day I went to the seaside of Yedo, hoping to see the view of the sea. I saw largest man-of-war of Dutch lying there, and it seemed to me a castle or a battery, and I thought too she would be strong to fight with enemy."[27] The excitement felt by this late Tokugawa youth is apparent. Niijima was acutely aware of Japan's need to create a navy and of the important benefits to be had from seaborne trade.

Niijima was chosen by his domain of Annaka to study Dutch, and he learned to read books on natural science. ("I read through the book of nature at home, taking a dictionary of Japan and Holland.") He had studied at the bakufu's Naval Training Institute for a time but found this inadequate and unsatisfying and decided that he must go overseas himself. Niijima was motivated by precisely the same simple-minded directness that Yoshida had shown, and as in Yoshida's case, Americans – the captain of the *Berlin*, who smuggled him out of Hakodate against instructions, and the captain of the *Wild Rover*, to which Niijima transferred in Shanghai and who accepted responsibility for him during the year-long voyage to Boston – found themselves drawn to him by the intensity of his passion. In Boston, the Alpheus Hardys, owners of the *Wild Rover*, after reading Niijima's poorly composed English explanation for coming to America, generously paid his school fees and supported him through his undergraduate education at Amherst College and his theological training at Andover Seminary.

When Niijima discovered that the captain of the *Berlin*, who had taken him on board, had been dismissed for having helped him leave Hakodate, he made the following diary entry:

Ah, I feel torn with guilt for having caused that good man such grief. But what is done is done, and cannot be undone. In the future, when my schooling is finished, I will do all I can to repay each and every one of his kindnesses to me. Maybe then I can make up for a small part of my wrongdoing against him.[28]

27 A. S. Hardy, *Life and Letters of Joseph Hardy Neesima* (Boston: Houghton Mifflin, 1892), p. 6.
28 Diary entry, 9/13/Meiji 1, in *Niijima Jō sensei shokan shū zokuhen* (Kyoto: Dōshisha kōyūkai, 1960), p. 239.

Westerners could no longer be considered "barbarians" by a man of such gratitude and conviction.

Individual Westerners, of course, could still provoke strong reactions. Niijima served as the captain's valet, "cleaning his cabin, waiting on him, washing his cups and saucers, and caring for his dog" – duties that he could stoop to perform only because there were no other Japanese to watch him. Having been trained in etiquette in Annaka, Niijima was well equipped to minister to the captain's needs, and we may imagine that he did so splendidly; but his samurai pride was often gravely injured. On one occasion, he was reprimanded for not obeying directions given in English by a passenger whose services he had requested as a language teacher. An expert swordsman, Niijima raced back to his cabin, took his sword, and prepared to cut down the passenger when he remembered his mission and stopped. No doubt such endurance and self-restraint were required more than once during the voyage.

After transferring to the *Wild Rover* at Shanghai, Niijima asked its captain to take him to America and presented him with the longer of his two samurai swords as a token of his gratitude. He also had the captain sell the shorter sword for $8.00 so that he might purchase a translation of the New Testament in classical Chinese. This captain, whom Niijima admired greatly, was unable to pronounce Japanese and so called Niijima "Joe." In 1876, Niijima formally adopted "Jō" as his first name. He later wrote his name "Joseph Hardy Neesima" in English, using "Hardy" to express his gratitude to the Boston shipowner couple who had cared for him and for whom he "felt a greater sense of gratitude than for his own parents." Niijima, an eldest son, justified his violation of filial piety and his illegal departure from Japan in terms of serving his "Father who art in Heaven." He became a Christian, found a new father and mother in the Hardys, and pursued his studies in America with total peace of mind.

In time, official Japanese policy turned to support what had been the goals of Niijima's decisions for disobedience and flight. By the time of the Iwakura mission to the West in 1871–3, when Niijima was still studying in the United States, he was asked to serve as official interpreter for his country's highest officials, and upon his return to Japan in 1874, he was able to win the confidence and help of high officials like Kido Takayoshi (a member of the Iwakura mission) in gaining permission to found his Christian college in Kyoto. By then, Japan's policy of "civilization and enlightenment" seemed virtually indistinguishable from Niijima's personal mission to convert his fellow Japanese to Christianity. At that time, Niijima clearly had a linear view of progress, and he saw Westernization, civilization, and Christianity as a single goal to be sought. As he put it in an appeal for support for his college in 1884: "It is the spirit of liberty, the development of science, and the Christian morality that have given birth to European civilizations. . . . We cannot therefore believe that Japan can secure this civilization until education rests upon the same basis. With this foundation the State is built upon a rock. . . ."[29]

Two points emerge from these two dramatically different careers. The first is that Yoshida Shōin, no less than Niijima Jō, began with a warm, trusting, and optimistic view of a West whose strengths he proposed to appropriate for his backward but beloved country. The second is that Niijima Jō, no less than Yoshida Shōin, though committing himself to the West totally in terms of personal relations and spiritual beliefs, did so in the conviction that he was contributing to the "foundation of the state."[30]

Learning missions to the West

Yoshida Shōin and Niijima Jō were not the only Japanese longing to experience the West directly; high-ranking officials in the very bakufu that prohibited travel to foreign lands strongly desired to see the West with their own eyes and create a navy equal to those of Western nations. As early as February 6, 1858, Japanese representatives negotiating the Treaty of Amity and Commerce between the United States and Japan were reported by the American consul, Townsend Harris, to have

proposed, if I [Harris] was willing, to send an ambassador in their steamer to Washington via California for that purpose! I told them nothing could possibly give me greater pleasure. That, as the United States was the first power that Japan even made a treaty with, I should be much pleased that the first Japanese Ambassador should be sent to the United States.[31]

Japanese documents record this incident as follows: "Your nation has sent a total of three missions (including this one) to obtain this treaty. Now that it has been concluded, would it be possible for us

29 "Meiji Semmon Gakkō setsuritsu shishu," in *Niijima sensei shokanshū* (Kyoto: Dōshisha kōyūkai, 1942), pp. 1158–9.
30 I have discussed the attitudes toward America of Yoshida Shōin, Niijima Jō, and other mid-nineteenth-century travelers in Hirakawa Sukehiro, *Seiyō no shōgeki to Nihon* (Tokyo: Kōdansha, 1974), pp. 139–99.
31 M. E. Cosenza, ed., *The Complete Journal of Townsend Harris* (Rutland, Vt.: Tuttle, 1959), p. 531.

to send a mission of our own to Washington for purposes of exchanging the documents?"[32]

Iwase Tadanari, who made this statement, probably did so in hopes of being sent himself, but two years of political upheaval, which included the Ansei purge, elapsed before the project was realized. Finally, in 1860, Shimmi Masaoki was selected as chief ambassador ("due to my father's achievements," as he put it); Muragaki Norimasa was deputy ambassador; and Oguri Tadamasa was superintendent and inspector (*metsuke*). Muragaki, a man of gentle disposition, left the detailed *Kōkai nikki* (Voyage diary) in which he described his feelings when he was summoned to Edo Castle and informed of his appointment:

Although we did dispatch "official envoys" to T'ang China in ancient times, that neighboring land was only a strip of water away; but America lies a myriad miles beyond our Divine Land, and when it is daytime there, it is nighttime here.

I humored [my daughters, boasting,] "a man could achieve no greater honor than to assume this heavy, unprecedented responsibility and thereby attain renown throughout the five continents." But on second thought I realized, "a foolish man like myself accepting this first of all missions to a foreign land? Should I fail to execute the shogunal decree, our Divine Land will suffer humiliations untold." Just then, the moon was shining so clear and bright that I felt moved to a toast in solemn thanks for shogunal confidence:

> Henceforth foreigners as well
> will gaze
> upon the moon
> of our Japan.[33]

The tension in this poem contrasts with the following, which Muragaki composed upon his arrival in San Francisco:

> Foreign lands as well,
> lie beneath the same sky.
> Gaze upward and behold
> the mist-veiled spring moon.

Clearly, the sense of self-importance enabling Muragaki to carry out his duties had weakened. Finally, the following poem expressed

---

32 Dated 12/23/Ansei 4, in *Dainihon komonjo: Bakumatsu gaikoku kankei monjo* (Tokyo: Tokyo teikoku daigaku, 1925), vol. 18.

33 Muragaki (Awaji no Kami) Norimasa, *Kōkai nikki* (Tokyo: Jiji shinsho, 1959). This work was translated by Helen Uno as *Kokai Nikki: The Diary of the Frist Japanese Embassy to the United States of America* (Tokyo: Foreign Affairs Association of Japan, 1958). That translation has been modified here.

his sentiments when he parted with the captain and crew of the *Powhatan* in Panama:

> Though a glance reveals
> that they are foreigners,
> the sincerity of heart they display
> differs not from our own.[34]

Thus Muragaki expressed his appreciation to the American crew. After traveling with them, he had discovered the universality of human nature.

After "the Tycoon's envoys" ratified the Treaty of Amity and Commerce between the two nations in Washington with Louis Cass, President James Buchanan's secretary of state, they made their way to New York. In his diary, Muragaki described in detail their welcome there on 4/28/1860. Walt Whitman also described the festivities in his "A Broadway Pageant." The poem describes not only Broadway, which on that day "was entirely given up to foot-passengers and foot-standers," but also the joy of seeing the union of East and West and the oneness of the universe.

The welcome received by the members of the mission became known throughout Japan after their return home, and the mistaken image of Westerners as barbarians was modified, albeit gradually and among a limited number of intellectuals. In Yokoi Shōnan's remote Kumamoto country school, lectures on the *Analects* were revised. Shōnan's gloss on the first entry reads:

[*Analects*]: "Is it not a joy to have friends come from afar?"

[Shōnan's gloss]: The phrase "have friends" means that when we appreciate learning and are eager to study, if we voluntarily approach, become intimate with, and speak to a man of virtuous repute whether he lives near or far away, that person will as a matter of course confide in us and become intimate with us in return. This is what is meant by the principle of "feeling and response" (*kannō*).

The term *friends* is not limited to scholar-friends. When we study to adopt the good points of any person, all men in the world are our friends.[35]

Then this scholar-statesman cited recent historical developments and advocated revising Japan's international relations on the basis of universal brotherhood:

34 Uno, *Kokai Nikki*, pp. 38, 51.
35 Yokoi Tokio, ed., *Shōnan ikō* (Tokyo: Min'yūsha, 1889), pp. 447–8.

Viewed from a wider perspective, this principle of "feeling and response" may be witnessed in the warm reception extended by the Americans to the recent bakufu embassy sent to their land. Their cordiality was deep indeed. By extending this meaning [of friends] to all people in the world, and not just to those in Japan, they are all our friends.

Because sentiments for *jōi* were intense in Kumamoto *han* in that era, a feigned champion of righteousness could have cut an imposing figure by dancing to this tune of the times. But in Shōnan's lecture notes, we see a different figure, that of a Japanese thinker responding in kind to the hand of friendship offered by Whitman and other Americans. Until after the Russo-Japanese War, when American attitudes toward Japan began to change, the Japanese people felt a friendliness toward Americans that differed from their feelings toward other Western powers.

Oguri Tadamasa, *metsuke* in the first bakufu embassy, refined his knowledge while in the United States. After returning to Japan, he served as commissioner for foreign affairs and then naval commissioner (*gaikoku*, then *kaigun bugyō*), exercised his capabilities in finance, sought assistance from France, and built the Yokohama and Yokosuka foundry and shipyard. After the bakufu's defeat at Toba-Fushimi in 1868, Oguri opposed concessions by the shogun, was captured, and executed.

However, the most famous member of this embassy traveled on an auxiliary vessel, the *Kanrin maru*, which was the first Japanese ship to cross the Pacific. Fukuzawa Yukichi, then a young student of Dutch, requested and received permission to escort Kimura Yoshitake on this trip to San Francisco. The chapter of his *Autobiography* entitled "I Join the First Mission to America" contains many interesting episodes, but perhaps the most surprising of these is that his reading of Dutch books and scientific training at the Ogata school in Osaka had given him enough of a background in natural science to facilitate his understanding of the explanations of the latest inventions made in America. By contrast, "things social, political, and economic proved most inexplicable." For example, when he asked "where the descendents of George Washington might be," an American replied, "I think there is a woman who is directly descended from Washington. I don't know where she is now." The answer was "so casual as to shock" this Japanese, who had more or less equated the social positions of Tokugawa Ieyasu and George Washington, both of whom had founded the political systems then existing in Japan and the United States.[36]

Katsu Kaishū (1823–99), the captain of the *Kanrin maru*, was originally a low-ranking Tokugawa official, but he rose to the highest positions of authority within the bakufu and ultimately became the person responsible for surrendering Edo Castle to the Restoration forces. Immediately after returning to Japan from this mission, Katsu earned the rancor of his colleagues by asserting that unlike the situation in Japan, all men in positions of leadership in America possessed leadership capacity. In the late Tokugawa era, knowledge of the West gradually proved effective in criticizing the existing order for its inability to deal satisfactorily with the crises confronting Japan.

After this first mission abroad, the bakufu sent large and small embassies abroad each year or every other year until its demise in 1868. The second embassy, led by Takeuchi Yasunori in 1862, toured the states of Europe to seek approval for postponing the opening of four additional treaty ports. The third mission, to France, was led by Ikeda Naganobu in a futile effort to secure the closing of Yokohama as a port. Shibata Takenaka led the fourth mission, which went to France and England in 1865 to negotiate conditions for constructing the Yokosuka foundry and shipyard. The fifth toured Europe and headed for Russia in 1866 when its chief ambassador, Koide Hidezane, conducted negotiations to establish the boundary between Japan and Russia on Sakhalin (Karafuto). The sixth mission, headed by the shogun Tokugawa Keiki's personal representative, Tokugawa Akitake, attended the Paris World's Fair in 1867. This last embassy was entrusted with the secret mission of persuading France to increase its aid to the bakufu, and it was still in Europe when the bakufu collapsed in 1868.[37]

Although these "envoys of the Tycoon" had specific diplomatic assignments for dealing with the domestic situation or foreign relations at the time of their appointment, intentionally or not, they also made important contributions to Japan's study and assimilation of Western civilization. In addition, when we consider the students sent to Europe by the bakufu and (illegally) by the domains of

36 "Seiyō jijō," in *Fukuzawa Yukichi zenshū* (Tokyo: Iwanami shoten, 1959), vol. 7, p. 95. Also Eiichi Kiyooka, trans., *The Autobiography of Fukuzawa Yukichi* (Tokyo: Hokuseidō Press, 1948), p. 125.

37 Haga Tōru discusses these embassies in *Taikun no shisetsu* (Tokyo: Chūō kōronsha, 1968). The diplomacy in which they participated is the subject of Ishii Takashi, *Zotei Meiji ishin no kokusai kankyō*, rev. ed. (Tokyo: Yoshikawa kōbunkan, 1966).

Chōshū, Satsuma, or Hizen, we realize that the movement to study "in barbarian lands," launched by Yoshida Shōin in 1854, had expanded and developed to the bakufu or national level. If we include the crew of the *Kanrin maru* on the first bakufu mission abroad, over three hundred Japanese traveled to foreign shores before the Meiji period.

Each of these missions investigated the institutions and civilization of the nations to which it was dispatched, but the second led by Takeuchi Yasunori was the most thorough and systematic, having been instructed "to pay particular attention to politics, school administration, and military systems." The activities of Fukuzawa Yukichi, Matsuki Kōan (Terashima Munenori), Mitsukuri Shūhei, and other students of Western learning were noted in pamphlets bearing such titles as "An Investigation of England," "An Investigation of France," and "An Investigation of Russia." On the Takeuchi mission, Fukuzawa, who had already been to America two years earlier, did more than gaze at Europe with the bedazzled eyes of a tourist; he had discerned the inevitability of the sociopolitical transformation that would soon take place in Japan and began to see himself as an enthusiastic "engineer of civilization." Thus the beginning of Fukuzawa's enlightenment activities in Meiji times can be gleaned from his travel in Tokugawa service.

Fukuzawa's *Account of My Voyage to the West* and *Notes on My Voyage to the West* are full of memos scribbled in a hodgepodge of Japanese, Dutch, English, and French. A glance at these works shows Fukuzawa to be a virtual walking antenna, eager to absorb any and all information in these foreign lands. Whereas other Japanese became caught up in the small facets of Western civilization, Fukuzawa sought to integrate these facets and observe the overall organization that made this civilization function. For example, his colleagues might admire the size of a locomotive, note how fast the train ran, or measure the width and height of its rails. But Fukuzawa went well past such concerns; his interests led him to investigate the composition of railroad companies, their banking activities, or the joint control enjoyed by England and France over Egypt's railways. In short, he tried to grasp not only the technology but also the social aspects of Western civilization. In his *Autobiography*, he wrote:

I did not care to study scientific or technical subjects while on this journey, because I could study them as well from books after I returned home. But I felt that I had to learn the more common matters of daily life directly from the people, because Europeans would not describe them in books as being too obvious. Yet to us those common matters were the most difficult to comprehend.

So while in Europe, "whenever I met a person whom I thought to be of some consequence, I would ask him questions and would put down all he said in a notebook. . . ."[38] After returning home, Fukuzawa organized the notes he had taken during these question-and-answer sessions, checked them against information found in books that he had bought abroad, and published them from 1866 to 1869 under the title *Conditions in the West* (Seiyō jijō).

Fukuzawa wrote the following account of one of these investigations in his *Autobiography*:

A perplexing institution was representative government. When I asked a gentleman what the "election law" was and what kind of a bureau the Parliament really was, he simply replied with a smile, meaning I suppose that no intelligent person was expected to ask such a question. But these were the things most difficult of all for me to understand. In this connection, I learned that there were bands of men called political parties – the Liberals and the Conservatives – who were always fighting against each other in the government.

For some time it was beyond my comprehension to understand what they were fighting for, and what was meant, anyway, by "fighting" in peacetime. "This man and that man are enemies in the house," they would tell me. But these "enemies" were to be seen at the same table, eating and drinking with each other. I felt as if I could not make much out of this. It took me a long time, with some tedious thinking, before I could gather a general notion of these separate mysterious facts. In some of the more complicated matters, I might achieve an understanding five or ten days after they were explained to me. But all in all, I learned much from this initial tour of Europe.[39]

Conditions in the West, the fruit of such labors, was the first systematic account of the structure of Western civilization written by a Japanese, and it was phrased in language that anyone could understand. In one sense, it was designed to heighten Japan's appreciation of the West, but in another, it provided a vision of the future Meiji state as envisioned through Fukuzawa's reformism. Thus, the bakufu missions abroad greatly contributed to the building of Meiji Japan by teaching numerous Japanese about the West and producing popular best-sellers such as Fukuzawa's *Conditions in the West* and Nakamura Masanao's translation of Samuel Smiles's *Self-Help*. The Meiji Restoration altered Japan's political leadership totally and

38　*Fukuzawa Yukichi zenshū*, vol. 7, p. 107; *The Autobiography*, pp. 142–3.
39　*Fukuzawa Yukichi zenshū*, vol. 7, pp. 107–8; *The Autobiography*, p. 144.

strengthened a resolve to learn from the West that was already forming by 1868. The greatest of all the official missions followed the Restoration. On December 23, 1871, the new Meiji government dispatched Ambassador-Plenipotentiary Iwakura Tomomi to America and Europe as the head of a forty-eight-member delegation that took with it fifty-nine students of the ex-samurai class, five of whom were women.

At this point, we should mention the subsequent course of antiforeign sentiment. On his way back to Japan in 1860, Katsu Kaishū playfully displayed on board the *Kanrin maru* the Western umbrella he had bought overseas. When he asked, "What would happen if I tried to use this in Japan?" other members of the delegation cautioned him not to invite assassination. In 1862, when Fukuzawa returned from his second trip, sentiment for *jōi* had become more intense. As a student of Western learning, Fukuzawa lived in constant fear of being cut down by xenophobic extremists, and for ten years he refused to go out after dark, choosing instead to concentrate on translations and his own writing. But by 1871, this sentiment had spent its force. The appearance among the members of the Iwakura mission of seven-year-old Tsuda Umeko, carrying a doll, symbolized the return of peace. The idea of a girl studying overseas would have been unimaginable before the Restoration, but after her long sojourn in America, Tsuda returned to Japan and founded what later became Tsudajuku University for Women, an institution that along with Fukuzawa's Keiō University and Niijima's Dōshisha University made important contributions to private higher education in modern Japan.

We can only marvel at the new Meiji government's stability, which allowed it to send the Iwakura mission to America and Europe for such a long period of time, even allowing for the fact that civil war had ended and peace had been restored. Only four years after its inception, the new government abolished the old domains and provinces of Tokugawa Japan and forced through the establishment of a modern prefectural system. Then only four months after that, leaders such as Iwakura Tomomi, Kido Takayoshi, Ōkubo Toshimichi, and Itō Hirobumi went abroad and, extending the originally planned length of their overseas stay by almost a full year, returned to Japan on September 13, 1873, after a tour that had lasted 631 days. The Iwakura mission's ostensible objective was to revise the unequal treaties ratified and exchanged in Washington by the first Tokugawa mission to America in 1860, but its members' real intention was to discover conditions in the West and adapt these to Japan in order to create a new Meiji state. The Meiji leaders realized that to revise the unequal treaties, they would have to restructure Japan by putting it on a par with Western states and reforming domestic laws and institutions to bring them into line with those of the Western powers. Though the Iwakura mission was larger than those sent by the bakufu, its purpose and task were essentially the same: to study and learn from the West. One piece of evidence for this continuity of purpose can be found in the embassy's membership. Although its leaders were court nobles and prominent power holders from the domains that had emerged victorious in the Restoration wars, the secretarial staff supporting these leaders included many veteran diplomats, such as Tanabe Ta'ichi, who had served under the bakufu and were knowledgeable about or had actually traveled to the West.

The mission looked at chambers of commerce, schools for the deaf and dumb, museums, shipyards, biscuit factories, girls' schools, prisons, telegraph offices, army maneuvers – all at a whirlwind pace. Kume Kunitake, a student of Chinese learning, went as scribe and published *A True Account of the Observations of the Ambassadorial Mission to America and Europe*, which describes the embassy's brisk day-to-day routine:

No sooner had our train arrived and we had unloaded our baggage at the hotel than our tour began. During the daytime we rushed about from place to place, viewing machines that peeled and locomotives that roared. We stood amidst the acrid smell of steel with smoke billowing around us and became covered with soot and dirt. Returning to our hotel at dusk, we barely had time to brush off our dirty clothes before the hour of our banquet approached. At the banquet we had to maintain a dignified manner; if invited to the theater, we had to strain eyes and ears to follow what took place on stage, and all of this led to exhaustion. No sooner had we retired at night, than morning greeted us with an escort sent to guide us around a factory. In this way, strange sights and sounds filled our eyes and ears; our spirits sagged and our bodies were exhausted by all the invitations we received to this and that event. Though we might have wished to drink a cup of water or stretch out and nap with bent elbow for a pillow, we could not, for any personal slovenliness on our part would constitute a lack of propriety in negotiations between Japan and foreign nations.[40]

40 Kume Kunitake ed., *Bei-Ō kairan jikki* (Tokyo: Iwanami shoten, 1977), vol. I, p. 12. For detailed information on the Iwakura mission, see Tanaka Akira, *Iwakura shistetsu dan* (Tokyo: Kōdansha, 1977); and Haga Tōru, *Meiji ishin to Nihonjin* (Tokyo: Kōdansha gakujutsu bunko ed., 1980), pp. 219–43. I have relied heavily on Haga for this presentation. For the Iwakura mission in English, see Marlene Mayo, "The Western Education of

The daily schedule of Ōkubo Toshimichi, who concentrated his investigations on industry and economic systems, no doubt resembled this. He questioned factory foremen, sought advice from legal scholars, exchanged speeches with city mayors, and discussed issues with the foreign ministers of various governments. In London, he experienced a blackout caused by striking electrical workers seeking higher wages and thus discovered the serious effects that labor disputes might have. He toured the East End after sunset to see the misery and wretchedness lurking beneath the surface of modern Western "civilization." Ōkubo concluded that "the prosperity of English cities occurred after the invention of the steam engine," and Kume noted that "the contemporary phenomenon of wealth and population in European states presented itself after 1800 and has become pronounced only in the last forty years." On the one hand, the members of the mission marveled at the cumulative nature of civilization in Europe, saying that "the light of civilization shines because knowledge has been accumulated through the ages," but at the same time, they braced themselves and stirred their often-flagging spirits by realizing that the gap between Japan and the West, which had just experienced the Industrial Revolution, could be bridged. Thus they resolved to overtake and surpass the West.

Like Fukuzawa's *Conditions in the West*, Kume's *True Account* was organized according to individual countries. Japanese thinkers ranked Western nations according to their relative "superiority" or "inferiority." The scholars of Dutch learning had already discovered that Dutch medical texts were mostly translations from German and thus learned of Germany's superiority in this field. In similar fashion, the Japanese, through their study of books, through traveling abroad, and through advice obtained from foreign teachers, chose to assimilate the best that each particular Western nation had to offer. Fukuzawa challenged his countrymen to turn away from scholars of Chinese learning, arguing that they were so oblivious to world developments as to be "little more than rice-consuming dictionaries," and to adopt Western culture, which was based on practicality. By the same token, he himself abandoned Dutch for English in 1859 after acknowledging the superior material civilization of the Anglo-Saxon nations. The Japanese modeled themselves after England for indus-

Kume Kunitake 1871–1876," *Monumenta Nipponica* 28 (1973). The daily experiences and observations of Kido Takayoshi can be followed in Sidney D. Brown and Akiro Hirota, trans., *The Diary of Kido Takayoshi*, vol. 2: *1871–1874* (Tokyo: University of Tokyo Press, 1985).

trial and naval development; Prussia, which defeated France in 1871, provided a model for military organization; France offered the model of its centralized police system and educational and legal patterns; and America stimulated agricultural development in the northernmost island of Hokkaido. The Iwakura mission found in Prussia a model of a late-developing modernizer that seemed particularly appropriate to emulate. In regard to Prussia, which then was exporting agricultural products to obtain the capital necessary to develop its mining and industry, Kume wrote: "In establishing its national policies, Prussia has much that closely resembles conditions in Japan. We should find it more profitable to study Prussian politics and customs than those of England or France."[41] It was only natural for the Meiji Japanese to turn to America and Europe rather than to Asian countries in formulating plans to modernize their nation rapidly, and they were wise to select the strong points of each Western nation to further this process. Their selectiveness, based on considerations of efficacy, seems totally different from the traditional Confucian view of a world order centered on China.

Japan's knowledge of and experience with the West may seem to have progressed further during the Taishō and Shōwa eras than during the Meiji. But on closer examination, we find that at least in regard to Japan's leaders, their knowledge of foreign countries did not improve qualitatively and quantitatively. The "elder statesmen of the Restoration," as they later were called, were on the one hand raised in accordance with traditional Tokugawa values, but at the same time, they also knew a great deal about the West. The Restoration activists exercised a shrewd sensibility in their contact with foreigners. For the Meiji government leaders, the Iwakura mission provided firsthand contact with the Western world. For most of them, it was their first trip, although Itō had gone to England as a young Chōshū student. What mattered was that the experience shared by Iwakura, Ōkubo, Kido, and Itō produced a consensus on Japan's future course. These men were convinced of the need for domestic reforms first of all, and upon returning home in 1873, they canceled the plans for invading Korea that had been prepared by the "caretaker" government in their absence. This was the first case of a split in views on national policy engendered by the experience or lack of experience of the outside world and the knowledge or ignorance of foreign affairs.

41 Kume, *Bei-ō kairan jikki*, vol. 3, p. 298.

TEACHERS OF "ARTS AND SCIENCES":
FOREIGNERS IN MEIJI GOVERNMENT EMPLOY

Japan's use of foreign employees in late Tokugawa and early Meiji times presents an interesting and useful perspective on the larger turn to the West, and it was also in some sense prophetic of the role of foreign advisers in the reconstruction of Japanese institutions after World War II. The relative success with which the Allied Occupation of Japan completed its work contrasts with the problem of American counselors in their efforts to channel reform in other developing countries. But when considered in regard to Japan's use of foreign advisers in the nineteenth century, it suggests that much of that "success" was actually Japan's. The Meiji government and society, like those of developing states in the twentieth century, were intensely nationalistic, but the country's skill in using and then replacing outside foreign employees is too often forgotten.

The rush with which Japan adopted foreign institutions and customs following the Meiji Restoration sometimes gave Westerners (and not a few conservative Japanese) the impression that Japan was scrapping its entire traditional civilization to appropriate all the material and spiritual attributes of modern Western states. Of course, much of this program was tactical. Britain's defeat of China, followed by the extension of unequal treaties to Japan in the wake of Matthew Perry and Townsend Harris, filled Japan's leaders with apprehension. Japanese felt themselves exposed to a military threat and concluded that if they were to enter the arena known as the family of nations, they too must equip themselves with the weaponry possessed by the Western powers. But they also realized that the basis of Western power was not limited to weaponry; to the extent that such power was based on a civil society that had undergone the economic and social transformations of the Industrial Revolution, Japan's quest for power also entailed the building of political and social institutions based on the Western model.

Although the overthrow of the Tokugawa bakufu was conducted under the slogan "revere the Emperor, expel the barbarians!" the Meiji regime that followed immediately implemented a policy of "open the country, establish friendly relations." After "expulsion" of the "barbarians" was rejected in light of the recognition of the international situation, the same nationalism that produced the slogan was transformed into a quest for "civilization and enlightenment." So too for "reverence" for the sovereign: The overthrow of the bakufu resulted not in a restoration of direct imperial rule as it had existed in antiquity, but in a new form of monarchy.

In pursuing its goals of following, achieving equality with, and even overtaking the West, the Meiji government created slogans for all aspects of its endeavors – "enrich the country, strengthen the army" (*fukoku kyōhei*), "civilization and enlightenment" (*bummei kaika*), and "revise the (unequal) treaties" (*jōyaku kaisei*). The government obtained the assistance of foreign teachers and technicians to achieve these goals. In their assimilation of Western culture, the Japanese, who had progressed from book learning to direct experience of the West, now adopted a state policy of inviting large numbers of foreign teachers.

Countries of origins and numbers

Immediately after the opening of the country, the foreigners under whom the Japanese studied were mainly Dutch, although the first systematic instructor in Western arts and sciences was a German, P. F. von Siebold (1796–1866), who arrived in Nagasaki as a physician with the Dutch trading post in 1823. While studying Japan's language, history, geography, animals, and plants, he practiced and taught medicine to Japanese students in a private academy set up for him, the Narutakijuku. In the Tokugawa years, Japanese curiosity began with Western medicine and astronomy, but by late Tokugawa times, their concerns had shifted to Western arms and military methods, reflecting the gravity of the international situation. In 1855, the bakufu set up a naval training institute in Nagasaki to which it invited a team of Dutch instructors to provide training in navigation. Thus Japan's first "foreign employees" were Pels Rijcken and a group of twenty-two instructors, who arrived in 1855, and Huyssen van Kattendycke and a team of thirty-seven, who came slightly later.

In 1858, parallel treaties were concluded with the United States, Holland, England, France, and Russia. Once Holland was no longer the sole avenue for studying Western civilization, Dutch prestige suffered precipitously, and as the Japanese discovered that England, France, Germany, and America were the leading Western powers, they discarded the Dutch language and began studying English, French, and German. Thereafter, students were dispatched to England, America, France, and (in Meiji times) Germany to study.

Initially, few foreigners were employed, and most of them were from France and Britain. In its final conflicts with Satsuma and Chōshū, the bakufu sought closer relations with France, whereas Satsuma and Chōshū looked to England. In 1862, the bakufu, with help from France, built a shipyard in Yokosuka and began a foundry in Yokohama as well as establishing a French-language school there. Oguri Tadamasa, a leading official in these final bakufu reforms, remarked to a colleague: "The Tokugawa may have to transfer this old house [the bakufu] to someone else, but it will look a lot better with a new storehouse on the premises."[42] In fact, the Meiji government did take the decrepit bakufu structure off the hands of the Tokugawa a few years later and received the new Yokosuka arsenal "storehouse" as a bonus. Moreover, it is important to note that not only the plant itself but also the foreign employees operating it were taken over by the new regime. The Meiji government acquired new facilities as well as precious human talent in the form of Japanese who had been sent abroad in the late Tokugawa period, but foreign employees were by no means the least valuable assets it inherited.

In the Meiji period, there was a rapid increase in the number of foreign employees serving in government and private capacities. The number of foreign government employees peaked in 1875 with approximately 520 persons employed, but by 1894 and after, the annual totals were fewer than 100. In contrast, the number of foreigners in private employ was small at first but reached a high of approximately 760 in 1897. By occupation in government, engineers and educators in the ministries of Industry and Education were most numerous, and in the private sector, the number of educators increased as time went on. Classified by nationality, among government employees, the British were most numerous as educators and engineers, followed by the Germans; in the private sector, American educators predominated. In regard to the relative influence of the different nationalities, it is interesting to note the changes in numbers of foreigners employed in the various government bureaus. In 1872, out of a total of 213 government-employed foreigners, 119 were from the United Kingdom, of whom 104 were engineers in the Ministry of Industry, and 49 were French, of whom 24 were shipbuilding technicians. By 1881, however, the statistics show 96 English, 32 Germans, 12 Americans, and 10 French. Areas in which particular

42   Fukuchi Gen'ichirō, *Bakumatsu seijika* (Tokyo: Min'yūsha, 1900), p. 266.

nationalities were particularly influential included the English in the ministries of Industry, Navy, and Communications; and the Americans in the development of Hokkaido.[43]

Budget figures are revealing: At some points, foreigners' salaries accounted for one-third of the Ministry of Industry's regular budget and one-third of the budget allocations for Tokyo Imperial University, the first modern university to be established in Japan. The foreigners' salaries clearly placed great strains on the budgets of all government ministries and bureaus, to say nothing of the costs of studying abroad. Yet perhaps it was precisely because of these great costs that the Japanese studied so assiduously under their expensive foreign teachers. These costs were heavy when the foreigners were conscientious and of good character, but when they assumed an attitude of superiority toward their Japanese employers, the costs must have seemed heavier still – all the more reason, no doubt, for the diligence with which the Japanese strove to master the new teachings.

What the Japanese desired

In November 1873, Itō Hirobumi, minister of industry, delivered a directive to mark the opening of the government's new Kōgakuryō, which later evolved into the Department of Engineering of Tokyo Imperial University. Itō pointed out that the new enterprises that Japan was developing should be considered the foundation of future greatness. To create a "great civilization" meant educating "high and low alike," and it had to be done quickly so that "Japan could take its rightful place among the nations of the world" in wealth and power. Because only a few Japanese had mastered the skills required up to that point, the country had "no choice but to employ many foreigners to assist us at the outset." But it was not enough to rely on the skills of others; to do so might bring temporary gains but not the "wealth and strength that will endure through myriads of generations." Consequently, Itō concluded:

It is imperative that we seize this opportunity to train and educate ourselves fully. On this solemn occasion, I urge all ambitious youths to enroll in this school, to study assiduously, to perfect their talents, and to serve in their various posts with dedication. If this is done, then as a matter of course, we

---

43 Umetani Noboru, *Oyatoi gaikokujin: Meiji Nihon no wakiyakutachi* (Tokyo: Nihon keizai shimbunsha, 1965), pp. 209–23. In English, see Hazel Jones, *Live Machines: Hired Foreigners in Meiji Japan* (Vancouver: University of British Columbia Press, 1980).

will be able to do without foreigners. We ourselves will fill the realm with railroads and other technological wonders that will form the basis for further developments to continue for a myriad generations. The glory of our Imperial Land will shine forth to radiate upon foreign shores, while at home, high and low will share in the benefits of a great civilization. Therefore, let all ambitious youths throughout the land proceed vigorously with their studies.[44]

It is clear that the Meiji leaders intended foreign employees to play only a subsidiary and temporary role in Japan's development and wanted Japanese nationals to be trained to replace them as soon as possible. The Japanese realized that in order to "lay the foundations for national wealth and strength that will last a myriad generations," they would have to "train and educate" themselves and that they had no choice but to develop and increase their own capabilities. It was also Japan's good fortune that even in the West, scientific and technological development had a history of only a few decades. And so although it was totally dependent on foreign teachers and technicians at the beginning, Japan succeeded in transplanting Western industrial techniques and in producing enough talented men to become surprisingly self-sufficient in the relatively short span of fifteen to twenty years. Tokyo Imperial University's engineering department had a total of 411 graduates between 1879 and 1885. This number of trained technological leaders was not far below the number of foreigners employed by the Ministry of Industry since the beginning of the Meiji period.

Tokugawa Japanese had gained a fair understanding of Western science, a fact that can be discerned in the observations made by Fukuzawa Yukichi during his 1860 visit to America. He was not in the least surprised by the modern phenomena of the telegraph, metalworking, or sugar refining. As is generally true for backward nations, however, Japan began its own development by availing itself of advanced Western science and technology.

The entry of Western modes of life

The numerous foreigners employed by the Meiji government facilitated Japan's turn to the West, not only by serving as teachers but also in the broader sense of introducing new life-styles. For example, at one time during the first half of the 1870s, there were as many as twenty foreigners (most of them English) employed at the govern-

44 Umetani Noboru, *Oyatoi gaikokujin* (Tokyo: Kajima kenkyūsho shuppan, 1968), p. 210.

ment mint, where it is reported that as early as 1870–1, Western clothing, the solar calendar, and Sunday holidays were adopted. Western clothing became compulsory for government officials in November 1872, when a directive established Western clothing as the official ceremonial dress. In 1876, frock coats were decreed standard business attire.[45]

Calendar reform took place in November 1872, when the government decreed that the third day of the twelfth month of the lunar calendar would become January of the next year.[46] This was how the solar calendar was introduced to Japan.[47] The rationale behind calendar reform deserves a slight digression. The solar calendar was not unknown during the Tokugawa period, thanks to Dutch studies. As early as 1795, Ōtsuki Gentaku and his *rangaku* friends had celebrated the eleventh day of the eleventh lunar month as "Dutch New Year's Day." The actual use of the solar calendar after its adoption in 1872, however, was not particularly rapid or widespread. The traditional lunar-solar "Tempō calendar," intricately connected with the pulse of agricultural seasons, suited the Japanese life patterns well. For a time, the new Meiji calendar was dubbed the "imperial court calendar," as opposed to the "Tokugawa calendar," to which the people were accustomed. Not until 1911 were the lunar listings of days removed from the calendars, and even today many Japanese feel a certain nostalgia for the old lunar calendar.

One reason that the new regime pushed through calendar reform so early probably stemmed from budgetary considerations. Because there was one intercalary month to be added to the lunar calendar every three years, changing to the solar calendar meant saving the intercalary month's expenditures. When the new government converted to the solar calendar in 1872 and "erased" two days, it withheld salaries for those days, not only for Japanese but also for foreign employees whose salaries were drawn on a monthly rather than a yearly basis. The government mint, which took the lead in adopting Western dress and the solar calendar, also pioneered in Western accounting methods, reserve funds for work injuries, medical clinics, and other matters hitherto unknown in Japan. In addition, it quickly introduced gas lights and telegraph lines, which became symbols of "civilization and enlightenment" in Japan, even

45 Tsuji Zennosuke, *Nihon bunkashi* (Tokyo: Shunjūsha, 1950), vol. 7, p. 18.
46 Satō Masatsugu, *Nihon rekigakushi* (Tokyo: Surugadai shuppansha, 1968), p. 479.
47 The Julian method of intercalation was used at this time, but the Gregorian method was adopted in 1900.

though none of these innovations was directly concerned with minting techniques.

Individual foreign teachers often had astonishing influence through the strength of their personal example and assumed almost oracular importance for young students who were only partly rooted in traditional values and eager to learn the inner strength of "civilization." The artillery Captain L. L. Janes in Kumamoto and the agronomist William Clark in Hokkaido proved to be more successful religious teachers than were the numerous missionaries who were sent to Japan after the government rescinded the prohibitions against Christianity in 1873, and major groupings of the small but influential Protestant church derived from the "Kumamoto Band" and "Hokkaido Group."[48] In addition, many of the customs inherent in "civilization and enlightenment" or capitalist enterprise were introduced by foreign employees of the Meiji government. Christmas, for instance, which became a holiday, came with the foreign residents. Many aspects of Western life were taught by the foreigners through daily affairs rather than through formal instruction.

THE JAPANIZATION OF WESTERN THOUGHT AND INSTITUTIONS

When Western value systems came into contact with Japanese values, there were three possible outcomes: The two could conflict; the values might be adopted totally; or they might be altered in the process of being accepted. Christianity provides one example of Japan's alteration and transformation of Western values. Another example can be found in Japan's civil code, which was drafted under the guidance of the French jurist G. E. Boissonade. By examining this draft, we may discover Japan's reaction to "teachers of arts and science" who attempted to introduce Western morality as well.

Social order was well maintained in Tokugawa Japan, but not because the Japanese of that era were bound by written laws. The unequal treaties concluded by the bakufu in 1858 posed a new problem and need in this regard. They were inequitable and humiliating; Japan was forced to relinquish tariff autonomy and concede extraterritoriality to Westerners. To obtain equal status with the

48 John F. Howes, "Japanese Christians and American Missionaries," in Marius B. Jansen, ed., *Changing Japanese Attitudes Toward Modernization* (Princeton, N.J.: Princeton University Press, 1965), pp. 337–68. For Janes, see F. G. Notehelfer, *American Samurai: Captain L. L. Janes and Japan* (Princeton, N.J.: Princeton University Press, 1985).

West, the early Meiji government would first have to prove that
Japan was a "civilized" country, deserving equal status and treatment, and part of that process involved compiling legal codes similar
to those possessed by the European states. Thus the adoption of a
Western-style legal system was not simply a domestic matter; it was
also essential to the resolution of an external problem that demanded
an urgent solution.

When the French legal system first came to the attention of the
Japanese in late Tokugawa, they greeted it with enthusiasm. The
Tokugawa official Kurimoto Joun, who traveled to France in 1867,
noted in his memoirs:

"Deciding a lawsuit with half a word" is something that requires the
wisdom of Tzu-lu and is beyond the capability of men of only average
abilities and intelligence. How much more impossible for a man without
human feelings. The complete elimination of argumentation in court would
have been impossible even for the sage Confucius. That, at any rate, was
what I thought until I learned of this Napoleonic code. . . . I was overwhelmed with admiration and envy.[49]

The reason for Kurimoto's praise was that two Japanese merchants
who had accompanied his party had been arraigned and brought to
court, where he saw the French judge "base his decision and pro-
nounce sentence in accordance with Article X, Provision Y of the
Napoleonic code."

In 1869, the Meiji government ordered Mitsukuri Rinshō to translate all five French law codes. At that time, Etō Shimpei suggested
that they "merely translate the French civil code verbatim, call it
the 'Japanese Civil Code,' and promulgate it immediately."[50] His
aim was to revise the unequal treaties: The laws need not be perfect,
and it would be sufficient if they were part of a new judicial system.
This would convince the West that Japan was indeed a "civilized"
nation.

A group under Etō's direction began compiling a civil code based
on Mitsukuri's translation. In 1872, the French lawyer Georges
Bousquet was hired to assist them, and the next year Gustave Emile
Boissonade de Fontarabie (1825–1910) followed;[51] the latter worked

---

49 This opening phrase is a quotation from *The Analects* of Confucius. Kurimoto Joun,
    "Gyōsō tsuroku," in Nihon shiseki kyōkai, ed., *Hōan ikō* (*Zoku Nihon shiseki sōsho*, vol. 4)
    (Tokyo: Tokyo daigaku shuppankai, 1975), p. 24.
50 Etō Shimpei, "Furansu mimpō wo motte Nihonmimpō to nasan to su," in Hozumi
    Nobushige, ed., *Hōsō yawa* (Tokyo: Iwanami shoten, 1980), pp. 210–13.
51 See Ōkubo Yasuo, *Nihon kindaihō no chichi: Bowasonado* (Tokyo: Iwanami shoten, 1977)
    for a discussion of this consultant.

in Japan until 1895. In addition to their work of compilation, these men served as instructors in Western legal concepts at the Ministry of Justice. Before this, Inoue Kowashi (1854–95), who deserves much credit for his work to implement Western institutions, had been sent to France by the Ministry of Justice, where he had studied under Boissonade, who was then a professor of law at the Sorbonne. In Japan, Boissonade cooperated with Inoue on many projects. In public law, he strove to establish concepts like the principle of legality and the principle of evidence and to abolish torture. He also drew up criminal and penal codes, which were Japan's first modern law codes. In private law, he worked on the civil code, drawing up sections on property, securities, and evidence. In addition, he was influential in determining what was to go into the sections on personal and family relations and property acquisitions. Boissonade's drafts passed final review in the Privy Council and were scheduled to go into effect in 1890. A noteworthy aspect of his draft was the ideal of equality between individuals in the inheritance of property. But these provisions drew sharp criticism from those who held that they would threaten the primacy of the house (ie), and as a result, implementation of the code was held up just before it was to become law. Boissonade's provisions were rejected and replaced by requirements that the household head inherit all property. In sum, the Meiji government placed more emphasis on maintaining the "house" (ie) as a structural unit than on respecting the individual's right to inheritance.[52] This "civil code issue" raged for several years.

The controversy over the new code had many facets, but in general terms, it can be viewed as a conflict between the universalistic, theoretical legal thought espoused by French jurists of natural law and a more particularistic and empirical set of ideas advanced by proponents of historicist legal thought who drew their arguments from English and especially German traditions. The latter group argued that the concept of "house" (ie) and the sentiments it engendered were an intrinsic part of particularistic and traditional Japanese society and values. Hozumi Yatsuka, a spokesman for the latter group, became famous for his catchphrase "Loyalty and filial piety will perish with the enactment of the civil code." He wrote:

52 On the compilation of the civil code and the "civil code issue," in addition to Ōkubo, *Nihon kindaihō no chichi*; see Ishii Ryōsuke, ed., *Meiji bunkashi: Hōsei-hen* (Tokyo: Genyōsha, 1954), p. 515. This work is vol. 2 of the Centennial Cultural Committee Series, *Meiji bunkashi* and was translated by William Chambliss as *Japanese Legislation in the Meiji Era* (Tokyo: Pan-Pacific Press, 1958).

With the spread of Christianity in Europe, a self-righteous "Father who art in Heaven" has come to monopolize the love and respect of all men. Perhaps for that reason, Westerners neglect the worship of ancestors and the Way of filial piety. With the spread of doctrines like equality and humanity, they slight the importance of ethnic customs and blood ties. Perhaps that is why no "house" system exists among them anymore; instead they create a society of equal individuals and try to uphold it by means of laws centered on the individuals.

Japan has never forgotten the teaching of ancestor reverence because of the coming of foreign religions. However, the spirit in which this civil code is drafted will bring repudiation of the national religion and destruction of our "house" system. The words *house* and *household head* do appear briefly, but the draft obscures the true principles of law, and thus, is worse than if it were a dead letter. Alas, these men are trying to enact a civil code centered on extreme individualism, ignoring three thousand years of indigenous beliefs![53]

Hozumi explained why the proposed civil code would lead to "the loss of Japan's individuality": (1) The section on property, by idealizing unlimited freedom of contract for individuals, might raise society's productive capacities, but at cost of widening the gap between rich and poor, thereby producing conflicts between owners and workers, "contradictions inherent in capitalism"; and (2) the section on personal and domestic relations, based as it was on an imitation of Western individualism, had been drafted with the idea that husbands and wives, and elder and younger brothers were separate individuals. Consequently, there was danger that the code would break up Japanese society, which had always been upheld by teachings of reverence for ancestors, who continued to be central to the house.[54] Instead, Hozumi advocated the enactment of a civil code that would emphasize "a spirit suited to the nation" and "the familial relations of the 'house system.'"

As a result of this civil code issue, the Diet (parliament) voted to postpone until 1896 the enactment of the civil code scheduled to go into effect the following year. It was still in limbo when Boissonade, who had poured heart and soul into the code during a residence of over twenty years in Japan, returned to France in 1895. Inoue Kowashi composed a commemorative poem in classical Chinese for Boissonade from his sickbed and died soon after. New forces came into play.

---

53   Hozumi Yatsuka, "Mimpō idete, chūkō horobu," *Hōgaku shimpō*, vol. 5 (August 1891).
54   On Hozumi's theory of state, see Richard Minear, *Japanese Tradition and Western Law: Emperor, State, and Law in the Thought of Hozumi Yatsuka* (Cambridge, Mass.: Harvard University Press, 1970).

The code was in effect recompiled by a new commission headed by Itō Hirobumi and Saionji Kimmochi, and their new code was finally enacted in 1898. Their two guiding principles, which together defined the Meiji civil code, are of great interest to us: (1) Indigenous Japanese institutions and practices should be taken fully into account; and (2) the strong points of legislative theories from all Western nations should be adopted, and not just those of France and Italy, as had been the case previously.

The section on property was left virtually unchanged. It incorporated principles of legal equality between the sexes and the former social-status groups as well as the principles of individual choice, personal ownership of property, and liability arising from negligence, all based on the spirit of individualism. It also contained a system of real and obligatory rights based on the idea of equal rights and duties. However, the section on social relationships was greatly revised to establish the power of the household head by means of special provisions for family heads, parents, and fathers. As a result, individuals were constrained by being placed within a status hierarchy of family relationships. According to Western historical concepts, Japan's civil code was thus based on a dual structure, whose two layers were logically inconsistent: the return of the individual to a gemeinschaft-type of "house" unit in personal relationships versus the recognition of that person's status as an individual in capitalistic society. A modern society is presumably made up of individuals, but the Japanese people were continually forced to adjust themselves to a "house system" in which each individual was rooted.

That the enactment of Japan's civil code went through these vicissitudes and that the end product came about by such contradictory compromises are hardly surprising. Quite the contrary: The civil code epitomizes the basic pattern taken by Japan's turn to the West. Etō Shimpei, who, as mentioned earlier, once suggested that Japan enact a word-for-word translation of the French civil code, is said to have given the following instructions to Inoue Kowashi when the Ministry of Justice sent him to France:

The most vital task for all of you who are being sent to Europe is to inspect various European countries and institutions and then adopt their strong points while discarding their weaknesses. You are not being sent to study about the conditions in each country and to import Western ways wholesale into Japan. Hence, you should no longer think in terms of learning from Westerners, but instead, observe them in a spirit of critical inquiry. As Japan proceeds along the path of civilization, it is vital to adopt Western institutions and ways to improve our governmental processes. Nevertheless we must not become so infatuated with the West that we fail to discern its defects. If that is the case, the institutions and ways we adopt with so much toil and trouble will not be fit for our use.[55]

In his memoirs, Inoue stressed that the Meiji constitution and all other areas of reform in which he had had a hand in implementing show the spiritual characteistics of Japan. In contrast, Saionji Kimmochi (1849–1940), who spent ten years of his youth in France and who placed his faith in the universality of civilization, criticized such particularism as follows: "Usually, what is termed 'particular to' a certain nation or race is a shortcoming or idiosyncracy. . . . Most traits that present-day educators in Japan babble about as being distinctively Japanese would distress men of learning. . . ."[56]

Hozumi Yatsuka, who overemphasized the importance of the "house system" and the "teaching of ancestor reverence," was derided by the intellectuals of his day. It must be noted here that when the sections on family relations and inheritance in Japan's civil code were drastically revised during the American Occupation in 1947, the concept of "house" was thoroughly repudiated. Many Japanese, however, still opposed such "morality" imposed from abroad and feared that Western-style individualism would weaken family ties and create new problems in caring for the elderly, a problem that was of great concern by the 1980s. Thus opposition to aspects of Western "morality" represented more than a conservative, emotional reaction, for it was reinforced by a desire to make Japan achieve "modernity" while avoiding the alienation and atomization of human relationships inherent in capitalistic society.

THE SPIRIT OF CAPITALISM: FIRST TRANSLATIONS
FROM WESTERN LITERATURE

Robinson Crusoe

The great number of translations from Western literature made during the Meiji period and after provides another striking indication of Japan's turn to the West. During the early decades, however,

---

55 Matono Hansuke, Etō Nampaku (Tokyo: Hara shobō reprint, 1968), vol. 2, p. 107.
56 Miyazawa Toshiyoshi, "Meiji kempō no seiritsu to sono kokusai seijiteki haikei," in Miyazawa Toshiyoshi, Nihon kenseishi no kenkyū (Tokyo: Iwanami shoten, 1968), pp. 134–5.

translators were concerned more with causes than with literature. From the last days of Tokugawa rule through the first decades of Meiji, numerous translations were really practical tracts of agitation, often known as "political novels," that reflected the conditions of the time. More often than not, they were translated to suit the convenience of those who supported a cause or political position. Regardless of their literary value or lack thereof, however, these translations are interesting for what they reveal about the way that Japanese in that era reacted to the foreign intercourse that followed the breakdown of national isolation.

Japanese intellectuals began reading accounts of castaways toward the end of the Edo period. Japanese castaways who returned to Japan were often interrogated by bakufu officials, who transcribed their accounts of conditions overseas. Against that background, two translations of *Robinson Crusoe* appeared before the Meiji Restoration. The first was a partial translation from a Dutch version, entitled *The Account of a Castaway* by Kuroda Kōgen, a student of Dutch studies, which was completed before Perry's arrival. The following preface to the Dutch edition was also included in Kuroda's translation:

Robinson Crusoe of England was a man with a desire to traverse the four quarters. He set out to sea and lost his ship in a tropical storm. He managed to stay alive but was cast adrift in a lifeboat, captured by pirates, and finally sold to a fisherman. Later, he escaped from that fishing boat and, while fleeing from pursuers, was unexpectedly rescued by a Portuguese merchant vessel. He grew sweet potatoes and became very wealthy, but his misfortunes at sea did not deter him from returning to it in a great vessel he constructed. He ran into many storms, was shipwrecked, and then marooned on a desert island. He used all his wits to survive on this island for twenty-eight years before an English ship chanced to come and take him home.

Any reader of these accounts cannot help but be overwhelmed with admiration. When it was published in England, readers devoured it and rushed to buy it in droves; at one point its publication reached forty thousand copies. Its Dutch translation is being read more avidly than was the English original. Moreover, this book supplements gaps in our knowledge of geography. Although there are numerous other accounts of sea voyages, these merely describe stormy seas or the contours of lands discovered; none reports anything like the miraculous nature of Crusoe's achievements. Readers who learn of his countless hardships and his resourcefulness in overcoming these cannot but develop their own mental faculties.

I personally feel that although life is full of vicissitudes, no one has experienced as many as Crusoe. Each account of his experiences on that deserted island has great relevance to our own understanding of affairs in society. You should never forget the sufferings Crusoe experienced and become conceited and self-indulgent.

Moreover, Crusoe was adept solely in navigation, not in any other technical skills. Yet the mind of man is indeed a marvelous thing! Once he landed on the deserted island, he sewed his own clothes, gathered his own food, built his own house, constructed his own ship, made his own pottery, grew his own vegetables – succeeded in meeting all his personal needs by himself. . . .[57]

This translator was apparently unaware that *Robinson Crusoe* was a fictional product of Daniel Defoe's pen and instead believed that it was a true account. Furthermore, *Robinson Crusoe* was not considered a children's story by the Japanese of that era but, rather, a true account of a castaway, meant to be read by adults.

Translations of this type suggest Japan's initial orientation toward the sea, as well as their yearning for information about foreign affairs. In the case of Niijima Jō, for example, his desire to find out about conditions abroad was accelerated by reading a translation of *Robinson Crusoe* lent to him by his teacher of Dutch studies. He then smuggled himself out of Japan. After spending well over a year at sea, he found himself in America in 1865, engaged in manual labor with no idea of what the future held in store for him: "Exhausted after each day's labor, I would fall asleep as soon as my head hit the pillow. When I awoke each morning, my entire body ached so badly that I could hardly move."[58] This continued for weeks. Then he bought a copy of *Robinson Crusoe* in the original English. This book, along with a Dutch book about Christ and a Bible translated into classical Chinese, was what induced him to become a Christian. Niijima too believed that Crusoe was a real person and seems to have compared his own experiences with those of that solitary castaway. When he was stranded in Boston, he was insulted by burly sailors and found out about the grim living conditions caused by post–Civil War inflation. In that black hour, he is said to have gained the strength to carry on by repeating Crusoe's prayer.

This is a most interesting account of the circumstances surrounding the conversion of one Japanese to Protestantism. Today we are used to reading editions of *Robinson Crusoe* rewritten for children and forget the emphasis on Divine Providence in Defoe's original. The author's intention, scholars tell us, was to edify readers and impress

57 Kokusho kankōkai, ed., *Bummei genryū sōsho* (Tokyo: Kokusho kankōkai, 1913), vol. 1, p. 136.
58 "Hakodate yori no ryakki," in *Niijima sensei shokanshū*, p. 1137.

them with the importance of moral behavior. *Robinson Crusoe* was a parable of the role of Providence in human affairs, and accordingly, Niijima's interpretation was probably truer to the original than is that of most modern readers.

Protestantism enlarged upon this idea of diligence and work based on the individualism of a God-fearing person, and for that reason, it is often associated with the flowering of capitalism. What Defoe depicted in *Robinson Crusoe* was an individual in relation to an absolute God, and that relationship made for an autonomous individual. Niijima perceived in Crusoe such a religious man, but he also saw the prototype of those who would later develop capitalism.

After returning to Japan, Niijima established the Dōshisha English School in Kyoto in 1875. His goal was to foster "talented men of conscience," a phrase that suggests Max Weber's "spirit of this-worldly asceticism." One might even suggest that with the abolition of feudal society, Niijima and his associates set out to reconstruct and transform the ethics of the samurai, who had been taught to "do everything humanly possible and trust in Heaven's fate" in Meiji society through the medium of Protestantism.

Except for a period in the 1880s when the number of converts to Protestantism seemed to be growing rapidly – a phenomenon not unrelated to the exigencies of treaty reform – the young Meiji church probably did not enroll more than about thirty thousand converts. They were a strategic and able group of educated and usually ex-samurai youths. Prejudice in Kumamoto brought L. L. Janes's "Kumamoto Band" to Niijima's Dōshisha, and the association of Protestantism with Western dynamism by adventurous and able youth made the influence of Protestantism much larger than the modest number of its adherents would suggest. Yet its significance can also be exaggerated, for adherents to the new faith came as often from a commitment to this-worldly values as they did to other-worldly, transcendent beliefs.

Self-Help

During the "civilization and enlightenment" of early Meiji, the first Western ideas to enter Japan were generally those associated with English and American thinkers like Mill, Bentham, Spencer, de Tocqueville, Guizot, and Buckle – utilitarianism, civil liberties, natural rights, and rational positivism. Slightly later, French republicanism associated with Rousseau arrived and spread. Together, these ideas destroyed the hierarchical status system of Tokugawa times and ushered in an ethos of "achieving success and rising in the world" (*risshin shusse*). This ethos was powerfully stated in the phrases of Fukuzawa Yukichi's *Gakumon no susume* (An encouragement of learning) in 1872: "People are not born exalted or base, rich or poor. It is simply that those who work hard at their studies and learn much become exalted and rich, while those who are ignorant become base and poor."[59] This later became the Meiji government's ideology.

Japan's traditional work ethic was instilled anew in early Meiji youths in the form of this demand for a modern education. As a result, an enthusiasm for "personal cultivation" spread. Under slogans such as "hard work and application" or "thrift, diligence, and effort," Meiji youths prepared to carry out their future duties and to acquire knowledge from the West in various capacities – as pupils in the newly created school system, as apprentices in traditional crafts, as live-in disciples in the homes of famous scholars, and as students studying in universities abroad.

In 1883, a new translation of *Robinson Crusoe* by Inoue Tsutomu appeared as *An Extraordinary Adventure: An Account of Robinson Crusoe, the Castaway*. In his preface, Inoue treated Crusoe as a fictional character, not as an actual person, but he also asserted that the novel was no mere adventure story and that it served to teach young Englishmen to overcome hardship. Inoue interpreted *Robinson Crusoe* in the following terms: "This book should not be thought of as trivial, for if men read it carefully they will see that it shows how an island can be developed by stubborn determination."[60]

But it is the reception given to *Self-Help* that best shows the dominant hold maintained by the work ethic in Meiji Japan as it was applied to rendering service to society. After Fukuzawa Yukichi, Nakamura Masanao was the most influential exponent of Enlightenment in the early Meiji era. Half of Nakamura's influence stemmed from his translation of John Stuart Mill's *On Liberty*; the other half, from Samuel Smiles's *Self-Help*. Nakamura was born in 1832 to a low-ranking samurai family but was admitted to the bakufu's Shōheikō academy on the basis of his scholarly promise. His educa-

59 "Gakumon no susume (shohen)," in *Fukuzawa Yukichi zenshū*, vol. 3, p. 30. This work has been translated into English by David Dilworth and Umeyo Hirano as *An Encouragement to Learning* (Tokyo: Sophia University Press, 1969).
60 Inoue Tsutomu's translation was published in Tokyo by Hakubunsha in 1883. See also George B. Sansom, *The Western World and Japan* (New York: Knopf, 1950), p. 419.

tion was fundamentally Confucian, but he was also drawn to Western studies and to Christianity, which he embraced in 1874. Just before the Restoration, he was sent to England as the supervisor of a group of young bakufu students. When he returned to Japan after a sojourn of a year and a half, he brought back copies of *Self-Help* (which was a gift from a friend) and *On Liberty*. At that time, the bakufu was collapsing, and Nakamura joined a group of loyal retainer-intellectuals who retreated to Shizuoka with the Tokugawa house.

Nakamura now became an educator and translator. He completed a translation of Smiles's *Self-Help* in 1871 and published it as *A Collection of Stories about Success in the West* and another of J. S. Mill's in 1872 as *The Principle of Liberty*. Both books were immediately successful, as the Japanese of that era were thirsting for knowledge of the West. *On Liberty* became a fountainhead of liberalism during the Meiji Enlightenment, and *Self-Help* was read by all Meiji youths. The latter work was a best-seller in England and America as well, selling 250,000 copies by the end of the nineteenth century. But in Meiji Japan, where it appeared as an account of real Western men whose experiences were anchored in real social conditions, it is said to have sold 1 million copies. It certainly was a best-seller, being reprinted into the 1920s.

In recent years, *Self-Help* has been dismissed as part of the "success-story genre," but Nakamura's goals were moral as well as materialistic, and he stressed (by length and language) moral responsibility and the national interest. His translation was couched in classical language congenial to samurai readers, but he achieved a sonorous style that still strikes a respondent chord in many people, especially his opening rendition of Smiles's language:

The proverb "Heaven helps those who help themselves" is a truism, empirically verifiable. In this adage lies the success or failure of everything in human affairs. "He who helps himself" means the ability to be autonomous and independent, to refrain from relying on others. The spirit of self-help is the basis from which man derives intelligence. In broader terms, when the majority of a nation's people "help themselves," that state is filled with vigor and is strong in spirit.[61]

When Nakamura, a model Confucian scholar who had studied in England, pointed to the path that Japan should follow, Meiji youths obeyed him implicitly. His puritan individualism and utilitarian

---

61 For Nakamura's original text from which this was translated, see Ishikawa Ken, ed., *Nihon kyōkasho taikei: Kindai hen 1* (Tokyo: Kōdansha, 1961), p. 25.

morality could be transplanted in Japanese soil without much opposition because they could be grafted onto traditional Japanese ideas almost naturally.[62] This is indicated by the following episodes.

In a book that Kōda Rohan (1867–1947) wrote to instill the success ethic in young people, the first book that its hero is said to have read is Ninomiya Sontoku's *Account of Recompensing Virtue* (Hōtoku-ki). But when Smiles's book became popular, Rohan changed the title of his hero's inspiration to make it Nakamura's translation of *Self-Help*. Yet the hero's exclamations, "The fruits of your labors will derive from Heaven's boundless abundance" and "This book made me what I am," fit either source of inspiration equally well.

Kunikida Doppo, in *An Uncommon Common Man*, sympathetically portrays Katsura Shōsaku, a youth fully imbued with the spirit of *Self-Help*. Katsura idealizes Watt, Edison, and Stevenson, saves his money, and goes to Tokyo to work his way through school. Though poor, he exhibits none of the heedlessness toward life's necessities that is usually depicted as a virtue (or a vice) in the traditional swashbuckling hero-gallant of East Asia. Instead, Katsura supports his brother while going on to become an electrical engineer who is earnestly "absorbed in the work he is performing." He walks around and around some equipment, checking to discover the cause of its malfunction and then repairs it. Such an uncommon common man who has set his mind to do something fits Smiles's description of "a man devoted to his trade," one who is "able to endure long periods of tribulation and possesses true mettle." The reason that Japan could follow the example of Western peoples (whom Nakamura hailed in exclamations like "Ah, how happy Western peoples are today!") so quickly and could enjoy the benefits of electrical lighting in rural villages so early is that the majority of Japanese shared Doppo's sympathy with Katsura: There was a large reservoir of uncommon common men toiling diligently in the Meiji era.

As might be expected in a nineteenth-century English work, Smiles lists many "creators of new inventions" among his heroes in *Self-Help*. He devotes several pages to an anecdote about Richard Arkwright's invention of the cotton reel. One admiring reader of this anecdote was Toyoda Sakichi, who himself succeeded in inventing an automatic loom in 1897. His descendents went on to make automobiles. The lessons preached by Smiles were quickly trans-

62   Marius B. Jansen, ed., *Changing Japanese Attitudes Toward Modernization* (Princeton, N.J.: Princeton University Press, 1965), p. 67.

planted into Japanese soil and became the foundation for "overcoming adversity" and for "earnest application" in Meiji youths.

The philosophy implied in these slogans – that possibilities were unlimited for the individual with ability and that everything depended on personal application – fit the realities of early Meiji society. This philosophy was also expressed in common parlance. However, one should also keep in mind the less glamorous reasons when explaining why this transplantation took place so smoothly. One reason is that at least superficially, the lessons contained in *Self-Help* are arbitrarily and conclusively stated. In both the original and the translation, the doctrines are asserted with categorical authority. This arbitrary though edifying style, which is rather at odds with the work's purpose, was probably congenial to men born and raised in a feudal, authoritarian value system. As George B. Sansom wrote, "It was unfortunate that, when at last the Japanese had time to consider the nobler efforts of the Western mind, it was the dreary ratiocinations of Herbert Spencer or the homiletic of men like Benjamin Franklin and Samuel Smiles which seemed best to stay their intellectual pangs."[63] A Japanese raised within the Tokugawa Confucian tradition could accept the injunctions of Smiles and Franklin precisely because he was accustomed to their style of homily.

In 1878, the Meiji empress translated Benjamin Franklin's "Twelve Virtues" into traditional Japanese poems. Regarding industry, Franklin had written in his *Autobiography*: "Industry: Lose no time; be always employed in something useful; cut off all unnecessary actions." The young empress, who had learned Franklin's "Virtues" from her Confucian imperial tutor Motoda Eifu as part of her education, transcribed this in traditional poetic form and "bestowed it upon the Tokyo Women's Normal School," whose students had previously accompanied her procession at the school's opening ceremonies. The poem, adapted to music composed by Oku Yoshihisa, soon gained popularity and was sung in every part of the country:

> If unpolished, even the diamond
>   loses its jeweled radiance.
> Without education, people too,
>   will ne'er emit true virtue.
> If one begrudges the sunlight
>   working throughout the day,

63 George B. Sansom, *Japan, a Short Cultural History* (London: Cresset, 1932), p. 504. See also Earl H. Kinmonth, *The Self-Made Man in Meiji Japanese Thought: From Samurai to Salary Man* (Berkeley and Los Angeles: University of California Press, 1981).

As ceaselessly as the hands of a clock,
all things can be accomplished.[64]

The tendency to modernize from above is discernible in all late modernizing countries, but in the Meiji era, when the need to "foster industry and promote enterprise" was felt especially keenly, the royal poetess saw in Franklin's "Virtues" a new morality for civil society and took the initiative of Japanizing and introducing it to the people through the medium of traditional poetry.

Of course, the virtues of diligence and application were not new to the Japanese people in the Meiji period. The school song composed by the empress was, to be sure, Franklin's injunction in one sense, but in other respects, it was fully Japanese. In Tokugawa times, there was a saying that "hardships polish one into a jewel." The thirteenth-century Zen monk Dōgen wrote: "The jewel becomes a jewel through polishing. Man becomes benevolent through training. No jewel shines in its natural state. No novice is characterized by keenness of insight from the very beginning. They must be polished and trained."[65] If we go back even farther, we will find virtually the same injunction in the *Book of Rites*: "Unless the jewel is polished, it does not become a jewel; unless men study, they do not learn the Way."[66] Precisely because this idea of character building had a long tradition in Buddhism and Confucianism in East Asia, the Japanese were able to educate themselves so diligently and in such a sustained fashion during the Meiji "civilization and Enlightenment" period. Indeed, Ninomiya Sontoku's asceticism of self-restraint and moral cultivation was an ethos that dominated the rural villages until the end of World War II, and his *Account of Recompensing Virtue* (Hōtoku-ki) is far from neglected even today.

Every age has its fashions. Today, for example, "becoming a success and rising in the world" sounds old-fashioned and pretentious, but when rephrased as "self-realization," the same aspiration becomes modern and chic. Similarly, in early Meiji times, when everything traditionally Japanese or Asian seemed anachronistic, young hearts were not inspired by quotations from Dōgen or the *Book of Rites*.

Masaoka Shiki, a great Meiji reformer of Japanese poetry, read Franklin's *Autobiography* when ill with tuberculosis and was deeply

64 See Inoue Takeshi, ed., *Nihon shōkashū* (Tokyo: Iwanami shoten, 1958), pp. 48–9.
65 *Nihon koten bungaku taikei*, vol. 81: *Shōbōgenzō, Shōbōgenzō zuimonki* (Tokyo: Iwanami shoten, 1965), p. 397.
66 This is from the chapter "Music" in *The Book of Rites*. See *Kokuyaku kambun taisei*, vol. 24: *Raiki* (Tokyo: Kokumin bunko kankōkai, 1921), p. 351.

impressed by it. Shimazaki Tōson, later a naturalist writer of great renown, used Franklin's *Autobiography* at a country school when he was a young teacher. These details illustrate what the Japanese were concerned about during the period of their nation's rise to statehood in the early Meiji era.

Finally, we must consider that just as the activities of citizens in Western societies, many of them Protestants, later supported nationalism, the "diligence and application" of Meiji youths also became linked with nationalism in Japan. Self-cultivation did not stop at the personal level for Meiji youths but became associated with preserving Japan's independence in the face of Western encroachment. Morality and application came together in service to the larger community. As Fukuzawa Yukichi put it, again in *An Encouragement of Learning*, "When we compare Oriental Confucianism with Western civilization, we discover that what is possessed by the latter and is lacking in the former is (1) mathematics in the realm of the tangible and (2) the spirit of independence in the realm of the intangible."[67] Fukuzawa advocated cultivating the individual's spirit of independence. Based on Mill's view that "the independence of a nation grows out of the independent spirit of its people," Fukuzawa proposed that every Japanese "establish his own independence, and then Japan would be independent." This proposition is identical to one put forth by Smiles quoted earlier: "When the majority of a nation's people 'help themselves,' that state is filled with vigor and is strong in spirit." So it is interesting to note that the Confucian spirit repudiated by Fukuzawa functioned quite smoothly in this process, as Confucianism held that "personal cultivation and regulation of family affairs" was requisite to "ordering the realm and bringing peace to all under Heaven." Each citizen's "personal cultivation" in the form of "self-help" led directly to "ordering the realm" in the sense of "national wealth and power" (or its synonym, "national independence"). Thus it was fortunate for Japan that "overcoming hardship through diligence" and "becoming a success and rising in the world" in private life were in complete harmony with Japan's fortunes as a state. In this sense, self-help was by no means at odds with traditional Japanese values; quite the contrary, it was reinforced by them.[68]

67 "Kyōiku no hōshin wa sūri to dokuritsu," in *Fukuzawa Yukichi zenshū*, vol. 3, p. 198. See also Kiyooka, tr., *The Autobiography*.

68 On the influence that Franklin and Smiles had on Meiji Japan, see Hirakawa Sukehiro, "Furankurin to Meiji Kōgō," in Hirakawa Sukehiro, *Higashi no tachibana, nishi no orenji* (Tokyo: Bungei shunjūsha, 1981), pp. 53–88.

THE RETURN TO JAPAN: A CONSCIOUSNESS OF SELF
IN MEIJI YOUTH

The reaction against slavish Westernization

During the first two decades of the Meiji era, it seemed as if the
entire nation was determined to Westernize itself completely, but in
the late 1880s, a reaction set in. Nevertheless, this "return to being
Japanese" was not a reversion to the blind xenophobia of late
Tokugawa times.

In 1887, Foreign Minister Inoue Kaoru was pursuing a policy of
Westernization symbolized by balls and garden parties in the
Rokumeikan that were designed as an aid to procuring treaty revi-
sions from the Western powers.[69] Inoue spoke of the "recovery of
judicial authority" for Japan, but in reality he was willing to accept
the Westerners' treaty demands that foreign judges continue to
preside in all cases involving foreign nationals. When an opposition
faction headed by Inoue Kowashi learned of this, it leaked certain
secret documents, thereby inciting fierce antigovernment agitation.
Among those documents was a criticism by Boissonade of the government's frivolous Westernization policy. Boissonade pointed out
that at that time in all areas – the armed services, administration,
finance, education – in which foreigners served as employees or
advisers, they were not permitted to obtain government posts or to
wield actual government authority. Any system under which judicial
authority was delegated to foreigners, he stressed, would be injurious
to Japan's national interests and would open the door to foreign
intervention in domestic affairs.[70]

It is noteworthy that foreign employees like Boissonade were
critical of Japan's craze for Westernization. Nevertheless, the "return
to being Japanese" was not triggered solely by the advice of such
well-intentioned foreigners. What is more important is that some
Japanese began to criticize Westerners in terms of the universal
principles of "civilization" they had learned from the West. One
example was the *Normanton* incident.

---

69   See Donald H. Shively, "The Japanization of Middle Meiji," in Donald H. Shively, ed.,
     Tradition and Modernization in Japanese Culture (Princeton, N.J.: Princeton University
     Press, 1971), pp. 77–119.
70   See "Bowasonaado gaikō iken," in *Meiji bunka zenshū*, vol. 6: *Gaikō-hen* (Tokyo: Nihon
     hyōronsha, 1928), pp. 451–2.

In 1886, the *Normanton*, an English ship, sank off the Wakayama coast. Its English captain and foreign crew scrambled to safety in lifeboats, leaving all the Japanese passengers to drown. Despite widespread public indignation, a consular court in Kōbe exonerated the captain and crew of charges of criminal negligence. The reaction was predictable: "The news spread like lightning throughout the four quarters, and all people , whether in or out of government, were overwhelmed with grief and righteous indignation. Newspapers were filled with editorials and articles treating the incident in a tragic or righteously indignant light."[71] This sense of outrage played its part in bringing to a close the craze for Westernization symbolized by Inoue Kaoru's balls at the Rokumeikan.

What provoked Japanese ire about the shipwreck and the court's verdict, in addition to the realization of racial prejudice, was the fact that the English captain and court had not lived up to the West's self-avowed standards. The Japanese originally were inspired by Smiles's *Self-Help* because of its many anecdotes of "benevolence even at the cost of death." For example, one story proclaims that when a British ship sank off the coast of Africa, the English army officers turned over the lifeboats to women and children. Nakamura's translation reads: "This group of heroes sank to the depths of that raging sea without a word of regret on their lips or a teardrop of lament on their cheeks." The hearts of Meiji readers were struck by "these gallant, yet quiet models of English manhood." The rule that "a captain goes down with his ship" was followed again and again until the end of World War II, not only in the Imperial navy but also in Japan's merchant marine. Japanese youths had devoted themselves to creating a modern Japan based on Western models precisely because the injunctions and exemplars contained in *Self-Help* seemed to conform to their own ethical ideals. When these overly idealized images were betrayed and exposed as false by the actual deeds of living Englishmen, the Japanese reaction was to explode with anger and indignation.

To be sure, this incident itself should not be interpreted as ending Japan's turn to the West. The "return to being Japanese" manifested by intellectuals was not a wholesale rejection of the West in favor of

71 For journalism on the Normanton Incident, see *Shimbun shūsei Meiji hennenshi*, vol. 6 (Tokyo: Rinsensha, 1936), pp. 350, 356–7, 361, 365. See also Richard T. Chang, *The Justice of the Western Consular Courts in Nineteenth Century Japan* (Westport, Conn.: Greenwood Press, 1984).

a total return to traditional foundations so much as a genuine appropriation of the best in Japanese tradition.

A composite sketch of Meiji nativism:
Lafcadio Hearn's "A Conservative"

In *The Western World and Japan*, George B. Sansom wrote as follows about the Japanese (in this case, Baba Tatsui) who reembraced their native land during the Meiji period:

An interesting chapter of modern Japanese history could be written by tracing the careers of clever young men educated in liberal surroundings in England or America who returned to Japan flushed with democratic enthusiasms and in course of time lapsed into a bitter nationalism accompanied by a strong dislike of the West, which had nourished their youthful ardours. Not long ago an able and experienced member of this class observed to me that most of his contemporaries, products of Western education, had turned against the Western democracies feeling that their liberalism was a sham.[72]

The phenomenon of the Westernized intellectual returning to native traditions is by no means restricted to Japan but is also found in thinkers and leaders in Russia and in other Asian countries. The trend toward a "return to Japan" was already evident in the 1890s, when Lafcadio Hearn wrote "A Conservative," a short story that he included in *Kokoro*. The piece is worth noting for the subsequent appeal it had to young Japanese. Its plot dealt with the intellectual development of a young man in changing historical conditions.

Hearn's protagonist was a high-ranking samurai born and raised in the castle town of a 300,000-*koku* domain. Trained in the martial arts and schooled in Confucian and other traditional values, he was disciplined to honor the spirits of his forebears and to scorn death. This warrior witnessed the coming of Perry's Black Ships; soon "barbarians" were employed as teachers within his castle town. After the Meiji Restoration, the protagonist left home to learn English in Yokohama under a foreign missionary. At first he believed that love of country required him to learn about enemy conditions in a detached, cool manner, in keeping with the dictum "Know the enemy." But before long he was deeply impressed by the overwhelming superiority of Western civilization and decided that because the basis of its power lay in Christianity, he was duty bound

72 Sansom, *The Western World and Japan*, p. 418.

as a Japanese patriot to accept this higher religion and encourage all his countrymen to convert. So intense was his conviction that he became a Christian against his parents' opposition. To discard the faith of his ancestors was cause for more than a moment's distress: He was disowned by his family, scorned by his friends, deprived of all the benefits accompanying his noble status, and reduced to destitution. Still, the samurai discipline of his youth enabled him to persevere with fortitude despite all the hardships to which he fell victim. As a true patriot and seeker of the truth, he ascertained where his convictions lay and pursued these without fear or regrets.

However, Hearn's protagonist was soon disturbed to discover that the knowledge derived from modern science, which had enabled his missionary-teachers to demonstrate the absurdity of Japan's ancient beliefs, could also be used to demonstrate absurdities in the Christian faith. The Western missionaries were often surprised and shocked to discover that the more intelligent their Japanese students were, the sooner they tended to leave the church. So it was with this youth, who became an agnostic in religious matters and a liberal in political affairs.

Forced to leave Japan, he went to Korea and then to China, where he earned his living as a teacher for a time before making his way to Europe. There he lived for many years, observing and obtaining a knowledge of Western civilization matched by few Japanese. He lived in many European cities and engaged in various types of work. The West appeared to him a land of giants, far greater than he had ever imagined. On both the material and the intellectual fronts, Western civilization seemed far superior to his own. Yet its power of intellect was too often employed to destroy the weak. With this realization, Hearn's hero gained two articles of faith: (1) Japan was being forced by necessity, not by choice, to learn Western science and to adopt much from the material culture of its enemies; nevertheless, (2) there was no compelling reason to discard completely the concepts of duty and honor and ideas of right and wrong inherited from the past. The prodigality inherent in Western life taught him to value the strength found in his country's honorable poverty. He would do his utmost to preserve and protect the best in Japan's traditions.

What was of value and beauty in Japanese civilization – things that could be comprehended and appreciated only after coming into contact with foreign culture – now seemed clear to him. Thus he had become a man longing to be allowed to go back home, and on the day that he set out for his return to Yokohama, he did so not as a blind xenophobe of *bakumatsu* times but as "a conservative" who was "returning to Japan."[73]

Hearn's character portrait can perhaps be considered a composite of the samurai-intellectuals who came to grips with Western civilization in the early Meiji era. It was so with many of the early Dōshisha student Christians, not a few of whom came as "band" members from Kumamoto where Hearn was teaching. Even Uchimura Kanzō, the leading member of the early Hokkaido Christian group, wrote of a moment in the United States when his homeland began to appear "supremely beautiful" to him. Another example can be found in the physician-writer Mori Ōgai, who, like Hearn's conservative, received a samurai education in a castle town. As a child, Ōgai was often warned by his parents in no uncertain terms: "You are the son of a samurai, so you must have enough courage to cut open your belly." Others, like Nakamura Masanao or Uchimura Kanzō, studied under missionaries and accepted Christianity out of a sense of patriotic duty. Many converts, however, subsequently repudiated Christianity. In fact, although this is a little-studied area in modern Japanese thought, the great majority of Japanese thinkers seem to have "returned" to Japan in some sense. "China activists" like Miyazaki Tōten and journalists such as Tokutomi Sohō were both Christians at one time.[74] Baba Tatsui was a liberal who took refuge abroad, and Shiga Shigetaka and the periodical *Nihon oyobi Nihonjin* (Japan and the Japanese) bring to mind the intellectual who returned to Japan bent on discovering its true "national essence."

Hearn's piece, in that it foreshadows a floodtide of *weltschmerz* stemming from an observation of the darker aspects of Western civilization, has something in common with Natsume Sōseki's later critique of modern Western civilization, and Hearn's short story contains many aspects of thought and action that match those of later Japanese intellectuals. Stated conversely, later Japanese

---

73 "A Conservative," in *Kokoro*, vol. 7 of *The Writings of Lafcadio Hearn* (New York: Houghton Mifflin, 1922), pp. 393–422. For a detailed analysis of "A Conservative," see Hirakaw Sukehiro, "Nihon kaiki no kiseki – uzumoreta shisōka, Amenomori Nobushige," *Shinchō* (April 1986):6–106.

74 Miyazaki's autobiography was translated by Etō Shinkichi and Marius B. Jansen as *My Thirty-three Years' Dream: The Autobiography of Miyazaki Tōten* (Princeton, N.J.: Princeton, N.J.: Princeton University Press, 1982). Tokutomi is treated by John D. Pierson, *Tokutomi Sohō, 1863–1957: A Journalist for Modern Japan* (Princeton, N.J.: Princeton University Press, 1980).

intellectuals, for all the surface brilliance and diversity of their variegated philosophical spectrum, have much in common with Hearn's hero on a deeper level of feeling. In these respects, "A Conservative" is a composite sketch and a precursor of many modern Japanese intellectuals.

The Japanization of education

Upon his arrival in Japan in the early Meiji period, Basil Hall Chamberlain, who later became the dean of foreign Japanologists, lectured on "the life of Nelson" and similar topics in his post as instructor in the then fledgling Imperial Japanese Navy. About the young Japanese naval officers, successors of the Tokugawa samurai, whom he taught, he wrote that they were "fairly fluent in English, and dressed in a serviceable suit of dittos, might almost be a European, save for a certain obliqueness of the eyes and scantiness of beard."[75] He noted that the Meiji naval officers were quite fluent in English. This held true beyond the students in Japan's naval academy, for the generation born around 1860 produced an elite better able to communicate in foreign languages than could its successors. Men like Okakura Tenshin (b. 1862), Uchimura Kanzō (b. 1861), and Nitobe Inazō (b. 1862) all wrote books in English; and Mori Ōgai (b. 1862) probably did more than anyone else to introduce Western literature to Japan.

Natsume Sōseki (1867–1916), who was born a few years later, graduated from Tokyo Imperial University in 1893, took over Lafcadio Hearn's chair as the first Japanese lecturer in English literature in 1903, and then in late Meiji left academic life to concentrate on his writing. His remarks about the capabilities of Japanese students in English over time provide a revealing insight into the Japanization of Meiji higher education. The students' command of English was declining, he noted, because of the proper and predictable progress achieved by Japanese education:

In my generation, all instruction at regular schools was done in English. In all courses – geography, history, mathematics, botany and biology – we used foreign-language textbooks. Most students who came a little before us even wrote their answers in English; and by my generation, there were some Japanese instructors who taught in English.[76]

---

75 Basil Hall Chamberlin, *Things Japanese* (Rutland, Vt.: Tuttle, 1971), p. 1.
76 "Gogaku yōseihō," in *Sōseki zenshū* (Tokyo: Iwanami shoten, shinsho ed., 1957), vol. 34, pp. 233–4.

In that era, he went on, English was only one aspect of an excessive subordination to foreign culture: "Men would show off by dangling gold watches, wearing Western dress, growing beards, and interjecting English phrases when speaking ordinary Japanese." Not only was English fashionable, but modern knowledge was as yet inaccessible in Japanese:

Because we had so much English training outside regular English classes, our ability to read, write, and speak developed naturally. But we all are Japanese in mind, and considering our independence as a nation, such an educational system is, in a sense, a disgrace. It invokes in us the feeling that we are no different from India, that we are subjects of England. We all agree on the importance of Japan's nationality; it is not something to be exchanged for a mere knowledge of English. Hence, as the foundations for our state's survival are solidified, the aforementioned educational system ought naturally to fall into disuse; and in fact, this is precisely what is taking place.

Not enough had been translated yet, and the use of many foreign textbooks was still unavoidable. But scholarship was universal, and once there were adequate materials and competent Japanese teachers, Japanese students were increasingly taught in their own language.

From the standpoint of widely diffusing scholarship in society, it would be best to teach in Japanese, the language in which our students have been brought up and which they use naturally. . . . The declining use of English is natural and to be expected.

But government policy also came into play and might even have proved more important than these cultural aspects. As Sōseki saw it:

The biggest cause for declining English abilities in Japan was man-made, in the form of a policy adopted, I believe, when the late Inoue Kowashi was minister of education [1892–6]. The decision was to teach all subjects except English in Japanese as much as possible. While emphasizing the importance of the Japanese language in teaching, Inoue sought to revive Japanese literary and classical Chinese studies as well. . . . This man-made decision to suppress the use of foreign languages [in education] is an overwhelmingly important factor behind the present decline in language abilities.

In early Meiji years, the modernization of institutions and ways was construed as "Westernization." However, in that the desire to modernize was generated by an external crisis that caused independence for the Japanese people and nation to be established as a categorical imperative, it was inevitable that Japanese students studying abroad would, upon their return home, appropriate the positions temporarily held by foreign employees in and out of government.

Inoue Kowashi, too, advocated modernization with less Westernization. Like many other Meiji leaders, his objective was not "the importation of things Western" but, rather, "Western-style production" in Japan. After the "political crisis of 1881," he submitted a political program to the government in which he outlined the educational policies that he thought the state should adopt. Two clauses in his program read:

The Promotion of Chinese Studies:

Since the Restoration, English and French studies have had high priority, and this has caused the sprouts of revolutionary thought to appear in our country for the first time. However, for teaching the Way of loyalty to ruler, love of country, and allegiance – values in danger of disappearing at present – nothing equals Chinese studies. We must revive these values and thereby maintain a balance.[77]

Encouraging the Study of German:

Under our present educational system, the only students who study the German language are found in medicine. Students studying law and related subjects all learn English and French. It is only natural that those who study English admire English ways, and that those who study French envy French government. But of all nations in present-day Europe, only Prussia is similar to us with regard to the circumstances of its unification. . . . If we want to make men throughout the land more conservative minded, we should encourage the study of German and thereby allow it, several years hence, to overcome the dominance now enjoyed by English and French.[78]

It was Inoue who, with Motoda Eifu, drafted the Imperial Rescript on Education promulgated in 1890. In the preceding passage, we can see that as early as 1881 Inoue wanted to return to East Asian traditions and to uphold national unity by means of a philosophy stressing virtues such as loyalty to ruler, love of nation, and allegiance to superiors.

However, we must not forget that among the generation that studied directly under foreign teachers in Japan, there was a clarity of understanding regarding international affairs that proved lacking in later days. Naval officers are a case in point. Officers in the Russo-

---

77 "Kangaku wo susumu," in Inoue Kowashi denki-hensan iinkai, ed., *Inoue Kowashi-den, shiryō* (Tokyo: Kokugakuin daigaku toshokan, 1966), vol. 1, p. 250.

78 "Doitsugaku wo okosu," in *Inoue Kowashi-den, shiryō*, pp. 250–1.

Japanese War for the most part fought on warships made in Britain. Unlike the officers in World War II, who fought on ships and flew in planes manufactured in Japan, they went to Britain or other foreign countries, observed how ships were built there, and delivered the finished products to Japan themselves. At times, they might witness British laborers staging strikes, for example, and this broad range of experience made navy men international-minded. After that generation retired in the 1920s, the naval officers, like the ships they commanded, were "made in Japan." This was true also for the leaders in all other areas of government. In the 1930s, the entire nation was seized by a very narrow nationalism. That nationalism was partly due to conditions external to Japan, but it was able to gain ground in part because of the parochialism of Japanese education in that era.

From the Charter Oath to the Imperial Rescript on Education

The Charter Oath issued in 1868 and the Imperial Rescript on Education promulgated in 1890 may be considered official proclamations that mark the beginning and end of an era. In regard to the West, the Charter Oath states:

Evil customs of the past shall be abandoned and everything shall be based upon the just laws of Nature.

Knowledge shall be sought throughout the world so as to strengthen the foundations of Imperial rule.

These two articles were declared by the victorious loyalists (sonnō-ha) to be the cultural and political policies to be undertaken by a unified new Japan. It is interesting to note that once the antiforeign loyalists had toppled the bakufu and seized power themselves, they immediately proclaimed a policy of peace and opened the country to foreign trade and diplomatic intercourse. This fact exposed the slogan "revere the emperor, expel the barbarians" for what it had really been – a catchphrase devoid of meaningful content that was used to unite and mobilize the energies of dissident samurai activists.

Yet the new Meiji government's declaration that "knowledge shall be sought throughout the world" should not be interpreted as a simple by-product of its policy to establish peace and open the country. Yoshida Shōin, who defied bakufu law, had also "sought knowledge throughout the world," and his purpose too was "to strengthen the foundations of Imperial rule." The commitment to abandon "evil customs of the past" was clearly indicative of the realization that Japan in 1868 was as yet unequipped to be a modern nation-state and showed a singular desire to learn from the West.

As opposed to the Charter Oath, which sought models to adopt in foreign nations perceived to possess cultural superiority, the Imperial Rescript on Education issued twenty-two years later in 1890 sought these models in a transcendent Japanese historical character. The rescript reads:

Be filial to your parents, affectionate to your brothers and sisters; as husbands and wives be harmonious, as friends true; bear yourselves in modesty and moderation; extend your benevolence to all; pursue learning and cultivate arts, and thereby develop intellectual faculties and perfect moral powers; furthermore, advance public good and promote common interests; always respect the Constitution and observe the laws; should emergency arise, offer yourselves courageously to the State; and thus guard and maintain the prosperity of Our Imperial Throne coeval with heaven and earth.[79]

These virtues appealed deeply to feelings traditionally held by the people. Moreover, the rescript asserts that "ever united," the Japanese people "have from generation to generation illustrated the beauty" of those virtues, thus pushing national unity and the source of national morality far back to the historical origins of the Japanese people. Conversely, such historicism posits the continued existence of national unity and morality throughout all periods of Japanese history, thereby giving birth to the concept of a historically transcendent "national essence" (*kokutai*).

Not that the rescript was anti-Western in thrust. The exhortations to "pursue learning and cultivate arts, and thereby develop intellectual faculties and perfect moral powers; furthermore, advance public good and promote common interests" are almost identical to those put forth by Smiles in *Self-Help*. Thus, although it is often characterized as a simple piece of Confucian reaction, elements meeting the demands of a new age are to be found in this document. The rescript did not assert that Japanese traditions were universal principles; rather, it proclaimed that values then regarded as universal in nature really conformed to traditional Japanese ways.

79 Translated in R. Tsunoda and W. T. de Bary, eds., *Sources of Japanese Tradition* (New York: Columbia University Press, 1958), pp. 646–7. For the genesis of the rescript, see also D. H. Shively, "Motoda Eifu: Confucian Lecturer to the Meiji Emperor," in D. S. Nivison and A. F. Wright, ed., *Confucianism in Action* (Stanford, Calif.: Stanford University Press, 1959), pp. 302–23.

Yet it is also evident that foreign nations disappeared from view in the rescript. One distinguishing characteristic of post-*bakumatsu* history is that unlike the period of national isolation, an inescapable influence was exerted on Japan by foreign, mainly Western, nations. In the Charter Oath, we find a declaration that for Japan, a latecomer to international society, to preserve national independence, the Japanese people must learn from foreign countries and progress along the road to civilization and enlightenment. By contrast, the only reference to Japan's relations with foreign countries mentioned in the Imperial Rescript on Education is "should emergency arise, offer yourselves courageously to the State; and thus guard and maintain the prosperity of Our Imperial Throne coeval with heaven the earth," which posits a hypothetical state of war.

The Imperial Rescript on Education, which totally ignored the existence of foreign countries and extolled the virtues of Japan's "national essence," was by no means indicative of recovered national self-confidence. The omission of foreign nations actually suggests a Japan filled with doubt and anxiety, a Japan unable to reject foreign influences completely and therefore driven to rely all the more on indigenous values. Such doubt and anxiety are revealed in the fact that, as opposed to the Charter Oath, the rescript depicts foreign nations in a negative, almost menacing, light. The rescript's aim is to create internal solidarity among the people by maintaining a common national morality, and a consciousness of that morality as stemming from shared origins in Japan's past. This aim is manifested from the beginning – "Our Imperial Ancestors [stemming from the sun goddess, Amaterasu] have founded Our Empire on a basis broad and everlasting, and have deeply and firmly implanted virtue; Our subjects ever united in loyalty and filial piety, . . ." – to the end: "It is Our wish to lay it to heart in all reverence, in common with you, Our subjects, that we may all attain to the same virtue."

Thus the Imperial Rescript on Education clearly decreed the end of a fervent turn to the West, whose start was symbolized by the Charter Oath. Whereas the Charter Oath posited "the just laws of Nature," a value assumed to be hitherto lacking in Japan, as a goal to be attained, the rescript asserted that a "national essence," whose values were already manifested in Japan's feudal past, should be the foundation for future action.

The Charter Oath can be compared to a small child just beginning to understand what is going on around him who seeks to absorb things from his environment; in short, it shows the desire to identify with the world. Conversely, toward the end of the 1880s, after deciding that its turn to the West had been too sudden and extreme, Japan sought an identity of its own, and part of this straining to confirm an identity can be seen in the Imperial Rescript on Education of 1890.

Japan, a non-Western nation, adopted from the West a tremendous amount of what was fundamental and essential to modernization during these twenty-two years. Without those ideas and institutions, the establishment of a national identity would have been impossible, and the existence of an independent Japan within a society of nations dominated and ordered by the West could not have been maintained. But at the same time, because of this wholesale borrowing from the West, the basic establishment of a "self," which had to be attained and upheld by the Japanese themselves, became a process filled with anxiety and uncertainty. In short, the assimilation of Western culture was dictated by reasons of state, yet such efforts were fraught with an uneasiness that Japan's cultural self-identity might be violated. Because this psychological problem – a sense of pride easily injured – lay constantly at the bottom of Japan's modernization process, the Japanese displayed what might be called a strange fanaticism in every subsequent foreign crisis involving the West. The fact that the slogan "defend the national essence" (*kokutai*) had such a powerful hold over Japanese hearts is undoubtedly also closely related to this psychological problem.

CHAPTER 3

MEIJI CONSERVATISM
KENNETH B. PYLE

The Meiji period bequeathed to modern Japan a powerful conservative tradition that dominated government and society in the twentieth century. Meiji conservatism took shape at the end of the nineteenth century in reaction to the sweeping reforms and Western influence that had held sway in the first two decades of Meiji. Those reforms, which brought to fruition the demands for change that had grown during the late Tokugawa, drew their inspiration from Western ideas and institutions that were the products of the Enlightenment and of the liberal philosophies that accompanied the emergence of commercial capitalism and a bourgeois class dissatisfied with traditional forms of government in Europe. The Meiji ruling group, after initially adopting many of the ideas and institutions of the Enlightenment, subsequently promoted a powerful conservative program in order to sustain its power and the social order on which it rested.

Conservatism, in the sense used here, is not simply a tendency to maintain the status quo. Rather, it is a distinctly modern phenomenon that first developed in the West in the late eighteenth and early nineteenth centuries in reaction to the dominant themes of the Enlightenment and to the implications of the French Revolution. Although conservatism had distinctive features in different European countries, owing to their divergent histories and social structures, certain common features became apparent wherever it arose in the West. It is worthwhile to examine our topic in the context of European conservatism, in part because the Japanese conservatives drew inspiration from their European counterparts and in part because comparisons will prove meaningful in understanding the nature of Meiji conservatism.

The origins of conservatism have generally been associated with

Edmund Burke and the reaction to the consequences of the French Revolution. However, students of this style of thought, like Karl Mannheim and Klaus Epstein, trace its origins more precisely to a reaction to the ideas of the Enlightenment. They show that conservative doctrines were already formed before 1789. To be sure, the polarities among categories of liberal, radical, and conservative were more sharply defined after the French Revolution, but it was the implications of the European Enlightenment that first called forth a coherent philosophy of conservatism.

The dominant themes of the Enlightenment in Europe included an optimistic faith in the ability of humans to mold their environment according to their own designs. This faith was rooted in the achievements of natural science and the belief that it was possible through the application of reason to construct a social order in accord with nature. In the same way that rational science had made progress possible in the mastery of the physical world, human affairs, too, could be improved because they were believed to be governed by natural laws whose workings, once discerned, could be used to bring ever-greater improvement in society. Accordingly, traditional values and beliefs associated with organized religious practice were dismissed in favor of a new view of humanity and its place in the world. By disseminating the new scientific knowledge and liberating humanity from the obscurantism and religious parochialism of the past, a new era would dawn. Government must become enlightened by recognizing the "rights of man" and by sweeping away the old class restrictions and establishing a new social equality through a wide array of reforms. It was necessary to eliminate all artificial restrictions, especially state regulations, that inhibited the natural workings of the economy. Because all human beings were subject to universal laws, all peoples and races were seen as progressing toward a uniform civilization. The Enlightenment, accordingly, embodied a negative view of the particularistic culture and traditions of all societies.

Those who opposed this new world view, who became known as conservatives, rejected the notion that society could successfully be remade simply through the application of the rational will. They stressed the idea of the historic growth of societies and the "collective wisdom" that existing customs and traditions embodied. Institutions would be more useful if they were the product of gradual growth than if they were constructed anew by individuals. Conservatives did not oppose change but said that it should be evolutionary.

Society was like an organism; it had grown as a whole, as a system with its parts interrelated and fitting one another. Such a holistic conception of society required that a change of institutions be made by gradual adaptation. Because nations were the products of organic growth, institutions could not be transferred arbitrarily from one nation to another. Conservatism and nationalism found a natural affinity in their glorification of the particular traditions and institutions of a people. The universalist themes of the Enlightenment, its affirmation of the potential similarity of all human beings and of the progress of all peoples and races toward a uniform civilization, were countered with the particular claims of distinctive national patterns of historical development.

THE CHALLENGE OF THE JAPANESE ENLIGHTENMENT

Modern Japanese conservatism had its origin in response to dominant themes of influence exercised by Western culture during the period of "civilization and enlightenment" or "Enlightenment" (*bummei kaika*) that held sway in the first two decades of the Meiji period. The full sweep of European Enlightenment and nineteenth-century liberal thought was introduced into Japan in a very short space of time. Positivism, materialism, utilitarianism – there was little opportunity to sort out and pursue the logical development of ideas. They were introduced in no particular order. For example, Nakamura Masanao published a translation of John Stuart Mill's *On Liberty* in 1871, but it was eleven years before Jean-Jacques Rousseau's *Social Contract* was translated by Nakae Chōmin.

The *bummei kaika* brought a wholesale delivery of the entire Western liberal tradition. The Enlightenment writers associated with the society known as the Meirokusha – Fukuzawa, Nishi, Tsuda, Mori, Kanda, Katō, and others – were among the most self-conscious initial advocates of the cultural revolution that swept over Japanese society in early Meiji. Subsequently, the ideologues of the People's Rights movement, like Ueki Emori and Nakae, further elaborated the political implications of the Western liberal tradition; and in the 1880s, a new generation of writers, of whom Tokutomi Sohō was the most representative, sought to press the *bummei kaika* ideals to their ultimate conclusion by demanding the Westernization of every aspect of Japanese society. Western liberal civilization challenged Japan's traditional beliefs, its traditional social organization, and its traditional system of government with such ceaseless persistence as to throw nearly every area of life into a state of turmoil. Here I will summarize only the main themes in the Enlightenment that subsequently evoked the conservative response.

First, *bummei kaika* thought was dominated by a negative view of Japan's traditional institutions and the learning that underlay them. Fukuzawa Yukichi summed up this sweeping rejection of his heritage:

If we compare the knowledge of the Japanese and Westerners, in letters, in techniques, in commerce, or in industry, from the smallest to the largest matter . . . there is not one thing in which we excel. . . . Outside of the most stupid person in the world, no one would say that our learning or business is on a par with those of the Western countries. Who would compare our carts with their locomotives, or our swords with their pistols? We speak of the yin and yang and the five elements; they have discovered sixty elements. . . . We think we dwell on an immovable plain; they know that the earth is round and moves. We think that our country is the most sacred, divine land; they travel about the world, opening lands and establishing countries. . . . In Japan's present condition there is nothing in which we may take pride vis-à-vis the West. All that Japan has to be proud of . . . is its scenery.[1]

Despite this thorough rejection of Japanese civilization, the *bummei kaika* writers held almost limitless hope for the future. As with the Enlightenment in Europe, there was an optimistic belief that human effort could master the sociopolitical environment, just as science had made it possible to master the physical environment. A second dominant theme of the Japanese Enlightenment stressed the cultural example of the West. Because universal laws of nature governed human behavior, if Japan developed in accord with these laws, it could progress in the same way that the Western nations had. Progress, in other words, was unilinear; it was determined by universal forces of historical development rather than by the particular trends of national history. Civilization in the West had progressed further along this universal path of development, and therefore, it could be looked to as an example. The liberal economist Taguchi Ukichi explained that the object of *bummei kaika* was not simply to "Westernize" Japanese society but, rather, to follow the path of universal progress that the West represented:

We study physics, psychology, economics, and the other sciences, not because the West discovered them, but because they are the universal truth.

1 Albert M. Craig, "Fukuzawa Yukichi: The Philosophical Foundations of Meiji Nationalism," in Robert E. Ward, ed., *Political Development in Modern Japan* (Princeton, N.J.: Princeton University Press, 1968), pp. 120–1.

We seek to establish constitutional government in our country, not because it is a Western form of government, but because it conforms with man's own nature. We pursue the use of railways, steamships, and all other conveniences, not because they are used in the West, but because they are useful to all people.[2]

Taguchi was bold and consistent in his pursuit of the *bummei kaika* themes. Civilized development meant not only that people would use similar machines; they would also think and behave in similar ways, eat the same kinds of food, wear the same kinds of clothing, live in houses of similar architecture, and enjoy the same kinds of art. In short, it was the implication of his *Nihon kaika shōshi* (A short history of civilization in Japan) that civilized people would become more and more aware of their common humanity and that no nation would have a peculiar message.

A third dominant theme of the Enlightenment was a wholehearted commitment to science, technology, and utilitarian knowledge. The classical curriculum in the schools had to be replaced by practical learning that was useful for day-to-day life. Fukuzawa's well-known condemnation of Tokugawa scholars as "rice-consuming dictionaries" concluded that "managing your household is learning, business is learning, seeing the trend of the times is learning."[3] The principles governing the physical universe could no longer be seen as identical with Confucian ethical principles. "First there are things and only afterward ethical principles"; Fukuzawa wrote in his *Bummeiron no gairyaku* (Outline of civilization), "it is not that principles come first and that things emerge afterward."[4]

As a fourth dominant theme, the Enlightenment writers promulgated a new view of humanity with revolutionary implications for society and the state. Fukuzawa's ringing words that opened *Gakumon no susume* (The progress of learning), "Heaven did not create men above men, nor set men below men," succinctly summarized a rejection of inflexible hereditary status. Signifying a new, open, and mobile society, he went on to explain that a young man's position in society should be determined by his grasp of practical

2 Kenneth B. Pyle, *The New Generation in Meiji Japan: Problems of Cultural Identity, 1885–1895* (Stanford, Calif.: Stanford University Press, 1969), p. 90.
3 Carmen Blacker, *The Japanese Enlightenment: A Study of the Writings of Fukuzawa Yukichi* (Cambridge, England: Cambridge University Press, 1964), p. 52.
4 Craig, "Fukuzawa," in Ward, ed., *Political Development*, p. 122. For the entire work, *An Outline of a Theory of Civilization*, trans. David A. Dilworth and G. Cameron Hurst (Tokyo: Sophia University Press, 1973).

knowledge. In *Bummeiron no gairyaku*, he wrote that the fundamental flaw of Japanese culture was its most basic institution – the Japanese family system. The *bummei kaika* writers blamed the family for destroying the spirit of individual initiative and independence on which, they believed, modern scientific civilization depended. They said that the family system inculcated values of absolute power on the one hand and unquestioning deference on the other and, therefore, that it provided the foundation for authoritarian government. What was necessary was the fostering of a new set of values on which democratic, constitutional, and enlightened government could be founded. The *bummei kaika* was by no means democratic in the twentieth-century sense of advocating universal suffrage or economic equality, but it did oppose old forms of social stratification and government by a closed elite. It favored an open and mobile society in which economic rewards would be commensurate with individual talent and effort. It stood for a new social ethic that would free the individual from group control – an ethic that would cultivate self-support, self-expression, and self-responsibility. The *bummei kaika* advocates frequently expressed hope of replacing the extended hierarchical family groups with independent nuclear households consisting of only parents and children and marked by the elevation of women to a new status. These writers generally argued for a parliamentary government that would function through rational deliberation and enlightened legislation, with responsible ministries and an impartial law-abiding administration. They espoused Manchester free-trade ideals and put their faith in an emerging internationalism. Fukuzawa, in a section entitled "Countries Are Equal" of *Gakumon no susume*, saw little future for a narrow nationalism: "A country is a gathering of people. Japan is a gathering of Japanese and England is a gathering of Englishmen. Japanese and English alike are members of a common humanity; they must respect each others' rights."[5] Taguchi Ukichi was typically even more bold and provocative in arguing an emerging internationalism. In an article in the first issue of the journal *Kokumin no tomo* in 1887, he described nationalism as a foolish and outmoded conception that had caused needless disputes. Nationality ought to be ignored, so that an Englishman living in Tokyo was "a Tokyoite" just as much as was a Kagoshima man living in Tokyo. *Kokumin no tomo*, the journal of Tokutomis Sohō that evoked enthusiastic response

5 Ibid., p. 118.

from educated youth, transmitted *bummei kaika* themes and ideals to a new generation of Japanese. *Heiminshugi*, as Tokutomi called his ideas, proclaimed the emergence of "a new Japan," making a clean break with its past and becoming a wholly Western, liberal, democratic, industrial society. There was no room here for a Japanese cultural identity.

EARLY MEIJI CONSERVATIVES: THE MORAL IMPERATIVE

It was in confronting individual elements and themes of the Enlightenment, or *bummei kaika*, that a conservative philosophy began to take shape. From the very outset of the Meiji period, of course, there was reactionary opposition to the reforms that were introduced. This opposition drew its greatest strength from the activities of those who were politically alienated from the new regime. Saigō, for example, left the government, returned to Satsuma, and led an uprising that sought to turn back the clock on many of the Meiji reforms. There were other reactionary efforts such as the Shimpūren in Kumamoto, which were prepared to use violence against the agents of Western-inspired reform.

In contrast with such reaction and a wish to return to the past, the beginnings of a coherent conservative philosophy depended on a reasoned response to the premises of the *bummei kaika*. Above all, it was the challenge that the Enlightenment offered to fundamental Japanese social institutions and values that evoked the beginnings of Meiji conservatism. Except for the imperial institution, the *bummei kaika* advocates could not have attacked any part of traditional society to which the Japanese felt a deeper emotional attachment than they did to the values that underlay family life.

Even the advocates of reforming these values found it difficult to practice their proposals within their own families. Fukuzawa, for example, had advocated a modern education and individual rights for women but brought up his own daughters in the strictest orthodoxy. Mori Arinori had published a reformist "Essay on Wives" in the periodical *Meiroku zasshi* but found trouble in being consistent. For his first marriage, he insisted that it be in the form of a contract – Fukuzawa was a witness! – to demonstrate the equality of the partnership. Subsequently, however, he dissolved the marriage, explaining that his wife had become "peculiar and flighty" as a result of the new relationship and that "to attempt a marriage like that with an uneducated Japanese woman was my mistake."[6]

The early Meiji education system was the prime target of conservative wrath because it replaced traditional Confucian moral teachings with a utilitarian spirit stressing a view of learning as an investment in worldly success. The preamble of the Education Ordinance of 1872 stated that the purpose of education was to enable a student to "make his way in the world, employ his wealth wisely, make his business prosper, and thus attain the goal of life." Some of the values that were introduced in the new school system may have had a basis in Japanese experience and in the background of the Meiji Restoration. Those values that emphasized ambition, hard work, the value of education, and the utility of science clearly had the force of history behind them. Other values, however, which were drawn from the Western liberal tradition and emphasized the natural rights of humans, the freedom of the individual, the rights of women, and so on, had little basis in Japanese experience and relatively little social support.

In fact, traditional ideals of loyalty and obligation, solidarity, and duty to superiors, which had deep roots in the family ethics and the feudal experience of Japanese, retained vast social support in Meiji and well into the twentieth century. This was partly owing to the "limited" nature of the Meiji Restoration, which had not brought to power a wholly new class espousing a revolutionary set of values. Above all, there was no revolutionary change in the basic nature of the farming classes. Extraordinary continuities in the mode of Japanese farming all the way up to World War II helped perpetuate old values in the countryside. Accordingly, it was no surprise that the clean sweep of traditional values wrought by the Enlightenment in the educational system should soon come under attack. Conservatives had a vast social basis for the reassertion of old values.

The beginnings of a coherent, conservative defense of traditional Japanese values can best be found in the thought of several Confucian-oriented writers who supported some of the Meiji reforms but who regarded the disappearance of a clear, accepted moral code as a failing of the new period. They concentrated their criticism particularly on the new educational system, advocating instead a return

6 Michio Nagai, "Mori Arinori," *Japan Quarterly* 11 (1964): pp. 98–105. For Mori's "Essay," see *Meiroku Zasshi: Journal of the Japanese Enlightenment*, trans. William R. Braisted (Cambridge, Mass.: Harvard University Press, 1976). For Fukuzawa's raising of his daughters, see Blacker, *Japanese Enlightenment*, pp. 157–8, note.

to prescribed, Confucian-based values. Their ideas had something in common with the views of intellectuals in the late Tokugawa years who advocated a combination of *Tōyō dōtoku* (Eastern ethics) with *Seiyō geijutsu* (Western techniques).

The two most prominent advocates of this position were Motoda Eifu and Nishimura Shigeki, both of whom were Confucian in their fundamental views. Motoda, who served as tutor and personal adviser to the Meiji emperor for twenty years beginning in 1871, was the more conservative of the two because he still held in significant ways to the universal applicability of Confucian values.[7] Though accepting the irreversibility of the Western technological adoptions, he maintained that Confucian ethics must remain the core of education. Virtue and knowledge could not be separated:

> The advocates of enlightenment completely mistake the basic meaning of virtue when they contend that whereas the province of wisdom is broad and boundless, the sphere of virtue is narrow and limited. Originally, virtue was a name which embraced myriad excellences, while wisdom was one part of virtue with no province outside it.[8]

Motoda began a crusade to restore traditional Confucian ethical training shortly after the Ministry of Education decided in 1872 to replace Confucian ethics in the courses in moral training (*shūshin*) with translations of American and French moral texts. As lecturer to the emperor, he was able to press his views within the government, often through documents drafted for the Meiji emperor to promulgate.

In 1879, he wrote a document describing the emperor's dismay at what he observed in schools on an imperial tour of inspection to the Tōhoku region. The damage that Western-style ethics texts was inflicting could be overcome if instruction were "founded upon the Imperial ancestral precepts, benevolence, duty, loyalty, and filial piety, and Confucius were made the cornerstone of our teaching of

---

7 Three essays by Donald H. Shively are useful in understanding the early stages of this Confucian-oriented protest: "Motoda Eifu: Confucian Lecturer to the Meiji emperor," in David S. Nivison and Arthur F. Wright, eds., *Confucianism in Action* (Stanford, Calif.: Stanford University Press, 1959), pp. 302–33; "Nishimura Shigeki: A Confucian View of Modernization" in Marius B. Jansen, ed., *Changing Japanese Attitudes Toward Modernization* (Princeton, N.J.: Princeton University Press, 1965), pp. 193–241; and "The Japanization of the Middle Meiji," in Donald H. Shively, ed., *Tradition and Modernization in Japanese Culture* (Princeton, N.J.: Princeton University Press, 1971), pp. 77–119. An essay more sharply focused on our interests here is by Matsumoto Sannosuke, "Meiji zempanki hoshushugi shisō no ichi dammen," Sakata Yoshio, ed., *Meiji zempanki no nashonarizumu* (Tokyo: Miraisha, 1958), pp. 129–64.

8 Shively, "Motoda," in Nivison and Wright, eds., *Confucianism in Action*, p. 315.

ethics."[9] Issued as an imperial rescript, the Kyōgaku taishi (The great principles of education) put the emperor's prestige behind the preservation of Japan's "customary ways" as part of every Japanese child's schooling. The rescript of 1879 regretted that "in recent days, people have been going to extremes. They take unto themselves a foreign civilization whose only values are fact-gathering and technique, thus violating the rules of good manners and bringing harm to our customary ways."[10] To reverse the decline in the moral climate required restoration of the "ancestral teachings" and, particularly, the "study of Confucius" to priority among the objectives of instruction.[11]

The rescript of 1879 spelled the beginning of the end of the Enlightenment era in education. A new minister of education decreed a greater centralization of education and stipulated that moral instruction in loyalty and filial piety be the chief end of education.[12] What was more, at the urging of Itō Hirobumi, the government issued the Public Assembly Ordinance in 1880 which denied to both pupils and teachers the right "to attend or to join as members in assemblies organized for the purpose of political lectures and debates."[13] Itō's primary intent was to undercut the influence of the People's Rights movement in the schools, but the ordinance also had the effect of adding to the conservative tide in education.

Nonetheless, although the liberal ideals that had guided education in the 1870s were mortally wounded by the initiatives of Motoda and other conservatives with the personal backing of the Meiji emperor, there were sharp disagreements among the conservatives. Itō, Inoue Kowashi, Mori Arinori, and others in the bureaucracy opposed the reintroduction of Confucian moral doctrine and the establishment of a "national doctrine" (kokkyō) through the educational system.[14] They favored a secular, statist approach in contrast with what they regarded as Motoda's reactionary and crude attempts at Confucian ideological orthodoxy. Itō already envisioned a modern though limited constitutional monarchy, whereas Motoda sought imperial rule and the unity of court and government.

9   Ibid., p. 327.
10 Herbert Passin, *Society and Education in Japan* (New York: Columbia University Press, 1965), p. 227.
11 Ivan Parker Hall, *Mori Arinori* (Cambridge, Mass.: Harvard University Press, 1973), p. 347.
12 Passin, *Society and Education*, p. 84.
13 Hall, *Mori Arinori*, p. 346.
14 See Helen Hardacre, "Creating State Shintō: The Great Promulgation Campaign and the New Religions," *Journal of Japanese Studies* 12 (Winter 1986): 29–63.

Despite these disagreements, the conservative trend gained momentum. Influential officials, particularly those around the emperor, began to compile new moral textbooks. Among them was Nishimura Shigeki, who had been a founding member of the Meirokusha and was one of the early advocates of Western institutions but whose *bummei kaika* enthusiasm faded after his appointment as a lecturer to the emperor in 1876. Outside the court, Nishimura's views often had greater influence than Motoda's did, as he was not so uncritical of Confucian values as Motoda was. Nishimura found fault with Confucianism as a comprehensive and universal doctrine and for its lack of progressive spirit, but he believed that it formed the basis for a code of moral values that could serve modern Japan. While pointing out the shortcomings of Confucianism, he proposed to adopt selectively from both Confucianism and Western philosophy in order to build a new morality for modern Japan. In practice, the result was a watered-down Confucianism:

The Confucian way, which has formed the morality of the Japanese people since the times of our ancestors, cannot be discarded even if we were to try to discard it. Especially the Four Books – the *Analects*, *Mencius*, *Great Learning*, and the *Mean* – in my opinion, can be said to be so far the best teachings in the world. Therefore, it is most proper to establish the foundation of moral education in Confucian books today.... When the Confucian Way is used, its spirit alone should be taken, and I hope the name Confucianism will not be used. The name Confucianism has for some time been disliked by the people, so that there are many who would not believe in the substance because of the name.[15]

In 1886, Nishimura published a treatise, *Nihon dōtoku ron* (Discourse on Japanese morality), in which he summarized his views. The faults with Confucianism, he wrote, were its lack of progressive spirit, its idealization of the past, and its rigid hierarchical views of the social order. Western philosophy alone, however, was inadequate because it did not give sufficient attention to personal conduct and was too contentious to provide a basis for a strong moral system. Japan would selectively have to build its own system, retrieving the basic Confucian spirit and updating it with appropriate maxims from Western philosophy.

Nishimura and Motoda also pressed during the 1880s for a "sacred rescript" to establish the basis of a moral orthodoxy for education. But Itō, who became prime minister in 1885, and Mori, whom he appointed education minister, opposed the idea of

15   Shively, "Nishimura," in Jansen, ed., *Changing Japanese Attitudes*, p. 238.

creating a rigid national orthodoxy. It was not until after Mori's assassination in 1889 that Nishimura and Motoda succeeded. In 1890, Premier Yamagata Aritomo and Minister of Education Yoshikawa Akimasa gave their support to the idea of an imperial edict because they thought it would contribute to the stability of the new constitutional era. The final document, issued shortly before the opening of the Diet (parliament) on October 30, 1890, was the product of drafts by many in the government, including Motoda. Until 1945, it remained the fundamental statement of ethical principles to govern the behavior of teachers and students and, in fact, the entire nation.

The Imperial Rescript on Education read as follows:

Our Imperial Ancestors have founded the Empire on a basis broad and everlasting. . . . Our Subjects ever united in loyalty and filial piety have from generation to generation illustrated the beauty thereof. This is the glory of the fundamental character of Our Empire, and herein lies the source of Our Education. Ye, Our Subjects, be filial to your parents, affectionate to your brothers and sisters; as husbands and wives be harmonious, as friends true . . . pursue learning and cultivate arts, and thereby develop intellectual faculties and perfect moral powers; furthermore, advance public good and promote common interests; always respect the Constitution and observe the laws; should emergency arise, offer yourselves courageously to the State; and thus guard and maintain the prosperity of Our Imperial Throne coeval with heaven and earth.

Conservatives faced a dilemma to which Nishimura alluded when he wrote that the name Confucianism should not be used in the document because "there are many who would not believe in the substance because of the name." In the new age, Confucian values lacked the automatic sanctions to command belief that they had once had when the entire Confucian world view was accepted. The dilemma is nowhere better illustrated than in the work of Inoue Tetsujirō, a conservative professor of philosophy at Tokyo Imperial University who was asked by the Ministry of Education to prepare a commentary on the education rescript. In his *Chokugo engi*, Inoue set out to justify traditional values to a new generation raised on scientific and utilitarian thought. His purpose, he said, was to explain a rational basis for loyalty and filial piety. He wrote that traditional values must be justified inductively if they were to command belief. Accordingly, he gave the values of the rescript a utilitarian explanation. Filial piety, for example, was justified by self-interest, for "inevitably everyone grows old and weak. . . . Therefore, if you want your children to feel filial tenderness for you in the future, you must set the example. . . . If you do not, you cannot expect anyone to take care of you."[16]

It was typical of this formative period of conservative thought that such clumsy attempts at rescuing traditional values should be made. Inoue's blatant utilitarianism was indicative of the conservatives' desperate attempt to justify the traditional values, to which they were still attracted, in terms of the new rationalist thought that was intellectually satisfying to them.

Other young conservatives found distasteful such a defense of traditional moral values. The brightest and most influential of a new conservative group that came to the forefront in the late 1880s was the young editor of the newspaper *Nihon*, Kuga Katsunan. Well-read in European conservative thought, he understood the kind of premises on which a viable conservative philosophy must be built. The fundamental claim of the Enlightenment – that Japan must follow the historical development of the West – must be combated. The *bummei kaika* writers contended that this process was a fixed, universal pattern of development to which all progressing nations must conform. Accordingly, they held that the values of *bummei kaika* were of universal validity. On both theoretical and practical grounds, Kuga attacked these premises. His editorials, which had a wide and influential audience, argued that the liberals failed to understand the meaning of history and of the nation-state that established the framework within which Japanese reform must take place if it were to be effective and enduring. He was fond of asserting that the Enlightenment theorists "failed to grasp the historic, that is to say, organic, relationship between the nation and the individual."[17] A Japanese acted not as a member of a bloodless humanity governed by universal values; rather, he acted as a member of his own vibrant people, inspired by Japan's own national spirit.

Kuga did not embrace traditional values, as Motoda and Nishimura had, from confidence in their universal validity. Nor did he try to legitimize them, as Inoue Tetsujirō attempted, in terms of the new rationalist thought. Instead, he gave them a nationalist justification. Referring to the rescript's provisions, he stated: "Filial

16   Pyle, *The New Generation*, pp. 127–8. See also Minamoto Ryōen, "Kyōiku Chokugo no kokkashugiteki kaishaku," in Sakata Yoshio, ed., *Meiji zempanki no nashonarizumu* (Tokyo: Miraisha, 1958), pp. 165–212. The standard reference on the framing of the rescript is Kaigo Tokiomi, *Kyōiku chokugo seiritsushi no kenkyū* (Tokyo: Tokyo daigaku shuppankai, 1965). For the development of nonofficial interpretations of that document, Carol Gluck, *Japan's Modern Myths: Ideology in the Late Meiji Period* (Princeton, N.J.: Princeton University Press, 1985).
17   Pyle, *The New Generation*, p. 97.

piety, brotherly affection, marital harmony, and the loyalty of all to
the Imperial Throne are Japan's distinctive national ethics. They are
the historic customs of the Japanese people, the basic elements that
support her society." He concluded pointedly that these values
"cannot be deduced by academic reason (*gakuri*), but (only) by the
emotions (*kanjō*)" of Japanese.[18]

Further, on practical grounds, Kuga added that the preservation
of traditional morals and customs was psychologically necessary to
the nation because they provided the binding, integrative basis on
which Japan's cultural identity and nationalism could be built. Kuga
feared the social disruption that the values of the *bummei kaika*
would cause, which in the heyday of Western imperialism could lead
to national destruction:

> If a nation wishes to stand among the great powers and preserve its
> national independence, it must strive always to foster nationalism
> (*kokuminshugi*). . . . If the culture of one country is so influenced by another
> that it completely loses its own unique character, that country will surely
> lose its independent footing.[19]

This argument became the most powerful in the conservative arsenal: that nations could not be subdued by force alone, that cultural
acquiescence could prove to be self-defeating.

Promulgation of the Imperial Rescript on Education was accompanied by much pomp and circumstance. Copies of the imperial
portrait and the rescript were sent to all the schools as sacred
symbols to be used for regular ceremonies. When Uchimura Kanzō,
a Christian recently returned from a period of extended study in the
United States before teaching at the First Higher School, abstained
from ceremonial obeisance to the portrait on the occasion of a
reading of the rescript at the school, it set off a controversy as to
whether Christianity was compatible with Japanese nationalism.
Inoue Tetsujirō wrote an essay denouncing Uchimura's behavior
that became the center of the controversy. His essay, entitled
"The Clash Between Religion and Education," held that Christian
beliefs in individualism, universal brotherhood, and denial of the
emperor's divinity could not be reconciled with the spirit of the
rescript.

Kuga, much more astute than Inoue, saw the controversy in a
somewhat different light. If Christianity could be stripped of its

18 Ibid., p. 127.
19 Ibid., p. 75.

foreign customs and ties and assimilated to Japanese circumstances, as Buddhism had been, then Christianity need not be regarded as inevitably in conflict with Japanese moral education. In a period of intense competition among nations, as a matter of national survival, moral education was necessary to foster the "common sentiments" of the Japanese people to enable them to work together to deal effectively with their domestic and international problems. Uchimura, in fact, later attempted to foster a Japanese-style Christianity shorn of its foreign customs and ties. It was not his goal to turn Japanese into "universal Christians" who, he said, "turn out to be no more than denationalized Japanese."[20] He founded the "nonchurch" movement (mukyōkai), which deliberately divorced itself from outside influences. But Christianity in Japan after the rescript and the rise of conservative ideological movements in the 1890s was on the defensive. Traditional values of Japanese society became inextricably intertwined with partriotism and loyalty to the Japanese nation. In the heyday of imperialism, to adhere to beliefs introduced by missionaries coming from the Western imperial nations was to leave oneself open to suspicion of disloyalty and subservience.

CONSERVATIVES AND THE PROBLEM OF FOREIGN RELATIONS

The struggle over the nature of moral instruction in education was the first issue around which conservative opinion began to crystallize. Another issue that early attracted the conservatives' attention was the problem of Japan's relations with the treaty powers. Until 1894, revision of the unequal treaties was one of the prime political issues whose influence was felt in both domestic and foreign affairs. More than any other issue at the time, it forced the conservatives to define their views of the Japanese nation.

The Enlightenment had posited a rather benign view of the treaty powers. Its advocates were disposed to overlook, at least for the time being, the violations of Japanese sovereignty imposed by the system of extraterritoriality that the powers maintained. Such infringements were attributed to Japan's backward nature; but as it adopted civi-

---

20 Marius B. Jansen, *Japan and China: From War to Peace, 1894–1972* (Chicago: Rand McNally, 1975), p. 99. For a study of Uchimura, see John F. Howes, "Uchimura Kanzō: Japanese Prophet" in Dankwart A. Rustow, ed., *Philosophers and Kings: Studies in Leadership* (New York: Braziller, 1970), pp. 180–207.

lized values and institutions, these infringements, they believed, would disappear. Nations as they progressed would become more alike, and with the advancement of civilization, conflicts among them would recede. The nation-state, in fact, would become less important.

Tokutomi Sohō, whose views as a young writer in the 1880s can be seen as the culmination of *bummei kaika* themes, saw the militant phase of civilization being replaced by an industrial phase. Under the influence of Herbert Spencer, Tokutomi foresaw the decline of warfare and emergent internationalism. The rise of industrial civilization was accompanied, he wrote, by free-trade policies and economic interdependence that would overcome divisions among nations. Economic, rather than military, strength would determine the survival of societies. Accordingly, the most important measures that Japan could undertake were the adoption of the modern technology, civilized institutions, and liberal values that were common to the advanced industrial societies. Reaction to such a sanguine world view became a major issue, evoking a conservative response to the *bummei kaika*.

The treaties to which the bakufu had submitted represented an infringement of Japanese sovereignty. They permitted foreign residents and trade in certain leased territories and ports, and under the system of extraterritoriality, foreign residents were subject to the jurisdiction of their consular courts. Japanese tariffs were under international control. For a quarter of a century after the Restoration, it was a primary goal of Japanese foreign policy to revise the treaties and join the international system on an equal footing with the Western powers. To achieve this goal, the Meiji leaders pursued a pragmatic course of adopting the legal institutions that were deemed necessary for acceptance into the company of civilized nations who controlled the international system of late nineteenth-century imperialism. Foreign Minister Inoue Kaoru put it succinctly in 1887 when he told his colleagues, "It is my opinion that what we must do is to transform our empire and our people, make the empire like the countries of Europe and our people like the peoples of Europe. To put it differently, we have to establish a new, European-style empire on the edge of Asia."[21]

The Meiji leaders went to great lengths to accommodate to the rules and mores of the international system. They pressed for adop-

21 Marius B. Jansen, "Modernization and Foreign Policy in Meiji Japan," in Ward, ed., *Political Development in Modern Japan*, p. 175.

tion of Westernized legal codes in order to impress on the powers the civilized progress of Japan and so to hasten treaty revision. Many of the other Meiji reforms, including constitution making, had treaty revision as one of their motives. The lengths to which the oligarchs were willing to go to accommodate their Western visitors were dramatized by the opening in Tokyo in 1883 of the Rokumeikan, a gaudy Victorian hall where foreign residents were entertained with Western music, cards, billiards, masked balls, and other social functions. A dancing master was hired from abroad to instruct the oligarchs and their wives in the "civilized" social graces.

Conservatives were outraged and made the Rokumeikan a symbol of cultural subservience to the Westerners, but it was Inoue Kaoru's efforts at treaty revision that elicited a clearer focus of conservative views of the importance of cultural autonomy. Inoue convened representatives of the treaty powers in Tokyo in 1886 and proposed a number of concessions in return for the abolition of consular jurisdiction. He offered to establish "mixed residence," which would allow foreigners to travel and engage in commerce in the interior, and promised determination of all Japan's legal codes "according to Western principles."

The intense conservative opposition to these proposals was led by Tani Kanjō, minister of commerce and agriculture. Tani was a former army general who, along with other military figures, had opposed some of the liberal trends of the 1870s and had organized a party to urge a conservative version of the constitution. The oligarchs had given him a cabinet position that took him on a tour of Europe where he was impressed by the spirit of nationality that was preserved from country to country. He returned from the trip at the time that Inoue was pressing his proposals. Tani expressed sharp opposition to them on the grounds that the promise to transform Japan's legal codes after the pattern of Western ones was humiliating and destructive of the Japanese spirit of nationality. Tani issued a dramatic resignation from the cabinet and led a vociferous opposition, both in the bureaucracy and outside the government, forcing Inoue to resign and ending his effort to revise the treaties.

Nonetheless, the government followed it with another effort at revision. This time the attempt was by the new foreign minister, Ōkuma Shigenobu, appointed in 1888. In his negotiations with the powers, Ōkuma extracted more concessions than Inoue had, but he did not gain an unconditional end to extraterritoriality. Moreover, the commitment to adopt Western legal principles remained a part of the agreement. When the details were revealed, controversy once again erupted; Ōkuma was driven from office; and negotiations were suspended.

The treaty revision controversy galvanized conservative opposition to *bummei kaika* views. It brought into focus the relationship between cultural borrowing from the West and the establishment of national self-esteem and pride. This issue was the prime concern of a new generation of intellectual conservatives. A group of young journalists and publicists emerged who expressed a more moderate conservatism than Motoda or Nishimura had. Educated after the Restoration in the new schools, they had been imbued with Western values from the early days of their education. They were not backward looking; they favored change and reform; but they believed it must be consistent with the Japanese character. Such concerns, they believed, were essential to national survival in an age of keen competition among nation-states and, particularly, in the heyday of Western imperialism. We have already considered Kuga Katsunan, the most articulate of them, the one most impressive for the clarity of his reasoning. He and others of this group formulated arguments against the Enlightenment notion of a universal civilization toward which all nations were progressing and against the belief that cultural distinctions from the West would ebb as Japan advanced. He held that the concept of "civilization" was relative, that social progress was not governed by universal laws. Not only was progress compatible with a diversity of cultures; but, in fact, "world civilization progresses through the competition of different cultures." He sought to distinguish his own views from the more traditionalist reaction by arguing for careful, selective borrowing:

We recognize the excellence of Western civilization. We value the Western theories of rights, liberty, and equality; and we respect Western philosophy and morals. We have affection for some Western customs. Above all, we esteem Western science, economics, and industry. These, however, are not to be adopted simply because they are Western; they ought to be adopted only if they can contribute to Japan's welfare. Thus we seek not to revive a narrow xenophobia, but rather to promote the national spirit in an atmosphere of brotherhood.[22]

22 Pyle, *The New Generation*, pp. 94–7. A treatment of Tani Kanjō and other conservatives of his group is found in Barbara Joan Teters, "The Conservative Opposition in Japanese Politics, 1877–1894," Ph.D. diss., University of Washington, 1955. See also Barbara Joan Teters, "The Genro-In and the National Essence Movement," *Pacific Historical Review* 31 (1962): 359–78; and Barbara Joan Teters, "A Liberal Nationalist and the Meiji Constitution," in Robert K. Sakai, ed., *Studies on Asia* (Lincoln: University of Nebraska Press, 1965), vol. 6, pp. 105–23.

When he argued for selective borrowing from the West, his liberal critics charged that this would make a "patchwork" of society, because there was a certain spirit and set of values that underlay and motivated institutions in Western society. Kuga argued, however, against a monolithic conception of Western societies, pointing to cultural differences among the European countries and their fierce preservation of their own separate nationalities. The artist and writer Okakura Tenshin, who was joining at this time with an American, Ernest Fenollosa, in a movement to preserve the distinctive Japanese traditions of aesthetics, made a similar point:

Where is the essence of the West in the countries of Europe and America? All these countries have different systems; what is right in one country is wrong in the rest; religion, customs, morals – there is no common agreement on any of these. Europe is discussed in a general way, and this sounds splendid; the question remains, where in reality does what is called "Europe" exist?[23]

To counter the *bummei kaika* themes of universalism and individualism, Kuga adopted the historicist and holist arguments characteristic of conservative theorists in any country. There was rarely apparent in his thought nostalgia for the past. Certainly there was no longing for an archaic utopia, for example, antedating Western or even Chinese influence on Japan. Rather, Kuga argued for the idea of the historic growth of society over time. This was, in short, moderate conservatism that sought piecemeal change – selective borrowing, for example – to improve society. Japan's development must be organic and holistic; it must grow gradually so that all the parts interrelated and worked together.

A group of young intellectuals and writers, with whom Kuga was closely associated, known as the Seikyōsha and led by Miyake Setsurei, founded a journal *Nihonjin* (The Japanese) in 1888 whose express purpose was the "preservation of the national essence" (*kokusui hozon*). The phrase became popular among writers of the day, and there was much debate over the nature of the national essence that should be preserved. The difficulty they had in this regard was indicative of a conservative dilemma. These young writers had a Western education and were perturbed by reactionaries who used their arguments to make a sweeping defense of traditional

23 Pyle, *The New Generation*, p. 74 note. For Fenollosa, see Lawrence W. Chisholm, *Fenollosa: The Far East and American Culture* (New Haven, Conn.: Yale University Press, 1963).

civilization. They sought a middle way between such traditionalism and the Westernism of the *bummei kaika*. In a word, they sought to be both modern and Japanese.

The fundamental issue in the deliberations of these young conservative writers is one not fully resolved today, namely: What is the nature of social progress? They, of course, fully accepted the notion of progress, but was it compatible with diverse social structures? Or did the functional necessities of industrial society inevitably overcome the diversity of social and cultural forms? Today, in the late twentieth century, there is plenty of evidence to show that industrial societies retain aspects of their traditional social structure, but for the Japanese in the late nineteenth century, as the first non-Western people to pass through the Industrial Revolution, the issue was particularly perplexing. Young liberals, like Tokutomi Sohō, who had a broad following in the 1880s and 1890s, believed that industrial development required passage through universal, evolutionary stages. As it advanced, Japan would inevitably come to resemble the more advanced Western nations; Japan's progress, in fact, could be measured by its success in acquiring similarities to Western societies.

Such views made Japanese self-esteem vulnerable. For example, when the first session of the Diet failed to operate smoothly, many liberals were depressed because the experience reawakened doubts about Japan's ability to establish successful parliamentary institutions that were regarded as the essence of the *bummei kaika.*

Miyake Setsurei's most successful contribution to formulating a conservative argument was an essay, *Shin-zen-bi Nihonjin* (The Japanese: truth, goodness, and beauty), written in 1891 amidst disappointment over the outcome of the first Diet. This essay set forth a concept of world civilization progressing through competition among nations having diverse talents that resulted from different experiences and environments. The culture of Western nations might be the highest stage that civilization had so far attained, but progress would require other cultural forms and values if civilization were to move on to a higher state. In other words, cultural nationalism was not only a matter of self-defense; as Kuga argued, it was also a contribution to the progress of man. In his preface, Miyake wrote: "To exert oneself on behalf of one's country is to work on behalf of the world. Promoting the special nature of a people contributes to the evolution of mankind. Defense of the homeland and love of mankind are not at all contradictory."[24] It was a billiant argument designed to appeal to the young by persuading them that preserving Japanese cultural values was not a reactionary stand against progress but was, rather, a contribution to the development of civilization in the world.

Miyake described the ways in which his concept of world civilization, with its corollary of national mission, could be pursued by the Japanese and thus contribute to the realization of the ideals of truth, goodness, and beauty, which he defined as the ultimate goal of world civilization. Japanese, because they were familiar with both Asia and Europe, could make a unique contribution to truth by correcting the Western-centric view of scholarship. Spencerian sociology, for example, did not deal adequately with Asia, and the Japanese could offer new scholarly theories based on broader knowledge than Western scholarship possessed. Similarly, Japanese had a mission to contribute to goodness by building their military strength, protecting Asian nations from Western imperialism, and thus promoting justice. Finally, the Japanese had a mission to conserve their unique conception of beauty, with its emphasis on the delicate and exquisite, rather than simply adopting the grand styles characteristic of Western art and architecture.

These young conservatives had many able spokesmen, and we cannot doubt their wide influence in appealing to the nationalist predilections of the first generation to go through the Western-oriented Meiji schools. They were instrumental in forestalling the treaty revision effort of Inoue and Ōkuma. They also lent support to the opponents of the new legal codes that had been drafted and that would have introduced many significant Western legal concepts. For a generation, Japanese bureaucrats and scholars had been working with foreign advisers to develop new codes to cover the law of the family and private transactions as well as the law of civil procedure. Tokugawa customary law, in unrecorded form and highly diverse from place to place, was incapable of dealing with the social relations and commerce of the Meiji state. Adherents of French or German or other Western legal traditions argued for the adoption of their favored patterns of legal codes. The complex controversies were important, to say the least, because of the effects that the codes were bound to have on the future social order. The growing influence of conservatism in the 1890s induced much greater caution. The Code

24   Pyle, *The New Generation*, p. 151.

of Civil Procedure went into effect in 1891, but the civil code was postponed and debated further until 1898, and the commercial code was delayed until 1899.

Similar controversies between the universalism of the Enlightenment and the growing influence of cultural nationalism and conservatism took place in many fields of human endeavor. Literature and the arts were directly affected. Okakura and Fenollosa led a movement against the prevailing adulation of Western styles in the arts. The *bummei kaika* had brought to adherents of Westernism control of the government apparatus of art training and patronage, but the traditional arts and crafts languished in neglect and disrepute. Okakura, a contributor to *Nihonjin*, and Fenollosa tried to chart a middle position between the liberal, utilitarian, and pro-Western circles, on the one hand, and the traditionalists and xenophobes on the other. They tried "to create a new basis for Japanese art in an amalgam of East and West, old and new, subjective and objective."[25] Similarly, literati struggled over new forms of prose. Tsubouchi Shōyō's *Essence of the Novel* in 1885 pointed the way toward a new realistic literature that Futabatei Shimei's novel *Ukigumo*, published two years later, in prose close to the colloquial, sought to attain.[26]

The 1890s was, in short, a kind of watershed in the public discussion of cultural issues raised by the Meiji reforms. Japanese conservatism in its formative phase became deeply imbued with cultural nationalism. The younger generation had clearly succeeded in articulating a more thoughtful and balanced conservatism than Motoda, Nishimura, and others had in the early 1880s. The perceptive journalist, Yamaji Aizan, distinguished between the two styles of thought:

Whereas the conservatism that appeared in 1881 and 1882 was nothing more than a rebirth of Chinese learning, the conservatism of the late 1880s represented the development of national consciousness. Of course, in the latter case, many backwoods priests and Confucianists were delighted to plunge into the movement but ... the leaders of the group had an understanding of Western culture. They absorbed the spirit of European nationalist movements, and regarded the attempt to make Japan over into a Western state as a most dangerous tendency. They observed that Western powers, through their language, literature, and customs, strove to preserve

25 John M. Rosenfield, "Western-style Painting in the Early Meiji Period and Its Critics," in Shively, ed., *Tradition and Modernization in Japanese Culture*, p. 204.
26 Translated by Marleigh G. Ryan as *Japan's First Modern Novel*: Ukigumo *of Futabatei Shimei* (New York: Columbia University Press, 1967).

their nationality. Ultimately, they reversed the intellectual trend, and national spirit (which those who did not sympathize called conservative spirit) finally prevailed.[27]

The successive public controversies over the unequal treaties with the powers diminished the appeal of the *bummei kaika's* benign view of international relations and helped make the conservatives' case for preserving cultural autonomy a basis for maintaining the strength of the Japanese state. Tokutomi saw his Westernism declining in influence before the growing strength of "the new conservative group." In an eloquent appeal, he admonished his countrymen:

> If you hate damage to national pride and therefore entrance into the civilized world ... then feeling for Japan will grow and feeling for the world will wane, then the ideal of the state will flourish and the ideal of the people will wither, then the spirit of conservatism will appear and the spirit of progress will die, and our country will have lost its vital energy. . . . Stop treaty revision, but don't halt the progress of nineteenth century Japan![28]

More than any other event, the outbreak of the Sino-Japanese War in 1894 and its extraordinary release of patriotic emotion gave sway to the conservative cause and overrode the universalism and liberal ideas of the Enlightenment. Not until 1945 was public opinion again so receptive to the appeals of reform as it had been in the early Meiji.

For a generation, an effective foreign policy had implied a successful reform movement. But by 1890, the mood was changing. The new order was largely in place, and the international environment was changing. East Asia became the locus of fierce competition among the powers. Yamagata and the heads of the military services concluded that the security of the Japanese islands could be imperiled by the way in which the vacuum of power on the continent was filled. The Western powers became primarily adversaries rather than models of reform.

Treaty revision was achieved, and national pride, so long submerged by the tasks of the *bummei kaika*, welled up with the great military victories of 1894–5. Abandoning his liberal views in a *volte-face* that attracted immense symbolic interest, Tokutomi Sohō exulted:

27 Pyle, *The New Generation*, p. 108.
28 Ibid., p. 106. For a comprehensive treatment of Tokutomi, see John D. Pierson, *Tokutomi Sohō, 1863–1957: A Journalist for Modern Japan* (Princeton, N.J.: Princeton Unviersity Press, 1980).

Now we are no longer ashamed to stand before the world as Japanese. . . . Before, we did not know ourselves, and the world did not yet know us. But now that we have tested our strength, we know ourselves and we are known by the world. Moreover, *we know* we are known by the world![29]

Fukuzawa, the leading symbol of an era now past, could scarcely contain his joy:

One can scarcely enumerate all of our civilized undertakings since the Restoration – the abolition of feudalism, the lowering of class barriers, revision of our laws, promotion of education, railroads, electricity, postal service, printing, and on and on. Yet among all these enterprises, the one thing none of us Western scholars ever expected, thirty or forty years ago, was the establishment of Japan's imperial prestige in a great war. . . . When I think of our marvelous fortune, I feel as though in a dream and can only weep tears of joy.[30]

THE EMERGENCE OF BUREAUCRATIC CONSERVATISM

The Meiji leaders looked at the problems of cultural nationalism and the lack of moral standards in a somewhat different light than did the journalists and intellectual leaders. The oligarchs were less concerned with the issues of cultural pride than with the practical problems of stabilizing the new order and, at the same time, mobilizing mass support for the national goals of economic and military power.

European conservative thought became increasingly relevant to the Meiji leaders in the early 1880s. They had already implemented many of the revolutionary ideas that they had held when they came to power, including the abolition of the rigid Tokugawa social order, the establishment of a national conscript army, the introduction of universal education and a new curriculum, and the promotion of an ambitious industrial policy. Other reforms still awaited completion, including the constitution, the local government system, parliamentary institutions, and the codification of law. But in the implementation of these programs in the 1880s, an increasingly conservative tone was evident. After the crisis of 1881, Meiji leaders, purged of liberal elements and determined to reestablish order and unity in political life, were less inclined to hold up their revolutionary example to the

29 Pyle, *The New Generation*, p. 175.
30 Kenneth B. Pyle, trans., "The Ashio Copper Mine Pollution Case," *Journal of Japanese Studies* 1 (Spring 1975): 347. From *Fukuzawa Yukichi zenshū*, 21 vols. (Tokyo: Iwanami shoten, 1958–64), vol. 15, pp. 333–7.

younger generation. Itō Hirobumi, for example, described the early
1880s as an age of "a transition":

The opinions prevailing in the country were extremely heterogeneous and
often diametrically opposed to one another. We had survivors from former
generations who were still full of theocratic ideas and who believed that any
attempt to restrict an imperial prerogative amounted to something like high
treason. On the other hand, there was a large and powerful body of the
younger generation educated at a time when the Manchester theory was
in vogue, and who, in consequence, were ultraradical in their ideas of
freedom. . . . A work entitled *History of Civilization*, by Buckle, which
denounced every form of government as an unnecessary evil, became the
great favorite of students of all the higher schools, including the Imperial
University. . . . At that time we had not arrived at the stage of distinguishing
clearly between political opposition on the one hand and treason to the
established order on the other.[31]

In order to realize the immense task of building an industrial
society in the course of their generation, the Meiji leaders had to find
some means to spur the populace to prodigies of self-sacrifice and
effort and, at the same time, to maintain social stability. This, of
course, is a fundamental problem of nation building, for modern
development entails the awakening of increasing numbers of people
to the national political community, and it engenders new divisions
of the population. The challenge that Meiji leaders faced, therefore,
was to balance economic development with political integration.
What is particularly impressive about the statecraft of the Japanese
leaders is the clarity with which they understood the historical process through which they were leading the nation. This owed much to
their sensitivity to the experience of the more advanced industrial
societies of the West. As Itō wrote in 1880 of the People's Rights
movement and the demands for democratic government to which
the Enlightenment had given rise:

The present political disturbance is symptomatic of a general trend
sweeping the whole world and is not limited to a single nation or province.
About a hundred years ago, the revolutions in Europe started in France and
spread gradually to other European nations. The momentum of those
revolutions gained strength and has come to constitute a tremendous force.
Sooner or later practically all nations . . . will feel the impact of this force
and change their form of government. The change from old to new was
accompanied by violent disturbances. The disturbances have lasted to this
very day. An enlightened ruler and his wise ministers would control and
divert the force towards a solidifying of the government. To achieve this, all

31 George M. Sansom, *The Western World and Japan* (New York: Knopf, 1950), pp.
    347–8.

despotic conduct must be abandoned, and there can be no avoiding a sharing of the government's power with the people.

Itō was confident that Japan could avoid the revolutionary violence that had accompanied the historical process elsewhere: "Even as we control the trends, there will be no violence, and even when ideas are given free rein, they will not lead the people astray. Progress will be orderly and we will set the pace of progress, and the passage of time will bring about the normalization of trends."[32] Itō believed that the trend toward popular participation in government was irreversible but that it could be controlled.

The oligarchs needed to find ways to avoid the severe antagonism in society that would undermine the effort to achieve their national goals. They found their answer to this need in the conservative reform tradition of German political-economic theories. Influenced by this tradition, the oligarchs foresaw the necessity of accommodating new groups into the political order so as to maintain the social consensus necessary to control the development of society. The concept of social monarchy was influential – up to a point – in the development of the oligarchs' attitudes toward the institutional framework. The thinking of Lorenz von Stein and Rudolf von Gneist was particularly influential in forming the oligarchs' conservative reformism. Stein saw the development of industrial capitalism as creating acquisitive instincts that if unchecked would lead to the dominance of the bourgeoisie at the expense of the other social classes. The result was likely to be social upheaval. Therefore, it was the necessary role of the socially conscious monarch and his bureaucracy to stand neutral above class interests and to act in the interest of the whole. In order to build a strong nation-state, the government would intervene in the economy to prevent class conflict and to maintain a harmonious social balance, integrating the lower classes into the national community "by means of social legislation and an active administrative policy that works for the physical and spiritual welfare of the lower classes."[33]

It was not only the Germans who gave conservative advice. There was plenty of it from other Western countries, much of it originating from evolutionist thought. Ivan Hall called it "overcompensating

---

32 George M. Beckmann, *The Making of the Meiji Constitution: The Oligarchs and the Constitutional Development of Japan, 1868–1891* (Lawrence: University of Kansas Press, 1957), app. 5.

33 Johannes Siemes, *Hermann Roesler and the Making of the Meiji State* (Tokyo: Sophia University Press, 1966), p. 32.

conservatism on the part of Westerners, a tendency to lean over backward away from their own liberalism in order not to push Japan too rapidly down the road of progress."[34] Herbert Spencer, for example, advised Mori that constitutionalism not be introduced too rapidly, that institutional growth follow an evolutionary or organic pattern: "I explained how botany teaches that vegetation transplanted from a foreign land will not produce the same flowers and fruits as in its native soil; that constitutions follow a principle identical with this botanical law."[35]

The Meiji leaders were committed to finding ways to accommodate and, thus, to control the increasing politicization of the lower orders. Yamagata, more conservative than many of his colleagues, wrote in his 1879 "Opinion on Constitutional Government" that although political parties and other forms of opposition to the government were wrong and immoral, the governed should be given an opportunity to participate in order to overcome divisions within society, popular estrangement from the government, and economic discontent: "If we gradually establish a popular assembly and firmly establish a constitution, the things I have enumerated above – popular enmity toward the government, failure to follow government orders, and suspicion of the government, these three evils – will be cured in the future."[36] It became an *idée fixe* of bureaucratic conservatism that the people should be brought into the governing process, not as a natural innate right but, rather, to achieve national unity. Thus, conservatives in Japan favored – in fact, conservatives generally took the initiative in bringing about – popular participation in local government, a national assembly, and, later, universal suffrage.

After Ōkuma, whose constitutional views were an extension of *bummei kaika* thought, was expelled in 1881, Itō went to Europe to prepare for the development of a conservative constitutional order and, in particular, to study Prussian experience firsthand. "By studying under two famous German teachers, Gneist and Stein," he wrote to a fellow oligarch,

I have been able to get a general understanding of the structure of the state. Later I shall discuss with you how we can achieve the great objective of establishing Imperial authority. Indeed, the tendency in our country today is to erroneously believe in the works of British, French, and American liberals and radicals as if they were Golden Rules and, thereby, lead

34   Hall, *Mori Arinori*, p. 321.   35   Ibid., p. 138.
36   Beckmann, *The Making of the Meiji Constitution*, p. 130.

virtually to the overthrow of the state. In having found principles and means of combatting this trend, I believe I have rendered an important service to my country, and I feel inwardly that I can die a happy man.[37]

Itō found in German constitutional thought the elements needed to legitimate the new order in terms other than natural rights philosophy. Popular participation in government would be permitted under conditions that channeled it in nationalist directions. Herman Roesler was retained as an adviser, but his ideas were filtered through the oligarchs' own determination to make the emperor into an unchallengeable and invulnerable centerpiece of the government, giving the Japanese people the sense of identity that conservative intellectuals had seen as so necessary to the new ear. As Itō wrote:

What is the cornerstone of our country? This is the problem we have to solve. If there is no cornerstone, politics will fall into the hands of the uncontrollable masses; and then the government will become powerless. . . . In Japan [unlike Europe] religion does not play such an important role and cannot become the foundation of constitutional government. Though Buddhism once flourished and was the bond of union between all classes, high and low, today its influence has declined. Though Shintoism is based on the traditions of our ancestors, as a religion it is not powerful enough to become the center of the country. Thus, in our country the one institution which can become the cornerstone of our constitution is the Imperial House.[38]

The imperial myth became the ideological glue that held together the new political structure. As we have seen, it was enunciated again in the Imperial Rescript on Education, laying the foundation for the more full-blown ideology of the family state. The new order was, therefore, at its core given a Japanese cast that departed sharply from the vision that the bummei kaika had held out for a new Japanese nation. Though embodying some limited aspects of liberal political principles, it was fundamentally based on a conception of a unique Japanese polity – the Japanese kokutai – which was rooted in the history and traditional cultural values of the people. Conservatives interpreted this kokutai in different ways. Itō held to a rational, secular view of the kokutai, which treated it as the product of a long evolutionary process and certainly capable of change and development in the future.

37 Nobutaka Ike, *The Beginnings of Political Democracy in Japan* (Baltimore: Johns Hopkins University Press, 1950), pp. 175–6.
38 Joseph Pittau, *Political Thought in Early Meiji Japan: 1868–1889* (Cambridge, Mass.: Harvard University Press, 1967), pp. 177–8.

But there was another interpretation that had more in common with the views of conservatives like Motoda. In this interpretation, the *kokutai* was a moral, religious, almost mystical entity. The Imperial Rescript on Education described the imperial house as "coeval with heaven and earth," almost a personification of the Confucian cosmological order. Conservative legal scholars like Hozumi Yatsuka, dean of the law faculty at Tokyo Imperial University and one of the most influential interpreters of the constitution at the turn of the century, elaborated this religious conception of the *kokutai* by stressing the themes of the family state and of ancestor worship. His was a blend of Confucian, Shinto, and German statist thought. Japanese society, according to Hozumi, was founded not on a social contract but, rather, on racial unity that was preserved through ancestor worship. All Japanese were ultimately descended from a common imperial ancestor:

The ancestor of my ancestors is the Sun Goddess. The Sun Goddess is the founder of our race, and the throne is the sacred house of our race. If father and mother are to be revered, how much more so the ancestors of the house; and if the ancestors of the house are to be revered, how much more so the founder of the country.[39]

Hozumi was the chief opponent of the French-influenced draft of a civil code that was debated from 1892 to 1898. The draft, based on natural rights theory, would have greatly curtailed the power of the family head. But Hozumi and other opponents argued that the Japanese *kokutai* was based on the authority of the househead, in both the family and the state. "Our family state," he wrote, "is a racial group. Our race consists of blood relatives from the same womb. The family is a small state; the state is a large family."[40] The section on family law in the revised civil code issued in 1898 represented a victory for Hozumi's views. The notion of the family state was, likewise, increasingly evident in the school texts for moral education. Hozumi, himself, headed the Ministry of Education Commission that recommended revision of the textbooks in 1908.

39 Richard H. Minear, *Japanese Tradition and Western Law: Emperor, State, and Law in the Thought of Hozumi Yatsuka* (Cambridge, Mass.: Harvard University Press, 1970), p. 73. For a splendid treatment in Japanese, see Matsumoto Sannosuke, *Tennōsei kokka to seiji shisō* (Tokyo: Miraisha, 1969).

40 Minear, *Japanese Tradition*, p. 74. For treatment of the civil code controversy, see Tōyama Shigeki, "Mimpōten ronsō no seijishiteki kōsatsu," in Meiji shiryō kenkyū renrakukai, ed., *Minkenron kara nashonarizumu e* (Meijishi kenkyū sōsho, IV) (Tokyo: Ochanomizu shobō, 1957). In English, see Dan Fenno Henderson, "Law and Political Modernization in Japan," in Ward, ed., *Political Development*, pp. 387–456.

The conservative interpretations of the new order were soon disseminated through the educational system. As we have seen, the tide had already turned in a conservative direction by the early 1880s, when the liberal morals texts were removed, and a reassertion of traditional values began. When Mori Arinori was appointed minister of education in 1885, the momentum picked up.

Mori, an apostle of the *bummei kaika* in the 1870s, helped push education in a conservative direction during the succeeding decade. He and Itō had conferred at great length regarding the role of education while they were in Europe in 1882. Both agreed that "the foundations of education should be established with a view to the future stability of the nation." Education should not be confused with the "aimless promotion of intellectual prowess" or with "the struggle to get ahead." Rather, its purpose was "to elevate the spirit of the entire nation."[41] Under Mori's leadership, the educational system was recast to place it at the service of the state rather than the individual. It was to create an elite of talent so as to promote "the economic growth and viability of the Japanese state."[42] Mori told local officials in 1887:

Reading, writing, and arithmetic are not our major concern in the education and instruction of the young. Education is entirely a matter of bringing up men of character. And who are these men of character? – they are the good subjects required by our Empire. And who are these good subjects? – they are those persons who live up fully to their responsibilities as Imperial Subjects.[43]

Mori's was a secular vision of the state that contrasted with the views of Motoda and later theorists like Hozumi, who approached a mystical conception of the Japanese state. Mori was, in fact, assassinated in 1889 for his purported slights in ritual during a visit to the Ise Shrine. At the time, Kuga reminded the readers of *Nihon* that the ceremonies conducted at Ise were not religious services to worship Shinto deities, but rather they were national political ceremonies to reverence the imperial household, because Ise had been built to honor the emperor's ancestors. The distinction was an important one for Kuga and for most conservatives: The imperial household was the most important symbol of Japan's historical continuity and its unique cultural traditions.

The growing popular reverence for the imperial institution was apparent after 1890. We have already seen the reaction to Uchimura

41 Hall, *Mori Arinori*, pp. 362–3.   42 Ibid., p. 458.   43 Ibid., p. 398.

Kanzō's reluctance to bow before the imperial portrait in 1891. The same year, a Tokyo Imperial University professor, Kume Kunitake, published an article describing Shinto as the "survival of a primitive form of worship." Writing in objective, historical fashion, he traced the origins of court ceremonies, of the imperial regalia, and of the Ise Shrine to forms of primitive worship in the Orient that had existed in prehistoric Japan. Shintoists attacked the article as sacrilegious and forced Kume out of his university position. Moderate conservatives like Kuga made no attempt to defend a literal belief in Shinto myths, but they abhorred detached objective criticism of the imperial court, which they regarded as an historic symbol of national unity, essential to national cohesion. Kuga wrote:

It is our moral obligation to refrain from making a public issue of anything that relates to the Imperial household, lest . . . what began as an academic dispute result in jeopardy to the security of the nation. People like Mr. Kume are aware of their status as scholars, but they tend to forget their obligation as subjects.[44]

The Enlightenment had never had a deep social basis for many of its ideas. There was a ready audience for conservative views, and the public mood of Japan changed dramatically. The pressures to conform, as Marius Jansen has pointed out, came not so much from the government as from "forces within Japanese society. Colleagues, neighbors, publicists, relatives – these were the people who hounded the Kumes, the reformers, and the liberals."[45]

The new ethics texts adopted the conservative ideology to explain the basis of the new political order. In the early 1890s, over eighty texts were privately produced. They stressed the sacred authority of the emperor, the family state, and ancestor worship. To maintain control of the new developing orthodoxy, the Education Ministry began in 1903 to compile an official set of ethics textbooks. There is some indication that the bureaucracy felt that the conservative trend was going too far, for the 1903 edition is regarded by many as representing a somewhat liberalizing trend. Nevertheless, they contained the basic teachings of the family-state ideology on which the subsequent edition of 1910 was built.[46] The new imperial ideology drew on the traditional language of loyalty and obligation and on a

44 Pyle, *The New Generation*, pp. 124–5.
45 Jansen, *Changing Japanese Attitudes Toward Modernization*, pp. 80–1.
46 Wilbur M. Fridell, "Government Ethics Textbooks in Late Meiji Japan," *Journal of Asian Studies* 29 (1970): 823–34. The standard authority is Karasawa Tomitarō, *Kyōkasho no rekishi* (Tokyo: Sōbunsha, 1960).

mythical past to imbue the new order with the aura of sanctity and legitimacy that would inhibit political opposition and dissent. As one scholar has put it, "The emperor became a substitute for the charismatic leader so prominent in the modernization of most non-Western societies of a later period, a substitute that was more permanent, more deeply rooted in the culture, and more invulnerable to attack."[47]

THE CONSERVATIVE APPROACH TO INDUSTRIAL SOCIETY

The Meiji leaders in their drive to promote industry had always advocated one of the main enlightenment themes, namely, the advancement of science, technology, and utilitarian knowledge. In that sense, they might not be considered conservatives. As Benjamin Schwartz observed in his essay on conservatism in modern China, modernization of industrialization would seem to be "the very antithesis of conservatism" because it involves "the systematic universal application of technological rationalism both to nature and society," which was one of the main premises of enlightenment thinking that the conservatives were said to oppose. Modernization, Schwartz continued,

thus seems to be the very paradigm of the deliberate effort to shape the social order according to conscious ideas in people's heads. Yet the fact is that as modernization has proceeded, it too has come to be viewed more and more as a sociohistoric process independent of human wills. It has thus also come to be viewed as a kind of organic societal growth which has already achieved a mature state of development. While there no doubt have been forms of aristocratic conservatism in Europe which resisted industrialization, the fact is that conservatism of the Bismarckian variety wholeheartedly based itself on bureaucratic and industrial nationalization and clearly perceived the link between industrialization and national power.[48]

The Bismarckian variety of conservatism – formulated under the impact of Germany's maturing industrialism, fear of social revolution, and the ideals of German unification – was uniquely relevant to Japanese circumstances and, in fact, exercised great influence on the Meiji bureaucratic leaders. German thought helped them anticipate

47   Robert A. Scalapino, "Ideology and Modernization: The Japanese Case," in David E. Apter, ed., *Ideology and Discontent* (New York: Free Press, 1964), p. 103.
48   Benjamin I. Schwartz, "Notes on Conservatism in General and on China in Particular," in Charlotte Furth, ed., *The Limits of Change: Essays on Conservative Alternatives in Republican China* (Cambridge, Mass.: Harvard University Press, 1976), p. 14.

the social and economic effects of industrialization and plan ways in which political initiatives could be taken to maintain conservative control of industrial society.

The German historical school of economics was particularly influential. It had risen in the nineteenth century to challenge the laissez-faire liberalism of Adam Smith. The historical school rejected the notion that the same body of theory was valid for all times and places. It rejected the materialism and universalism of both the Manchester school and the socialists. Instead, it saw economic issues as inseparable from the society, culture, and history in which they arose. Economic issues, moreover, could not be left free to work themselves out as the Manchester liberals had contended. Economics should be studied from an ethical point of view, with the purpose of advancing the good of the whole society. German historical economics, therefore, favored the intervention of the state to maintain social welfare. Otherwise, pursuit of individual self-interest would lead to class cleavages and to social revolution. The socially conscious monarch and his bureaucracy were the only neutral force in the conflict of social classes. In order to build national greatness and to prevent the alienation of the lower classes, it was necessary to protect them from exploitation and to integrate them into the political community. Under the influence of these economists, Bismarck's government proposed factory inspection laws, social insurance plans, state encouragement of consumers' and producers' cooperatives, state ownership of railroads, and minimum wage laws.

Conservatism in the modern world since the French Revolution came to have a direct relationship to social revolution. As one observer put it, "The historic mission of political conservatism in the West has been not to defeat but to forestall revolutions, not to crush but anticipate them."[49] In Japan, bureaucratic conservatism had as a principal motivation the forestalling of social revolution.

German historical economics came to have very great influence in shaping bureaucratic conservatism in Japan. Its introduction was primarily the work of Kanai Noburu (1865–1933), who was the first major academic economist in Japan, the one most responsible for introducing the new industrial economics, and the teacher of many of Japan's subsequent academic and bureaucratic

49   Clinton Rossiter, "Conservatism," in *International Encyclopedia of the Social Sciences* (New York: Macmillan and Free Press, 1968), vol. 3, p. 292.

leaders.[50] The writings of his school greatly expanded the understanding of incipient social problems inherent in the process of
industrialization that Roesler had touched on in his advice to the
oligarchs.

In 1890, after four years of study in Europe, principally in Germany where he had immersed himself in studying the historical
school and in observing Bismarck's conservative policies, Kanai
was appointed professor at Tokyo Imperial University. Kanai's
early writings criticized the bummei kaika writers, attacking their
universalism and arguing that economic theory must be based on the
particular history and cultural heritage of a nation. They had followed Manchester views. Fukuzawa, for example, wrote in Seiyō jijō
that economics, like chemistry and physics, was governed by fixed
laws. Similarly, Taguchi Ukichi, one of the most bold and consistent
of the enlightenment writers, wrote in his Keizairon no rompō (1884):
"Economic truth does not change according to the times or the
national conditions. The law that is useful in one country is useful in
every country. . . . One plus two is always three."[51] Kanai rejected
the free-trade notions and the faith in individual pursuit of self-
interest that the bummei kaika had introduced. He held that liberalism had failed in Europe because it permitted conditions in the new
industrial societies to deteriorate until revolution became a serious
possibility. Kanai was instrumental in introducing discussion of the
social problems (shakai mondai) created by industrialization and the
positive role required of the state to prevent such problems. He
wrote in 1891:

If workers are treated like animals, then after several decades unions and
socialism will appear. If now we concentrate on protection, we can prevent
unions and the spread of socialism. This is the policy of prevention. An
illustration of the failure to act is not far to seek; it is in every country of the
West.[52]

Kanai's theme of preventive action became an important element
in Meiji conservative thought. The timing of Japan's industrialization gave it an opportunity to learn from the experience of the more
advanced Western societies, to act early to forestall social problems.

50 Kanai is described in Sumiya Etsuji, Nihon keizaigaku-shi (Kyoto: Mineruva shobō, 1958).
51 Kawai Eijirō, Meiji shisōshi no ichi dammen: Kanai Noburu o chūshin toshite, reprinted in
    Kawai Eijirō zenshū (Tokyo: Shakai shisōsha, 1969), vol. 8, p. 195. This account of
    economic thought in Meiji, centering on Kanai and written by his son-in-law, himself a
    well-known political economist, is a valuable source.
52 Kenneth B. Pyle, "Advantages of Followership: German Economics and Japanese Bu-
    reaucrats, 1890–1925," Journal of Japanese Studies 1 (1974): 143.

A second theme in Kanai's writing was his emphasis on thought guidance (*shisō zendō*) as an important preventive for social unrest. He held that social problems originated as much in the awakened consciousness of the lower classes as they did in objective living conditions. Accordingly, it was necessary for the state to lead the lower classes toward a positive and harmonious social attitude. Another important theme of Kanai's that was also essential to the conservative view was his emphasis on social solidarity as necessary to success in foreign affairs. He wrote:

Ultimately the highest object of social policy in modern times is to bring back together again the various social classes which are daily becoming more and more separated; and it must establish a socially cooperative life based on intimate relations of mutual help and interdependence. . . . That is to say, social policy, which is the greatest need in domestic politics, is not just a noble human ethic, it is an effective method to achieve success in foreign policy.[53]

Social policies of the government would introduce reforms, not as a matter of justice or right but because they would strengthen national cohesion. Max Weber, in his 1895 Freiburg inaugural lecture, explained the motivation of German economists: "It is not the purpose of our work in social policy to make the world happy, but to unite socially a nation split apart by modern economic development, for the hard struggles of the future." And he added, "Not peace and human happiness we have to pass on to our descendants, but the maintenance and up-breeding of our national kind." Japan was not yet "a nation split apart by modern economic development."[54] Japanese conservatives were determined to prevent that.

In 1896, Kanai's disciples established the Shakai seisaku gakkai (Organization for the Study of Social Policy), a group modeled on the Verein für Sozialpolitik, which had been formed by the German historical economists in 1872 to advocate state intervention in the economy in order to ease class conflicts through social welfare legislation. The Gakkai became the principal professional organization for Japanese economists, including nearly everyone teaching economics in universities as well as those in the bureaucracy and in business who were considered economists.

Increasingly, after the Sino-Japanese War, the Meiji conservatives found themselves as much concerned about the socialists and other

---

53 Ibid., p. 144.
54 Ralf Dahrendorf, *Society and Democracy in Germany* (New York: Doubleday Anchor, 1967), p. 41.

radicals as they were about the liberals. The declaration of principles issued by the Shakai seisaku gakkai defined a middle course between the liberals and the socialists. It professed to discern already in Japan the beginning of a clash between labor and capital:

We oppose laissez-faire because it creates extreme profit consciousness and unbridled competition, and aggravates the differences between rich and poor. We also oppose socialism because it would destroy the present economic organization, obliterate capitalists, and therefore impede national programs. We support the principles of the present private enterprise system. Within this framework we seek to prevent friction between classes through the power of government and through individual exertions and thereby preserve social harmony.[55]

Kuwata Kumazō, who was a prime mover in the founding of the Shakai seisaku gakkai, wrote in an 1896 essay, entitled "The State and the Social Problem," that although the nineteenth century had been one of political revolutions, the new century promised to be one of economic revolutions. Whereas the Western countries were accomplishing the economic revolution in the same way as they had accomplished the political revolution – at the cost of great strife and bloodshed – Japan could avoid this, as it had already proved: "The fact that the Japanese people established a constitutional system without shedding a drop of blood is a matter of great distinction in modern history. In the coming economic revolution, too, why should it be impossible to solve this great problem peacefully?" He argued that German social policy was appropriate to the Japanese experience because of Confucian injunctions to a ruler to take a benevolent interest in the well-being of his people and to instruct them in moral principles. Kuwata, who lectured on industrial policy at the Imperial University of Tokyo and served on many governmental commissions, recommended specific measures that the government should enact:

1. Factory legislation to regulate working hours, conditions, and female and child labor.
2. Regulations to protect the interests of tenants.
3. Poor relief laws.
4. Compulsory workers' insurance.
5. Credit cooperatives to protect and aid small farmers.
6. Progressive tax policies to ease the burden of low-income groups.

55 Pyle, "Advantages of Followership," pp. 145–6.

After the Sino-Japanese War, with the political order established and underwritten by a powerful ideology and with the goal of treaty revision accomplished, the Meiji leaders had to turn their attention to the problems of the industrial revolution. It was a new era. The term *shakai mondai* (social problem) become a frequent theme of public discussion. The naive optimism about the future that had characterized the *bummei kaika* was fading and was replaced by a more balanced assessment of what was entailed by modern economic development. The term *bummei byō* (civilization sickness) became a common phrase to indicate the problems that afflicted Western industrial societies – class hostilities, labor strife, destruction of the peasant village, decadence, materialism, radical ideologies, the decline of cooperation, and its supporting values. Would Japan be inevitably afflicted by the same problems as it passed through its industrial revolution? Many Japanese feared so. There were already harbingers. Socialist writings appeared in the 1890s, and the first socialist groups, small as they were, were accorded much attention. The first socialist party did not have a long history – it was closed down by the Home Ministry several hours after it had announced its formation in 1900.

The Ashio Copper Mine problem was seen as an early symptom of *bummei byō*. The mine, situated at the headwaters of the Watarase River, near Nikkō, represented one of Japan's important industries. Through the application of modern technology, the mining complex had undergone impressive expansion, but in the process, through deforestation, the river's watershed was destroyed. Floods brought appallingly polluted waters downstream, inundating villages and contaminating fields in the northern Kantō plain. In 1896, thirteen thousand households were flooded, and a national protest movement began. Ashio became a symbol of the sacrifice of agriculture to industry and of community values to economic growth.[56]

Ashio was only one of the more dramatic indications to the Japanese of what was likely to come as the industrial revolution proceeded. By the turn of the century, there was a rising awareness of the need to take preventive measures and a sense that Japan had a special advantage as a "follower country" to profit from the Western experience. The young economist (later to be a socialist), Kawakami Hajime, wrote in 1905:

56 See "Symposium: The Ashio Copper Mine Pollution Incident," *Journal of Japanese Studies* 1 (1975).

We have the history of England's failure and there is no need to repeat that history. Are there not opportunities for countries that lag behind in their culture? . . . The history of the failures of the advanced countries (*zenshin-koku*) is the best textbook for the follower countries (*kōshin-koku*). I hope that our statesmen and intellectuals learn something from this textbook.[57]

As the comments of one official, Kaneko Kentarō, indicated, the Japanese bureaucrats were sensitive to the lessons of history. We should learn from the "sad and pitiful" history of British industrialization, because, Kaneko added, "it is the advantage of the backward country that it can reflect on the history of the advanced countries and avoid their mistakes."[58] This style of thought soon infused the thinking of officialdom, even at the highest levels. Ōkuma Shigenobu wrote in 1910 that Japan was in an advantageous position to secure the cooperation of labor and capital: "By studying the mistaken system that has brought Europe such bitter experience in the past several decades, businessmen, politicians, and officials in Japan can diminish these abuses." Relying on the force of laws and family customs, they could "prevent a fearful clash" and plan the conciliation of capitalists and laborers. Similarly, Prime Minister Katsura wrote in 1908:

We are now in an age of economic transition. The development of machine industry and the intensification of competition widens the gap between rich and poor and creates antagonisms that endanger social order. Judging by Western history, this is an inevitable pattern. Socialism is today no more than a wisp of smoke, but if it is ignored, it will some day have the force of a wild fire, and there will be nothing to stop it. Therefore, it goes without saying that we must rely on education to nurture the people's values; and we must devise a social policy that will assist their industry, provide them work, help the aged and infirm and, thereby, prevent catastrophe.[59]

Thus, by the turn of the century, a conservative approach to industrial society had taken root in the bureaucracy. It was heavily influenced by Bismarckian social policy and German economic thought. It was influenced, as well, by the conservative belief that Japanese society was indeed different and should be unique, that by preserving its own values of social harmony it could avert the social consequences of industrialism evident in many Western societies.

---

57 Pyle, "Advantages of Followership," pp. 129–30.
58 Ronald P. Dore, "The Modernizer as a Special Case: Japanese Factory Legislation, 1882–1911," *Comparative Studies in Society and History* 11 (1969): 439.
59 Horio Teruhisa, "Taisei sai-tōgō no kokoromi to teikoku ideorogii no keisei," *Nihon seiji gakkai nempō* (1968): 164. See also Pyle, "Followership," pp. 130, 159.

Finally, and perhaps most important, it was motivated by the urgency of the time. Success in foreign affairs depended on a united nation and rapid economic growth.

THE SOCIAL PROGRAM OF THE CONSERVATIVES

The most clearly defined initial objective of the bureaucratic conservatives in addressing industrial society was the passage of a factory law to regulate the working conditions of industrial labor. Actually, far in advance of an organized labor movement demanding it of the government, the bureaucracy took the initiative in drafting it and in organizing support for its passage. In fact, the bureaucracy's efforts were so early, Dore points out, that when the Ministry of Agriculture and Commerce began to study foreign factory laws in 1882, there were fewer than fifty factories using steam power in all of Japan![60]

In the 1890s, the Ministry of Agriculture and Commerce circulated to various chambers of commerce the draft of a law that would establish minimum health and safety standards and limit the working hours of women and children employed in factories.[61] After the Sino-Japanese War, the government pressed factory legislation with greater urgency. Beginning in 1896, the government convened a series of national conferences to discuss the state of the economy. Bureaucrats brushed aside the contention of businessmen that working conditions in Japan were good, with the argument that it was necessary "to create the laws necessary to maintain in the future the balance between capital and labor, and harmonious relations between employers and employees, thereby protecting in advance against any disorders."[62] At the same time, steps were taken to prevent the growth of union powers. The Public Peace Police Law of 1900 virtually denied the unions the primary function of organizing.

A factory law was eventually passed in 1911, and in the meantime, there were other steps taken in the cities to prepare for industrial society. On the whole, however, before World War I, the bureaucracy depended primarily on its police power to maintain control in the urban sector and, for a number of reasons, showed far more

60 Dore, "The Modernizer as a Special Case," p. 437.   61 Ibid., pp. 437–8.
62 Byron K. Marshall, *Capitalism and Nationalism in Prewar Japan* (Stanford, Calif.: Stanford University Press, 1967), p. 54. Discussion of bureaucratic efforts to develop factory and labor legislation can be found in Sheldon Garon, *The State and Labor in Modern Japan* (Berkeley and Los Angeles: University of California Press, 1987).

concern for the countryside. First, that was where 80 percent of the population still lived at the turn of the century. If the new order were to have a powerful counterrevolutionary bulwark, it would most effectively be in the towns and villages. Second, industrialization in Japan frequently had a rural setting and was dependent on village labor and farm side employments. The commercial spirit had already begun to invade the countryside and to affect the solidarity of the village community. Third, ever since the *bummei kaika* had made its effect felt on the cities, the towns and villages had come to symbolize the essence of what was historically Japanese. Finally, there was traditional sanction for such a view. Tokugawa political thought had regarded agriculture as the basis of society. Ogyū Sorai put it this way: "To take care of the roots and to keep the branches under control, this is the principle taught by the sages of old. The root is agriculture; the branches, industry and commerce."[63]

The Shakai seisaku gakkai devoted much attention to studies of the way in which industrialization in Western countries had led to the disintegration of the peasant village. Already, this society's members saw dangers in the countryside. Rising government expenditures for industrial capital formation and military enterprises were creating a growing tax burden for the citizenry. Central government expenditures tripled in the decade before the Russo-Japanese War, and responsibilities for public works and education were increasingly delegated to local government. Local taxes rose sharply, and the town and village assemblies, which were dominated by wealthy families, enacted a variety of regressive taxes. This growing tax burden, the increasing concentration of landownership, and the attractiveness of the city to ambitious peasant youth portended social problems in the countryside that the government could ill afford. As Tani Kanjō wrote in 1898, a secure yeomanry was critical to Japan because it would serve as a barrier to radical ideologies, provide a reliable source of able-bodied soldiers, and ensure self-sufficiency of food in time of war. To prevent destruction of the cohesiveness and harmony of the village, the Gakkai proposed a tenancy law to regulate landlord–tenant relations, and the establishment of credit facilities and industrial cooperatives.

The bureaucracy thus came to the conclusion that if the cohesion of the countryside could be preserved, then the tensions that industrialism was certain to create could somehow be managed. The

63 Ronald P. Dore, *Land Reform in Japan* (London: Oxford University Press, 1959), p. 57.

oligarchs, particularly Yamagata, had always regarded local administration as critical to the future stability of their rule. For that
reason. Yamagata had taken an intense, firsthand interest in the
establishment of the new system of local government, which culminated in the Town and Village Act of 1888.

To infuse this system with the new national ideology and to
establish a stable conservative social base for the difficult transition
to an industrial economy, the government embarked on an ambitious and comprehensive program of conservative reforms in the
countryside. The Rural Improvement movement (*chihō kairyō undō*),
which the Home Ministry launched at the turn of the century, was
the archetype of the bureaucratic approach to modern Japanese
social problems. It demonstrates the pragmatic effort of Japanese
conservatives to make limited reforms within a nationalist framework as a means of cushioning society from the traumatic effects of
the industrial revolution. The objectives of the movement were to
promote both economic development and social harmony. It thus
sought to strengthen the financial resources of the new administrative towns and villages and to build national loyalties among all
classes at the local level.

One of the most impressive manifestations of social-policy
thought in the bureaucracy's approach to rural society was its promotion of agricultural cooperatives. Through the efforts of a leading
bureaucrat, Hirata Tōsuke, who was a close associate of Yamagata
and who had studied social policy in Germany, the Diet passed in
1899 the Industrial Cooperatives Law, which encouraged the establishment of credit, consumer marketing, and producers' cooperatives. Just as the factory law had not depended on the demands of
discontented laborers for its promotion and passage, so the Industrial Cooperatives Law was not the result of demands from farmers
or farm pressure groups. Rather, the bureaucracy took the initiative
in drafting it in order to prevent the kind of agrarian impoverishment
and disruption that had occurred in the West. Hirata's justification
of the measure is noteworthy for us here. He regarded cooperatives
as a form of "social education" that would establish a strong collectivism at the local level. They would become "communities working
in behalf of the nation" (*kokka no tame no kyōdōtai*). Hirata reasoned
that if "we come to have the great class divisions that exist in every
Western country, it will be cause for immense concern and regret.
Therefore before this calamity occurs we should let the lower class
people share in the blessings of civilization along with the great

capitalists." Cooperatives would "protect the security of society" and promote economic development by helping the small producer who was "the center of the industry."[64] Following the enactment of the Industrial Cooperatives Law, the government mounted a vigorous propaganda campaign throughout the countryside. It relied on the teachings of the Tokugawa peasant-scholar, Ninomiya Sontoku, which stressed mutual aid and cooperation in the village, conciliation and cooperation between landlord and tenant, careful long-term planning and budgeting, the dignity of manual labor, thrift, and the payment of taxes as a moral obligation. Ninomiya's followers had, in fact, formed societies known as *hōtokusha*, which had functioned as crude credit associations. By 1921, over 13,700 cooperatives had been organized in conformance with the new law, and nearly one-half the farm families were members of a cooperative.

The Rural Improvement movement took a number of steps to strengthen the new administrative towns and villages that, following the Town and Village Act of 1888, had been formed by joining many of the old hamlets. By the time of the Russo-Japanese War, over 76,000 natural villages or hamlets (*buraku*) that had existed in the Tokugawa period had, through mergers, been reduced to some 12,000 administrative towns and villages. The intention was to transfer resources, including all communal lands and property, from the hamlets to the new administrative units.

As part of the same effort, the Home Ministry announced in 1906 its determination to enforce a sweeping merger of Shinto shrines at the local level so that hamlet shrines would be replaced by a single central shrine in each administrative village. Worship at the hamlet shrines had centered on the daily concerns of local inhabitants – such matters as clement weather, good harvests, and healthy offspring. Under the new program, worship was to focus chiefly on the imperial family and national festivals.[65] Priests were placed under the disciplinary regulations of regular civil government officials.

Inspiration for this program, as Hashikawa Bunzō and others noted, came from the visits that bureaucrats made to the West where

64 Kenneth B. Pyle, "The Technology of Japanese Nationalism: The Local Improvement Movement, 1900–1918," *Journal of Asian Studies* 33 (1973): 51–65. The best description of the Local Improvement movement in Japanese is by Miyachi Masato, *Nichi-Ro sengo seijishi no kenkyū* (Tokyo: Tokyo daigaku shuppankai, 1973). Another major work is by Kano Masanao, *Shihonshugi keiseiki no chitsujō ishiki* (Tokyo: Chikuma shobō, 1969).

65 Wilbur M. Fridell, *Japanese Shrine Mergers, 1906–1912* (Tokyo: Sophia University Press, 1973). See also Hashikawa Bunzō's excellent essay on the bureaucracy's efforts to extend its power to the local level: *Kindai Nihon seiji shisō no shosō* (Tokyo: Miraisha, 1968), pp. 35–73.

they were impressed with the cohesive power of religion and the dominance of churches in local society. The instrumental use of religious rites to support the state, of course, can be traced back in Japanese history to the ideas of Ogyū Sorai and beyond. In this way, what Itō had envisioned as the cornerstone of the nation – the imperial ideology or what was later called state Shinto – was established at the local level. This was not something that welled up spontaneously from the people and their folklore and traditions. To the contrary, there was much resistance at the local level to the attempt to merge shrines and override the simple local devotions of the past.

The bureaucracy, however, persisted in other methods to create national loyalties and inculcate the national ideology at the grass-roots level – most effectively through organizations that Ishida Takeshi has called half-bureaucratic/half-popular organizations – because they were organizations that had their origins at the local level and that were used by the bureaucracy as effective vehicles of the new nationalism and were encouraged to develop much more elaborate structures. The most important of these organizations were the youth groups (*seinenkai*) and the military associations (*zaigō gunjinkai*).[66]

The modern youth group movement was begun in the 1890s by a Hiroshima Prefecture schoolteacher, Yamamoto Takinosuke, who published in 1896 a tract entitled *Inaka seinen* (Rural youth). In this and subsequent writings, he exhorted and praised rural youth as the backbone of the nation: They exemplified virtues of hard work, thrift, filial piety, and national spirit. They were uninfected by the "civilization sickness" (*bummei byō*) that afflicted city youth. The Home Ministry, seeing the value that such grass-roots organizations could have in mobilizing support at the local level, set out to organize village youth groups in a national hierarchy under its guidance. By the end of the Meiji period, youth groups were said to number 29,320, with a membership of 3 million.

The local military associations (*zaigō gunjinkai*) had similar grass-roots origins. Established after the Satsuma Rebellion as fraternal organizations for former members of the military, they took leadership of youth activities, community service projects, and patri-

66 Ishida Takeshi, *Meiji seiji shisōshi kenkyū* (Tokyo: Miraisha, 1954) and Ishida Takeshi, *Kindai Nihon seiji kōzō no kenkyū* (Tokyo: Miraisha, 1956) are the standard sources. Also essential is Fujita Shōzō, *Tennōsei kokka no shihai genri* (Tokyo: Miraisha, 1966). In English, see Richard J. Smethurst, *A Social Basis for Prewar Japanese Militarism* (Berkeley and Los Angeles: University of California Press, 1974).

otic ceremonies. The government organized them into a national hierarchy, and by the end of the Meiji period, virtually every community in the nation had a branch. The youth groups and military associations became mass organizations (along with the credit associations) at the grass-roots levels and were increasingly effective in the twentieth century as instruments for mobilizing nationalist support of the great effort required to achieve military and industrial success.

The keynote of the Rural Improvement movement was sounded by the issuance of the Imperial Rescript of 1908, known as the Boshin shōsho. As Sumiya Mikio observed, this rescript symbolized the government's intention to press a campaign of national mobilization, exhorting all Japanese to unite in hard work, thrift, and cooperation so that the nation could achieve its destiny as one of the world's great military and industrial powers.[67] In part it read:

In order to keep pace with the constant progress of the world, and to participate in the blessings of its civilization, the development of the national resources is manifestly a requisite of prime importance.... We desire all classes of Our people to act in unison, to be faithful to their callings, frugal in the management of their households, submissive to the dictates of conscience and calls of duty, frank and sincere in their manners, to abide by simplicity and avoid ostentation, and to inure themselves to arduous toil without yielding to any degree of indulgence. The teachings of Our revered Ancestors and the record of our glorious history are clear beyond all misapprehension. By scrupulous observance of the precepts thus established, the growing prosperity of our Empire is assured.

The ease and speed with which mass mobilization was achieved under bureaucratic initiative is sometimes exaggerated and is still the subject of controversy. What was clearly accomplished by the late Meiji period was mobilization for nationalist purposes of the "local notables" – village headmen, school principals, prominent landlords, and Shinto priests. It was this stratum of grass-roots leadership that Yamagata had referred to as the "strong middle men" (chūken jimbutsu) who could mediate between the new national administrative system and local society. Charged with responsibility for achieving the national destiny, they attained enhanced respectability by exercising patriarchal leadership of the youth groups, the industrial cooperatives, and the military associations.[68]

---

67 Sumiya Mikio, *Nihon no shakai shisō* (Tokyo: Tokyo daigaku shuppankai, 1968), pp. 65–6.

68 A recent assessment of the success of bureaucratic efforts at the local level is by Ariizumi Sadao, "Meiji kokka to minshū tōgō," in *Iwanami kōza Nihon rekishi*, vol. 17 (*kindai* 4) (Tokyo: Iwanami shoten, 1976), pp. 221–62.

THE LEGACY OF MEIJI CONSERVATISM

By the turn of the century, the public mood of Japan had been transformed, and a powerful conservative orthodoxy held sway. The millennial vision of the Enlightenment had faded, and liberals and reformers were in disarray. Their optimism had given way to ambivalence. Many of them now had a more balanced perspective on the impact of the science and industry in which the *bummei kaika* advocates had put their faith. The new technology was creative but also destructive. It offered new hope and opportunities, but at a high cost in human disruption and hardship. The reformer, Tanaka Shōzō, expressing moral revulsion toward the commercialization of values and the decline in cooperation, said in the Diet in 1910 that modern civilization was destroying "moral structures that have taken five hundred or a thousand years to build." Reflecting on the Ashio pollution case, he wrote in his diary that "progress of material, artificial civilization casts society into darkness. Electricity is discovered and the world is darkened."[69] Some of the liberals like Tokutomi Sohō, the leader of the reform cause, had abandoned the faith and thrown in their lot with the conservatives. The journalist and reformer Kinoshita Naoe wrote of his disillusion with the Spencerian vision of the future that Tokutomi had offered in the 1880s: "Weren't we fools! We were afire with hope when we first heard Spencer's prophecy that society was evolving from the militant to the industrial stage, that wars would cease, that loyalty and patriotism would disappear, and that there would be a golden age of peace and freedom!" Instead, material civilization had brought "depravity, ruin, and normlessness."[70]

Liberal despair over the course of industrial civilization was compounded by the oppressive orthodoxy that pervaded public discourse. Most young Japanese had little of their predecessors' optimism about reforming society. They felt powerless to change the social and political order. "The atmosphere that surrounds us youth," the poet Ishikawa Takuboku wrote, "is suffocating. The influence of authority pervades the entire country. The existing social organization reaches into every nook and cranny." It was this kind of despair that radicalized socialists like Kōtoku Shūsui and impelled them to extremes.[71]

69   Alan Stone, "The Japanese Muckrakers," *Journal of Japanese Studies* 1 (1975): 402.
70   Ibid., p. 404.
71   Pyle, *The New Generation*, p. 200. On Kōtoku, see F. G. Notehelfer, *Kōtoku Shūsui: Portrait of a Japanese Radical* (Cambridge, England: Cambridge University Press, 1971).

Even moderate conservatives were dismayed at the extent to which the conservative reaction had gone. Those like Miyake Setsurei and Kuga Katsunan had attacked some of the main themes of the Japanese Enlightenment, including its dismissal of Japanese history, its naive internationalism, and its adulation of Western society and politics. But by the turn of the century, they were appalled at the distortion of their ideas. The term they had originated, "preservation of the national essence" (*kokusui hozon*), had become a pretext for opposing needed reforms. Moderate conservatives had argued for cultural autonomy, for a modern industrial society that was in keeping with historical traditions, but they lamented the narrow views that now stigmatized change as inconsistent with the national character.

This dramatic reversal of the liberal cause came about because many of the main themes of the *bummei kaika* had lacked a strong social constituency to defend them. When they were challenged, particularly from within the government and the imperial court, as in the case of the liberal education reforms, they were easily displaced. The extreme adulation of the Western cultural model could not sustain itself once the vogue had passed and, particularly, once the motivation of treaty revision had disappeared. Free trade and internationalism never had many self-interested supporters and, in the age of imperialism that dawned in the 1890s, could scarcely be sustained. Many of the new social values introduced during the Enlightenment ran counter to the mores of the Japanese but, above all, were incompatible with the institutions of the countryside, where the great majority of the populace had its roots. Finally, by the turn of the century, there was an emerging awareness that industrial society in the Western countries was subject to disruptions and strife that made it much less worthy of emulation. For these reasons, the public mood changed rapidly in the 1890s.

The oligarchs led this change in mood, placing the full weight of their power behind the new conservative tide. Historiographical controversy regarding Meiji conservatism has tended to center on assessment of its motivations and its legacy. E. H. Norman's classic work, *Japan's Emergence as a Modern State* (1940), locates the motivation of the Meiji leadership in the desperate exigencies of the time:

Time was short, resources scanty, and it is a cause for amazement that Japan's leaders accomplished so much rather than a cause for blame because they had to leave so much undone in the way of democratic and liberal reform. . . . Speed was a determining element in the *form* which modern Japanese government and society assumed. The *speed* with which Japan had simultaneously to establish a modern state, to build an up-to-date defense force in order to ward off the dangers of invasion . . . , to create an industry on which to base this armed force, to fashion an educational system suitable to an industrial, modernized nation, dictated that these important changes be accomplished by a group of autocratic bureaucrats rather than by the mass of the people working through democratic organs of representation. These military bureaucrats were so far in advance of the rest of their countrymen that they had to drag a complaining, half-awakened nation of merchants and peasants after them.[72]

In a later work, written in 1943 during the height of the Pacific War, Norman was more negative and harsh in his assessment. Repression and counterrevolution were the driving motives of the oligarchs. In *Soldier and Peasant in Japan*, he wrote that

any possibility of a steadily rising standard of living, a broadening out of popular liberties (all of which would have directed Japanese energies into channels other than . . . expansion, aggression, and wars) was resolutely blocked by the calculating Japanese Metternichs. . . . As soon as the people of Japan could stand upright and breathe the intoxicating air of freedom following the overthrow of the Bakufu, they were burdened with fresh exactions and taxes; their relative advance in terms of social and political freedom was soon drastically checked.[73]

This judgment has been widely shared by postwar Japanese historians who have elaborated themes of a nascent democratic-populist movement that supported the People's Rights movement and subsequently resisted bureaucratic institutions of control in the 1890s and later. Historiography in the West, which has tended to emphasize the success of Japanese modernization, has accorded a more favorable assessment. Most striking in this regard is Professor George Akita's judgment that the Meiji leaders were enlightened heroes determined to share their power with their countrymen by "force-feeding 'liberalization' to a citizenry reluctant to accept the rights and duties of participation in government affairs. When the results were not what had been expected and were threatening the socio-political structure, the Meiji leaders continued to take further steps calculated to relax their own hold."[74]

It is important for us to remember that there were different shades

72 John W. Dower, ed., *Origins of the Modern Japanese State: Selected Writings of E. H. Norman* (New York: Pantheon, 1975), p. 154.
73 Ibid., p. 23.
74 George Akita, *Foundations of Constitutional Government in Modern Japan, 1868–1890* (Cambridge, Mass.: Harvard University Press, 1967), p. 174.

of conservatism within the bureaucracy. Some bureaucrats were moved by a primary reliance on the imperial myth to circumscribe narrowly the limits on institutional innovation; others were more pragmatic and tolerant of change. There was, in fact, a strong strain of conservative reformism in the bureaucracy that was motivated by nationalist concerns. These reform-minded bureaucrats came to the conclusion, principally from their sensitivity to the experience of the Western industrial societies, that to prevent social disruption and maintain a strong nation-state, it was necessary for a government to adopt an early social policy and intervene in the economy to accommodate the lower classes into the political order. Their strategy for building this national solidarity was twofold. On the one hand, they pressed for social reforms like factory legislation and agricultural cooperatives. On the other hand, they relied on schools, youth groups, military associations, and the shrines to propagate the collectivist ethic.

This dual strategy characterized the government's approach to the problems of industrialism in the post–World War I years. Reform-minded bureaucrats worked for institutional changes that would conciliate tenant–landlord and labor–management problems. Similarly, they pressed for extension of the suffrage. Along with their social policy, they promoted the national ideology as a means of mass mobilization. The Local Improvement movement, which served as a model of this dual strategy, was followed by a succession of bureaucratically sponsored movements in the 1920s and 1930s, each one designed to maintain social cohesion and to prod the populace to the greater efforts required by the forced march to industry and empire.

This conservative strategy of early establishing institutions and an ideology to cope with social problems helped Japan avoid some of the horrors to which the Industrial Revolution gave rise in England – but it had its price. Ralf Dahrendorf, reflecting on the German experience, wrote that an "early social policy serves to prevent rather than to promote the reality of the citizen role" and that "social policy always went too far in holding citizens in tutelage."[75] In Japan, too, the bureaucratic strategy weakened support for parliamentary politics and for open confrontation of competing ideas and interests. A premium was placed on national unity. Reforms did not keep pace with the growing social problems. As problems of the economy

75 Dahrendorf, *Society and Democracy in Germany*, pp. 70–1.

worsened, threatening Japan's precarious international position, the rhetoric of national strength and exclusiveness was continuously strengthened. Meiji conservatism had set a pattern for handling the problems of industrial society that tended under these circumstances to lead to more and more extreme measures.

CHAPTER 4

SOCIALISM, LIBERALISM, AND MARXISM, 1901–31

PETER DUUS AND IRWIN SCHEINER

In the 1890s, many observers at home and abroad discovered that Japan had finally entered the mainstream of world history and had indeed become a principal actor in that history. As Ōkuma Shigenobu remarked at the end of the Sino-Japanese War, "Japan is no longer a Japan for Japan, but a Japan for the world." Although some Japanese viewed the end of their cultural and political isolation as cause for unrestrained self-congratulation, others were ambivalent about its implication for the future. If Japan became more like other modern nations, its material and political development might continue, but only at the expense of social harmony or cultural integrity. As the country moved into a new century, there was uncertainty over the shape of Japan's future.

One vision of the future saw Japan as eternally unique, able to maintain its traditional culture and values even in the midst of rapid economic and political change. This point of view, which we might call the "particularist" or "exceptionalist" perspective, found champions in the Seikyōsha writers of the early 1890s, who urged that the nation's cultural essence (*kokusui*) be preserved in the march toward modernity.[1] Given the polychromatic character of Japan's cultural past, however, it was difficult to identify this cultural essence. Unlike China, which boasted of an easily identifiable great tradition, Japan had none. Where, then, were the Seikyōsha writers to find the *kokusui* – in the myths and legends of the Shinto tradition, in the sensibilities of Heian culture, in the harsh ethos of the warrior class, in the boisterous arts of the Tokugawa townsmen, or in the austere puritanism of Tokugawa Confucianism?

---

1 On the Seikyōsha writers, see Kenneth B. Pyle, *The New Generation in Meiji Japan: Problems of Cultural Identity, 1885–1895* (Stanford, Calif.: Stanford University Press, 1969).

Although the Seikyōsha writers were conspicuously vague about what made Japan unique, neotraditionalist scholars like Hozumi Yatsuka and Inoue Tetsujirō found it in a blend of Confucian morality and nativist myth that they shaped into a civil religion for the state. They converted the familiar idea of the *kokutai*, long employed in the Edo period to sanctify a hierarchical sociopolitical order with the emperor at its apex, into an explanation for the durability, uniqueness, and superiority of Japanese social and political mores. Simultaneously sacralizing the emperor as the descendant of Amaterasu and secularizing him as the source of worldly political values, they likened his role to that of the benevolent father, concerned for his subjects/children but requiring their undivided allegiance. The family-state (*kazoku kokka*) concept, an ingenious ideological construct influenced by an organic conception of the state imported from the West, was powerful and pervasive: It informed the drafting of textbooks, the education of schoolteachers, and the training of lesser functionaries in the police, the military, and the judicial service. Although never formally adopted as a state creed, it became the basis of a highly particularistic nationalism that displaced critical political thought in the minds of its true believers.[2]

Even though the particularist/exceptionalist perspective on Japanese society enjoyed official respectability, many intellectuals found it difficult to accept. As products of a system of higher education whose curriculum depended on the "new knowledge" (*shinchishiki*) from the West, they were more inclined to a cosmopolitan conception of Japan's future, one that placed Japan fully in the mainstream of world history, subject to the same developmental laws and heading for the same future as were the more advanced nations of the West. Intellectuals of the late Meiji and Taishō periods frequently referred to the *jisei* (trends of the times) or *sekai no taisei* (trends in the world) to validate their proposals for political or social change. These words, which seem almost empty of meaning to the outsider, implied that there were discernible regularities or patterns of change in society, often unilinear in character. When linked with the concepts of social progress (*shakai shinpo*) or social evolution (*shakai shinka*), they conveyed the idea that the new was better than the old and that society improved over time. If the exceptionalist

2 For an excellent study of the origins of state ideology, see Carol Gluck, *Japan's Modern Myths: Ideology in the Making in the Late Meiji Period* (Princeton, N.J.: Princeton University Press, 1985).

perspective chose to focus on timeless essences, cosmopolitan intellectuals looked at patterns of flux and often found in them historical inevitability.

Like the theorists of the family state, these intellectuals drew much of their vocabulary, conceptual and semantic, from Western thought. The notion that there were fixed norms governing all societies was a familiar one, embodied in the Confucian concept of "principle" (ri), but it could not account for the dynamics of history, except in cyclical patterns of decline and restoration. The discovery that society could move to ever-higher levels of prosperity, rationality, or efficiency was perhaps the central intellectual revolution of the Meiji period. The notion of progress was to be found in nearly every tome and tract on social thought translated into Japanese, whether it came from a radical Rousseau or a conservative Bluntschli. To some degree, the concept of progress was complicated by the less optimistic social Darwinist ideas so influential in the 1880s, yet more often than not, social Darwinism, when applied to domestic rather than external developments, was construed in a positive sense, with the stress on the fittest who survived rather than on their struggle for existence.

The idea that there were regular patterns of social progress implied the basic commonality of humankind and the existence of a universal human psychology transcending the peculiarities of social, geographical, and historical context. Whereas the exceptionalist perspective extolled a unique "Japanese spirit" that was inaccessible to the alien mind, the cosmopolitan perspective often saw identical impulses at work in all persons and in all societies. This led to a simplified, even conventionalized, description of human behavior, but it also suggested that Japan was not a psychological lost continent inhabited by a separate species. The idea of social progress was also easy to associate with programs of social and political reform: If the future were always better than the past, then it could be used to rebuke the present as well.

In the early 1890s, the cosmopolitan viewpoint found its most undiluted expression in the writing of Tokutomi Sohō and his circle.[3] In Shōrai no Nihon, Tokutomi described Japan as being in a transitional stage of development, moving like the advanced Western societies from a militaristic-aristocratic to an

---

3   On the development of Tokutomi's thought, see Kenneth B. Pyle, *New Generation*, and John D. Pierson, *Tokutomo Sohō, 1863–1957: A Journalist for Modern Japan* (Princeton, N.J.: Princeton University Press, 1980).

industrial-democratic society. Drawing on the writings of mid-Victorian liberalism, from John Stuart Mill to Herbert Spencer, Tokutomi argued that the tendency of human history was toward freedom, equality, prosperity, and peace. At times, Tokutomi hovered on the edge of a rigid historical determinism, giving scant heed to the vagaries of historical accident or the impact of human will on history. But by the mid-1890s, he had somewhat modified his conception of the future from a simplistic model of a laissez-faire society to one in which individualism was tempered by collectivism or state interventionism, even though he remained committed to a unilinear concept of historical development.

Even those most closely attached to a theory of universal human development, like Tokutomi, had only to look around to realize that social laws did not work in a vacuum but in a concrete time and place. When applied to Japan, laws of universal development often had to be bent to fit. For example, Tokutomi described the Meiji Restoration as an incomplete or unfulfilled revolution. Although he saw it as the culmination of long-term trends toward liberty that had brought down the old order, paradoxically and perhaps illogically, he saw these trends thwarted, stymied, or aborted in the post-Restoration era. Later, Marxist debates on the character of the Restoration and the development of capitalism in Japan wrestled with the same problem. "Trends of the times" often seemed to have a different velocity and follow a different trajectory in Japan. Though traveling toward the same destination as were the advanced nations of the West, Japan appeared to move on a bypath rather than the main highway.

Then, too, the model of the future presented by the advanced societies of the West was itself in a continuous process of transformation. Japan might have the "advantage of followership," but it had to follow a constantly moving target. Cosmopolitan perspectives on the future in the early twentieth century therefore kept shifting, and so this chapter discusses several of its varied exponents – the late Meiji socialists, the democratic liberals of Taishō, and the Marxists and other left radicals of the 1920s. Often in contention with one another, they still shared a common discourse that made Japanese history part of universal history, and they agreed in rejecting the idea that Japan was unique in its structure and development.

THE EMERGENCE OF SOCIALISM

If Tokutomi Sohō was one of the first Japanese intellectuals to apply a scheme of universal historical change to the history of Japan, he was also one of the first to discern lines of fracture in Japanese society. In contrasting the "commoners" (*heimin*) and the "aristocrats" (*kizoku*), however, Tokutomi was referring not so much to structural as to historical and generational divisions. The aristocrats were representatives of the "Old Japan," the parvenu Meiji leaders and a handful of holdovers from the ancien régime, who wished to turn the clock back to an era of privilege and caste. The commoners were everyone else, the ordinary workers and peasants as well as the well-to-do landed farmers, whose interests were tied to the present and future "New Japan." It was they who would benefit from the expansion of market freedom, equality of opportunity, and political enfranchisement promised by the laws of social development. Tokutomi saw the commoners and the privileged few as being at odds, but he did not suggest that one segment of society should be set against another or that there were exploiters and exploited in Japanese society. In short, he did not suggest the possibility of class conflict.

By the late 1890s, however, a number of observers feared that as the process of industrialization quickened, the gap between rich and poor would widen, and social harmony would weaken. In 1898, a group of law professors at Tokyo Imperial University led by Kuwada Kumazō (1869–1932) and Kanai En (1865–1933) organized the Social Policy Association (Shakai seisaku gakkai) to discuss the social problems associated with industrialization. Influenced by the successful social reforms of Bismarck and the ideas of conservative social reformers such as Lujo Brentano, Gustav Schmoller, and Adolf Wagner, members of the association argued that the pursuit of profit and unbridled competition that accompanied industrial growth under a laissez-faire policy would erode social stability and encourage social conflict. Basically procapitalist in their views, they attacked neither private property nor the market mechanism per se. Rather, they contended that the harshness of a laissez-faire system should be tempered by the introduction of factory legislation, workers' insurance programs, relief for poor people, and other measures of social policy. Socialism, however, was anathema to them, as it would impede national progress, pulling society back to a more primitive collectivist stage. In any case, these politically conservative professors saw no reason to think that socialism would be necessary in Japan. "The fact that the Japanese people established a constitutional system without shedding a drop of blood is a matter of great distinction in modern history," observed Kuwada in 1896. "In the coming economic revolution, too, why should it be impossible to solve this great problem peacefully?"[4]

If these conservative scholars hoped to save capitalism from its worst instincts by allaying class conflict through a timely adoption of social policy, the socialist movement, which emerged at about the same time, had no qualms about attacking capitalism itself from a radical perspective. The manifesto of the Social Democratic Party, published on May 20, 1901, proclaimed, "Our party, in response to the general trend at work within the world, and understanding the tendency of the economy, wishes to abolish the gap between rich and poor and secure a victory for pacificism in the world by means of genuine socialism and democracy." To achieve these ends, the socialists offered the standard fare of the Second International: public ownership of land and capital, nationalization of the means of communication and transportation, universal brotherhood, disarmament, and international peace. They also called for the abolition of the House of Peers and a reduction in the Japanese army and navy, sources of political and social inequity specific to Japan. Unlike the members of the Social Policy Association, the socialists were clearly at odds with their society.[5]

The socialist movement had its origins in a group that began meeting in 1898 at the Unitarian Society in Tokyo to study the writings of European socialist pioneers such as Saint-Simon, Proudhon, Fourier, and Marx, as well as American social reformers such as Henry George, William Bliss, and Richard Ely. Forty members of this group formed the Socialist Society in 1900, and it was from their ranks that the Social Democratic Party was organized in 1901. The party's founding members represented a social profile of the study group. All but one (Kōtoku Shūsui) were Christians; two had participated in the *jiyūminken* (popular rights) movement and later became journalists (Kōtoku Shūsui and Kinoshita Naoe); one was a university professor (Abe Isoo); and two were professional

---

4   Kenneth B. Pyle, "Advantages of Followership: German Economics and Japanese Bureaucrats, 1890–1925," *Journal of Japanese Studies* 1 (Autumn 1974): 147.
5   Hyman Kublin, *Asian Revolutionary: The Life of Sen Katayama* (Princeton, N.J.: Princeton University Press, 1964), pp. 129–56.

labor organizers or political activists (Katayama Sen and Nishikawa Kōjirō).[6]

During their first decade as a self-conscious movement, the Meiji socialists passionately indicted the moral failings and cultural decadence of their society. Whether materialists or Christians, the socialists depicted late Meiji Japan as corrupt and degenerate, dominated by special interests. In 1899, on the eve of declaring his calling as a socialist, the journalist Kōtoku Shūsui (1871–1911) lamented that since the Restoration, "national virtues had been supplanted by a vicious struggle for monetary gain." Seven years later, the editors of *Shin kigen* (New era), a Christian socialist journal, inveighed against a Japan "owned by the nobility and the rich classes who are degenerate and marked by corruption." And Katayama Sen, writing in the labor newspaper *Rōdō sekai* (Labor world), deplored the selfishness of national politicians and described the Meiji government as incompetent and irresponsible. In short, socialists of all stripes saw the political and economic leadership of Japan as morally bankrupt.[7]

The late Meiji socialists did not distinguish moral criticism from social analysis, nor did they feel the need to do so. The Christian socialists, perceiving themselves as servants of the social gospel of Jesus, believed that socialism was the secular instrumentality to bring social and economic justice to Japan. Non-Christian leaders of the movement, often political journalists disillusioned with the Jiyūtō (Liberal Party) and the other political parties because of their accommodation with the Meiji government, identified themselves with the *bakumatsu* revolutionaries who had assailed the *bakufu* for its corruption. Christian or non-Christian, these men conceived of socialism as a means of social and moral regeneration, and they argued that government activity and economic organization had to be judged by their ethical effect on society. Their writings deliberately blended value judgment with factual statement. Even while following Marx's analysis of capitalism, they could not accept his moral agnosticism. If Marx had deliberately limited himself to an analysis of the structural

6 Yamaji Aizan, "Genji no shakai mondai oyobi shakaishugisha," in Kishimoto Eitarō, ed., *Shakaishugi shiron* (Tokyo: Aoki shoten, 1955), pp. 95–115; Kublin, *Asian Revolutionary*, pp. 129–56.
7 Sharon Lee Sievers, "Kōtoku Shūsui, The Essence of Socialism: A Translation and Biographical Essay," Ph.D. diss., Stanford University, 1969, pp. 129–31; *Shin kigen* (Tokyo: Shinkigensha, September 10, 1906), no. 11; Kishimoto Eitarō and Koyama Hirotake, *Nihon kindai shakai shisōshi* (Tokyo: Aoki shoten, 1959), pp. 81–5.

and historical causes of capitalist development, or claimed to do so, the Japanese socialists elaborated on its injustices and amorality.[8]

To be sure, the socialists generally followed the conventions of Western Marxist analysis. Consider the criticism of capitalism in Kōtoku's *Shakaishugi shinzui* (The quintessence of socialism) and Katayama's "Waga shakaishugi" (My socialism), believed by most scholars to be the two finest pieces of Marxist writing in Meiji Japan.[9] Like Marx, they praised the contributions of capitalism to the progress of modern society, and they marveled at its material production. Kōtoku and Katayama also concerned themselves with the paradoxes of capitalist development. With grotesque inconsistency, the greater part of humanity grew progressively poorer and more miserable under capitalism even as production grew by leaps and bounds. "Concurrent with the displacement of more and more workers by improved machinery," wrote Kōtoku, "there is a daily increase in the labor supply." Following Engels, he argued that capitalism created an "industrial reserve army," an extraordinary surplus of workers who fought with one another over a decreasing number of jobs. Even the fully employed suffered. Under capitalism, workers lost all control of the "means of production." As Katayama observed, the wealth produced by workers was expropriated by the capitalists, and the workers became a dependent class, losing their freedom. In part, both men asserted, this was a consequence of the anarchy spawned by free competition and its ideology of the "survival of the fittest, the strong devouring the weak." In their view, class conflict was inevitable, a systematic consequence of the sharp divide between "a class called capitalists who monopolize the productive machinery and possess its products and a class of workers who possess nothing but their own labor."[10]

Kōtoku and Katayama touched on all the basic precepts of Marxism: the "labor theory of value," the theory of "surplus value," the

8   Kōtoku Shūsui, *Teikokushugi: Nijūseiki no kaibutsu* (Tokyo: Iwanami shoten, 1954), conclusion; see Sievers's translation in "Kōtoku Shūsui," of Kōtoku's *Shakaishugi shinzui*, chap. 6; Katayama Sen, "Waga shakaishugi," in Kishimotō Eitarō, ed., *Katayama Sen, Tazoe Tetsuji shū* (Tokyo: Aoki shoten, 1955), pp. 112–16.
9   However much or little they read of Marx – a question often debated in recent studies – much of Kōtoku's and Katayama's terminology was Marxist, and with some exceptions it was accurately used. See Kōtoku, *Shakaishugi shinzui* (Tokyo: Iwanami shoten, 1955), preface.
10 See Katayama, "Waga," pp. 23–4, 32, 34, 36, 39–41, 49–50, 56, 60, 80–2, 91–3, 98–9; Kōtoku, *Shakaishugi*, pp. 142–5, 164, 178.

"industrial reserve army," and the contradictions that inevitably "exist between socialized production and capitalist ownership." But both men parted from Marxist theory on a crucial point. Marx and his European followers insisted that theory had to be embedded in an historical perspective. Change, class, and class conflict each must be understood historically. "For the time being," Marx wrote, "class antagonisms are the motor of historical (social) development. Progress depends upon them." The internal contradictions of bourgeois society, Marx argued, were in fact both its propellant and essential to its functioning. For the Marxist, as George Lichtheim wrote, contradictions "cannot be legislated out of existence though they can be overcome 'at a higher level,' i.e., after history has reached the stage of the classless society." To the Meiji socialists, however, contradictions were seen not as the motor of history but as paradoxes to be deplored as the source of social injustice. Influenced by the ideas of social Darwinism as well as Marxism, they conceived of history as driven by ineluctable and impersonal evolutionary forces and often suggested that large historical changes were somehow inevitable. Yet they did not analyze the causes of historical dynamics or offer any systematic explanation of historical inevitability. There was almost an element of fatalism in this view of history. As Kōtoku wrote, "Revolution depends on Heaven, not on the strength of man."[11]

The Meiji socialists also conceived of the bourgeoisie differently than Marx did. For Marx, the bourgeoisie had once been a "national class," a progressive class representing the interest of the whole society against its retrograde members, but as the pauperization of the masses accelerated, the class had lost its progressive role. In the *Communist Manifesto*, translated by Kōtoku and Sakai Toshihiko in 1904, Marx and Engels described the demise of the bourgeoisie as "unfit any longer to be the ruling class in society." The Meiji socialists, on the other hand, were curiously ambivalent about the historical role of the European bourgeoisie, whom they often referred to as "the middle class." The Japanese socialists understood the bourgeoisie normatively, abstractly rather than historically, and never structurally. Nothing better expressed their view than Kōtoku's

11 Katayama, "Waga," pp. 32–3, 41–2, 69–70, 86–7; Kōtoku, *shakaishugi*, pp. 153–8, 182, 200; George Lichtheim, *Marxism: An Historical and Critical Study* (London: Routledge & Kegan Paul, 1961), pp. 46, 382–5; Hayashi Shigeru et al., ed., *Heimin shinbun ronsetsushū* (Tokyo: Iwanami shoten, 1961), pp. 188–97; Kōtoku Shūsui, *Hyōron to zuisō* (Tokyo: Jiyūhyōronsha, 1950), p. 27.

statement: "The purpose of socialism is simply to create a middle class out of all society."[12]

In contrast with Marx, the Meiji socialists continued to stress the still progressive role of the bourgeoisie. In the West, said Kōtoku, it was the middle class that embodied the revolutionary spirit and became a force for action. In searching for a middle class in Japan's immediate past, both Kōtoku and Sakai found their analogue in the *shishi jinjin*, the "righteous patriots" who created the Meiji Restoration. They characterized the bourgeoisie, like the *shishi*, as moral exemplars, men who had "ideals" (*risō*), and men who (borrowing a Western concept) had "character" (*jinkaku*). Like the samurai class, the European bourgeoisie was neither indolent like the aristocracy nor economically deprived like the lower classes. By identifying the Meiji Restoration with the bourgeois revolutions of Europe, Kōtoku was suggesting that only a similar moral elite free of the constraints of status and economic deprivation could lead a socialist revolution. In fact, as we shall see, the socialists directly identified themselves with both *shishi* and bourgeoisie by describing themselves as heirs of the Meiji Restoration.[13]

Like the European Marxists, the Meiji socialists began with a critique of capitalist society, but it was the moral insensitivity of capitalism and its cruel social consequences that drew their most severe criticism. Both Kōtoku and Katayama called the inequity of economic distribution under capitalism a great crime. Under capitalism, Kōtoku wrote, not only did the workers face eleven hours of unremittingly harsh labor every day, but through expropriation, the product of their labor was "enjoyed by the indolent and the pleasure-seekers." Above all, what enraged both Kōtoku and Katayama, as well as their fellow socialists, was the corrupting effect of capitalism on civilization. Capitalism was a "curse on humanity," said Katayama; free competition created "an amoral and animalistic outlook on life." There was "nothing in life so cruel as the persistence of unemployment, endemic to the capitalistic world," wrote Kōtoku, because it turned men to thievery and women to prostitution and plunged the "great majority of the world's

12 Lichtheim, *Marxism*, pp. 86–8, 142–54, 387–90; Kōtoku, *Shakaishugi*, pp. 183–4; Matsuzawa Hiroaki, "Meiji shakaishugi no shisō," in Nihon seiji gakkai, ed., *Nihon no shakaishugi* (Tokyo: Iwanami shoten, 1968), pp. 26–7.
13 Sievers, "Kōtoku Shusui," pp. 34–7, 94; Kōtoku, *Shakaishugi*, pp. 183–4; Matsuzawa, "Meiji shakaishugi no shisō," p. 45; John Crump, *The Origins of Socialist Thought in Japan* (New York: St. Martin's Press, 1983), p. 133; Saigusa Hiroto, *Nihon no yuibutsuronsha* (Tokyo: Eihōsha, 1956), p. 17; Nakamura Katsunori, *Meiji shakaishugi kenkyū* (Tokyo: Sekai shoin, 1966), p. 60.

humanity . . . into oblivion." "What," he added, "was to become of truth, justice and humanity?"[14]

Like socialists everywhere, Katayama, Kōtoku, Abe, and their fellow activists argued that reform and protest were only stopgap measures, not capable of correcting the basic evils that permeated the social organization of Japan. Also like many socialists, they had no quarrel with the material progress that industrial development had brought, and indeed they often praised it. What horrified the socialists, provoked their criticism of Meiji society, and animated their advocacy of socialism was the ascendancy of economic values and the disappearance of a moral center. They deplored the acquisitive ethic of the uncontrolled marketplace, the greed and the competitiveness that eroded moral relationships among the members of society. Although industrialization brought the benefits of prosperity, the cash nexus eroded the moral bonds of society.[15]

The socialists aspired to combine material progress with a social order suffused by compassion and impelled by morality. As Kōtoku wrote in 1901, the function of socialism was to bring harmony to society by removing the economic cause of strife; social harmony was its objective, and it was to be achieved not by laws or government discipline but by giving morals primacy over economics. Katayama once described socialism as "the *civilized society of our grandparents but with production carried out by steam, electricity and compressed air,* that is, a society where a working man can obtain the greatest power and pleasure." Kōtoku spoke of the eradication of the "base desires" impelled by the atmosphere of free competition and called for their replacement by "competition for ideals, justice and the like . . . competition among good men." Sakai Toshihiko argued that if it were possible to achieve a unity of private and public interest, "the hateful thing called *economic relationships* in society disappears and a relationship of love, warm and pure, spreads its wings freely." Abe more specifically asserted that "if the present social organization is reformed and each man is relieved of money worries, then we may look for a great change in morality." Sex crimes, crime itself, and in fact all problems arising from social relationships would disappear.[16]

For the socialists, social conflict, political venality, and a return to

14 Katayama, "Waga," pp. 33–5, 84–6, 104, 112–16; Kōtoku, *Shakaishugi,* pp. 78, 136–7; Matsuzawa, "Meiji shakaishugi no shisō," pp. 25–6.
15 *Shin kigen,* no. 5, March 10, 1906; Kōtoku, *Teikokushugi,* foreword, chap. 1; Kōtoku, *Shakaishugi,* pp. 145, 181–3; Katayama, "Waga," pp. 24–5, 41–9, 59–62; 100–2.
16 Kōtoku, *Shakaishugi,* pp. 164–201; Katayama, "Waga," pp. 104–5, 116, 126; Kōtoku, *Hyōron to zuisō,* pp. 25–6; Matsuzawa, "Meiji shakaishugi no shisō," pp. 22, 36–7.

outmoded behavior were merely symptoms of the gross structural inequities in their society. Current evils, according to a writer in the *Yorozu chōhō*, a newspaper employing a number of socialist reporters, "may be ascribed not so much to the fault of those who are corrupt and degraded but to the system and organization of present society that caused them to fall into such a condition." At the same time, these evils demonstrated the Meiji government's responsibility for the spiritual and intellectual corruption of the individual and of society. "Our politicians," Kōtoku wrote, "have forgotten the original purpose of the revolution [the Meiji Restoration] and its original spirit [which was] based on freedom, equality and fraternity." As a result, further progress had been brought to a standstill. As Kōtoku wrote in yet another essay, the once-radical party movement had lost its spirit of opposition, and its leaders had become no more than government sycophants. By 1904, Sakai, as well as Kinoshita and Kōtoku, had given up hope that an independent and morally upright middle class would make its appearance in Japan; instead, there was only a corrupted bourgeoisie, a hedonistic "gentlemen's gang" (*shinshibatsu*), besotted by extravagant indulgence in geishas and other luxuries.[17]

Increasingly, socialism became a moral creed to which its adherents bore witness. The socialists conceived of themselves as a moral elite, true heirs to the spirit of the Meiji Restoration. Kōtoku described himself and his colleagues as "righteous patriots" (*shishi jinjin*) who would carry out a "great cleansing of society." All socialists, whether Christian or materialist, described socialism as an "ideal" or a "way," whose achievement, so it seems, was to be accomplished by religious acolytes. Acceptance of socialism and its goals was for its followers an act of self-abnegation and self-transcendence. In his prison letters, Kōtoku later wrote disparagingly of his past pride; he spoke of the need to rid himself of "what was unclean and ugly wherein I sought profit and name." He added, "Those who sacrifice their natural instincts most are truly those most advanced in morality."[18]

Socialists also took as their goal the creation of "men of character"

17 Matsuzawa, "Meiji shakaishugi no shisō," pp. 24, 38–9; Kōtoku, *Teikokushugi, passim*; Hayashi, *Heimin shinbun ronsetsushū*, pp. 153–4; 161–5, 192; Nakamura, *Meiji shakaishugi kenkyū*, pp. 59–60; Mitani Taichirō, "Taishō shakaishugi no 'seiji' kan – 'seiji no hitei' kara 'seijiteki taikō e," in Nihon seiji gakkai, ed., *Nihon no shakai shugi* (Tokyo: Iwanami shoten, 1968), p. 69; *Shin kigen*, no. 1, November 10, 1905.
18 Matsuzawa, "Meiji shakaishugi no shisō," pp. 41, 57; Saigusa, *Nihon no yuibutsuronsha*, p. 17; Sievers, "Kōtoku Shūsui," p. 37; *Chokugen*, April 16, 1905.

(*jinkakusha*). Overcoming false individualism was a significant part of the socialists' task, argued Abe Isoo, and their ultimate objective was the creation of "cosmopolitan men" with universalistic ideals and goals.[19]

Yamaji Aizan (1864–1917), a contemporary social commentator and popular historian, observed that the socialists attracted young supporters because of their "seemingly religious devotion" to moral goals and reform in the face of government persecution. University students, like the socialists, thought of themselves as potential political and social leaders. But as Taoka Reiun (1870–1912), another social commentator and socialist sympathizer, wrote, these young men were "uncompromising, rough-mannered people with spirit" who either found government positions "inaccessible" or lost out to "clever sycophants." Socialism therefore was attractive not only because it attempted to solve social problems but also because it offered moral sustenance to those who felt themselves wrongly barred from office. Socialism gained their attention, as Kōtoku contended, because it took as its objective "the cooperation of all the people of society." It spoke to the frustrations of these restless (and as some argued) morally uprooted young people, by promising a society "completely based on the human feeling of brotherly love and humanity." It attracted their sympathy by suggesting that "men of character" must ultimately triumph in a society in which leaders and led had lost their moral focus.[20]

THE COLLAPSE OF THE SOCIALIST MOVEMENT

The Meiji government feared that the appearance of socialist doctrine in Japan portended social upheaval. The movement questioned the legitimacy of class divisions, propagated the idea of class warfare, and criticized fundamental institutions such as the military forces of a strong administrative state. In 1900, the Yamagata government promulgated the Public Peace Police Law, intended to check the activities of labor and socialist organizations. Under the provisions of these regulations, in 1901 the Social Democratic Party was disbanded within twelve hours of the publication of its manifesto, and editions of newspapers that had published its manifesto were confiscated. According to Abe Isoo, the authorities offered not to close

---

19 *Chokugen*, April 16, 1905; *Rikugo zasshi*, no. 177, September 1895.
20 Yamaji, "Genji no shakai mondai oyobi shakaishugisha"; Matsuzawa, "Meiji shakaishugi no shisō," pp. 9, 36.

down the organization if the socialists agreed to strike from their manifesto two items: the abolition of the House of Peers and the reduction of arms expenditures. And although the authorities objected to the manifesto's references to destruction of the class system, interestingly they offered no objections to socialist principles such as the public ownership of land and capital or to political reforms such as universal manhood suffrage or the secret ballot. This clearly reflected an implicit official recognition that most of the manifesto presented no clear and present danger to the Meiji state and that its authors were not revolutionaries.[21]

The socialists objected to the state as an instrument of political oppression and to the corruption of officials, but none of them (with the possible exception of Kinoshita) objected to the state per se before the Russo-Japanese War. As Abe Isoo argued, the state could in fact be an instrument for the establishment of a socialist economy: "There are two sides to the nature of the state these days, namely, the state as a political entity and the state as an industrial entity. . . . The path to socialist politics is the gradual decline of the *authoritative* agencies in politics and the development of economic agencies." In short, the state was acceptable as an agent of material progress but not as an agent of social or political control. It was even possible, Katayama wrote, to contemplate the realization of socialism under the Meiji constitution. In fact, with the exception of Kinoshita, who openly called for rejection of the *kokutai* myth, Meiji socialists criticized neither the Meiji constitution nor the role of the emperor.[22]

Central to the socialist program was the idea of public ownership of the means of production – variously referred to as *seisan kikan*, *shakaiteki kyōyū*, and *kokuyū*. But for the most part, the Meiji socialists focused narrowly on the social welfare and managerial aspects of

21 Gluck, *Japan's Modern Myths*, pp. 174–7; F. G. Notehelfer, *Kōtoku Shūsui: Portrait of a Japanese Radical* (Cambridge, England: Cambridge University Press, 1971), pp. 66–8; Abe Isoo, "Meiji sanjūnen no Shakai Minshutō," *Nihon shakai undōshi* (special issue) *Shakai kagaku* 4 (Tokyo: Kaizōsha, 1928), p. 77.

22 It is interesting to note that Kōtoku wrote in 1902 that historically emperors in Japan had sought the well-being of the people and hence "were in complete accord with the principles of socialism" (Crump, *Origins of Socialist Thought*, pp. 126–7). Similar sorts of arguments were advanced by Abe as well, clearly in an attempt to establish the compatibility of socialism and the emperor system. For quotation from Abe, see Matsuzawa, "Meiji shakaishugi no shisō," p. 58; and for details, see Abe Isoo's articles in *Shin kigen*, nos. 1–8, 11, 12; Kōtoku, *Shakaishugi*, p. 68; Kōtoku, *Hyōron*, pp. 11–17; Hayashi, *Heimin shinbun ronsetsushū*, pp. 162–5; for quotation from Katayama, see Kishimoto Eitarō and Koyama Hirotake, *Nihon no hikyōsantō marukusushugisha* (Tokyo: San'ichi shobō, 1962), p. 10; for quotation from Kinoshita, see Nakamura, *Meiji shakashugi kenkyū*, pp. 38–42; and Yanagida Izumi, *Kinoshita Naoe* (Tokyo: Rironsha, 1955), p. 126.

the socialization of the means of production. In their discussion of public ownership, they disregarded any analysis of the state as the political instrument of the ruling class and ignored the revolutionary role of the working class. More socialist than democratic, they took immediate aim only at the creation of a social-welfare state or some sort of state socialism. They conceived of the state as basically administrative and tried to depoliticize it by emphasizing its managerial functions. (Abe in fact thought of the ideal socialist state as being "one big insurance company.") By making the state managerial rather than political, they hoped to reduce political corruption, with the aim of achieving distributive justice.[23]

The socialists were less concerned with the revolutionary takeover of government than with ensuring that the material and economic needs of the people were fulfilled. Unless poverty and deprivation were ended, it would not be possible to bring about the moral regeneration of society. As Kōtoku said in 1899, "According to Confucius, the people should be made rich before teaching them." This view was shared by Sakai Toshihiko, who wrote, "If we desire to advance the general population beyond the desires of food, clothing, and shelter, we must carry out a fundamental reform of society; we must form a society that guarantees the general population food, clothing, and shelter. In other words, we must make socialism a reality."[24]

For most of the decade after 1901, all socialists agreed on the efficacy of a parliamentary policy. The electoral success of the German Social Democratic Party, which they regarded as a mentor and model, gave them heart. Although Abe Isoo knew that socialist victory in Japan lay decades in the future, he confidently predicted in 1903 that "the final victory will be ours." Commitment to parliamentarianism assumed that the achievement of socialism would not require political violence. As the editors of the *Heimin shinbun*, the principal socialist newspaper, argued in 1904, "The only way to achieve socialism is to seize power, and to seize power the majority of the Diet seats must be taken. To seize the majority in the Diet, public opinion in favor of socialism must be created." The socialists

---

23 Meiji socialists read both Richard Ely, who praised the social welfare state, and Albert Schaeffle, who set forth state socialism as the ultimate form of socialism. For a bibliography of readings, see Kōtoku, *Shakaishugi*, introduction; and Yamaji, "Genji no shakai mondai oyobi shakai-shugisha." For a discussion of terms used by socialists, see Matsuzawa, "Meiji shakaishugi no shisō," pp. 31–2. For a discussion of the state, see Kōtoku, *Shakaishugi*, conclusion; and Abe Isoo, *Meiji Shakaishugiron* (Tokyo: Wabei kyokai, 1907), pp. 14–20.

24 Quotations are from Matsuzawa, "Meiji shakaishugi no shisō," pp. 39–40.

therefore not only committed themselves, as we have seen, to agitating, spreading propaganda, and publicizing their position; they also allied themselves with Diet politicians who called for the establishment of universal manhood suffrage.[25]

The socialists had no doubt that Japan would some day become a socialist state. Even before the founding of the Social Democratic Party, Kōtoku wrote, "Socialism is manifestly the great ideology and idealism of the twentieth century. . . . Socialism is the great principle that is to save the world; it is not a fantasy; it is a realistic proposition." But even though they looked forward to revolutionary change, the socialists did not think that it had to be achieved through violence or direct action. The function of the socialist movement, as Kōtoku saw it, was to act as the "midwife" of revolutionary change. "Revolution is destined; it is not brought about by human efforts. It must be led, but it cannot be manufactured. It is not something one can bring on, nor is it something one can escape." The role of the "revolutionist" therefore was to "judge what the conditions of society are and to guide the general trend of its progress so that we may hope to create a peaceful revolution." As a means to this end, Kōtoku supported universal manhood suffrage, which he saw leading to socialist control over the Diet and local government. But he did not expect the people to seize control by themselves. He saw them instead as the beneficiaries of the moral elite who would be brought to power by their votes. His assumption, like that of the other socialists, was that "men of character" like themselves would guide the country peacefully toward its socialist transformation. In fact, the socialist movement drew on the burgeoning educated elite rather than on mass organizations or the masses.[26]

25 Kōtoku, *Shakaishugi*, pp. 198–200; Kōtoku, *Hyōron*, pp. 20–3; Hayashi, *Heimin shinbun ronsetsushū*, pp. 156–61; Kishimoto and Koyama, *Nihon no hikyōsantō*, pp. 90–1; Matsuzawa, "Meiji shakaishugi no shisō," pp. 32–3, 40; Abe Isoo's article in *Rōdō sekai*, August 1, 1898.

26 Matsuzawa, "Meiji shakaishugi no shisō," pp. 32, 59–63; Kōtoku, *Shakaishugi*, pp. 195–200; Sievers, "Kōtoku Shūsui," p. 59; Yamaji, "Genji no shakai mondai oyobi shakaishugisha," *passim*. In 1907, the Metropolitan Police Bureau in Tokyo announced that there were a total of 25,000 socialists in the country, with 14,000 of them residing in Tokyo. The police acknowledged that this was a "rough figure" and did not explain the criteria by which they determined who was a socialist, but the report confidently categorized with exceptional (if suspect) precision the social status of many socialists: 3,200 workers, 7,500 students, 50 politicians, 180 soldiers, 60 priests or ministers, 10 judicial officials, 45 doctors, and 200 "unknown." A less optimistic tally by the Japanese Socialist Party itself that included the name of every person who appeared on the party rolls during its years of existence indicates a membership of only 200. Nakamura Katsunori, "Nihon Shakaitō no soshiki to undō," *Hōgaku kenkyō* 33 (October 1960): 28–31.

It was not until February 1906, after the establishment of the first Saionji cabinet, that the socialists were permitted to organize a legally recognized party able to run candidates for office, openly solicit members, and hold conventions. Though the names of several ironworkers, a few printers, a *jinrikisha* puller or two, and some miners from the Ashio copper mine appeared on its membership list, the Japanese Socialist Party (Nihon shakaitō) founded in February 1906 was essentially composed of middle-class intellectuals; its leaders were writers, reporters, and scholars, many of whom had been socialist activists early on. Legal restrictions, particularly the Public Peace Police Law, inhibited recruitment. No school-teacher, Shinto or Buddhist priest, woman, nonadult male, or student could join a party. The latter exclusion particularly hurt the Socialist Party, as it was the students more than any other part of the population who read the socialists' publications and flocked to their meetings. Neither was there a labor movement to offer its support, as the Public Peace Police Law made unions practically impossible; and socialist organizers never really did try to rally workers to their ranks. As a result, the Japanese Socialist Party, as Arahata Kanson put it, had "plenty of commanding generals without troops to move."[27]

In any case, the Japanese Socialist Party survived only a year, largely because its members were accused of engaging in subversive political disturbances. During the spring and summer of 1906, the Japanese Socialist Party, along with the National Socialist Party (Kokka shakaitō) led by Yamaji Aizan, led a popular protest against a proposed increase in Tokyo's city tram fares. The campaign achieved its purpose, and the proposed fare increase was canceled. Katayama Sen declared it "the first victory of the red flag in Japan," but it proved to be a Pyrrhic one. The police arrested and jailed ten socialists active in the campaign, including Nishikawa and Ōsugi Sakae (1885–1923), and the cabinet agreed to keep a close eye on the Socialist Party, waiting for an opportunity to crack down on it.[28]

The opportunity came the following February when Sakai Toshihiko opened the party convention with a strong protest against the government's use of army troops to suppress a riot of some 3,600

27 Nakamura, "Nihon Shakaitō no soshiki to undō," pp. 29–34; Kishimoto and Koyama, *Nihon no hikyōsantō*, pp. 37–62.
28 Nakamura, "Nihon Shakaitō no soshiki to undō," pp. 38–45; Kishimoto and Koyama, *Nihon no hikyosantō*.

miners and other workers who had bombed, burned, and virtually destroyed the facilities at the Ashio copper mine in Tochigi Prefecture. Government officials had quickly blamed the riot on the socialists, especially on their party journal, *Heimin shinbun*, even though there was little proof of their involvement. At the party convention, Sakai called the government's use of military forces against the rioters "a grave blunder." Most of the resolution he proposed on behalf of the party's executive committee was more programmatic, a reiteration of the ideas and demands made by socialists throughout the decade. It proclaimed that the party sought "fundamentally to reorganize the existing social structure" so that the means of production would be owned in common by society, and it stated that the party should "arouse the workers' class consciousness," seeking to develop their "solidarity and discipline." The executive committee also expressed its "deep sympathy with all types of revolutionary movements struggling throughout the world." Five days after the convention opened, the government disbanded the party because of the subversive content of speeches and debates carried on at the convention.

The 1907 convention was also marked by a tactical rupture in the ranks of the socialist movement. Missing from the executive committee's resolution, conspicuously so as it had been an integral part of the socialist credo since 1901, was a declaration of the party's commitment to legal or constitutional tactics. A year earlier, the party had promised "to advocate socialism within the limits of the law of the land," and for years the socialists had worked to broaden the electoral franchise. But now the executive committee avoided any discussion of the party's parliamentary role and merely suggested that party members were free to follow their own inclinations about involvement in the universal manhood suffrage movement. Neither Sakai nor the executive committee sought to repudiate parliamentary or legal tactics but merely wanted to mend the growing rift within the party. Kōtoku Shūsui had demanded that the party adopt the tactics of "direct action" and asserted that the general strike was the "means for future revolution." Tazoe Tetsuji (1875–1908), on the other hand, had demanded that the party reassert its commitment to the universal suffrage movement and the primacy of parliamentary tactics. The executive committee sought to find a compromise middle ground.[29]

29 Nakamura, "Nihon Shakaitō no soshiki to undō," p. 28; Crump, *Origins of Socialist Thought*, pp. 250–2; Kishimoto and Koyama, *Nihon no hikyōsantō*.

During 1906, Kōtoku had discerned a shift in the "tide of the world revolutionary movement" away from parliamentary tactics toward more radical tactics of anarchosyndicalism. His discovery came in part as the result of his reading of Peter Kropotkin's anarchist tracts while in prison and in part as a result of his association with the International Workers of the World in California in 1905–6. Moreover, he was impressed by the successful tactics of the Russian revolutionary uprising during and after the Russo-Japanese War. If the Russian revolutionaries could act with such boldness and determination in a society that appeared much more backward than Japan's, how much more appropriate for Japanese revolutionaries to do so. Kōtoku had come to think that parliamentary action, instead of advancing the cause of socialism, seemed instead to be emasculating it. The European socialist parties stood in danger of becoming nothing more than "alternative bourgeois [*shinshi*] parties" incapable of functioning as revolutionary parties of the working class. In an appeal to Japanese youth, Kōtoku wrote, "*The revolution* to come is not the revolution of politics, not the revolution of the electoral law, nor that of parliament. . . . [T]he revolution of the future, it goes without saying, is the socialist, the anarchist revolution."[30]

For Kōtoku, the meaning of revolution had changed, and so had the role of the socialist activist. He now advocated the use of "direct action," specifically a general strike, to paralyze society. "[I]f the [upper classes] had their food and clothing cut off, they would truly know the power of the workers. . . . [I]f the police know the truth of the socialist system can they really shoot their brothers and parents?" A general strike would not only make the ruling class aware of the workers' collective power but would raise the consciousness of the workers as well. "To achieve our objectives, which is a fundamental revolution in the economic system, and the abolition of the wage system, it is more urgent to awaken the consciousness of ten workers than to get a thousand signatures on a petition for universal suffrage."[31]

In opposition to Kōtoku, Tazoe argued for the parliamentary tactics on the grounds that strikes and other extraparliamentary tactics would not ultimately improve the economic position of

30 Hayashi, *Heimin shinbun ronsetsushū*, pp. 135–44. For a good translation of Kōtoku's "The Change in My Thought," see Crump, *Origins of Socialist Thought*, pp. 341–51; Mitani Taichirō, *Taishō demokurashiiron* (Tokyo: Chūō kōronsha, 1974), pp. 71–3; Nakamura, *Meiji*, p. 73; Matsuzawa, "Meiji shakaishugi no shisō," p. 34.

31 Sievers, "Kōtoku Shūsui," p. 108; Nakamura, *Meiji*, pp. 74–5; Kishimoto and Koyama, *Nihon kindai shakai*, pp. 100–3.

the workers. The locus of the capitalists' power was in the Diet, and if the workers were to challenge that power, they had to resort to parliamentary methods. He criticized the faddishness of Kōtoku, who urged that the Japanese radical movement keep pace with the latest shift in trends abroad; he himself thought that the socialist movement had to develop doctrines appropriate to the social and political situation in Japan. Within the party, only Katayama supported Tazoe, whereas Kōtoku's view appealed to younger members of the movement such as Ōsugi Sakae and Yamakawa Hitoshi.[32]

The debate between Kōtoku and Tazoe reflected a deepening awareness of the need for an appropriate way to raise the consciousness of the working class in order to accomplish the overthrow of capitalist society. The issue at stake between them was not the moral corruption of their society, on which they were agreed, but the way in which that corruption should be rooted out. Kōtoku wanted to raise the consciousness of the workers through the drama of "direct action," Tazoe through reliance on organization and votes. Kōtoku thought Tazoe's method was self-defeating, as any compromise with the political institutions of capitalism was corrupting. He feared that a parliamentary socialist party would ultimately come to terms with the ruling class, as the Jiyūtō had. If, as Yamakawa suggested, Kōtoku "denied politics," then Tazoe affirmed it. This divergence in views over whether to work within the given political structure or to overthrow it from without foreshadowed the tactical dilemma later to be debated in the 1920s by intellectuals and activists with a firmer grasp of Marxism. Both Kōtoku and Tazoe, though aware of the need to raise the workers' consciousness, still regarded the workers as tools or instruments for change rather than as men aware of their own needs and interests, and both still saw themselves as members of an enlightened moral minority.[33]

The socialist movement suffered an enormous setback in 1911 when the government hanged Kōtoku Shūsui and eleven others, including his lover Kannō Sugako, for the crime of conspiring to assassinate the emperor. The "Great Treason incident" (taigyaku jiken) was the culmination of a prolonged campaign to suppress the socialist movement. Although the socialists and their publications had been subjected to official harassment before 1907, the powerful elder statesman Yamagata Aritomo had increased his

32 Kishimoto and Koyama, Nihon kindai shakai; Kishimoto and Koyama, Nihon no hikyōsantō.
33 Kishimoto and Koyama, Nihon no hikyōsantō; Mitani, Taishō demokurashiiron, p. 75.

pressure on the first Saionji and second Katsura cabinets to suppress all social movements. Frightened by the Ashio incident, the first large-scale strike in Japan, as well as by other incidents of social protest, Yamagata felt that a period of "social destructionism" (*shakaihakaishugi*) had begun. Police agents stepped up their harassment of socialist newspapers by banning individual issues, arresting editors, and interfering with their newspaper distribution. Even the journals published by Katayama's parliamentary faction, which clearly asserted their belief that socialism could be achieved by legal means, were dealt with as harshly as were those associated with the anarchists.[34]

The arrest and execution of Kōtoku, leader of the anarchist wing, was intended to damn the entire socialist movement as subversive and a threat to the emperor and nation. But in fact, the government prosecutors were never able to prove that Kōtoku had more than an early and temporary interest in the conspiracy to assassinate the emperor. At the trial, they focused on his "intent," not on any overt acts he committed. In any case, the trial ushered in what has been called the "winter years' (*fuyu no jidai*) of socialism. Nothing, or nearly nothing, could be published, and obviously no one dared to organize a political party or any other kind of political group. In his autobiography, Arahata even recalls that the government banned an entomological work entitled *Konchū shakai* (Insect society) because it contained the dreaded word *shakai* (society).[35]

MINPONSHUGI

Although the "winter years" were bleak for the socialist movement, they were years of thaw for more moderate and cautious intellectuals – most of them contemporaries of younger socialists like Yamakawa Hitoshi, Ōsugi Sakae, and Sakai Toshihiko – who advocated greater democratization of the political process. Like the Meiji socialists, these young democratic liberals lamented the ethical poverty of politics and the meaningless struggles for power among the country's self-serving leaders, but they were more optimistic that the political system would soon change from within as the result of long-term evolutionary processes. The transition to a new imperial reign, from

34 Gluck, *Japan's Modern Myths*, pp. 170–6, 188, 219, 227; Crump, *Origins of Socialist Thought*, p. 304; Oka Yoshitake, "Generational Conflict after the Russo-Japanese War," in Tetsuo Najita and Victor Koschmann, eds., *Conflict in Modern Japanese History* (Princeton, N.J.: Princeton University Press, 1982), p. 217.
35 Notehelfer, *Kōtoku Shusui*, pp. 185–6.

Meiji to Taishō, symbolized for them the passing of the old and a coming of the new, a break in political time. "The trend of the times demands a new politics, and they demand new men," wrote Maruyama Kanji in 1914. "To resist is like trying to make water run up hill. By new politics, I mean a politics that does not exclude Japan from the rest of the world; by new men, I mean those who will move with the currents in the world. The road the Taishō era must travel cannot veer from the trend toward democracy."[36] Japan, like the rest of the world, was being swept along in a great democratic tide, and the "era of the popularization of politics" lay ahead. Visible everywhere were signs of an "awakening of the people" (*jinmin no jikaku*) or an "awakening of the nation" (*kokumin no jikaku*).

What initially gave the democratic liberals grounds for optimism was the steady escalation of popular demonstrations and street movements during the years following the Russo-Japanese War. Beginning with the anti–Portsmouth Treaty movement of 1905, these popular outbursts had culminated in the first "movement to protect constitutional government" (*kensei yōgo undō*) of 1912–13 and the protests over the Siemens affair in 1914. Their political meaning, however, was ambiguous. Although public demonstrations were solid evidence of the new "trend of the times" about which Maruyama spoke, they were also symptomatic of the failure of the constitutional process. "The reason we see these mob explosions today," observed Ukita Kazutami, "is that there is no public opinion adequate to check the government's use of its authority."[37] Denied other legal and constitutional means of making their views known, crowds had taken to the streets, rallying in public to denounce the nation's leaders, their policies, their selfish hold on power. Often demonstrators fell prey to the agitation of rabble-rousers and turned violent. The upsurge of popular political unruliness marked a breakdown in the national consensus and social harmony, a growing rift between the goals of the government and the goals of the people.

The liberal democratic intellectuals had no doubts about where to place the blame for this breakdown in national consensus. The fault lay not in capitalism or capitalist morality but in the backwardness of Japanese political development. The persistence of "bureaucratic government" (*kanryō seiji*) or "clique government" (*hanbatsu seiji*)

36 Maruyama Kanji, "Minshuteki keikō to seitō," *Nihon oyobi Nihonjin*, January 1913.
37 Peter Duus, "Liberal Intellectuals and Social Conflict in Taishō Japan," in Tetsuo Najita and Victor Koschmann, eds., *Conflict in Modern Japanese History* (Princeton, N.J.: Princeton University Press, 1982), p. 46.

perpetuated authoritarian politics and obsolete national priorities. In 1912–13, protestors had called for the "overthrow of clique government" and the "protection of constitutional government." Control over the government lay in the hands of a "privileged class" (*tokken kaikyū*) that selfishly arrogated to itself the right to decide the nation's destiny. With the same vehemence that the Meiji socialists had attacked the "gentlemen's gang," and for many of the same reasons, the Taishō democrats assailed the "aristocratic cliques" (*monbatsu*), "bureaucratic cliques" (*hanbatsu*), and "militarist cliques" (*gunbatsu*) who dominated politics. Unlike the socialists, however, they did not attack "capitalists," nor did they express any interest in restructuring the political economy along the lines suggested by the Second International.

The democratic liberals' overriding concern was with the political process. Reform of that process was the key to ending political conflict and strengthening the nation. Unlike the socialists, the liberals did not debate whether to pursue "parliamentary action" or "direct action." Their model was the liberal bourgeois representative democracies of the West, and commitment to the parliamentary process basically defined their political position. The democratic liberals had no quarrel with the state, or the idea of loyalty to the state, but only with the way that "bureaucratic government" demanded that loyalty by docile obedience. They envisaged a political society made up of involved citizens, not passive subjects. Only if the parliamentary process were democratized, only if it were made more responsive to public opinion, and only if the people assumed greater control over the government, they argued, could the nation be held together.

Given their focus on the political process, the Taishō liberals did not concern themselves much with the "locus of sovereignty," an issue that had bedeviled constitutional theorists since the 1880s. In 1912, the journalistic debates between Uesugi Shinkichi, the heir of Hozumi Yatsuka, and Minobe Tatsukichi, author of the "organ theory" (*tennō kikan setsu*), had again brought that issue to public attention. Uesugi argued that sovereignty lay in the emperor, whereas Minobe argued that it lay in the state, of which the emperor was merely an "organ" or "mechanism" (*kikan*). For the democratic liberals, this question seemed unrelated to the realities of politics. Yoshino Sakuzō, while a law student at Tokyo Imperial University, had come under the influence of Onozuka Kiheiji, who encouraged his students to investigate governmental policy and political practice.

Onozuka contended that "political science" (*seijigaku*), that is, the study of political systems as they functioned historically, was as important as "juridical science" (*kokkagaku*), that is, the abstract analysis of the state as a legal concept. What counted for Yoshino, as well the other democratic liberals, was not where sovereignty lay but how it was to be exercised.

The publication of Yoshino Sakuzō's lengthy essay on constitutional government in 1916 (*Kensei no hongi o toite sono yūshū no bi o nasu michi o ronzu*) brought the democratic liberals' position into sharp focus.[38] The purpose of his essay was to describe the essential features of a democratic constitutional structure – the protection of individual rights, the separation of powers, the role of a representative assembly, and responsible cabinets – and to suggest why this model was appropriate for Japan. Like other liberals, Yoshino deliberately avoided issues of juridical theory, that is, how to interpret the letter of the constitution, and concentrated instead on its "spirit," the values that gave it life. (As Ōyama Ikuo later observed, it was not possible to "interpret a system of law apart from the national spirit [*Volksgeist*].")[39]

The "spirit of constitutional government," Yoshino implicitly argued, could be discovered only if one searched for its historical roots. Like most advocates of democratic reform, Yoshino read modern history as the history of expanding liberty, the collapse of authoritarianism in the face of rising popular power. This "Whig interpretation" of history, a legacy from the Meiji era, had first surfaced in the 1880s and 1890s among the advocates of constitutional government and a national assembly.[40] It tacitly assumed that yearning for freedom was a universal instinct and that the spread of constitutional government was its product.[41] Hence, Yoshino asserted, although constitutions might differ from country to country in their particu-

---

38 The essay appeared in the January 1916 issue of *Chūō kōron* and has been reprinted in Ōta Masao, ed., *Taishō demokurashii ronshū* (Tokyo: Shinsuisha, 1971), vol. 1, pp. 244–312. For an interesting treatment of Yoshino's thought, see Tetsuo Najita, "Some Reflections on the Political Thought of Yoshino Sakuzō," in Bernard S. Silberman and H. D. Harootunian, eds., *Japan in Crisis: Essay on Taishō Democracy* (Princeton, N.J.: Princeton University Press, 1974). Also useful is Peter Duus, "Yoshino Sakuzō: The Christian as Political Critic," *Journal of Japanese Studies* 4 (Spring 1978): 301–26.

39 Ōta, *Taishō*, vol. 1, p. 412.

40 Cf. Peter Duus, "Whig History, Japanese Style: The Min'yūsha Historians and the Meiji Restoration," *Journal of Asian Studies* 33 (May 1974): 415–36.

41 Cf. the following statement by Nagai Ryūtarō: "There is a law that the trend of civilization moves from autocracy to freedom. That human beings crave freedom and require equality is a natural desire, just as feathered creatures crave flight in the sky, and beasts of the field seek water from mountain streams when they thirst." *Shin Nihon*, March 1915, pp. 73–4.

lars, all constitutions were the "inevitable product of modern civilization," and all shared a "common spiritual root."

It should not surprise us that Yoshino found the "common spiritual root" of all constitutions to be *minponshugi*, a term that became central to the political lexicon of the 1910s. *Minponshugi* was Yoshino's translation of the word *democracy*, but as his essay pointed out, the Western term conflated two separate meanings: the idea that "legally, state sovereignty lay in the people" and the idea that "politically, the fundamental goal of the exercise of state sovereignty lay in the people." Democracy in the first sense, popular sovereignty, was better called *minshushugi*. It was clearly not applicable to Japan, whose constitution unambiguously lodged sovereignty in the emperor. Rather, it was democracy in the second sense that Yoshino meant by *minponshugi*. The concept was political, not legal or juridical. On the one hand, it meant that "the exercise of political power, that is, the 'purpose of government,' is in the welfare [*rifuku*] of the general populace [*ippan minshū*]"; on the other hand, it also meant that "the determination of the goals of the exercise of political power, that is, 'policymaking,' depends on the will [*ikō*] of the general populace."[42]

Interestingly and ironically, Yoshino had borrowed the word *minponshugi* from Uesugi Shinkichi, his conservative colleague in the law faculty of Tokyo Imperial University, who argued that Japan had always been a country with a "monarchical sovereign [*kunshu*]" but had never been a "monarch-centered [*kunpon*] polity" like the France of Louis XIV. Rather, it had been a "people-centered [*minpon*] polity" responsive to the needs and welfare of all the people, and the basic moral imperative of the imperial family had always been *minponshugi* ("the principle of people centeredness"). Uesugi was clearly stating that the Japanese monarchy was benevolent and that imperial sovereignty was compatible with popular welfare. But Yoshino used *minponshugi* not to defend the imperial institution or the *kokutai* but, rather, to show that "democracy" (= *minponshugi*) posed no threat to the imperial institution or the *kokutai*. He wanted to refute the view that democracy was a form of "dangerous thought." Danger lay not in *minponshugi*, said Yoshino, but in *minshushugi* – popular sovereignty – an idea that could lead to sedition in the hands of a radical like Kōtoku Shūsui. One of the reasons that Yoshino's essay had such an impact was that it bril-

42 Ōta, *Taishō*, vol. 1, p. 266.

liantly reconciled the democratic political process with the peculiarities of the Japanese constitutional structure, demonstrating that it was possible for Japan to participate in the "world trend" toward democracy without sacrificing its national essence.

In practical terms, Yoshino, like the other democratic liberals, asserted that *minponshugi* meant following the practices of modern representative parliamentary democracy. Even though representative institutions were a less-than-perfect embodiment of *minponshugi*, they did rest on the principle that the "people" (*jinmin*) should select their own leaders, and they did guarantee that policy would reflect the will of the people. Like other democratic liberals such as Minobe Tatsukichi or Nagai Ryūtarō, Yoshino also argued that a commitment to representative government, and hence to *minponshugi*, had been national policy since the Charter Oath of 1868 had called for the convening of assemblies and broad public discussion. Representative government was compatible not only with the ancient tradition of imperial sovereignty but also with the goals of the Restoration.[43]

Yoshino's essay immediately provoked debate. "*Minponshugi! Minponshugi!*" remarked one ironic observer. "These days night does not fall nor the sun rise without *minponshugi*. Anyone who does not talk about *minponshugi* is regarded as an eccentric badly out of touch with things."[44] Despite Yoshino's attempt to reconcile democracy with the *kokutai*, conservatives like Uesugi attacked the idea of representative democracy as incompatible with the Japanese monarchical order. Some liberals criticized Yoshino for making vague and simplistic distinctions or presenting a model of representative government already out of date, and still others offered their own pet neologisms – *minshūshugi*, *minseishugi*, *minjūshugi*, and *minjishugi* – as alternatives to *minponshugi*. But nearly all the leading liberal intellectuals – Kimura Kyūichi, Minobe Tatsukichi, Sasaki Sōichi, Ōyama Ikuo, and Kawakami Hajime – immediately accepted Yoshino's dichotomy between *minshūshugi* and *minponshugi* (if not always his terms) as well as his implication that democracy was compatible with the *kokutai*. There was also a solid consensus behind his programmatic proposals: an end to "bureaucratic government," the establishment of responsible cabinets, the subordination of the upper house to the lower house in the Diet, and, most important of all, the broadening of suffrage. "The expansion of the suffrage, together

---

43 Ōta, *Taishō*, vol. 1, p. 275.   44 Ōta, *Taishō*, vol. 2, p. 101.

with strict enforcement of [election] control laws, is the most urgent task facing our nation," Yoshino wrote in 1916.[45]

The advocates of *minponshugi* were no more populist than were the Meiji socialists, however, and they too expected the representative process to produce a moral elite (or a meritocratic elite) not unlike themselves. Before 1918, when Yoshino, Ōyama Ikuo, Nagai Ryūtarō, and other democratic liberals called for an expanded suffrage, it was the enfranchisement of all educated middle-class males that they had in mind. They wanted to substitute educational qualifications (or other tokens of social responsibility such as completion of military service or assumption of household headship) for the tax-paying qualifications on the right to vote. The lower orders – "those below the middle class" – were not yet ready for full political participation, nor were women. To be sure, the democratic liberals saw no intrinsic reason that the general populace should not be enfranchised in the long run, but they felt that the constitutional system was only a generation old and that it was difficult for the people to absorb the idea of self-rule or political representation after centuries under autocratic regimes. At the beginning of his *minponshugi* essay, Yoshino had lamented that even many members of the educated classes, who should be the "leaders of a nation's culture," did not fully understand the working and spirit of constitutional government; how much more difficult it would be then for the lower classes. The democratic liberals covered their ambivalence toward the masses, however, by contending that the people had to be prepared for full political enfranchisement through "political education" and a "transformation of their knowledge and morality." Raising their political consciousness was the first step in bringing them into the political process.

The democratic liberals also seem to have assumed that suffrage reform would take care of the problem of leadership. If the suffrage were broadened to include the educated middle classes, vote buying, bribery, and other forms of electoral corruption would decline, and "men of character" (*jinkakusha*) would stand for election. There was less agreement on just how the elected should represent those who elected them. On the one hand, it was obvious that representatives should reflect the will of the people, or at least public opinion. But the people did not always know what was best for them. As Yoshino often put it, the relation between the people and their representatives

45 Ōta, *Taishō*, vol. 1, p. 298.

was like that between patients and physicians: The patients know that they are ill, but the doctors know how to cure them. "True *minponshugi* politicians make public opinion and lead it, but afterwards carry on government in accordance with public opinion," suggested Kawakami Hajime.[46] Like the Meiji socialists, the democratic liberals yearned for the emergence of knowledgeable and moral leaders, and they often pointed out that democratic countries in the West produced men like Wilson, Poincaré, and Lloyd George – eloquent, literate, and even scholarly intellectual aristocrats who were nonetheless able to respond to the popular will.

As we have already suggested, it was the growing rift between the government and the people that concerned the democratic liberals. The ultimate practical justification of their program was that democratization of the political process created national harmony and consensus. Representative government, the democratic liberals believed, would intensify commitment to the nation. The flaw of despotic or authoritarian government – such as the domination of government by "privileged classes" in Japan – was that it did not encourage voluntary commitment to national goals. Yoshino, Ōyama, Kawakami, and others used terms like *kanmin dōkyō* (cooperation of people and officials), *kunmin dōchi* (joint rule by sovereign and people), *kunmin dōsei* (joint government by people and sovereign), or *banmin dōchi* (joint rule of all the people) to describe the essence of constitutional government. These faintly traditionalistic terms were intended to suggest that democratic politics was an integrative process, creating solidarity within society by creating a sense of jointness or commonality.

Ōyama Ikuo developed these ideas into a theory of democratic nationalism. Drawing on the sociological theories of politics he had studied in the United States, he argued that the state rested on both the individual's instinct toward community ("associative consciousness" [*dōrui ishiki*]) and a "sense of common interest" (*kyōdō rigai kannen*). If the state suppressed the demands of the individual, then the whole society would be weakened. But if "associative consciousness" were strengthened and a "sense of common interest" were clarified, then the individual would spontaneously contribute to the welfare of the whole society. "We believe that true national unity [*kyōkoku itchi*] springs from an intense consciousness of the people's

46   Kawakami Hajime, "Minponshugi to wa nanizoya," *Tōhō jiron*, October 1917.

common interests [*kokumin kyōdō no rigai*]," wrote Ōyama Ikuo in 1917, "and this intense consciousness of common interest will come once the people have assumed joint responsibility for the management of the state as a result of the spread of the right to vote."[47] Democracy, in other words, was the "end point" (*shūten*) of nationalism. "Nationalism," he wrote, "must ultimately end in democracy." This argument rested on the assumption, which Ōyama shared with the other democratic liberals, that the state was not only legitimate but neutral, standing above partisan, sectional, or class interests.

It was in their nationalism that the *minponshugi* liberals set themselves farthest from the Meiji socialists. Whereas the socialists had been strongly opposed to the Russo-Japanese War and had proclaimed the international solidarity of the working class when Katayama shook hands with Georgy Plekhanov at the Second International meeting in 1904, the democratic liberals took pains to point out that *minponshugi* was compatible not only with imperialism but also with militarism. Only anarchists believed in cosmopolitan liberty, observed Ōyama, whereas imperialism was expressive of the national spirit. In the midst of World War I, it was difficult for the *minponshugi* liberals to be pacifist when the forces of democracy were pitted against the forces of autocracy, and militarism in the narrow sense of using military force was seen as compatible with democracy. At the end of the war, many liberals began to speak of internationalism as well, but they construed that to mean not a supranational cosmopolitanism transcending national boundaries but an attempt to create harmonious relationships among nation-states by peaceful diplomatic means.

TOWARD RADICALISM

The outbreak of the rice riots in 1918 confirmed the democratic liberals' claim that dire consequences would result if government were not more responsive to popular needs. As the *Tōyō keizai shinpō* editorialized shortly after the disturbances, "Unfortunately the political process in our country works effectively only for the property-owning minority, whereas the classes without property are hardly given any security at all. In one sense it is possible to say that those without property have no government at all. Herein lies the true

47 Ōyama Ikuo, "Kokka seikatsu to kyōdō rigai kannen," *Shin shosetsu*, February 1917.

cause of the riots."[48] Such disturbances occurred, said Yoshino, because governments do not lend an ear to the demands of the people. Nagai Ryūtarō pointed out that the riots revealed not only that the bureaucratic authorities were out of touch with the people but also that the Diet "neither possessed the will to understand the economic hardships of the people nor made efforts to eliminate them."[49]

To the liberals, the rice riots indicated that the "awakening of the people" seen dimly on the horizon in 1914 had arrived and that events in Japan echoed the broader "trend of the times." The triumph of the democratic powers in World War I, the collapse of autocratic regimes in Germany and Austria-Hungary, and the explosion of popular democratic and nationalist movements in central Europe confirmed the "world trend" toward democracy. On the other hand, the triumph of the "extremist" (that is, Bolshevik) government in Russia gave practical significance to the idea that democratization was essential to preserving social solidarity. The new Bolshevik government, wrote Ōyama Ikuo, was a "decadent form of democracy."[50] If a similar sort of upheaval were to be avoided in Japan, it was essential to forestall the growth of class consciousness and class conflict foreshadowed by the rice riots, and that could best be done by the passage of a universal manhood suffrage law.

In the wake of the rice riots, many leading *minponshugi* intellectuals moved toward greater political activism, but because many were academics or journalists, they saw their task as raising political consciousness rather than seizing political power. At the end of 1918, Yoshino brought together a group of his students to begin a systematic study of universal suffrage and electoral reform, and he joined with Fukuda Tokuzō, Ōyama Ikuo, and other liberal academics to found the Reimeikai, a society aimed at "enlightening" the Japanese public by discussing new political ideas. Other small organizations of young intellectuals, journalists, and politicians such as the Kaizō dōmeikai came together to discuss democratic reforms.[51] With the support of liberal professors like Yoshino and Ōyama, reform-

---

48 Quoted in Inoue Kiyoshi and Watanabe Tōru, eds., *Kome sōdō no kenkyū* (Tokyo: Yūhikaku, 1962), vol. 5, p. 240.
49 Nagai Ryūtarō, *Kaizō no risō* (Tokyo, 1920), pp. 9–10.
50 Ōyama Ikuo, "Rōkoku kagekiha no jisseiryoku ni taisuru kashōshi to sono seiji shisō no kachi ni taisuru kaidaishi," *Chūō kōron* 33 (May 1917).
51 For an informative discussion of several of these organizations, see Itō Takashi, *Taishōki "kakushin" ha no seiritsu* (Tokyo: Hanawa shoten, 1978).

minded students at the major national and private universities began to organize political societies of their own, such as the Shinjinkai at Tokyo Imperial University and the Minjin dōmei at Waseda University. To the extent that most of these groups or their members engaged in overt political activities, they did so through support of, or participation in, the universal suffrage movement of 1919–20.[52]

But if the rice riots confirmed the position of the *minponshugi* liberals, it also revealed the limitations of their position. The advocates of democratic reform, although they repeatedly stressed the importance of "social policy" as a part of *minponshugi*, had been less attentive to the distribution of wealth within Japanese society than to the distribution of power. The rice riots – as well as the wave of strikes and other labor disputes that broke out at the end of World War I – made clear that most of the population lacked economic security as well as political rights. Ōyama Ikuo characterized the riots as a kind of "retaliatory confiscation," and Fukuda Tokuzō said the riots had occurred because the people had been pushed to a "point of extreme need" at which their right to survive overrode property rights. Still others pointed out that the basic cause of the riots was popular resentment at the great gap between rich and poor. Unlike the Hibiya riots and other post-1905 popular demonstrations, the rice riots had little to do with questions of governmental control or foreign policy. At stake, rather, were issues such as the existence of social division, unequal distribution of wealth, pervasive economic hardship, and the unresponsiveness of the propertied class to any of these problems.[53]

What made the resolution of these issues particularly urgent was the spread of labor unrest. Before World War I, the police, invoking Article 17 of the Public Peace Police Law, had been able to contain the growth of working-class organizations, but wartime economic dislocations had provoked labor–management friction. In many factories, disgruntled workers began to organize strikes and unions. In 1914, there had been only 49 labor unions in Japan, but by 1919, there were 187, with a total membership of

52 On the universal suffrage movement, see Matsuo Takayoshi, *Taishō demokurashii no kenkyū* (Tokyo: Aoki shoten, 1966); Matsuo Takayoshi, "Dai-ichi taisengo no fūsen undō," in Inone Kiyoshi, ed., *Taishōki no seiji to shakai* (Tokyo: Iwanami shoten, 1969). The best Western-language treatment of the student movement in the 1920s is by Henry D. Smith II, *Japan's First Student Radicals* (Cambridge, Mass.: Harvard University Press, 1972).

53 A collection of comments on the rice riots by important political and intellectual figures can be found in Inoue and Watanabe, eds., *Kome sōdō no kenkyū*, vol. 5.

100,000. The most important of these, the Yūaikai, founded by Suzuki Bunji as a "friendly society" in 1914, commanded a following of 30,000. The issues of social and economic justice raised by the rice riots were not a passing phenomenon but a cause for continuing concern.[54]

By the end of 1918, neologisms like *minponshugi* were gradually abandoned in favor of more straightforward terms like *minshushugi* or simply *demokurashii*. More important, the idea of democracy was construed more broadly to embrace not only the political process and political institutions but also the social structure itself. It came to imply the elimination of social privilege, the guarantee of economic equality of opportunity, and a fairer distribution of wealth. "True democracy," wrote Hasegawa Nyozekan in 1919, meant increasing the equality of opportunity not only politically but socially and economically as well; and Ōyama Ikuo argued that the purpose of "true democracy" was to construct a society in which all members could "live like human beings" and in which there was an "increase in opportunities for each individual to act in a positive way politically, socially, and economically." Now everything was game for democratization, even education and the arts.[55]

It was clear as the supporters of *minponshugi* began to debate the meaning of "true democracy" that lines of fracture were appearing in their ranks. In 1919, Fukuda Tokuzō, who joined with Yoshino Sakuzō to found the Reimeikai, distinguished between "capitalist political democracy" (*shihonteki seiji minshushugi*) and "social democracy" (*shakai minshushugi*), by which he really meant "socialist democracy." Neither, he said, represented "true democracy," as they favored the interests of one segment of society over another. The holistic conception of democracy central to the *minponshugi* argument was denied by a class-based definition of democracy.[56] Yoshino Sakuzō agreed with Fukuda that he opposed "social democracy" if that meant siding solely with the position of the workers' interests. The notion of a society divided against itself was repellent to democratic liberals of his stripe, and so was the political violence associated with socialist revolution. A true democrat could never become an "extremist," said Yoshino, because he saw the democratic political process not as a means to an end but as valuable in itself. One wing of the democratic movement was there-

54 The standard treatment of the Yūaikai in English is by Stephen S. Large, *The Rise of Labor in Japan: The Yūaikai, 1912–1919* (Tokyo: Sophia University Press, 1972).
55 Ōta, *Taishō*, vol. 2, pp. 347–50, 475–82.   56 Ōta, *Taishō*, vol. 2, pp. 460–75.

fore turning its face firmly against any theory of class conflict or social conflict.

Curiously, however, Yoshino did not object to a socialist program of reform as long as it could be achieved through the constitutional process. Socialism stood for social policy. "A democrat [*minponshugisha*] does not necessarily have to be a socialist," he wrote in 1919, "but there is nothing to prevent him from being a socialist."[57] While continuing to advocate political reform – universal manhood suffrage, an end to the political autonomy of the military, abolition of the Privy Council, reform of the House of Peers, and so forth – Yoshino supported the legalization of labor union activities and social welfare policy after 1918. In short, Yoshino and other moderates like Fukuda, Abe Isoo, and Nagai Ryūtarō adopted a nondoctrinaire, non-Marxist kind of social democracy or social meliorism that linked democratic political reform to social welfare policy. Significantly, many of them were eventually involved in the organization of the moderate right wing of the "proletarian party movement" in the mid-1920s.

But there were other advocates of *minponshugi* who wanted to move beyond political democratization to more sweeping and radical schemes of social reorganization. "Reconstruction" (*kaizō*) or "liberation" (*kaihō*) became their new catchwords. In 1919, a spate of new journals appeared, focusing on labor problems, social problems, social reform, and socialism, many of them started by former advocates of *minponshugi*. In January, Kawakami Hajime began publication of *Shakai mondai kenkyū* (Studies in social problems), and Hasegawa Nyozekan and Ōyama Ikuo founded *Warera* (We ourselves); in April, *Kaizō* (Reconstruction), a new general interest magazine appeared, and in June, so did *Kaihō* (Liberation). Some former liberals, most notably Kawakami Hajime, declared themselves Marxists, but others, like Ōyama Ikuo, were moving toward a vaguer (and perhaps romantic) identification with the working classes. And still others, like Hasegawa Nyozekan, were drawn to new models of social and political organization emerging in the West. Articles began to appear on alternative forms of political representation, including guild socialism or the Soviet system, in which economic interests rather than territorial interests were represented. The era when parliamentarism could be equated with democracy was at an end, and the issue had become not whether the

---

57 Yoshino Sakuzō, "Minponshugi, shakaishugi, kagekishugi," *Chūō kōron*, June 1919.

"people" were represented in the political process but whether the emerging "fourth estate" (*daiyon kaikyū*) (that is, the working-class proletariat) was.[58]

The shift toward a more radical political position sprang from growing doubt about whether political democratization could guarantee social harmony and national unity, or indeed whether it was anything more than a political sham. The issue had been raised by Yamakawa Hitoshi, one of the younger members of the Meiji socialist movement, who wrote a series of penetrating critiques of both Yoshino and Ōyama. He dismissed Yoshino's distinction between *minshushugi* and *minponshugi* as a sophistry equivalent to saying that pork consisted of "two unrelated concepts – meat and fat."[59] (Perhaps, he added, Yoshino thought that fat was not suited to weak Japanese stomachs and so denied that it was pork.) But more to the point, in attacking Ōyama, Yamakawa denied the possibility that the state or the representative process could create social unity. Far from being neutral, states, governments, and parliaments were the instruments by which one class dominated others to its own material advantage. What dominated men was not their "associative consciousness" but their material interests. The usual state of all societies was not unity but conflict and the collision of material class interests. Only in primitive societies, in which people shared their goods and made decisions in common, was conflict absent – and only in primitive societies could one find democracy. Viewed through Yamakawa's Marxist perspective, history was not the history of liberty, nor did it find its culmination in the rise of parliamentary democracy. Rather, it was the history of the rise and fall of classes struggling for domination.

The impact of this conflictual view of history and social dynamics can perhaps best be seen in the defection of Ōyama Ikuo from his earlier defense of *minponshugi*. After he and Hasegawa Nyozekan founded their journal *Warera*, he spoke less and less of "class harmony," a national "sense of common interest," or "national unity." As the struggle between labor and capital seemed to intensify in 1920–1, Ōyama began to doubt that the intellectual could be a neutral or disinterested observer of the conflict, and eventually he concluded that the intelligentsia had to stand with the workers against their exploiters. Gradually, he shed his commitment to a theory of democratic nationalism as well; he denied the possibility of

58 Ōta, *Taishō*, vol. 2, *passim*.   59 Ōta, *Taishō*, vol. 2, pp. 20–8.

reconciliation between labor and capital; he branded constitutional government in Japan as "crippled"; he attacked the social organization as flawed and unfair, giving all the advantages to the capitalists and none to the workers; and he expressed doubts about how representative the Diet was and whether the existing system of representation was effective at all.

With the publication in 1923 of his major theoretical work *Seiji no shakaiteki kiso* (The social foundation of politics), the transition was complete.[60] Ōyama now looked at political phenomena as the expression of a power struggle among social groups. He argued that human social life was dominated by interest relationships, especially economic interests, and that "the motor of social evolution" and the "origin of political and social inequality" lay in the struggle among social groups (including classes) that regarded all other social groups as enemies and ruthlessly pursued their own interests. The state therefore was not a neutral instrument for the common good but a means of domination by the triumphant group or class. Concepts like "people" (*kokumin*), "public interest" (*kōri kōeki*), "national morality" (*kokka dōtoku*), and "national spirit" (*kokumin seishin*), which had been so much a part of Ōyama's analytical vocabulary in the 1910s, he now regarded as inventions of the dominant bourgeoisie to deflect resistance by the working class.

In adopting a theory of conflict to explain politics, Ōyama saw himself as trading a sentimental or idealistic position for one that was "empirical" and "scientific." As Kawai Eijirō later pointed out, one of the weaknesses of Taishō liberalism was its lack of an explicit philosophical or theoretical base. The *minponshugi* arguments for democratization did not grow out of a comprehensive understanding of how societies were organized, nor did it link political analysis to an understanding of basic human drives. Instead, it relied on an implicit optimistic faith in the inevitability of progress, in the triumph of morality over interest, and in the possibility of social harmony. Even the "Whig view" of history crumbled when it was discovered that there was a history of human oppression as well as a history of human liberty. The theoretical poverty of democratic liberalism left it vulnerable to competition from "social science" theories of the sort that Ōyama embraced, but even more so from the social and historical theories of Marxism that took on new life in the 1920s.

60 The text may be found in *Ōyama Ikuo zenshū* (Tokyo: Chūō kōronsha, 1947), vol. 1.

THE REVIVAL OF SOCIALISM

The "winter years" of socialism ended when the main survivors of the radical wing of Meiji socialism – Yamakawa Hitoshi, Ōsugi Sakae, Arahata Kanson, and others – broke their long silence on political and social issues. What emboldened them in part was the Russian Revolution of 1917. The mere news of the overthrow of the despotic czarist regime, Yamakawa often observed, had a profound effect on the radical socialists and anarchists. In May 1917, a resolution prepared by Yamakawa and Takabatake Motoyuki, and approved by thirty other socialists, expressed hope that the Russian Social Democrats would take the lead in ending the European war and launch an international struggle of workers against capitalism in all belligerent nations. Yamakawa and Takabatake enthusiastically greeted the seizure of power by the Bolsheviks in October as well. Aleksandr Kerensky's overthrow was right and proper, argued Takabatake, as he had attempted to use the soviets of workers and soldiers as a springboard to conciliation with the "gentlemen's gang." The Bolshevik victory confirmed their belief in the efficacy of direct action. The success of the Russian Revolution was assured, said Yamakawa, when Lenin and his proletarian followers refused to come to the aid of Kerensky's bourgeois democracy, and just as certainly the failure of the German revolution was assured by the German proletariat's support of bourgeois state capitalism.[61]

Yamakawa's theoretical analysis of the Bolshevik revolution – which he described as a "socialist revolution," in contrast with the "bourgeois revolution" in France – would probably have been acceptable to the Bolsheviks themselves. It also set the terms for a future analysis of the political status of the Japanese bourgeoisie and the revolutionary potential of the Japanese masses. "Russia," said Yamakawa,

had begun its second revolution. Its first was a dual revolution, both a political revolution by the new bourgeoisie against the despotic

---

61 Ōsawa Masamichi, *Ōsugi Sakae kenkyū* (Tokyo: Dōseishi, 1968), pp. 274–7; Koyama Hirotake and Koyama Hitoshi, "Taishō shakaishugi no shisōteki bunka," *Shisō* 466 (April 1966): 121; George Beckmann and Okubo Genji, *The Japanese Communist Party, 1922–1945* (Stanford, Calif.: Stanford University Press, 1969), pp. 15–16; Mitani, *Taishō demokurashiiron*, pp. 93–100; Kishimoto and Koyama, *Nihon no hikyōsantō*, pp. 80–1; Watanabe Haruo, *Nihon marukusushugi undō no reimei* (Tokyo: Aoki shoten, 1957), pp. 42–3, 46, 143–9, 186–7; Thomas A. Stanley, *Ōsugi Sakae: Anarchist in Taishō Japan* (Cambridge, Mass.: Harvard University Press, 1982), pp. 128–9; Watanabe Toru, "Nihon no marukusushugi undō ron," in *Kōza marukusushugi*, vol. 12: *Nihon* (Tokyo: Nihon hyōronsha, 1974), pp. 187–92.

bureaucratic state and a social revolution by the working masses against capitalism. These two revolutionary forces became one for the purpose of overthrowing the despotic state.... Up to that stage the Russian Revolution followed the course set by the great French Revolution. The divergence comes in the fate of the mass armies of each revolution. In the French case, the masses were conquered by the bourgeois forces, while in Russia, although the bourgeois political revolution was accomplished in the same manner, the masses were equipped, both intellectually and in matters of organization, to push toward socialist revolution.[62]

Few Japanese socialists, however, including Yamakawa, had heard of Lenin before, and none showed any understanding of Leninist theory. (In this, the Japanese were little different from the Europeans, as it was not until 1921 that translations of Lenin's work revealed that he had a systematic theory.) In 1917, Sakai Toshihiko described Lenin as an "anarchist." At first, Yamakawa called him a "syndicalist" who used "direct action" to make a revolution, and in 1921 he characterized him as an "orthodox Marxist," to be contrasted with a figure like Karl Kautsky, the German social democratic leader, who had turned from revolutionary Marxism to bourgeois liberalism. Only gradually, as more and more of Lenin's work made its way into Japanese, were the implications of his ideas fully understood. For the time being, he was mainly admired as a revolutionary hero who succeeded in establishing a radical popular government in Russia.[63]

The veterans of Meiji socialism were also heartened by new stirrings of unrest among the people. Although the *minponshugi* liberals had viewed the rice riots with apprehension, the socialists saw them entirely in positive terms, as evidence of a growing class consciousness among the people. The socialists were also pleased by the growing militance of the labor movement. In 1919, at its national convention, the Yūaikai adopted a new name – the Greater Japan Federation of Labor and Friendly Association (Dai Nihon rōdō sōdōmei yūaikai) – and promulgated a new and more militant program that included demands for the legalization of trade unions, the establishment of a minimum wage, the passage of universal manhood suffrage, an eight-hour workday and a six-day workweek. During the war years, the Yūaikai

62 Watanabe, *Nihon marukusushugi undō no reimei*, pp. 47–8.
63 Watanabe, "Nihon no marukusushugi undō ron," pp. 43–4, 175–86; Kishimoto and Koyama, *Nihon no hikyōsantō*, pp. 66, 73–5, 85; Beckmann and Okubo, *The Japanese Communist Party*, p. 13; Koyama and Koyama, "Taishō shakaishugi no shisōteki bunka," p. 121.

had concentrated on resolving labor conflicts, but the Japan Federation of Labor took to the streets, organizing rallies to oppose the Peace Police Law and to support the universal manhood suffrage movement.[64]

On May 1, 1919, Sakai Toshihiko's journal *Shin shakai* publicly announced that it would fly the "flag of Marxism." Although Sakai and Yamakawa, who had joined his staff, announced that they would eschew politics for the moment, it was clear that they thought the country was on the verge of massive change. In the fall of 1919, Sakai wrote, "There is a strong sense that the end of the year marks the end of an age. The new year will be upon us soon. . . . I have a sense that we will for the first time step into a world of our own." A "socialist craze" seemed to be sweeping the country.[65]

The main participants in this "craze" were not only erstwhile liberals like Ōyama Ikuo and Kawakami Hajime, who rejected a commitment to parliamentary (that is, bourgeois) democracy for more radical social and political critiques, but also a new generation of university students and recent graduates who ultimately were to dominate the political and theoretical leadership of both the Communist and the non-Communist Marxist left in the 1920s. Students, of course, had been involved in the Meiji socialist movement; they probably accounted for a majority of the ten thousand subscribers to the *Heimin shinbun* and provided the readership for other socialist periodicals as well. But during the late Meiji period, few students joined in the socialist activities or agitation for social reform. They were, in the phrase of the political scientist Maruyama Masao, "merely admirers of a liberty which involved neither self-control nor responsibility." In his memoirs, Yamakawa disparaged many of the student followers of Meiji socialism as "rucks, misanthropic cynics, and malcontents – in short, those who had dropped behind in the competition of capitalist society." By contrast, young men like Yamakawa, Arahata, and Ōsugi who became active in the movement as journalists or agitators did not graduate from college or university but deliberately chose lives of moral and political commitment

64 Beckmann and Okubo, *The Japanese Communist Party*, pp. 22–3, 102; Watanabe, "Nihon no marukusushugi undō ron," p. 152.

65 Watanabe, "Nihon no marukusushugi undō ron," pp. 44–5, 149–50; Beckmann and Okubo, *The Japanese Communist Party*, p. 12; Arahata Kanson, "*Kindai shisō to Shinshakai*," *Shisō* 460 (October 1962): 115–25; Koyama and Koyama, "Taishō shakaishugi no shisōteki bunka," p. 119.

instead of clambering up the conventional educational ladder of success.[66]

The students who became radicalized in the 1920s and 1930s, however, were "exemplary" students, confident of promising careers in academia, business, or the bureaucracy if they wanted them. Students who joined leftist movements, a Ministry of Education report observed, were "modest," "decent," "sober," and "diligent" young men. Investigations of the family backgrounds and personalities of arrested leftist students showed that 65.9 percent of those questioned fell into these categories and were classified as "good"; only 4.6 percent were typified as "hypochondriacal," "weakwilled," or "unrestrained" and classified as "bad." A report published by the ministry in 1933 refuted the prevailing assumption that only people who were unhealthy could become susceptible to "dangerous thoughts." "[T]he greatest number of leftist students under investigation," the report lamented, "were modest and sound in character."[67]

Not only did "exemplary" higher school and university graduates enter left-wing movements, but a number who became Marxist theoreticians returned to their alma maters as professors. Fukumoto Kazuo, Miki Kiyoshi, Kushida Tamizō, Sano Manabu, Hattori Shisō, and Hani Gorō became leading academic economists, philosophers, historians, and critics. As members of the academic establishment, they gave Marxism social cachet, moral respectability, and intellectual influence. Members of this intellectually accomplished group, many of whom received government grants for postgraduate study in Europe, transformed the relatively simple and often vulgar Marxism of the Meiji socialists, who had virtually ignored the dialectical dynamics of social change, into sophisticated and sometimes antagonistic theories of political action and social revolution.

What the new generation of student converts to the left shared with the older generation of socialists, to whom they first turned for leadership, was a belief that capitalism and the bourgeois state were on the brink of collapse. The "world trend" was toward social and

66   Matsuzawa Hiroaki, *Nihon shakaishugi no shisō* (Tokyo: Chikuma shobō, 1973), pp. 65–7; Maruyama Masao, "Patterns of Individuation and the Case of Japan: A Conceptual Scheme," in Marius Jansen, ed., *Changing Japanese Attitudes Toward Modernization* (Princeton, N.J.: Princeton University Press, 1965), pp. 489–531, pages cited are 508–9, 514.
67   Maruyama, "Patterns," pp. 520–1.

political liberation, and the final stage of capitalism was well on the way. But the anarchist and Marxist leaders and their student followers did not think that revolution would drop like a ripe plum from a tree. The accomplishment of a Japanese social and political revolution lay in the hands of a self-conscious, class-conscious, and well-organized proletariat. Some older socialists who had been associated with the proparliamentary wing of the Meiji movement – Sakai Toshihiko, for example – at first cooperated with the liberal intellectuals in the organization of the universal suffrage movement, but by 1921 even Sakai had quit the movement and criticized it as "foolish." The more radical Marxists and anarchosyndicalists argued from the beginning that only through workers and their unions, not through Diet politics, universal suffrage, or even a socialist party, could they bring down the capitalist state.[68]

Undoubtedly, faith in the revolutionary potential of the Japanese workers and the Japanese labor movement was encouraged by the fact that activists in the Japan Federation of Labor in the spring of 1920 began to advocate the tactics of "direct action," opposing the universal suffrage movement and parliamentary tactics. The failure of a universal manhood suffrage bill to pass the Seiyūkai-controlled Diet in 1919 and 1920 probably deepened their disillusionment with parliamentary politics. Even Suzuki Bunji, who had begun his career as a moderate Christian social meliorist, called for the "thorough reform of present society" and described the Japanese industrial system as "violent and despotic." "We must first topple this despot," he said. "The inevitable consequence of the awakening of the workers will be the making of a new industrial system and organization."[69]

The awakening of the Japanese working class became the most significant and immediate project of the radical left. Only the proletariat, the Marxists and anarchosyndicalists argued, could be the active subject of a socialist revolution, and only the liberation of the working class could lead to the emancipation of the whole society. In contrast with their Meiji predecessors, the new generation of leftists also insisted that the workers' class consciousness could never be taken for granted; it had to be cultivated. In the imagination of both radical ideologists and student activists, the worker became simultaneously the potential hero of liberation as well as the object of

---

68 Watanabe, "Nihon no marukusushugi undō ron," pp. 154–5, 168–70.
69 Ibid., pp. 149–50, 70. Ōsawa, *Ōsugi Sakae kenkyū*, p. 184.

tutelage, a child whose mind and will had to be nurtured and guided.[70]

Even though Meiji socialists had condemned the horrendous conditions under which workers labored and lived, few had become involved in working-class movements, and most had been indifferent to the workers' potential as conscious revolutionaries. At best, as in the writings of Kōtoku, the workers were conceived of as a mass whose participation in a general strike might trigger revolution. In part, this attitude of the Meiji socialists resulted from the weakness of the labor movement and the legal restrictions on unionization, but as Yamakawa later pointed out, it also derived from the socialists' obsession with pure theory. By contrast, in the 1920s, in order to capture worker support for their own movements, radical leaders and their student followers brought their theories and theoretical conflicts directly to the workers themselves, taking part in their organizations and their debates over tactics.

ŌSUGI SAKAE AND ANARCHOSYNDICALISM

One of the most attractive and influential radical leaders in the early 1920s was Ōsugi Sakae, a former disciple of Kōtoku and the main theorist of the anarchosyndicalist position. What made him so appealing to young university students and graduates is clear from his writings, which overflow with feelings of boredom, oppression, and idealism that fostered a diffuse rebelliousness and a sense of affinity with the workers. But above all, Ōsugi appealed to the young because of his conception of revolution as personal emancipation. "It is only when we have developed a personal philosophy," he wrote in 1917, "that we become free. . . . No matter what happens then, we cannot become slaves."[71]

Students and graduates vividly expressed the mix of sentiments and impulses that attracted them into later agitation. At once altruistic and self-absorbed, they identified their own search for autonomy and their desire for relief from feelings of "suffocation" (ikizumari) with the emancipation of the workers. As one wrote, commitment to the cause of the workers allowed them to break the fetters of "trivial knowledge . . . formality and convention." They spoke of their desire to express "true feelings"; they sought "a life that would be lived sincerely"; they wanted to fulfill themselves; and

---

70 Ōsawa, Ōsugi Sakae kenkyū, pp. 183–5.
71 Arahata, "Kindai shisō to Shinshakai," pp. 117–19; Ōsawa, Ōsugi Sakae kenkyū, p. 148.

they dreamed of "an overflowing self" (*jiga no jūitsu*). Only as rebels and only as servants of "the multitude in their own country," wrote one, could they live life sincerely. At times, this relationship with workers was described as a romance, a near physical infatuation, even a self-seduction. "I search for a lover," Kataoka Takeo wrote in the journal *Demokurashi* in 1919. "The laborer is my lover. I cannot wait until that pale face becomes cheerful. To bring a smile is the first step of love." Identification with the worker and his cause allowed young members of the elite to transcend themselves by becoming a "vanguard."[72]

Students and graduates in the early 1920s often wrote that the "discovery of social problems" made them rebels, even though no single idea or clear ideology inspired their actions. As Asō Hisashi (1891–1940) wrote, students felt they "knew the trend of the times." Their vocabulary was eclectic, neither specifically anarchosyndicalist nor Marxist. "To the people," the slogan used to exhort their fellows to join the worker's cause, had been borrowed from the nineteenth-century Russian populist cry, *v narodni*, but the Russian *narodniki* (populists) believed that a postrevolutionary social order would be constructed on the basis of the village community, an idea derided by Marxists and never a part of the Leninist canon. Although some graduates described themselves as "heralds" of revolution, as Asō suggested, they sought "to clothe the workers in all the books that they themselves had read." They would give workers "freedom (*jiyū*), justice (*seigi*), humanism, socialism, anarchism, revolution, syndicalism, and the IWW (Industrial Workers of the World)."[73]

The workers, however, were not attracted to the students by socialism or any other ideology but by their anarchistic attitude. What workers understood about students, one labor activist wrote, was "that they [students] burned with the same spirit. [To them also] capitalism was an unpardonable system." In a memoir written decades later, one worker recalled: "Ideas of Marxism, syndicalism, labor unionism all entered my head at one time. I didn't understand the distinctions very well."[74] But one simple thought was quite clear: "If workers organize, if we stop the factory smoke, we come into our own world. When we stop the smoke of the chimney, it will chasten the powerful. This would be the means of correcting the social evil."[75] Workers shared with students a feeling that resistance had to

72 Matsuzawa Hiroaki, *Nihon shakaishugi*, pp. 65–9, 156.
73 Ibid., pp. 62–3, 148–52, 156–9.   74 Ibid., pp. 158–9.   75 Ibid., pp. 160–1.

be total. As one worker wrote, "we would prefer an honorable defeat, even a miserable defeat . . . [never] cooperation or moderation." And still another said: "We will lose our families . . . we will lose human pleasure. We will live only by a revolutionary resistance toward capitalism." It was these ideals that brought students and workers to Ōsugi Sakae and anarchosyndicalism.[76]

It was inevitable that Ōsugi and other anarchosyndicalists would turn against Bolshevik policies in Russia, reject the suppositions of Marxist-Leninists, and become bitter antagonists of all Marxists in the Japanese social and labor movements. Ōsugi initially had hailed the coming of the Russian Revolution because he believed it had been achieved by "direct action," in which the masses had risen spontaneously and driven out Kerensky's bourgeois regime. In Japan, as elsewhere in the world, anarchosyndicalists found gratifying this image of the revolution. They had long argued that revolution could be accomplished by a spontaneous uprising of all of the oppressed classes, which, in the course of widespread insurrection, would topple the state and replace it by some sort of autonomous community. In the early 1920s, the anarchosyndicalist strategists believed that the overthrow of capitalism could be accomplished by purely industrial organization and struggle, and they rejected any kind of political activity or participation in bourgeois institutions. At the inaugural convention of the Japan Federation of Labor in 1919, for example, anarchosyndicalist militants objected to the organization's support for universal suffrage, and they rejected all proposals that implied the compatibility of unions with the imperial values of capitalism. And in a debate over direct action (*chokusetsu kōdō*) versus parliamentarianism at a 1920 meeting of the federation, the cry of a Kyoto anarchist delegate, "We reject the Diet," was greeted with applause from anarchists at the convention. If led by a militant rank and file, the anarchosyndicalists believed, the labor union alone could become the instrument of the proletariat in its struggle against the bourgeoisie and its state.

The anarchosyndicalists also refused to subordinate the economic struggle of the proletariat to the coming revolution. Characteristically then, labor unions led by anarchosyndicalists favored confrontation rather than conciliation, preferring to sabotage a factory rather than to seek a contract. As one militant Japanese anarchosyndicalist put it, "We do not say unions are useless. But they are effective only

76 Ibid., p. 146, n. 43, 93, 167.

in building, not in the work of destruction – destruction must come before building." In the brief period from 1920 to 1923, when the anarchosyndicalists commanded a prominent position in the labor movement, they tried to incite the workers to carry out massive strikes that would paralyze the entire economy and to incite the workers' hostility against the existing order. Tokyo celluloid workers, watchmakers, and printers and Yawata steel workers, influenced by anarchosyndicalist organizers and other direct-action militants, carried out violent strikes, smashed machines, and sabotaged workplaces. Inspired by the anarchosyndicalists, workers in 1920 at the Fuji Gas Spinning Company resolved "even to die" for the cause.[77]

By late 1922, anarchosyndicalist influence in the union movement had begun to weaken. Because of their insistence on spontaneity rather than organization and coordination, their demand for individual union autonomy rather than the acceptance of the federation's centralized authority, and their failure to achieve much by direct confrontation, the anarchosyndicalists lost influence to reformists and Communists. The news that the Soviet Union had begun to persecute anarchists such as Emma Goldman and to disregard the will of local soviets while centralizing all power in the party and central committee impelled Ōsugi to announce his disgust with Bolshevism and to break off all contact with Japanese Marxist-Leninists. For Ōsugi, the establishment of the New Economic Plan, or NEP (which he believed was little more than a disguised attempt to establish state capitalism), and the reinstitution of national industrial discipline represented the end of the revolutionary era in Russia.[78]

Anarchosyndicalists had a vision of a secular millennium; they sought a future in which workers autonomously united to govern themselves in small communities. Workers needed neither a party nor an ideology, the French anarchosyndicalist George Sorel had argued; it fact, they should reject both as part of the bourgeois game in which workers were subject to the tyranny of bourgeois rule. For Ōsugi, the encouragement of worker resistance, the necessity of

77 Stephen S. Large, *Organized Workers and Socialist Politics in Interwar Japan* (Cambridge, England: Cambridge University Press, 1981), chaps. 1, 2; Ōsawa, *Ōsugi Sakae kenkyū*, pp. 263–9, 277–8, 311–12; Watanabe, "Nihon no marukusushugi undō ron," pp. 175–92, 206–16.

78 Large, *Organized Workers*; Ōsawa, *Ōsugi Sakae kenkyū*, p. 317; Watanabe, "Nihon no marukusushugi undō ron," p. 192.

unceasing conflict, and the call for disorder had the function of not merely disrupting contemporary society but of also liberating the workers (and those who sought to aid them) from history and hierarchy. Men must begin anew, with a "clean slate" (*hakushi*), Ōsugi believed. But "clean slatism" did not imply a belief in the natural spontaneity of the masses: Self-emancipation, the self-recovery of the masses, demanded an effort and a transformation of the consciousness of the workers by the workers themselves.[79]

In an essay entitled *Chitsujo binran* (The breakdown of law and order), Ōsugi wrote that the majority, bound by the thought and actions of their rulers, had been sacrificed to the "rules" of the few. By "disorder," a breakdown of law and order that he equated with "rebellion," workers could overcome "old values." Without rebellion, the individual could not attain "true existence" (*shin no sei*). Thus the breakdown of rules – in effect, the alienation of the workers from their past – became the only means by which the potential of both the masses and the individual could be achieved. "Living" in the modern world, for Ōsugi, meant "rebelling." Life without rebellion was not life but nonlife, death itself.[80]

Ōsugi exemplified in his life and thought the full sum of militant student ambivalence and aspiration. He doubted his ability to lead the workers because he believed he was crippled by his bourgeois or even petty bourgeois attitudes. Nonetheless, he offered the workers his leadership and the gift of his ideas, advising them that only by a life of constant rebellion could they overcome the tyranny of contemporary society. He summoned intellectuals to the cause of the workers, at times describing them as something like a vanguard. However, he questioned their revolutionary trustworthiness, identifying them as members of the bourgeoisie and hence no better than "passing friends among the enemy" (*teki no naka no yūjin*). But he also suggested that intellectuals could be useful to themselves and to the workers if they understood the workings of modern society, subsumed themselves to "become one" (*ittaika*) with the workers, and used the agency of workers to "practice rebellion."[81]

Even more consistently than his anarchosyndicalist predecessor Kōtoku, Ōsugi lived a life of dramatic resistance. He had a flair for confrontation. At one time or another, he repudiated all the conven-

79 For Sorel, see Leszek Kolakowski, *Main Currents of Marxism*, vol. 2: *The Golden Age* (New York: Oxford University Press, 1978), p. 163; Ōsawa, *Ōsugi Sakae kenkyū*, pp. 171, 259.
80 Ōsawa, *Ōsugi Sakae kenkyū*, pp. 171–2, 184.
81 Stanley, *Ōsugi Sakae*, pp. 115–19; Ōsawa, *Ōsugi Sakae kenkyū*, pp. 115–19, 130, 183–4, 260; Mitani, *Taishō demokurashiiron*, p. 85.

tions of his society, including the orthodoxies of his radical allies as well as those of his opponents. Although he liked the spirit of democracy, he hated what "the legal and political scientists call democracy and humanism." "Socialism," too, "I hate," he said, finding that orthodox socialism put too much emphasis on material determinism in the evolution of society and not enough on individual freedom. It is only a part of the truth, he asserted in criticism of socialism, that "new economics creates a new morality." No creed, no ism, no theory seemed wholly satisfactory. "For some reason," he wrote in February 1918, "I hate anarchism a bit."[82]

Underlying the ambivalence expressed in all of Ōsugi's arguments and attitudes was a belief, somewhat like that of his hero Nietzsche, that no fact was independent of interpretation and no vision of reality untainted by prejudice and perspective. Hence life became at its best a heroic act of interpretation in which the individual and the masses could transcend their society. Intellectuals, for example, had throughout history been thoroughly implicated in the ideological defense "of the ruling class and the deception of the oppressed classes." But if intellectuals abandoned their hegemonic role, desisted from imposing their ideology on the workers (an attitude, Ōsugi observed, prevalent among even socialist intellectuals), and resolved to be one "with the essence of the labor movement," they could overcome their class attitudes. In fact, Ōsugi's concern with individual freedom and his recommendation that individuals abandon their egos in order to find themselves (*jibun o torimodosu tame ni, jiga o kidatsu suru*) place him among the ranks of radical libertarians and in clear opposition to the Marxist socialists.[83]

Not surprisingly, then, in an essay published in 1919, Ōsugi quoted from Nietzsche to the effect that the "perfection of individuality" is the ideal, and even if only a vision, it is one with the direction of life. "The essence of life," he wrote, "is always to find a way out of an impasse." As an anarchosyndicalist, Ōsugi turned this vision of self-transcendence outward toward society and sought social revolution. He rejected Marxism (as he also questioned nineteenth-century notions of rationalism and mechanical inevitability) not only because of its emphasis on necessity but also because he found its proposition that "new economics creates a new morality" only a part of the truth. A new morality, he insisted, must be created within the old order so

82   Stanley, *Osugi Sakae*: Ōsawa, *Ōsugi Sakae kenkyū*, pp. 117–18, 174.
83   Ōsawa, *Ōsugi Sakae kenkyū*, pp. 168, 183.

that it can become the basis of the new. Ōsugi thus believed that all men, not merely one special being, had the will to power of the "superman" (chōjin). Workers could therefore transcend their society collectively and autonomously; alienated from the present and their consciousness transformed, they could become the pace-setters of the future. And like the workers, the alienated radical student activists could share in the achievement of a new world.[84]

YAMAKAWA HITOSHI AND THE
"CHANGE IN DIRECTION"

The murder of Ōsugi by a military police captain in September 1923 robbed the anarchosyndicalist movement of its only charismatic leader. The movement, however, had been devastated a year earlier when the Comintern became more interested in Japan and when Japanese leftists acquired a better understanding of Leninist theories of revolution. Some leftist factions began to call themselves Bolshe-viks, and many Marxists acquired a new understanding of Lenin's ideas about the dictatorship of the proletariat and the proper role of a socialist or communist party vis-à-vis the masses. With the forma-tion of the secret Japanese Communist Party in July 1922, these issues became the focal point of controversy between the Marxists and the anarchosyndicalists in the labor movement.

At the 1922 annual meeting of the Japan Federation of Labor, an alliance of Communists and labor reformers had engineered the adoption of a resolution favoring a highly centralized or-ganization based on national industrial unions. Rejecting the anarchosyndicalist principles of union decentralization, autonomy, and self-government, in which any union had the right to join or withdraw from any association at any time, the convention called for political as well as standard union economic tactics – all anathema to Ōsugi. Despite Ōsugi's growing distaste for the Soviet Union, the convention also passed a resolution supporting the communist re-gime in Soviet Russia.[85]

Ōsugi had not only been defeated by Japanese Bolsheviks, but his longtime ally, Yamakawa Hitoshi, emerged as the ideological leader of the Bolshevik faction and the hero of the meeting. Yamakawa's

84 Ibid., pp. 163–6.
85 See Large, Organized Workers, chaps. 1, 2; Beckmann and Okubo, The Japanese Commu-nist Party, pp. 46–47; Ōsawa, Ōsugi Sakae kenkyū, pp. 267–9; Watanabe, "Nihon no marukusushugi undō ron," pp. 174–5, 205–11, 229–30; Matsuzawa, Nihon, pp. 101–2.

July–August 1922 essay, "A Change in Course for the Proletarian Movement" (Musan kaikyū undō no hōkō tenkan), provided the slogan for the conference, "into the Masses" (*taishū no naka e*); and his denunciation of the anarchosyndicalist "idealization of revolution" (*kannenteki kakumei*) received the approbation of Communists and labor reformers alike. Present at the convention as an auditor, as was Yamakawa, Ōsugi bitterly described the whole of the "Bolshevik gang" – Yamakawa, Sakai, and Arahata – as a "bunch of crooks."[86]

Just as the Bolshevik-Reformist defeat of the anarchosyndicalists represents a decisive shift in the prevailing tactics and dominant ideologies of the labor movement, Yamakawa's essay marks a critical juncture in the intellectual history of Japanese radicalism and particularly its theories of revolution. Rejecting the creed of millenarianism, which had dominated the thought of radicals since Kōtoku, Yamakawa also expressed his objections to the radicals' misdirected expressions of moral indignation and criticized the tactical stupidity of radical spontaneity. "Ten or twenty enthusiasts," he wrote,

get together, dream about the next day of revolution and make big talk. . . . At best they would satisfy their "rebellious spirit" by taking "revolutionary action" against a policeman and spending a night under police detention. Although they reject the capitalist system, they actually do not lay a finger upon it.[87]

Yamakawa described the Japanese proletarian movement as having two aspects, a socialist movement and a labor movement. He castigated the former, including himself, for being overly concerned with the clarification of principles and the purification of ideology. As a result, socialists had isolated themselves from the proletariat as a whole, "[drawing] apart from the ordinary union members around them and even more so from the masses of the working class." They thus failed in their duty to raise the masses toward a maximum standard of class consciousness, instead allowing them to fall under the spiritual influence of the capitalists. Although Yamakawa praised the union movement, he found it lamentable that the advanced members, the organized workers, found themselves "separated from

86 Kishimoto and Koyama, *Nihon hikyōsantō*, pp. 95, 143–7. For quotation from Ōsugi, see Stanley, *Ōsugi Sakae*, p. 140. For Yamakawa's essay discussed in the next paragraphs, see Yamakawa Hitoshi, "Musan kaikyū undō no hōko tenkan," in *Yamakawa Hitoshi zenshū*, vol. 4, ed. Yamakawa Kikue and Yamakawa Shinsaku (Tokyo: Keisō shobō, 1967), pp. 336–45.
87 Beckmann and Okubo, *The Japanese Communist Party*, p. 51.

the ordinary worker." And finally, he criticized both for their "passive attitude" toward bourgeois government. Workers little realized, he wrote, that victories won on the economic front can be jeopardized by politics.

On any front where capitalism expresses authority and control, we must move on . . . to an attitude of positive struggle. The political front is the place where the authority and control of the bourgeoisie find their most naked and direct expression. . . . Simply to reject the existing system of bourgeois politics ideologically cannot bring the slightest injury to it.[88]

"Change of Course" offered a tactical solution to both the isolation of the vanguard from the masses and the political passivity and fecklessness of both. Ultimately, Yamakawa explained, "Our goal is the destruction of capitalism. . . . Any reform short of that can never liberate us." But if the mass of workers do not demand the abolition of capitalism and instead "demand the improvement of their immediate daily life, our present movement must be based on this popular demand." Even though the "movement must become more practical" in order to bring vanguard and mass together through their mutual struggle, he hoped that the vanguard could raise the demands of the workers and persuade them to expand their goals. "Change of Course" did not signal, Yamakawa insisted, "a fall from the principle of revolution to reformism" but, rather, an accommodation to worker demands in order to build a "concrete" movement for the achievement of the final goal. The vanguard must therefore take its ideology to the masses, retain its revolutionary consciousness, and, he insisted, never dissolve within the masses. Thus the second charge of the essay, "advance toward a political struggle," urged upon the vanguard the need to lead the proletariat toward recognizing that their call for "rights of livelihood" and for the settlement of the unemployment problem were demands aimed at the state. Hence the practical economic struggle could not be separated from the political one. Although in this essay Yamakawa did not discuss political parties or indicate a change in his attitude toward universal suffrage, he urged upon the proletarian movement a new sort of political action. "If the proletariat truly rejects bourgeois politics, it must not be simply passive. . . . It must put up proletarian politics against bourgeois politics."[89]

Quite clearly, then, Yamakawa had repudiated both his own past

88 Ibid., p. 52.   89 Ibid., pp. 46–7.

position (and Ōsugi's continuing position) that standard union economic demands were politically ineffectual. Instead, he offered a
near Leninist interpretation of the indispensable role of the vanguard
in creating a revolutionary and social democratic consciousness
among the proletariat. But in Yamakawa's discussions of the vanguard, and ultimately in his evaluation of the roles of trade unions
and the secret vanguard party (that is, the Japan Communist Party
[JCP]), he parted from Leninism. Lenin argued, and so would the
JCP, that only the vanguard and organizers could guide the workers
beyond the horizons of bourgeois society to revolution. Left to their
own devices, workers could never, autonomously, become conscious
revolutionaries. "Since," Lenin wrote, "there can be no question of
an independent ideology formulated by the working masses themselves in the process of their movement, the only choice is either
bourgeois or socialist ideology." For Lenin, no working class, however powerful the trade unions it created, was capable of attaining
consciousness of the fundamental opposition between their class as
a whole and the existing social system. "We have said," he wrote,
"that there could not have been social democratic consciousness
among the workers. It would have to be brought to them from
without."[90]

Yamakawa, however, had long been ambivalent about the Bolsheviks' domination of the Russian workers. In a February 1922 essay,
he was unwilling to testify fully to the "desirability" of the "leadership" or "dictatorship of the party"; he had merely accepted it as
necessary, given the yet undeveloped class consciousness of the
common people. Even earlier, in his criticism of *minponshugi* theories, Yamakawa had berated Yoshino and Ōyama for feigning a
belief in majority rule but in reality calling for the rule of an "enlightened few." Democracy, he wrote, demands rule by the people, who
are never ignorant of the real needs of society. And several months
after the publication of his "Change of Course" article, he roundly
denied the charges by an anarchosyndicalist that he had sold out the
working class to an intellectual vanguard. By a vanguard, Yamakawa
insisted, he meant only the organized and hence more class-
conscious members of the working class.[91]

90 This discussion of Lenin uses Leszek Kolakowski, *Main Currents of Marxism*, vol. 2, chap.
    16; for quotations, see pp. 386, 387.
91 Yamakawa Hitoshi, "Rōdō undō ni taisuru chishiki kaikyū no chii," in *Yamakawa Hitoshi
    zenshū*, vol. 3, ed. Yamakawa Kikue and Yamakawa Shinsaku (Tokyo: Keisō shobō,
    1967), pp. 26–39; *Yamakawa zenshū*, vol. 2 (Tokyo: Keisō shobō, 1966), pp. 82–91, 106–
    8; *Yamakawa zenshū*, vol. 5 (Tokyo: Keisō shobō, 1968), pp. 191–9.

Yamakawa, in fact, never completely accepted Lenin's belief in the indisputable need of a vanguard to lead the workers to a revolutionary consciousness. He may or may not have been a Kautskyian, as the theoretician Fukumoto Kazuo later argued, but his insistence after 1919 that the workers' class consciousness was bound to develop through their struggle with capitalism and that labor organizations served both as organs of struggle for the workers' demands and as nuclei in the creation of new social styles was certainly closer to the thought of Kautsky than to Lenin. Even in his "Change of Course" article, which members of the JCP contended had been written under party orders (Yamakawa's denial was supported by Arahata), he wrote that class consciousness is comprehensible not simply for the few with enough erudition to discern it; it inevitably grows in the mind of every member of the working class, though not always at the same rate or to the same degree.[92]

By 1924, Yamakawa's differences with the JCP had become clear. Arguments over proper revolutionary theory and tactics led to an extensive struggle that took several forms. In the labor unions, reformists (or pragmatists, as they are sometimes called) and Marxists clashed over the role of unions in a bourgeois state. Inside and outside the unions there was a sharp split over revolutionary theory between the independent Marxists, led by Yamakawa, and those associated with the JCP. Throughout, it was Yamakawa who dominated: his perception of the proper tactics of the Japanese working class toward a united front with the bourgeoisie, his analysis of the character of the Japanese bourgeoisie and the workers' class consciousness, and his interpretation of the revolutionary potential of organized workers and the nature of the Japanese state. Yamakawa defined the policies and practices of a non-Communist Japanese Marxist and provoked a theoretical debate among all Japanese Marxists. Ultimately, Yamakawa and the JCP, particularly the theoretician Fukumoto Kazuo, confronted each other over issues of theory and practice expressed in Comintern doctrine. As a result, Japanese Marxists began a debate on the origins and development of the modern Japanese state that stimulated the social scientific analysis of modern Japanese history and thoroughly embedded Marxism in the intellectual life of Japan. But for Yamakawa or Fukumoto and all their fellows, the function of historical analysis, like that of social theory, was never merely academic. It provided the "scientific" basis

92 Watanabe, "Nihon no marukusushugi undō ron," pp. 182, 198–200.

for their criticism of the Japanese state, an intellectual perspective from which to criticize liberal formulas, and conceptual guidelines for a revolutionary movement.[93]

WHOSE REVOLUTION IS IT?:
FUKUMOTO VERSUS YAMAKAWA

Within three years of the publication of "Change of Course," Yamakawa's strategic assumptions and theoretical conceptions were challenged by Fukumoto Kazuo (1894–1983). A graduate of the law faculty of Tokyo Imperial University who became a lecturer in economics and law at Matsue Higher School, Fukumoto had recently returned from several years of government-sponsored study in Germany. While there, he had steeped himself in the Marx–Engels classics and the works of Lenin, Rosa Luxemburg, and Karl Liebknecht. Using his encyclopedic knowledge of theory, a quality that particularly impressed young radical university students, Fukumoto by 1926 had revived the JCP and taken over its leadership.[94] As Hayashi Fusao, a leader of the *Shinjinkai*, wrote:

The one thing that could not be doubted was his extreme erudition. The passages he quoted were all crucial lines that I had never read. Neither Yamakawa, nor Sakai... had once quoted these for us. These fresh contents forced me to realize the ignorance of Japanese Marxists – or at least so I, as a student theorist, thought.[95]

Fukumoto had also learned the skills of sectarian vituperation. Shortly after his return in 1924, in a public address at Kyoto Imperial University, he neatly undercut the arguments of the prestigious Marxist professor of economics, Kawakami Hajime, caricaturing him in front of his students as an "empiriocritic" (*keikenhihan*), a man who espoused a philosophy that Lenin had written a whole pamphlet to vilify. But in his first essays in *Marxism* (Marukusushugi), the major theoretical journal of the proletarian movement, Fukumoto confined himself to denouncing Yamakawa's "Change of Course" as a "vulgarization of Marxism." He slandered Yamakawa as an "economist," a Leninist term of opprobrium to

93 Ibid., pp. 184–5, 230–5; Koyama Hirotake and Sugimori Yasuji, "Rōnōha marukusushugi," in *Shōwa no hantaisei shisō*, vol. 3, ed. Sumiya Etsuji (Tokyo: Haga shobō, 1967), pp. 278–334.
94 Koyama Hirotake, "Nihon marukusushugi no keisei," in *Shōwa no hantaisei shisō*, pp. 106–9.
95 Jeffrey Paul Wagner, "Sano Manabu and the Japanese Adaptation of Socialism," Ph.D. diss., University of Arizona, 1978, p. 58.

describe those who believed that economic struggle alone can lead to political transformation without the direct intervention of a party devoted to political struggle. He accused Yamakawa of failing to understand the "underlying principles" of a "change of course." In essence, Fukumoto was merely providing theoretical documentation to demonstrate what already should have been clear: Yamakawa was not a Leninist.[96]

Fukumoto was a Leninist, however; or at least he believed that he had preserved the essence of Lenin's doctrine in his maxims for a purified proletarian movement. Fukumoto accepted as axiomatic that "our true change of course" depended on "raising proletarian consciousness through . . . theoretical struggle." As described by Lenin, he wrote, a correct "change of course" for the proletarian movement "is a qualitative process of change within a dialectic process." In tactical terms, this meant that the proletarian movement must shift from trade union struggles to socialist political struggle. Like Lenin, Fukumoto did not believe that the proletariat could comprehend on its own the aptness or necessity of such a strategy. Rather than rely on changes in objective conditions, the proletariat must, by a subjective leap, gain a "genuine class consciousness" (a consciousness that Fukumoto equated with the possession of Marxist "knowledge" [ninshiki]). Only a "true vanguard party," a Communist party, would be a veritable source of socialist consciousness; only such a party "could use, direct, promote, or transform all political opposition, thereby making the proletarian movement a genuine class movement."[97]

After his return to Japan, Fukumoto decided that the broader tasks of the political struggle had to be set aside temporarily in order to deal with the corrupting influence of Yamakawa's "change of course" and his conception of a united-front party. Yamakawa had envisaged and helped create, as he himself wrote in 1924, "a proletarian political movement uniting the largest possible part of the workers' movement in an organization that was as free as possible from bourgeois influence." Yamakawa believed that the leadership of this "united front" should fall to the organized proletariat in urban

96   Iwasaki Chikatsugu, *Nihon marukusushugi tetsugakushi* (Tokyo: Miraisha, 1971), pp. 31–3; Furuta Hikaru, *Kawakami Hajime* (Tokyo: Tōkyō daigaku shuppankai, 1959), pp. 138–49; Kishimoto and Koyama, *Nihon no hikyōsantō*, p. 112; Koyama, "Nihon marukusushugi no keisei," p. 110.

97   Iwasaki, *Nihon marukusushugi tetsugakushi*, pp. 32–5; Koyama, "Nihon marukusushugi no keisei," pp. 110–16; Kishimoto and Koyama, *Nihon no hikyōsantō*, pp. 129–37; Matsuzawa, *Nihon*, pp. 194–200.

factories and the organized tenants in rural districts. The creation of such a party disturbed Fukumoto: Neither a vanguard party nor an illegal revolutionary corps, such an organization could never promote the revolutionary consciousness of the masses. In fact, Yamakawa had urged that it not be solely a proletarian vehicle. Rather, he believed, it should serve the broad democratic interest of the *lumpen*, all the unorganized, the colonial masses, the outcaste *burakumin*, and even the lower elements of the petty bourgeoisie. Yamakawa also recommended that the vanguard elements dissolve themselves within the united front and "allow every fraction to express its views fully at the party congress and to be recognized fully within the party." Fukumoto felt that such a view, which ran counter to Lenin's conception of a party composed of professional revolutionaries dictating policy, would be disastrous. Lenin had found "fractionalism," the organized activity of groups of members who were free to express minority views, to be destructive to the ultimate aims of a revolutionary party. Fukumoto believed, moreover, that his own desire to create a Marxist consciousness among the proletariat would come to naught in a united-front party: The vanguard would be dissolved in the mass. He argued that Yamakawa's conception of the natural growth of proletarian consciousness was, at best, mere "opportunism." Worse yet, Fukumoto wrote, Yamakawa had led the movement toward a belief in "spontaneity" and "infantile leftism," both thoroughly condemned by Lenin.[98]

Fukumoto therefore set as the immediate task of the Marxist left the establishment of a correct and unified theoretical program for the proletarian movement: "to give life to, deepen, and spread Marxism and Marxist influence." Following Lenin, he called for the creation of a Marxist vanguard that would follow a policy of "unity through separation" (*bunri-ketsugō*), a process by which genuine Marxists would be separated from false Marxists and reformists. This became the absolute prerequisite for the achievement of unity. In later years, this glorification of ideological purity, the insistence on the priority of intellectual struggle over political praxis, and the worship of dogma would be denounced by both the Comintern and JCP. But for the moment (and some believe that it permanently damaged the

98 Matsuzawa, *Nihon*, pp. 199–200. For a discussion of united-front strategies in Japan and the West, see Inumaru Yoshikazu, *Nihon no marukusushugi sono*, vol. 2: *Kōza gendai no ideorogii* (Tokyo: San'ichi shobō, 1961), pp. 39–40, 57–8; Koyama, "Nihon marukusushugi no keisei," pp. 89–92, 110–26; Koyama and Sugimori, "Rōnōha marukusushugi," pp. 283–8, 311–25; Iwasaki, *Nihon marukusushugi tetsugakushi*, pp. 34–5; Kishimoto and Koyama, *Nihon no hikyōsantō*, pp. 110, 125.

movement), it turned the JCP into a confederation of mandarins and quite possibly made the Marxist movement of Japan the most theoretically sophisticated in the world.[99]

Obviously, Yamakawa could not accept Fukumoto's propositions. A proletarian party, he wrote, "should represent the highest expression of the revolutionary demands of the proletariat, not simply an abstraction based on strategies for the establishment of a new society; it should incorporate all elements of the proletariat and reflect its current interests and demands."[100] Yamakawa quickly reconfirmed his belief in a united-front party: It, and neither a secret nor a vanguard party, should take the lead of the Japanese proletarian movement.

Yamakawa opposed the reconstitution of the JCP and refused to join it. He also explained later that he believed that the "existence of the party in 1922–3 had been to the detriment of the overall movement." He opposed the reorganization of the party on empirical and historical, not theoretical, grounds. "I felt that conditions being what they were in Japan, another Communist party at this time [1926] would not be any better. What suited Russia would not necessarily fit Japan." Yamakawa argued that only through an analysis of Japanese capitalism, an examination of the specific political structure of the Japanese ruling class, and an understanding of the historical peculiarity of the development of the modern Japanese state and society could a proper strategy for the proletarian movement be developed.[101]

Yamakawa took as the basis for his analysis Marx's typology of the capitalist stages of development, which described how the bourgeoisie in Europe had constituted itself as a class in opposition to the rule of feudalism and absolutism. But with a conceptual flexibility similar to Marx's social analysis in *The Eighteenth Brumaire of Louis Napoleon*, Yamakawa observed certain historical anomalies in the way that the Japanese bourgeois had acquired political rule. Thus he suggested an analysis at odds on critical points with that offered by the Comintern and JCP.

In 1922, the draft platform of the JCP (*koryō sōan*) had defined Japan as "semifeudal." Although the state was controlled by a definite part of the commercial and industrial capitalists, the draft pointed out, "remnants of feudal relationships" were manifest in its

99 Kishimoto and Koyama, *Nihon no hikyōsantō*, p. 137; Koyama, "Nihon marukusushugi no keisei," pp. 112–14; Iwasaki, *Nihon marukusushugi tetsugakushi*, pp. 32–4.
100 Koyama, "Nihon marukusushugi no keisei," pp. 91, 94–7.   101 Ibid.

structure. This semifeudal character was most clearly shown "in the important and leading role of the peers and in the basic features of the constitution." Moreover, Japanese capitalism "still demonstrates characteristics of former feudal relationships. . . . And the greatest part of the land is today in the hands of semifeudal landlords." The draft continued, "The emperor, who heads the Japanese government, [is] the biggest landlord of all." Members of the JCP at that time, particularly Sakai Toshihiko, chose to suppress this part. Given the semifeudal character of the Japanese state, the party recommended a joint struggle of proletariat and bourgeoisie to overthrow the imperial government as the correct political strategy, that is, a bourgeois revolution.[102]

Yamakawa accepted neither this strategy nor the historical interpretation on which it was based. "The center of power in our society," he insisted, "has decisively shifted from the bureaucracy to the bourgeoisie." When the Seiyūkai party rose to power and its leader, Hara Takashi, became prime minister, Yamakawa argued, "the political power of the bourgeoisie existent today was thus consolidated." But paradoxically, this transfer of power "explains the withering of democracy in Japan." Yamakawa explained this paradox by contrasting Japan's capitalist development with that of Britain. "Britain took fifty or seventy years to pass peacefully through the gradual establishment of bourgeois democracy, and under the most favorable circumstances." But Japanese bourgeois capitalism had grown up under the "tutelage of bureaucratic politics." Whereas British capitalism grew quickly in a period of free trade, Japanese capitalism was "warped" and the "political development of the country perverted . . . because it took place under the wing of medieval bureaucratic politics." In contrast with the European bourgeoisie, Yamakawa continued, the Japanese bourgeoisie "had no revolutionary period. What succeeded feudal aristocratic politics [in Japan] was not bourgeois democracy but, rather, bureaucratic militarist politics." Nor did the Japanese bourgeoisie ever "directly attack the bureaucracy in order to take state power." When the Japanese bourgeoisie consolidated their political power, they did so without any sense of a distinctly bourgeois class consciousness: They acted "almost without conscious purpose, in a fit of absence of mind." In fact, the Seiyūkai became the "representative bourgeois party . . . because it joined with and identified with the bureauc-

102 For a full translation of the draft platform, see Beckmann and Okubo, *The Japanese Communist Party*, pp. 279–82; Inumaru, *Nihon no marukusushugi sono*, vol. 2, p. 45.

racy." Given these circumstances and the fact that Japanese capitalism had appeared during the imperialist stage in the development of world capitalism, Yamakawa concluded that "Japan had no leeway to elaborate a bourgeois democracy, or at least very little. Our age of bourgeois democracy, if it appears at all, will be very brief."[103]

As a result of his analysis of Japanese history, Yamakawa believed that the proletarian movement had simultaneously to seek the abolition of feudal institutions in society and to complete the democratization of Japan's political institutions. But given the rapidity of Japanese development, the proletariat – like the bourgeoisie – had not had enough time to constitute itself as a singular and conscious class. It thus faced the danger of "being absorbed by bourgeois and petty bourgeois political movements." It was on these grounds that Yamakawa believed it necessary for the proletarian movement to take the lead (and to do so immediately) in "uniting the largest possible part of the workers' movement in an organization that is as autonomous as possible from bourgeois influence."[104]

By contrast, Fukumoto did not ignore historical circumstances, but he saw historical changes in abstract global terms. Following Lenin and Luxemburg, he insisted that contemporary capitalism had reached its final and moribund stage of imperialism. Its collapse was imminent. Like Europe, Japan faced revolution, and its proletariat needed the guidance of a Leninist vanguard to accomplish its revolution.[105]

Ultimately, neither Yamakawa nor Fukumoto, neither the JCP nor Yamakawa's "united front" of laborers and farmers was victorious. All fell victim to government suppression. Fukumoto and Yamakawa also faced attack from the Comintern and many fellow leftists. The JCP expelled Fukumoto from the central committee in 1927, accusing him of Trotskyism, among other things. The Comintern described Fukumoto's insistence on "unity through separation" as an error "that will isolate the party from the mass organizations of the proletariat." Yamakawa, his opponents wrote, encouraged "passivity." By ignoring the role of the vanguard, they charged, he left the proletarian movement powerless to transcend events and so reduced both to following them. Nonetheless, through

---

103   *Yamakawa zenshū*, vol. 5, pp. 77–82; Koyama, "Nihon marukusushugi no keisei," pp. 81–7; Koyama and Sugimori, "Rōnōha marukusushugi," pp. 282–4.
104   Koyama, "Nihon marukusushugi no keisei"; Koyama and Sugimori, "Rōnōha marukusushugi," pp. 281–2.
105   Koyama, "Nihon marukusushugi no keisei," pp. 114–16.

their debates, Yamakawa and Fukumoto made the entire left aware that a conceptual understanding of history was important to the analysis of contemporary affairs. As Yamakawa had made clear, the strategic concerns of the present were predicated on a correct understanding of the past. If nothing else, this insight raised the level of the historiography of the Meiji Restoration.[106]

IDEOLOGICAL DIALECTICS:
THE PARADOX OF JAPANESE MARXISM

No simple dichotomy between Leninists and non-Leninists or between Communist and non-Communist Marxists can do justice to the ideological complexity of Japanese Marxism in the 1920s and early 1930s. To be sure, Leninist theory and Comintern theses usually set the terms of discourse about proper political praxis for Marxists inside and outside the Japanese Communist Party alike. But throughout this period, a flood of translations and commentaries on the work of Marx, Kautsky, Rosa Luxemburg, and others kept the Japanese abreast of developments in European non-Leninist Marxism. (For example, a translation of Kautsky's *Karl Marx' Ökonomische Lehren*, a gloss on the first volume of *Capital*, became a best-seller, as did Marx's work itself.) Radical students like Fukumoto, Miki, and Hani who went to study in Weimar Germany also brought back what Alvin Gouldner called "critical Marxism" – a Marxism infiltrated by neo-Hegelian, neo-Kantian, and Heideggerian ideas. The Japanese socialists might not have heard of Lenin in 1917, but ten years later, Japanese Marxists were well aware of the main currents of Marxist thought in both Western Europe and the Soviet Union.[107]

Paradoxically, Marxism gained intellectual force and influence in the late 1920s and early 1930s even as the government intensified its crackdown on the Communist Party and defections from the movement increased. The intellectual significance that Marxism attained as a principium can be explained in part by the totality with which its

---

106 Koyama, "Nihon marukusushugi no keisei," pp. 99–100, 134; Takeuchi Yoshitomo and Suzuki Tadashi, "*Shinkō kagaku no hata no moto ni* to *Yuibutsuron kenkyū*," *Shisō* 465 (March 1963): 108–10.

107 Kishimoto and Koyama, *Nihon no hikyosantō*, p. 79. For a good discussion of these problems, see Iwasaki, *Nihon marukusushugi tetsugakushi*, chap. 1; Alvin Gouldner, *The Two Marxisms* (New York: Oxford University Press, 1980). For comparable Western Marxist developments, see Martin Jay, *The Dialectical Imagination* (Boston: Little, Brown, 1973), esp. pp. 76–80, 121–4, 272. A recent study of the Marxist debates in Japan is Germaine A. Hoston, *Marxism and the Crisis of Development in Prewar Japan* (Princeton, N.J.: Princeton University Press, 1986).

theory of dialectical and historical materialism explained human
social, economic, and political behavior. In Fukumoto's words,
"Everything must be understood as forms in motion, in contradictory development and as part of a totality, that is, must be grasped
dialectically." It is also true that Leninist ideas regarding the importance of theoretical purity and the hegemonic role of the rational
intellectual appealed to the traditional bias of the Japanese
mandarinate, as did the more general tendency of Western Marxism
in the 1920s to give priority to theory over praxis and to emphasize
cognitive clarity and consciousness. Although many academic Marxists like Miki, Fukumoto, and Hani were later attacked for their
abstractness and their overemphasis on theory, a fault that some say
has plagued Japanese Marxism ever since, it may have been precisely
these qualities that made their writings so widely read.[108]

But Japanese Marxism also attracted the attention of intellectuals
because of the apparent catholicity with which its chief ideologues
integrated contemporary Western ideas into their theories. The extent of this can only be suggested. For example, Fukumoto was
expelled from the JCP not merely because he insisted on the priority
of theory but also because he emphasized the humanist element in
Marx and asserted the priority of the transformation of consciousness in revolutionary practice. These ideas he had borrowed from
Karl Korsch, a neo-Hegelian Marxist, and from Georg Lukacs, who
had introduced Weberian ideas to Marxism. In contending that
Japan was on the verge of revolution, a position totally at odds with
the Comintern and the JCP, Fukumoto followed Rosa Luxemburg,
who had argued in a pre–World War I debate with Lenin that in the
imperialist stage of world history, crisis was universal throughout the
capitalist world.[109]

For some Japanese Marxists, the humanist side of Marx's thought
was tremendously appealing. In his interpretation of Marx's concept
of commodity fetishism – usually explained by most Marxists as the
simplest and most universal example of how the economic forms of
capitalism conceal underlying social relationships – Kawakami
Hajime found evidence that Marx had been concerned not with
material things but with human relationships. In most of his work
after 1927, Kawakami explored this humanistic relationship through

108 Takeuchi and Suzuki, "*Shinkō kagaku*"; Iwasaki, *Nihon marukusushugi tetsugakushi*, pp.
     39–41; Matsuzawa, *Nihon*, pp. 199–200.
109 Yamanouchi Yasushi, "Iwayuru shakai ishiki keitai ni tsuite," *Shisō* 568, 569 (October
     1971, November 1971): 23–37; 87–100.

a study of the Marxist classics, having found in neo-Kantian Marxism a way to integrate dialectical materialism and humanism. The younger Miki Kiyoshi, just at this time, infused his Marxism with theories of knowledge borrowed in part from Heideggerian existentialism. In his analysis of the dialectic between productivity and the relations of production, Miki introduced a primary *logos* of "existence," arguing in highly un-Marxian language that "man, in the process of life, is forced to advance an interpretation, in some manner, of his own quintessence."[110]

What Fukumoto, Kawakami, Miki, and many of their peers brought into Marxism was a belief in the significance of the human actor and the role of human self-consciousness in carrying out revolutionary praxis. The theory of revolution and social praxis that intellectuals found in Marxism offered a positive philosophical alternative to the ahistoricity and passivity of the prevailing academic philosophy of "self-cultivation," *kyōyōshugi*. Whereas self-cultivation encouraged individuals to indulge themselves in a world of individuality, Marxism offered a philosophy of action.[111] And it linked that philosophy of action with a universalistic or cosmopolitan conception of how human society developed, in Japan as elsewhere.

110 Iwasaki, *Nihon marukusushugi tesugakushi*, pp. 102–8, 116–20, 128–32, 178–9; Yamanouchi, "Iwayuru shakai"; Ōuchi Hyōe, ed., *Miki Kiyoshi zenshū*, vol. 3 (Tokyo: Iwanami shoten, 1976–8), pp. 8–9.
111 Iwasaki, *Nihon marukusushugi tetsugakushi*, pp. 178–9; Takeuchi and Suzuki, "*Shinkō kagaku*," pp. 110–11.

CHAPTER 5

JAPAN'S REVOLT
AGAINST THE WEST

TETSUO NAJITA AND H. D. HAROOTUNIAN

INTRODUCTION

Throughout most of Japan's modern history, the West has contributed to its formulation of theories of culture and action. At one level, the image of a monolithic West replaced an earlier interpretation of China as the "other." In the twentieth century and especially after World War I, Japan's conceptualization of the West affirmed a theory of militant and articulate revolt against the "other," usually imagined as a collective threat to Japan's national independence and cultural autonomy. The construction of the "other" required that it be portrayed as the mirror image of the indigenous culture. It was this representation of the "other" that clarified for the Japanese the essence of their own culture. This reversing of images was no less true in the Tokugawa period, when an idealized China had constituted the "other," than in the twentieth century, when a monolithic West did. If the "other" defined what was exceptional in Japanese culture, it also offered a model of excellence against which such distinctiveness could be measured. Just as Tokugawa writers focused on the world of the ancient sages, changing it into an unhistorical abstraction whose values existed only in pure form in Japan, so twentieth-century thinkers imagined a Japan destined to reach new levels of achievements realized by no single Western nation. Through this doubling of images, they shaped a theory of action aimed at maintaining a pure, indigenous cultural synthesis protected from outside elements that might disturb the perceived equilibrium. It was precisely because Japanese saw the urgency of keeping their culture uncontaminated and hence preserving its essence against the threatened external pollution that many felt justified using militant forms of political and cultural action.

Although desperate and even violent resistance against the West spread among nationalistic groups in the 1920s, reaching a climax in the mid-1930s, the concern for keeping Japan's culture pure prompted others to try more moderate ways of preventing Japan from assimilating too closely with the West. The impulse behind these efforts can be traced to the cosmopolitanism in the 1920s and the general conviction that Japan had contributed its own unique voice to a global civilization whose diversity was unified by a broad conception of humanity. Yet the emphasis on Japan's special contribution to world civilization narrowed easily in the political environment of the late 1920s and early 1930s to a preoccupation with the status of Japan's uniqueness. Many believed that by realizing the best of East and West, Japan had achieved a new cosmopolitan culture. The recognition of having achieved this unprecedented synthesis validated the subsequent belief that Japan was uniquely qualified to assume leadership in Asia, although much of the rhetoric that the writers used referred to the world at large. Whereas an earlier cosmopolitanism promoted the ideal of cultural diversity and equivalence based on the principle of a common humanity, which served also to restrain excessive claims to exceptionalism, the new culturalism of the 1930s proposed that Japan was appointed to lead the world to a higher level of cultural synthesis that surpassed Western modernism itself.

The ambiguity between the capacity of an indigenous culture to withstand change and the claims of new knowledge demanding transformation was at the heart of the Meiji Restoration of 1868. On the one hand, the Meiji restorers announced, in the opening decree proclaiming the Restoration, that the aim of the new policy was to return to the "events of antiquity and the Jimmu emperor's state foundation." This meant returning to origins, a mythical time before Japan had been corrupted by Buddhism and Chinese civilization, and to the unalloyed practices of native experience. Yet at the same time, the new government declared in the Charter Oath its determination to "search for new knowledge throughout the world" and to "eliminate old customs" "based on the universal way." The former intention led to a belief in cultural exceptionalism and even to presumptions of superiority in Japan's relations with foreigners. It also emphasized the basic similarity of all Japanese before the differentiating and alienating influence of foreign cultures, and it called attention to the real separation between demands of similitude (Japan) and difference (the "other"). The latter inspired the creation of the modern state and the transformation of Japanese society, classically expressed in the 1870s and 1880s as the establishment of "civilization and enlightenment" (*bummei kaika*). Hence the call to origins authenticated all those proposals directed toward what was essential and spiritual and what was irreducibly Japanese, even though society had changed visibly and materially. The search for new knowledge, on the other hand, was identified with progressive development, modernity, and the West. The terms of cultural uniqueness increasingly stressed ends and essence, and the pursuit of rational knowledge privileged means and instrumentality. In the end, the conflict was expressed in a struggle between culture – or the nation's distinctive spirit – and modern civilization – especially as expressed as functional political structure – and desperate efforts to overcome this polarization. Only Japan's defeat in the Pacific War and its dazzling economic recovery offered the occasion to complete the unfinished business of realigning these opposite claims and concealing their inherent contradiction in an improbable synthesis of Japan and the West.

RESTORATIONIST REVOLT

The particular militancy of the Japanese revolt against the West stems from the historical model of the loyalist samurai who overthrew the Tokugawa *bakufu* in the 1860s and established the Meiji state. In this model, there were two related but distinct orientations in the theory of a restorationist action. One emphasized the necessity of resolving the question of domestic politics by ridding the country of incompetent leaders and ineffective institutions. It was believed that unless domestic problems first were solved, the nation would be left defenseless against the hostile ambitions of Western colonial powers. The other orientation focused on the foreign problem and sought to solve it through frontal military strategies. Whereas the theories of Kita Ikki and their ultimate incorporation in the mutiny of radical young officers on February 26, 1936, exemplify the first orientation, the calculated attack on Pearl Harbor in 1941 – after a decade of trying to resolve the foreign problem – represents the second orientation.

Beginning in the 1920s, with the assassination of Prime Minister Hara Takashi in Tokyo Station in 1921 and continuing thereafter in single acts of terror, the radical restorationists shunned public debate and conciliation as a way of resolving domestic political problems and instead used strategies of direct and violent action in order to shock and even shatter the confidence of political and industrial leaders. Drawing on the historical analogy of the sixteenth century when the "lower overthrew the upper" (*gekokujō*), activists reminded their contemporaries that the idea of loyalty did not always mean compliance with the commands of superiors, that it could also mean righteous rebellion against incompetent and insensitive leaders. Indeed, this idea of loyalty functioned as a double-edged sword to cut down the constitutional leadership and to remove all obstacles from achieving the goal of expelling the Western presence in Japan and Asia.

Although it would be difficult to reduce all aspects of the Japanese revolt to a single doctrine or mode of action – as the ramifications were complex and branched over diverse areas of the culture – there are, nonetheless, some general characteristics that most of the groups and thinkers shared. Western conceptions of legal reason and rational cultural norms, often conveyed in the idiom of progress, rationalism, modernization, or simply Westernization, all came under scrutiny and were invariably modified but more often rejected as extensions of structures of power aimed at expanding Western interests. Moreover, such Western notions were seen as manipulating the indigenous cultural values in ways that were inimical to the legacies of a distinct history, particularly the aesthetic impulse of an elegant inheritance, and contrary to the communitarian experience vivified by the collective memory of the folk. Often these aesthetic and communitarian values were signified by the vague yet provocative phrase calling attention to the "national political essence" (*kokutai*), a concept that conjured up mythical associations of a mystical union of spirit and body and that evoked a distinctive past and the creative potential for a unique future. The conception of *kokutai* captured in a single verbal compound the entire range of ideological virtues that defined what it meant to be Japanese, as opposed to the "other."

The Japanese revolt also tended to link the resolution of Japan's problems with the revival of Asia as a world area, to emphasize the commonality of Asian peoples in their struggle to eliminate Western colonialism. Here, Japanese attitudes corresponded to the shift noted earlier from the Meiji enlightenment and its faith in rational progress to a preoccupation with an indigenous cultural spirit free from the constraints of alien logic and science. Thus, during the industrial and social revolutions that followed the Meiji Restoration,

Japanese leaders spoke confidently of "leaving Asia" – *datsu-A* – meaning principally the zone of Chinese civilization, and "entering Europe" – *nyū-Ō* – but this pattern was reversed in the twentieth century. Now leaders urged a "reentry into Asia" and an "abandonment of Europe," *nyū-A, datsu-Ō*. This reversal in phraseology was significant both politically and culturally. Politically, it referred to a growing expectation that Japan, as a newly industrialized nation in Asia, should rightfully assume responsibility for developing that area. But a closer reading of the slogan suggested Japanese hegemony in Asia and the removal of outside interference. Culturally, the call to reenter Asia heralded the reidentification of Japan with its continental roots, a return to its original sphere of civilization and the maintenance of Japan's unique place in it.

This was early and powerfully articulated by the art historian Okakura Tenshin or Kakuzō (1862–1913), who in a series of books (*The Ideals of the East*, 1902, and *The Book of Tea*, 1903) sought to establish Asia's cultural equivalence to the claims of Western hegemony. Okakura first formulated the principles that all Asians shared: "Asia is one," he wrote in *The Ideals of the East*, "The Himalayas divide, only to accentuate, two mighty civilizations, the Chinese with its communism of Confucius, and the Indian with its individualism of the Vedas." But, he added, this geographical divide has not "interrupted" a common inheritance marked by a "love for the Ultimate and Universal." It was precisely this shared disposition for the ultimate and universal that had enabled Asians everywhere to produce the great religions of the world and to emphasize the ends, not the means, of life that Okakura believed distinguished the maritime civilizations of the West. Although Asians had a mutual view of the world, Japan, he proposed, represented this cultural consensus through its aesthetic values. Indeed, Japan functioned as the key to this great cultural code, attesting to "the historic wealth of Asiatic culture" and therefore illuminating "its treasured specimens." Japan, Okakura announced, "is the museum of Asiatic civilization." What he meant by this strategy of substituting the part for the whole is that the artistic accomplishments of the Japanese had encapsulated the "history of Asiatic ideals" to form "sand-ripples" on the national consciousness with "each successive wave of Eastern thought." Long before writers like Watsuji Tetsurō identified the elements of the two different cultural styles, Okakura proposed that Japan alone assimilated two different ideals in an enduring tension: the Asian love for grand visions of "universal sweep" grounded in the concrete and particular and the Western propensity for science and "organized culture" "armed in all its array of undifferentiated knowledge, and keen with the edge of competitive energy." But Okakura was certain that the Japanese example would withstand the challenge of science and industry, to preserve the Asian "spirit" and to lead to a higher synthesis of both.[1]

The twentieth century witnessed a powerful cultural and political ground swell of resistance and revolt against the domination of Asia by Western powers, in which Japan assumed the role of leading this Asian renaissance. Yet before Japan could undertake this leadership role, it felt it necessary to cleanse its own society in a great "spiritual" restoration aimed at lowering the nation's reliance on Western modes of political and economic thought and organization. The various attempted coups and assassinations of the early 1930s – often under the authorizing banner of "restoration" (ishin) or "reconstruction" (kaizō) – all shared the conceptual assumption that the times demanded direct action promising the establishment of a new order in Japan, unified and freed from the corrosive influence of the West. Indeed, thinkers and activists such as Okawa Shūmei, Inoue Nisshō, Tachibana Kōsaburō, Kita Ikki, Gondō Seikei, and others represent nothing less than a program to "expel the barbarians" in the name of culture and spirit, or jōiron, as this sentiment was defined in the 1860s before the Meiji Restoration.

Another dimension of these theories of action prompted various evaluations relating to the performance of the modern Japanese state. It was widely believed that the Japanese state had been created in response to the threat to the nation's independence posed by the encircling Western powers. But underlying this conviction was the deeper fear of the structure of law enabling the formation of the modern state. This siege mentality in Japan led to the paradoxical conclusion that the best defense against the Western nation-states was the construction of a modern, legal state of its own. In other words, from the beginning, distrust of the West accompanied the act of state building in Japan, as the following quotation from Kido Takayoshi, one of the early leaders of the Meiji Restoration, illustrates:

There is an urgent need for Japan to become strong enough militarily to take a stand against the Western powers. As long as our country is lacking in military power, the law of nations is not to be trusted. When dealing with

---

1   Okakura Kakuzō, *Ideals of the East, with Special Reference to the Art of Japan* (Rutland, Vt.: Tuttle, 1970), pp. 1–9, 206–7, 236–44.

those who are weak, the strong nations often invoke public law but really calculate their own gain. Thus it seems to me that the law of nations is merely a tool for the conquest of the weak.[2]

The magnitude of the challenge suggested here reveals the urgency requiring the revolutionary samurai to construct the Meiji state. Yet a principal consideration of these Meiji state builders was to make sure that the Japanese state, as they envisaged it, would minimize and eventually obliterate the perceived disparity between Japan and the superior Western powers. Such a mission required continuous demonstration that Japanese achievements were equal to Western accomplishments. But ironically, it was precisely the need for demonstration that escalated the conflict that Japan hoped to avoid. For although Japan underwent with breath-taking speed a political and industrial transformation in order to establish a new relationship with the Western countries, the real and perceived challenge of a permanent condition of national peril never disappeared. Rather, this sense of continuing siege led to the belief that the challenge should be speedily resolved once and for all, in what many came to call the "war to end all wars" (saishū sensō). Many were convinced that such a war would definitively expel the West from Asia, would make the continent free for Asians, and thus would complete Japan's own "spiritual" revolution. Simultaneously, movements of dissent were unleashed against the modern state itself for its failure to realize the original vision of the Meiji Restoration, owing to the diverting influence of excessive Westernization, hence the "bureaucratization" of the constitutional system.

Among such proponents of revolt against domestic politics, one group dramatized the inadequacy of the state's constitutional structure and sought to alter it through violent confrontation. The other group rejected the primacy of structure altogether as a Western aberration and instead invoked the power of the spirit to bind all Japanese together in common, not divided, purpose. The major theorist for the former group was Kita Ikki (1883–1937), whereas Gondō Seikei and Tachibana Kōsaburō best represented all those groups that dreamed of replacing hierarchical structure with communitarian brotherhood. Nonetheless, there was considerable overlapping between these groups. In fact, some activists, notably Ōkawa Shūmei, were accomplished scholars who moved easily be-

2 Miyoshi Masao, As We Saw Them (Berkeley and Los Angeles: University of California Press, 1979), p. 143.

tween the various restorationist factions as strategists and planners of coups d'état.

Kita Ikki

Kita Ikki's restorationist theory of action originated in late Meiji nationalism and socialism. In Kita's first major treatise, "The Theory of National Polity and Pure Socialism" (*Kokutairon oyobi junsei shakaishugi*, 1906), Kita proposed an identity between ancient political society and socialism and equated the traditional absence of private property with the diminished role of state structure. To him, the emperor symbolized the common ownership of property and hence a communal form of social existence. He therefore regarded the idea of the national polity (*kokutai*) as an appropriate "historical" model for the present to emulate in order to remove inequality and the sources of contemporary divisiveness; it also justified undertaking political action to install the communalistic ideal. Although Kita remained faithful to this ancient ideal of community, he modified his overall thinking significantly in the course of his career as a theorist and activist.

The crucial turning point altering Kita's angle of vision came with his involvement in Sun Yat-sen's revolutionary movement in China in 1911. Following the revolution and China's subsequent effort to construct a viable state, Kita, though refusing to surrender his earlier communalism, became convinced of the importance of the imperial figure as a unifying principle of politics. In his estimation, the Chinese revolution failed precisely because of its leadership's inability to establish a persuasive centralized political order. In the end, he observed, they fell back to relying on an illegitimate monarchy that only aggravated the problem and forestalled its resolution. While still in Shanghai, Kita began to draft his program for total political reorganization, in a tract called "An Outline Plan for the Reorganization of the Japanese State" (*Nihon kokka kaizō hōan*, 1919). Soon to become a major manifesto read by a wide variety of malcontents in the military and civilian populations, Kita's "Outline" explained the contemporary political malaise in Japan and the reasons that it called for radical action. He identified what many had felt uneasy about in the political environment of the 1920s but what had not yet been articulated. Implicit in Kita's treatise was a perspective on what he called the crisis of the time, a plan for resolving the domestic failure and a sanction for direct action and the seizure of power in the emperor's name.

Underlying Kita's writings is a sense of national crisis unleashed by capitalist and bureaucratic exploitation and leading to extreme inequality and misery in society that, he feared, would sap the strength and energy of the people. The existing constitutional order, he reasoned, had necessitated divisive party and interest politics (an observation shared by a number of contemporaries along the political spectrum), created new privileged classes, and separated the public realm from the general populace. Kita committed himself, therefore, to revolutionary upheaval as the surest antidote to the evils of the modern Japanese state and its mode of distributing resources. Although he never abandoned his earlier communitarian vision of socialism, derived from his reading of ancient mythohistory, he supplemented it with an organizational scheme that would replace the existing constitutional structure. In his earlier text on the national polity, Kita had failed to raise the question of industrial production; he was satisfied to base his conception of communitarianism on an ancient agrarian model. But in his later work, he recognized the role of industrialism in modern socialism. It was this perception that prompted him to find a new organizational model to replace the established constitutional order. To achieve his revolutionary aim, Kita advocated overthrowing the prevailing leadership in a swift and conclusive coup d'état. By reconstituting the structure of authority, he believed, Japan would rid itself of Western political institutions and economic practices as a necessary condition for a final confrontation in Asia. Kita called this program a "national renovation" (*Nihon kaizō*) based on the ideal of the "people's emperor" (*kokumin tennō*).

The imperial principle was vital to Kita's overall plan for a revolutionary reorganization of the state. He saw the importance of the emperor not so much as an institution that had survived from ancient times but as a symbol of community. His view came close to the conception of the early Meiji rebels Etō Shimpei and Saigō Takamori, who demanded the installation of what they called a "people's emperor" free from the meddling mediation of bureaucrats. In Japan, Kita argued, the imperial institution had been preserved to represent the national culture, but its potential as a social monarchy had been suppressed by the rise of bourgeois and bureaucratic politics within the constitutional order. It was precisely this principle of social cohesion that made the

Meiji Restoration the proper solution to Japan's domestic and foreign problems in the nineteenth century but that subsequent leaders violated by reconstructing the state and society as sanctuaries for private interests and privileges. Kita was indifferent to the idea of a divine emperor. When he was executed for his role in the mutiny of 1936, he was ordered to recant by saying "long live the emperor" as a final act of reverence and submission. He is reported to have refused by replying that he had vowed long ago never to joke about his own death.

In his "Outline," Kita proposed first to suspend the Meiji constitution in the name of the emperor, that is, the national community, in order to liberate both the monarch and the people from the constraints imposed by a bureaucratic polity.[3] Revealing his awareness of the history of modern revolutionary movements elsewhere, he envisaged a true Japanese revolution like the earlier upheavals in France and Russia. He was convinced that such an event would inaugurate a new era in the twentieth century. Unlike earlier revolutions that had destroyed the monarchy for purposes of political and economic renewal, Kita's theory of revolution depended on establishing the principle of a "people's emperor" as a necessary condition for the eventual implementation of a socialist order. In Asian societies such as China and Japan, he noted, the maintenance of the imperial principle of authority was vital to any radical reconstruction. Without it there would almost certainly be chaos and disorder, such as he had witnessed in China. Behind this view lay Kita's conviction that "true" revolutionary movements were shaped by the specific geographical area rather than the necessities of history. Here he undoubtedly broke with prevailing Marxist theories of revolution that were being debated by many of his contemporaries. Although Kita professed admiration for Marx and Kropotkin, praising them as pioneers in the development of socialism, he believed that his conception of revolution was, by contrast, mediated by Asian realities, to which the concept of class conflict was not appropriated. From this "new" perspective, he saw a Japanese revolution clearly marking a historical break from what came before: The new socialist order in Japan would be achieved without class warfare yet would include the new forces of industry and science. A socialist revolution in Japan, moreover, would be the first step in a chain reaction leading to the liberation of all Asian countries from Western political and economic

---

3   Kita Ikki, "Nihon kaizō hōan taikō," in *Gendai Nihon shisō taikei*, vol. 31: *Chōkokka shugi*, ed. Hashikawa Bunzō (Tokyo: Chikuma shobō, 1964), pp. 283–347.

domination. As examples, Kita cited China and India where independence movements had already begun.

Kita's plan called for dismantling the structure of privilege that had been sustained by the Meiji state. The peerage would be abolished, and universal manhood suffrage would be instituted. Surplus land would be redistributed among the landless according to size and need of each household. Although allowing for the retention of personal property, Kita recommended the confiscation of "industrial capital." As this wealth was transferred to the new state, the power of big bourgeoisie, as it had been constituted, would be effectively diminished; and through the mediation of a new order, widespread deprivation would be ended. It was Kita's purpose to relocate industrial production and its management in new state agencies. Corporate bodies would hereafter direct major enterprises such as steel and iron, banks, maritime trade, railways, and mining. Moreover, he envisaged specialized agencies to administer agriculture and labor affairs. Although he was sensitive to the needs of the countryside, he was principally concerned with reorganizing the cities in order to rationalize the mobilization and distribution of industrial resources. The destruction of privilege, the reconstitution of community, the regulation of working conditions, such as the establishment of an eight-hour workday, equality of employment for both men and women, and numerous other proposals shaped this theory of mobilization.

Throughout the "Outline," Kita revealed his concern for the plight of the general population. His remedies stemmed from an earlier socialism: worker ownership of companies, the state's responsibility for the parenting of children and schooling (tuition, books, meals, and so on), and a comprehensive social welfare program for the aged, poor, disabled, and orphaned. Included here was the vision he shared with other contemporary socialists and internationalists that a universal language be taught to all youngsters in place of national languages such as French and English ordinarily used in international communication. Kita, therefore, prescribed the teaching of Esperanto as the second language after Japanese to be taught in all of the schools and the total abolition of the use of Chinese ideographs.

The ultimate aim of socialism in Japan was to force the retreat of the West and to create a new civilization based on the revival of all of Asia. Japan was uniquely suited because it had maintained the highest principle of sovereignty – the imperial monarch – despite the incursion of Western political and social institutions and thus had withstood, as had no other Asian society, the challenge of modernism. The Japanese flag, he boasted, would one day be emblazoned on the minds of all Asian peoples. The "darkness" spread over Asia by the Versailles Treaty, especially the duplicity of the United States, he promised, would be lifted in the near future when Japan engaged the West in a conclusive naval confrontation, just as the Greeks in ancient times defeated the Persians in the battle of Salamis. Although the Greek victory represented the triumph of West over East, Japan's forthcoming success would signal the reemergence of East over West. Only through such an "ultimate war" would peace and power in Asia be secured.

Not surprisingly, Kita ended his "Outline" with a passage from the Lotus Sutra, the central text of the Buddhist Nichiren sect, calling attention to the saint's determination to lead the populace from passion and chaos to light, knowledge, and salvation. Nichiren's mission was to save Japan and all humankind, which meant Asia. Throughout much of his later career, Kita identified with the twelfth-century Buddhist reformer Nichiren and often chanted from the sacred scriptures of the Lotus Sutra. He found a source of resolve in Nichiren's hostility toward the existing political order and in his intense faith in his new power as a bodhisattva to save Japan from the Mongol invasion. Kita no doubt saw himself as a latter-day saint in a time of grave national peril, as had been the case in Nichiren's time.

Gondō Seikei

Although Kita's "Outline" was the most articulate and comprehensive program for radical reorganization, it was not the only proposal for violent action against contemporary political and industrial leaders. Kita's platform gave special attention to the question of industrial capital and recommended ways to redistribute the wealth of the bourgeoisie while disenfranchising them of political power. Yet his principal aim was to reorganize the industrial workplace, usually large factories, in order to improve the lot of city workers. In a sense, his national socialism represented a confirmation, rather than a rejection, of both industrialism and the cities. If by mobilizing the cities, Kita sought a solution to the conditions of urban existence, others, closer to a nativist agrarian tradition, saw both industrialism and the cities as the problem for, rather than a solution to, the countryside. And although Kita emphasized the importance of a reconstituted state structure, theorists such as Gondō Seikei (1868–1937), Inoue Nisshō (1886–1967), and Tachibana Kōsaburō (1893–1974) dramatized the ideal of an Asian agrarian community independent of the state and a sacred sanctuary free from the erosions of contemporary history. Moreover, this romantic view of society was shared by many important cultural theorists in the 1920s and 1930s who increasingly saw in the promise of community the only possible alternative to the divisiveness of modern political and social relations. Where they differed from more programmatic agrarian nativists was in their refusal to translate their ideals into a theory of violent action. Yet all agrarianists, like Kita Ikki, emphasized the imperial institution as central to any conception of community and frequently referred to the polity as a popular union of the emperor and people, the *kunmin kyōchi*. The people were seen as an embodiment of a common essence that derived from the local land and the tutelary shrines that defined all within a marked-off space as "brothers" under the divine protection of spiritual entities. Far from the corrupt cities and the sites of industrial capitalism, the possibility of communal brotherhood, the agrarianists believed, continued to exist as an accessible reality, even though in recent times it had been attacked by the forces of modernity. Included in these new corrosive forces were not only interest politics and bureaucracy but also the whole panoply of Western rationalism, which many vociferous agrarianists saw as deceptive and alien to a community life close to nature. In the writings of people like Gondō and Tachibana, rational instrumentality separated people from community, and thus from themselves, as interest displaced reciprocity.

Gondō's analysis of the contemporary situation stemmed less from the perception of inequality, as Kita's analysis had, than from the erosion of communal ties and agricultural work that, Gondō believed, had always been the bedrock of traditional Asian societies. He compared the societies of ancient Asia with those of the West and concluded that the former were based on agricultural cultivation by the peasantry, whereas the latter were founded on animal domestication by herders, a view that prefigured Watsuji Tetsurō's later geographical typology. In fact, Gondō was convinced that the origin of agricultural production reached back so far that its recollection had lapsed in the social memory of the people. To remind the Japanese of this forgotten agricultural endowment, Gondō turned to "reading" the nature myths and first fables from the "age of the gods" when the folk first cleared lands to grow grain and irrigate paddies to cultivate rice. Yet Gondō also argued that this agricultural act was necessitated by the recognition that because the gods blessed humans with the gift of life, they were obliged to reciprocate by making this land habitable for each successive generation.

In his principal essay, "Principles of Popular Self-Government" (*Jichi minsei ri*, 1936), Gondō summoned the authority of a divine ordinance attributed to the sun goddess – Amaterasu – to support his claims: "The five grains are necessary, as they give life to the people."[4] This deceptively simple phrase indicated to Gondō the natural basis underlying the construction of civilized life; to reproduce the conditions of social life as they had been imparted by the gods in each generation was to produce civilization itself. It was this lesson that subsequent generations had forgotten as they were lured to the blandishments of modernity. Indeed, it was at this point that human community had become a possibility. The supposition that humans were autonomous was erroneous, Gondō reasoned, because it disregarded the natural relationships into which all persons must enter. When people are engaged in agricultural work, they are naturally part of a set of communal relations; reciprocity renders the self into a "nonself," inasmuch as the individual becomes a part of the whole. Moreover, there are corresponding moral and legal norms that regulate the life of the community that prevent the freedom of the individual from becoming absolute. Because these norms were wedded to the natural human quest for mutual nourishment and satisfaction, they were not to be confused with large, artificial, bureaucratic organizations and overarching state structures. The moral dignity of the natural individual in a communitarian context of abundance and happiness was central to Gondō and represented what was genuinely human.

If the most basic human relationships and interactions reveal the principle of mutual assistance and relief, then the village must represent the natural basis for "self-government" among the people. The symbolic authorization for such local self-rule was the indigenous tutelary shrines that, from antiquity, sanctioned the sacred character of Japanese life. From this perspective, Gondō saw the imperial institution not as the source of constitutional authority, as many contemporaries imagined, but as the sacred symbol of the natural community. In his view, the creation of the land by the imperial

4   Gondō Seikei, "Jichi minsei ri," in *Gendai Nihon shisō taikei*, vol. 31, pp. 239–82, esp. p. 241.

ancestors was identical to this principle of a sacred community. In ancient times, he wrote, "politics" was referred to as a solemn religious ceremony – *matsurigoto* – ministered by a priest-king who formed a national community from this unification of the sacred and secular. For Gondō, as well as his contemporary, the ethnographer Yanagida Kunio, Japan the imperial land was simply a large tutelary shrine.

Disclaiming that this ancient pattern was unique to Japan, Gondō emphasized its "Asian" dimension. Ancient China had also known tutelary shrines, he argued, and they were used to mark off provincial boundaries. Yet they were also synonymous with the production of the five grains and thus symbolized community life itself. The shrines transformed the earth into something divine, and agricultural cultivation was a form of religious supplication. As a result, there was no distinction made between secular administrative duties and the management of the sacred fruits of the land. Without local management of land and its produce, societies could not have survived. Nothing in modern times could alter that basic truth regarding the continuation of human society in the future.

Gondō's thinking regarding the natural community prompted his followers to reject the modern state in Japan as an artificial bureaucratic construction imported from the West and disengaged from the realities of the agricultural experience. What troubled him the most was the imposition of an artificial, centralized administration over the tradition of local self-control. The new bureaucracy was thus oppressive and distant from the people; it had even denied the imperial institution from playing its familiar role as priest-king overseeing the people's local management of the sacred village. Without a system of local self-government steeped in peasant cultivation of the soil, the spirit of the nation, Gondō feared, would be dissipated, its continuity into the future jeopardized. And he attributed the cause of this contemporary crisis to the short-sightedness and insensitivity of the modern state, centered in Tokyo, a city he especially disliked for its impersonality and its indifference to the needs of Japan's farming population. Concerned only with industrial production, the government was removed from the sacred agrarian foundations of Japanese civilization. Gondō begged the Japanese to resist the continuing migration of farmers into the cities and called for their return to the land as the only hope for retaining genuine human community. The rural landscape, like the Egyptian pyramids, emptied of humans and hope, resembled a ruin portending the death of Japanese civilization. The depth of Gondō's pessimism and the rage it generated led him to advocate direct action. Rejecting legal reforms as inadequate to Japan's needs and unlikely to succeed, Gondō envisaged an awakening of the people's consciousness stirred spontaneously by heroic deeds to save the sacred sources of Japanese life. The "evil" manipulators of the large bureaucratic, industrial, and military complexes, he believed, must be challenged and overthrown in order to realize the aim of a true "restoration." Here it is evident that Gondō's summons to act quickly in a desperate situation attracted radical activists searching for a program and malcontents seeking ways in which to channel their resentment.

Tachibana Kosaburō

The tendency in agrarian fundamentalism to elicit radical and often reckless action was best dramatized by the case of Tachibana Kōsaburō. Before graduating from the First Higher School, the elite educational institution from which students embarked upon prestigious careers in the bureaucracy, Tachibana decide to return to his native province in rural Japan. Although it is difficult to plumb motives, Tachibana's own testimony explaining this decision suggests that he felt compelled to deal directly with the spiritual and material misery of the countryside. In his mind, there was no real distinction between spiritual and physical malaise. A complex thinker with an enormous theoretical grasp, Tachibana acknowledged his indebtedness to the examples of Tolstoi, Gandhi, the history of Western socialism, and the early ideas of Kita Ikki. He sought to combine the various themes into a coherent synthesis of radical humanism and agrarian fundamentalism. In the late 1920s and early 1930s, Tachibana turned to the strategy of direct and violent action against the existing order, inspiring sympathetic young officers in both services to commit even greater acts of daring and terrorism, which included the assassination of Prime Minister Inukai Tsuyoshi in the so-called May 15 incident. Tachibana was also implicated in the bombing attacks on the headquarters of the Seiyūkai, one of Japan's leading political parties, and on the Mitsui Bank in central Tokyo.

The central thread of Tachibana's ideas appeared in the preamble of his summons to action, "The Basic Principles of Japanese Patriotic Reform" (*Nihon aikoku kakushin hongi*, 1932). In this text,

Tachibana announced: "There can be no people who are separated from the land. There can be no national society separated from the people."[5] Despite its circularity, the call rang resonantly throughout Japan and invoked specific associations concerning the plight of the countryside among those who, because of their own agrarian origins, were most grieved by the unrelieved rural misery. Perceiving a general national crisis, much in the same manner as did Kita and Gondō, Tachibana promised resolution through a reidentification of people with land as the source of the necessary spiritual regeneration that would culminate in a patriotic reordering of the nation itself. By this reordering, he meant providing direct relief to the people in order to "save them" (*kyūkoku saimin*). To accomplish this goal, however, it was necessary to uproot Western capitalistic and materialist civilization in Japan. Tachibana referred specifically to eliminating such institutions as political parties, interest groups, and large industrial combines known as zaibatsu.

Although noted as a romantic and utopian thinker, Tachibana rejected characterizations that discounted his ideas as mere abstractions dissociated from the actualities of historical conditions. The primary aim of his program was "to liberate the people" from false and arbitrary governance. Unfortunately, most Japanese had been persuaded to see their world in terms of Western concepts and things and to think of nothing else but money. The condition of life had reached this unhappy state because the Japanese, implicated in a global market, were compelled to sell not only goods in the conventional sense but also labor, land, women, and ultimately the nation itself. Nothing escaped the iron demands of exchange value. The villages' simplicity and undifferentiated community life were torn apart by the ravaging force of money and commodities. The privileged classes, political parties, and the industrial combines, all located in the cities, effectively robbed Japan of its basic conditions of social existence and sent the nation down the road to slavery. Convincing evidence for this conclusion was the devastating extent to which Japan already had been drawn into the corrupting network of world finance that produced the Great Depression. What men in power had failed to grasp, Tachibana observed, was the divergent historical bases accounting for the development of Asian and Western societies. Like Gondō, Tachibana believed in the agrarian and village community as the original starting point of civilization

5   Tachibana Kōsaburō, "Nihon aikoku kakushin hongi," in *Gendai Nihon shisō taikei*, vol. 31, pp. 213–38, esp. p. 213.

in Asia, whereas the cities constituted the substance of Western history.

Tachibana also was convinced that Western modes of thinking were totally inappropriate to Asia. Marxism and dialectical materialism, with their privileging of class struggle to resolve social contradictions, were too rigid and formalistic to be applicable to Japan and Asia. The Japanese were not inclined to "assassinate reality," as he put it, by employing such abstract and limiting logic. The historical source for Western thought was rooted in the remote experiences of the ancient Greeks, whose idea of "logos" authorizing speculation and science had led them to believe that all things and events resulted from a dialectical process. When compared with Asian modes of thinking, the differences became readily apparent. Thus in the great Asian intellectual and religious systems such as Buddhism, Hinduism, Confucianism, and even ancient Christianity (which Tachibana considered to be an oriental religion), the dialectical differentiation between self and others, subject and object, are completely overcome. For this reason, human reciprocity, the triumph of nonself over self, was the central principle in Asian civilization. The idea of humans conquering nature was offensive and alien to Asia, even though it had been used to justify the rise of capitalism everywhere. Yet this materialistic view of life now infected Tokyo and other Asian capitals. Ornamental evidences were visible everywhere, in large department stores, banks, newspapers, and industrial factories of every conceivable variety. When this new urban landscape was juxtaposed with the rural scene of Asia, it would be impossible to avoid conclusions regarding the fate of the Japanese people. What indeed, Tachibana asked rhetorically, would become of those ideals of mutual faith and trust that have defined community life in Japan since the beginning? Japan had no alternative but to abandon the capitalism of the large cities and to return to the true spirit of Asian origins and the promise of holistic national community free from fragmentation and division.

Tachibana's assessment of contemporary realities based on a conceptual differentiation between East and West convinced him that only through direct action could Japan overcome the pernicious influence of Westernization. Such a liberation from the West would simultaneously generate similar acts of separation throughout Asia. All this should be accomplished without relying on Western assistance. In Japan, he believed, a "patriotic revolution" was possible by activating the historical union between emperor and folk. The force of this union would sweep away illegitimate rule, as the past had always shown and made manifest for all to see the spiritual light of the national essence. Tachibana even speculated that the agrarian revolution begun in Japan would spread throughout the world and rid it of individualism and materialism.

Tachibana's strategy called for the formation of a "patriotic brotherhood." All Japanese shared the idea of a communal brotherhood symbolized by the national essence itself. He also believed that the culminating event could be realized only by brothers in blood (*shishi*) who would fearlessly and unselfishly lay down their own lives to save the people in accordance with the emperor's wishes. The members of this brotherhood would be recruited from all social classes and thus would represent a more perfect whole signified by the imperial will. Clearly, Tachibana aimed at a revolutionary upheaval in which the fate of the folk would once more be redirected to the establishment of an agrarian communalism. He was not recommending a mass movement but, rather, a vanguard action initiated by blood-sworn patriots pledged to violence and terror.

Nakano Seigō

Although the major theorists of the restorationist revolt often occupied positions on the margins of Japanese society, explaining both their resentment and their radical summons to return to the country-side, others closer to the mainstream were involved in similar modes of thinking concerning the problematical status of Japanese and Asian cultures. A well-known journalist and leader in the 1920s of one of Japan's major political parties, the Minseitō, Nakano Siegō is an example of one who tried to bridge the concerns of the center with those of the periphery. Noted for his fiery and moving speeches, Nakano began his career as a journalist and identified with Miyake Setsurei's influential circle of intellectuals, the Seikyōsha and the magazine *Japan and the Japanese*.[6] Nakano became the principal spokesman for the cultural program promoted by this circle. The political basis of the nation, he repeated in his speeches and writings, was the "people," a collection of spiritually idealistic individuals symbolized by the social monarchy. The emperor, therefore, was the people's emperor, a view widely held by the agrarianists; he was not

6 See Tetsuo Najita, "Nakano Seigō and the Spirit of the Meiji Restoration in Twentieth-Century Japan," in James Morley, ed., *Dilemmas of Growth in Prewar Japan* (Princeton, N.J.: Princeton University Press, 1971), pp. 375–421.

the captive of elites ensconced in the constitutional and industrial order. Thus, although the Meiji Restoration had succeeded in maintaining Japan's independence against the threat of colonialism, it had also produced a system of elitism contrary to the ideal of popular national community. Indeed, the new elites had led the people astray into the path of uncritical conformism with Western ideas, manners, and things and had diverted them from their true and abiding purpose. Nakano believed the time had come to contest this deception by reidentifying with the true tradition of spiritual autonomy represented in the philosophic intuitionism (Ōyōmeigaku) of such heroic figures as Ōshio Heihachirō and Saigō Takamori. Given the failed expectations of the Meiji Restoration, Nakano called for a "second restoration" that would result in the "reorganization of the state" (kokka kaizō) and join the emperor and people into a powerful egalitarian order. He emphasized that such a reorganization would also signal Japan's leadership in the liberation of colonized countries throughout Asia to realize their own indigenous popular spirit. In Nakano's thinking, the opposition to domestic bureaucratism was closely associated with an expansive vision of Asian liberation, "Asia for Asians," a theme that was monotonously repeated in the 1930s by ideologues bent on justifying Japan's own imperialist adventures on the continent.

Ōkawa Shūmei

Yet an even better example of this mode of thinking was Ōkawa Shūmei (1886–1957), who, though not a "brown shirter" like Nakano, was involved in a range of activities that bridged the world of officialdom and militant paramilitary organizations. Ōkawa was, above all else, a scholar who brought impressive credentials and intellectual accomplishments to the vision of Japan's reconstruction and Asia's liberation. A respected scholar of Islamic studies trained at the newly established Institute for Oriental Studies (Tōyōkenkyūjo) at Tokyo Imperial University and noted for his translation of the Koran, Ōkawa was devoted to the study of Asia's major religious systems as a condition for "returning" to the sources of his own indigenous tradition.

In a reflective essay describing his own reidentification with the Japanese spirit (Nihon seishin kenkyū, 1939), Ōkawa acknowledged that after many years of spiritual confusion, he had rediscovered the native place of the Japanese soul (waga tamashii no *kokyō*).[7] Recognizing this return as a religious experience similar to conversion, he confessed how recovering the Japanese spirit resolved the psychological contradictions in his youthful mind that had so long afflicted him. He further analogized the return as the culmination of a long, perilous ascent up the side of a steep mountain. But Ōkawa's "mountain" was a metaphor for an uphill struggle to overcome personal cultural despair; it was not simply a specific "local place," as had been the case with Gondō and Tachibana. What Ōkawa found, therefore, was not the utopian village of romantic agrarianists but the moral tradition tempered by the major religious and philosophic systems of Buddhism and Confucianism which, he believed, had always emphasized the close relationship between proper ethical conduct (*dōgi*) and religion (*shūkyō*). This combination of morality and religion was exemplified best in the spirit of the samurai class. En route to this discovery, Ōkawa observed the spiritual confusion and agony among vast numbers of people. He grieved over what he imagined was the absence of purpose in society, which he felt was caused by the failure of the existing political order to provide clear direction. Much of the imagery he used to characterize Japan's contemporary predicament called forth spiritual malaise, isolation, and alienation. The actual world before him was devoid of both peace and compassion. In his lengthy retrospective "The Gates of Paradise" (*Anraku no mon*, 1951), Ōkawa recalled that a psychological dislocation bordering on a fatal illness had spread throughout all of Asia.[8]

Ōkawa's "return" to Japan, then, included concern for the "awakening" of the Asian continent. Although he saw the importance of revolutions in the West as a model for overthrowing imperialism and facilitating an Asian renaissance, he believed that Asians must liberate themselves through collective movements and common purpose. The urgency behind his view was the belief that Europe and Asia stood in a relationship of master and slave; Europe had plundered the soul of Asia and had robbed it of its dignity and creative spirit. In an essay called "Revolutionary Europe and Renascent Asia" (*Kakumei Europpa to fukkō Ajia*, 1992), Ōkawa meditated on the consequences of the domination of Asia by Europe and saw its solution in an Asian renaissance.[9] The Russo-Japanese War of 1905

7 Ōkawa Shūmei, "Nihon seishin kenkyū," in *Gendai Nihon shisō taikei*, vol. 31, pp. 137–43.
8 Ōkawa, "Anraku no mon," in *Gendai Nihon shisō taikei*, vol. 9: *Ajia shugi*, ed. Takeuchi Yoshimi, pp. 254–321.
9 Ōkawa, "Kakumei Europpa to fukkō Ajia," in *Gendai Nihon shisō taikei*, vol. 9, pp. 239–53.

was the turning point in the awakening of independence movements in Asia. The possibility of freedom was dramatized by Japan's victory over a Western power in this war. Ōkawa's argument also rested on an appreciation of Asia's cultural contributions to human civilizations. Many of the inventions used by the West to subjugate the East – the printing press, gun powder, and the like – had been developed in Asia. And all of the great religions, Ōkawa observed, had originated in Asia. It was for this reason that the peoples of Asia should not be cowed into accepting the status of inferiors that had been accorded them. During the past several years, he emphasized, the "yellow races" had been made to feel unworthy by being called the "white man's burden." Even though the Russo-Japanese war had sparked the first glimmerings of hope, there was still much that needed to be done to reach the goal of liberation and to create a new world history. The Asian renaissance must be based on the reconstruction of traditional societies into modern states. And an essential ingredient in this transformation was the installation of representative government. Here, he pointed to the failings of the Chinese revolution and its ill-advised reliance on Western powers; the Japanese example offered the only possible promise of a genuine independence.

For Asian independence movements to succeed, Ōkawa was convinced that each must reconstitute its society into an ideal state, an idea he derived from his interpretation of Platonic idealism. He argued that this ideal had been distorted by the Western experience, notably by Christ and Marx. Although he initially admired these two men, he acknowledged that a reading of Plato had changed his mind. In his view, Plato's state was divided into three parts, the leaders, who are endowed with "reason," the military who possess "commitment," and farmers, artisans, and merchants who provide for the needs of the "spirit." Yet Ōkawa's interpretation of Plato was closer to the idealized representation of the Tokugawa order or indeed even Mencius' "ethical realm" than it was to the philosopher's idealized polity. If people were helped to prosper, were protected, and were nourished, they would serve as a firm and healthy foundation in the quest for the ideal good. In the ideal state, private interests and passions, such as Ōkawa observed in the conduct of party politics, must be suppressed for the public good; the state must, at all times, avoid corruption and elitist competition over issues relating to interest. The ideal of the good must be grasped to overcome short-term gains of partisan rivalries. Here, he compared the Platonic state with

the Mencian idea of kingly justice, ōdōron, and identified its traditional idealization of "letters," bu, with the Greek philosopher's
concept of "philosophy" as the basis of civilized governance. Later
he linked the Confucian tradition itself to the teachings of Plato.
Within Japanese intellectual history, the philosophies of Kumazawa
Banzan (1619–91) and Yokoi Shōnan (1809–69) disclosed to him a
similar spirit consistent with this idealistic tradition.

Ōkawa's spiritual peregrinations spanned the globe, often disclos-
ing a close kinship with the cosmopolitanism of the 1920s. Along
with his discovery of Plato's political idealism, his intellectual curiosity led him to probe the recesses of Western civilization for figures
who had been able to transcend the constraints of Christianity.
Ōkawa believed that like-minded cultural heroes could be found in
both East and West, people who reflected a cosmopolitan idea in
their personal effort to overcome race and region. Leonardo da Vinci
thus represented the great complexity of the human spirit devoid
of Christian associations. He felt similar admiration for Dante,
Spinoza, and Ralph Waldo Emerson. Ōkawa especially prized
Emerson because of his discovery of individual "intuitionism,"
which went beyond Christianity, time, and place and reminded
Ōkawa of the Tokugawa "intuitionism" that Nakano Seigō also
admired. Yet it is also true that Emerson's appeal lay in the presumed relationship between New England "transcendentalism" and
the Indian religions. In any case, the spiritual resources that Ōkawa
sought in the West were those that were functionally equivalent to
Asian religiosity. He saw in this universal spirituality the means by
which Asians might throw off the yoke of Western domination, and
the solution to Japan's own psychological dislocation under the
impact of modernity and industrialism. Ōkawa's "cosmopolitanism"
was therefore closely related to what he believed to be the general
malaise of the human spirit in modern life. In it, individual self-
awakening and the spiritual renaissance of Japan and Asia were really
one and the same thing. Through the mediating role of the "Japanese spirit," Ōkawa believed, it would be possible to gain release
from the "prison" and "hospital" of modernity and realize fully the
promise of the ideal state.

Ōkawa's conception of the ideal state and its offer of deliverance
from modern alienation led him to conclude that the existing order
was prevented from accomplishing this task because it was dogged
by corruption and partisan rivalries. Here Ōkawa used his idea of
spiritual renaissance as a plea for action to purge political practice; to

rid domestic life of the Western presence was the condition for expelling imperialism from Asia. As a student of Asian philosophy, Ōkawa had become interested in the fate of modern India and the imposition of British despotism in that country. The British had drained India of its spirituality. Hence, the cleansing of politics at home was directly related to the broader goal of returning Asia to Asians. The incorporation of capitalism in Japan, especially at the accelerated rate witnessed after World War I, produced conditions in Japan that had come to resemble those found in Western countries. Labor disturbances, tenant protests, conspicuous consumption by the new rich, and ruthless party politics all had worked against the spiritual needs of the people. Moreover, the Japanese were experiencing social conditions that earlier in Russia had led to revolution, in Hungary, abortive uprisings, and in Italy and Germany, fascism. What appeared on the horizon were "reconstructionist movements" (*kaizō undō*) consisting of various action-oriented groups dedicated to spiritual renaissance and political reorganization. Sometime in the late 1920s, Ōkawa joined them.

It was clear to Ōkawa and others that the object of reconstruction was domestic politics. This goal must be reached by any means, which, in the early 1930s, meant violence and terror. Indeed, violence was a necessity because of its "cleansing" propensities. It was not simply expelling the Western presence from Japan and Asia but purging the spirit of putrefaction and pollution. Absolution of the personal soul (*watakushi no tamashii*) paved the way for the realization of the national spirit (*kokka no seishin*). The implicit Pan-Asianism that Ōkawa and other contemporaries advocated provided an ideological mapping for the construction of large-scale strategies to eliminate Western power from Asia in an ultimate encounter or, as it was increasingly expressed, "the war to end wars." That is to say, the spiritual reconstruction summoned by writers such as Ōkawa converged with plans to launch a war either on the Asian continent against the Soviet Union or in the Pacific against Great Britain and the United States. Yet the reasons for an Asian renaissance and its intended meaning were not always the same as the diplomatic and political causes leading to military confrontation. But the merger of a spiritual ideology and military aggression often produced self-serving justifications of Japan's own presence in Asia and its destiny to lead the yellow races to a new order. If war were necessary for the "spiritual awakening" of Asia, peace would bring a "new order of coprosperity" under Japanese leadership. For example, in 1939, a pamphlet entitled the "Shōwa Restoration" openly declared that the "war to end wars" was a historical necessity and the agency of progress.[10] After World War I, the argument ran, the global trend was for states to reconsolidate into larger groupings. These new blocks were the Soviet Union, Europe, North and South America, and Asia. But according to the pamphlet, there were only two major spheres that required attention: Asia, which represented the just, and the West (Europe and North America), which was despotic. The inevitable clash between the forces of light and darkness would occur in the Pacific, where the two blocks converged. Such a war would inaugurate a millennium of peace and autonomy for all of Asia. It was also the destiny of the Japanese state itself, founded on the principle of "imperial justice," to achieve not only a Japanese "restoration" but one extending to Asia as well, a *Tōa ishin*, as it was called in the late 1930s.

CULTURALISM

Despite Ōkawa Shūmei's own plunge into the stream of direct action, his thinking was linked to a deeper and more complex opposition to the West as it was being articulated in the 1930s. This resistance was the product of a widely shared intellectual shift from "cosmopolitanism" to "culturalism" (*bunkashugi*). The pattern of this movement exceeded the limited outlook of the radical right and its resentments to include many of the leading writers and critics of the day, such as Tanizaki Junichirō (1886–1965), Nishida Kitaro (1870–1945), Watsuji Tetsurō (1889–1960), Yanagida Kunio (1875–1962), and Yokomitsu Riichi (1898–1947). What linked this group of writers and thinkers was not so much a program of action, as promoted by the radical right, but, rather, their search for spiritual and critical resources in the world's civilizations. This quest made culture problematical and made defining its contours and meaning a more-than-adequate substitute for politics and violent action. The search for value led first to an examination of Western culture, which invariably sent the seekers to a "return" to the "native place of the spirit" (*Nihon kaiki*). After less than a decade, Japanese writers and intellectuals abandoned the cosmopolitan civilization for the familiarity of traditional culture. Those who had been most deeply engaged in discussions on "human cultivation" (*kyōyōshugi*) and

10 Tōa remmei dōshikai, "Shōwa ishin ron," in *Gendai Nihon shisō taikei*, vol. 31, pp. 381–412.

"character" (*jinkakushugi*) as the condition for cultural renewal were often the same men who had turned to Western intellectual history to gain critical inspiration and who had been attached to one of the major philosophic movements in Europe in the 1920s, Neo-Kantianism. It is hardly surprising that the middle-class intellectuals in Japan who flocked to Neo-Kantianism saw themselves in an analogous relationship to the German bourgeoisie, which had constituted its main support earlier. Here was an idealistic and humanistic system of thought that privileged the role of individual consciousness and moral awareness in perceiving the world as it is. Yet the categories with which this world is grasped, a world that never could be known in itself, determined what that world should be. It was also one of the premises emphasized by the Kantian revival that the immediate subject–object distinction was deceptive and required an act of sublation. The objective world and subjective intention were not dialectical equivalents; the objective world was "determined" by the actions stemming from subjective consciousness. Thus, Japanese Neo-Kantians recognized that because individual consciousness made the world or the categories with which to comprehend it, such activity would result in the creation of value. In other words, they believed that consciousness functioned primarily to judge value, as it could never really know the world as it is; the highest values acknowledged by a critical consciousness are the true (*shin*), the good (*zen*), and the beautiful (*bi*), and it is culture where such values are realized.

Miki Kiyoshi

The philosopher Miki Kiyoshi (1897–1945), an early adherent to Neo-Kantianism, proposed that literature and philosophy, found in the ideal of self-cultivation, were essential to a science of culture, whereas physical science and technology belonged to material civilization. Clearly, "civilization" became a pejorative concept in the 1920s and came to mean material progress and human debasement, whereas culture was associated with creative self-realization. The important implication of this polarization of civilization (*bunmei*) and culture (*bunka*) was the belief that individual self-cultivation could not be reached through capitalism and technological industrialism. Another contemporary of Miki's, Kuwaki Gen'yaku (1874–1946), writing in the 1920s, announced that culturalism was a force that disclosed internalized human values endowed with universal meaning. Culture was understood as the product of human creation and contrasted with the natural order, which was merely mechanical and repetitive. Others argued that because culture is created by humans, it must reflect the internal spirit. Yet to equate culture with interiority was to disengage the inner self, as many writers called it, from the external world of politics and technology. Such a separation persuaded thinkers and writers, bent on a quest for self-cultivation, to remove themselves from the corruptions of the outside world and to refrain from trying to change it. The search for value in the creation of culture, signifying universalistic meaning, transcended the particular historical and existential context in which they were produced. The emphasis on the capacity of the self to create universalistic values turned writers and intellectuals away from questions of social responsibility and political action. In the final analysis, their philosophical aim was to construct a domain of pure creative spirit independent of the world of existing structures. Although the impulse toward culture as the manifestation of universal value was initially informed by cosmopolitanism, thus dramatizing the possibility of a unique Japanese contribution to a universal human culture that recognized no national boundaries, the affirmative role of a particular cultural inheritance could easily dissolve into cultural exceptionalism. The hermeneutic "horizon of prejudices," the realm of historical experience accessible to an observer, narrowed into provincial national culture. This was especially apparent during the years of domestic and diplomatic turbulence in the late 1920s and early 1930s.

During this cosmopolitan interlude, the Japanese turned to producing cultural histories and texts testifying to Japan's unique contribution to a global culture and praising its accomplishments as equivalent to Western achievements. A common theme in many of these "histories" was the concentration on Japanese culture before the modern era. Some of the better-known works in this genre were Watsuji's "Studies in the History of Japanese Spirit" (*Nihon seishinshi kenkyū*, 1926), the sinologist Naitō Torajirō's "Studies on the Cultural History of Japan" (*Nihon bunkashi kenkyū*, 1924), the humanist philosopher Abe Jirō's "Studies in Arts and Crafts of the Tokugawa Period" (*Tokugawa jidai ni okeru geijutsu no kenkyū*, 1928), Tsuda Sōkichi's exposition of the manifestation of popular spirit in literature, *Bungaku ni arawaretaru waga kokumin no shisō* (1921), and Kuki Shūzō's "The Structure of Tokugawa Aesthetic Style" (*Iki no kōzō*, 1929). All of these works positioned values and ideals such as beauty, goodness, and truth as central to Japan's creative endowment and as examples of how culture manifested the inner workings of self and spirit. Indeed, what many of these texts tried to make clear was not the history of cultural development but, rather, the journey of the spirit. Watsuji's "Studies" attempted to grasp "the existence or life of the Japanese throughout the ages in order to show how the self realized itself as it passed through a number of cultural artifacts."

The most comprehensive philosophical synthesis of the problem of culture and values was formulated by Nishida Kitarō. An entire generation of writers, intellectuals, and thinkers in the 1920s and 1930s fell under the powerful influence of Nishida, in either agreement or dissent. One of Nishida's key concepts was his theory of "place" (basho), which represented the existential space in which universal value is actualized. In his earlier and well-known treatise, "Studies of the Good" (Zen no kenkyū, 1911), Nishida formulated a theory of "pure religious consciousness." To conceptualize this state, he drew heavily on the philosophy of pure existence found in the tradition of Zen Buddhism. From this perspective, he constructed an elaborate metaphysical framework for "place" as the locus of universal creation. Denying that it was his purpose either to revive Zen or to preach it, Nishida claimed to be looking for a philosophically stable basis of "life" that could transcend the limitations of material interest, historical change, and the Western bourgeois concept of egoism. His critics, particularly the Marxist thinker Tosaka Jun (1900–45), a former student of Nishida's, found Nishida's thinking to have confused "existence" with its "interpretation" in his search for metaphysical certainty. But Nishida continued to emphasize, without compromise, the superiority of knowledge and interpretation over historical actuality. He saw the category of the universal negative (mu) as the location of "place" unconstrained by history, individual ego, and Western definitions of absolutes such as the Judeo-Christian God.

The implications of Nishida's ontology were worked out by his students, many of whom were later associated with what was called collectively the "Kyoto school." The best known among them was Miki Kiyoshi, who was deeply affected by Nishida's "Study of the Good" and his study of German idealism. As a young intellectual, Miki was drawn to the humanistic ideas of twelfth-century Buddhism as formulated by Shinran, in contrast with Nishida's lifelong interest in Zen. And it is quite likely that Miki saw in Nishida's synthesis of Buddhism and German idealism a model for his own philosophic program. First as a pupil in Kyoto and then later as an exchange student in Germany for three years, Miki explored a diversity of ideas ranging from Neo-Kantianism, originally learned from Nishida, to Marxist and existentialist thought.

Yet the most philosophically distinct position for which Miki came to be known was his phenomenological and hermeneutical understanding of reality as it occurs in time.[11] Based on his studies in Germany, which included a close reading of Wilhelm Dilthey, Miki argued that without a phenomenological interpretation of events, humankind would be left with only meaningless "action." In particular, Miki emphasized events' temporal and spatial dimensions as the key to human meaning. Like many of his contemporaries in Europe and Japan, Miki was convinced that the principal temporal or historical problem of the day was capitalism and its culture. In his view, capitalism had spawned an egoistic and inequitable culture, and any assessment of meaning must include the possibility of going beyond the historical limitations imposed by capitalism. Miki was not advocating a simple restoration of feudalism and did not hint at a return to some essential spirit. Rather, he saw events as a world historical process and its dialectic. Yet this dialectic was produced by a combination of temporality and spatial specificity. Here he proposed a conception of "space" comparable to Nishida's idea of "place." By space, Miki meant the area of Asia that had been under Western domination and subject to the sway of capitalism and the ideas of "modernism" associated with historical force. Events within Asia, he argued, must contain the potential for a new meaning, such as the possibility of creating a different order that would go beyond the historical limitations set by Western capitalism. Specifically, Miki emphasized a new "cooperativism" for Asia, which would join the various societies in accordance with "Asian humanism" (Tōyōteki hyumanisumu), referring vaguely to Buddhist principles of compassion and mutual assistance. He also described this humanism as representing a synthesis of gemeinschaft and gesellschaft, traditional community and modern society. This new order would be an advancement over capitalism, as it would be the result of a dialectical encounter between capitalism and Asian society and thus would contain elements of both but yet be vastly different.

11 See, for example, Miki Kiyoshi, "Kaishakugaku teki genshōgaku no kisogainen," in Kindai Nihon shisō taikei, vol. 27. Miki Kiyoshi shū, ed. Sumiya Kazuhiko (Tokyo: Chikuma shobō, 1975).

Miki also pointed to the importance of resolving the problem of class. He regarded "cooperativism" as the means to achieve the goal of first exposing "class" as a fixed category of social existence and then overcoming it altogether. The "public sphere" should always override the interest of classes based on narrow interests and provide the space within which new divisions of labor would be formed based on the acquisition of knowledge and skills. In his vision of cooperativism, informed by the principle of *techné*, the technocratic idea would become central to public life and replace criteria mandating the class lines developed under capitalism. Here Miki revealed a kinship with Max Weber's earlier assessment of the political effects of capitalism and his subsequent effort to formulate a new vision of governance founded on the primacy of expert knowledge rather than the maximization of profit. Miki, like Weber, envisaged a nonhereditary technocracy as a new stage of development that would abandon social divisions based on class. He also distinguished between cooperativism based on technocratic proficiency and the romantic communitarianism advanced by the extreme right. Although right-wing polemicists had offered a critique of capitalism, liberalism, and communism, they had failed to provide a critical basis for action, other than turning back the clock, and had slipped into incoherent and dangerous forms of folkism (*minzokushugi*) in their desperate attempt to distance themselves from both modernism and Marxism.

Miki turned his interpretative strategy to account for the China incident of 1937, which sparked Japan's full-scale invasion of China. He used the occasion to raise the question concerning Japan's future course. But he believed that this question could be answered only by grasping the "world historical meaning" of that decisive event. He understood the relationship between war and culture and saw the former as a causal condition in the transformation of the latter. Events in Russia and Germany after World War I provided him with ample evidence to support this conclusion. Writing shortly after the China invasion, he saw that the war there would produce far-reaching cultural consequences in both Japan and China. He compared these consequences with the revolutionary changes in Russia after 1917. In Japan, too, he believed that the status of its culture after the war could provoke a response from all sensitive and thoughtful intellectuals. War, he wrote, necessitated the establishment of control over popular thought and action and compromised creativity. Under such circumstances, poets might compose jingoistic songs but never real poetry. Systems of control, however, could never eradicate the creativity of the human spirit. Hence he was convinced that this spirit would remain active throughout wartime in order to shape the new culture that would appear with the reestablishment of peace.

Thus Miki refused to see the China incident simply as an act of naked invasion. Rather, he grasped the event as the starting point for the true unification of Asia based on a new order of cooperativism and the ideals of Asian humanism. As if he were able to speak for the "cunning of reason" itself, the Hegelian knowledge of hindsight, he believed that the event's larger meaning was to create a new spatial realm, free from the constraints of capitalism and poised to embark on a new development of world history. The promised liberation of Asia, Miki proposed, would signal an advancement to a new, yet-to-be-understood, historical stage beyond discredited forms of modernism. It was for this reason that Miki called on his society and those in power to understand the deeper historical meaning of the event. Moreover, it was his interpretation of the possible meaning of events that helps explain Miki's decision to join the Shōwa Research Society (Shōwa kenkyūkai) established in 1938 and composed of leading scholars of the time, such as Ryū Shintarō, Shimizu Ikutarō, Rōyama Masamichi, and Hayashi Tatsuo. These were scholars and intellectuals who, again like Weber, believed that the fundamental crisis of twentieth-century capitalism – the efficient distribution of resources and power – necessitated bureaucratic organization. Accordingly, they felt that such bureaucratic structures should be managed by scientifically trained experts, free from party and interest, who could, with the right kind of knowledge, ascertain the general interest and formulate the appropriate policies. It was in this sense that they saw their role in government and seized the opportunity to influence the course of action taken by the state, an issue that was first recognized in the 1930s but that remains a continuing legacy of this century. In particular, members of the Shōwa Research Society wished to improve upon capitalism by supplying politically rational management – planning – of the state comparable to the economic rationality of technology and industrialism. In effect, this meant finding ways to overcome conflict and its enduring threat that the state hitherto had not been able to resolve.

Miki saw his own participation in this group as an example of technocratic expertise serving public policy. He had long believed it important to recruit for managerial posts in government experts who had demonstrated their mastery of certain kinds of knowledge, and he saw his own role as an expert influencing policies in accordance with his informed cooperativist vision of a better future. Far from shaping policy and determining the course of events, as Miki and others in the Shōwa Research Society hoped, the reverse occurred: The expert intellectuals participated little or not at all in the actual decision making, and the ideas they advanced, like Miki's conception of a cooperativist Asia, were ultimately used for propaganda by the war mobilization structure (*kokka sōdōin*). Miki himself lived precariously throughout the war years and eventually was imprisoned by the very government he had earlier tried to serve. Before his death in prison, Miki wrote his last work on Shinran and seemingly returned to the point at which he had begun his intellectual odyssey as a young student and which initially had attracted him to Nishida Kitarō.

CULTURAL PARTICULARISM

If Miki assessed the impact of war on culture negatively and yet recognized the necessity of intellectuals and writers preparing themselves for peace, the philosophers of the Kyoto school inverted this formulation to regard war as a requisite condition for determining national culture. These philosophers, students of Nishida, formed a group called the Kyoto faction and identified with the philosophy faculty of Kyoto University. The principal members were Koyama Iwao (1905–), Kōsaka Masaaki (1900–69), Suzuki Shigetaka (1907–), and Nishitani Keiji (1900–). It was their purpose to make Nishida's more formal concepts more tangible so that they could direct national policy and action. These thinkers wrote a series of books and articles in the late 1930s dealing largely with the historicist implications of Nishida's ideas for the current political situation. Their statement was summarized in a symposium in 1941 entitled "The World Historical Position and Japan" (*Sekaishiteki tachiba to Nihon*) and later published in the widely read periodical *Chūō kōron*.[12] This group's central purpose was to construct what they called a "philosophy of world history" that could both account for Japan's current position and disclose the course of future action. But a closer examination of this "philosophy of world history" reveals a thinly disguised justification, written in the language of Hegelian

12   Published in book form in 1943 by Chūō koron.

metaphysics, for Japanese aggression and continuing imperialism. In prewar Japan, no group helped defend the state more consistently and enthusiastically than did the philosophers of the Kyoto faction, and none came closer than they did to defining the philosophic contours of Japanese fascism.

The Kyoto philosophers specified Nishida's ontological concept of "space" to mean the "world stage" where all human and social problems will be resolved under Japan's leadership role. History, or the world stage, consisted of the interaction of "blood" and "soil," a conclusion already reached by a number of Nazi apologists. Yet Japan was uniquely appointed to resolve the struggle of history because philosophically it had successfully synthesized Eastern humanism and Western rationalism and thus moved to a higher stage of human development. This accomplishment demanded the dismantling of Western hegemony. Thus despite their use of abstract philosophical language, the Kyoto philosophers unashamedly spoke on behalf of Japanese imperial expansion as the creative moment of a vast historical movement to a new level of human excellence. The historical present was pregnant with meaning for state and culture. In fact, the Kyoto faction rarely differentiated between these two categories, using them interchangeably. In the world, the state realized its fullest ethical potential in war. War was the central event, they believed, by which states came into existence. It would continue as the agency to forge a new order. The self-awareness of the state, as Kōsaka put it, would be sustained by war. "Only as the folk experience war do they become aware of the state and its subjective nature." "Place," then, was not the formal category that Nishida had envisaged but, rather, the "world, which served as the moral training ground of the state."[13] For Kōsaka, war was the test that validated or invalidated the state's moral status. And through war alone is the world's historical meaning made manifest. If war is waged for a proper cause, then the state will authenticate its ethical subjectivity. But if it is lost, Kōsaka cautioned, it will have been fought for unethical and uncultural reasons. Echoing Leopold Ranke, he proposed that world history would turn into world judgment.

The members of the Kyoto faction openly acknowledged their admiration for European fascism and its own struggle with the forces of modernity. They saw it as part of the larger world movement in which they had identified Japan's historical destiny. The purpose of

13   From Takeuchi Yoshitomo, *Shōwa shisō shi* (Tokyo: Minerva shobō, 1958), p. 406.

this movement was the overthrow of communism and the establishment of a new future order. As homegrown fascist writers, Kōsaka and Koyama insisted on the necessity of strict state control of domestic society; the elimination of intellectual heterodoxy, however moderate or unpolitical; and rigid conformism in behavior and conduct. Although it is tempting to associate Miki Kiyoshi's own intellectual dependence on Nishida, and his subsequent involvement in Konoe's "brain trust" to the fascism of the Kyoto faction, the two programs were worlds apart. Miki addressed his philosophy to a new future that would liberate the creative human spirit under conditions of peace. The Kyoto faction glorified the state as the ideal embodiment that justified Japan's leadership role in a war of revolt against the West.

Although it is often suggested that the revolt against the West was a militant and jingoistic movement populated by putschists, assassins, or "Japanese-style fascists" – such as some of the members of the Kyoto faction – this characterization misrepresents the compelling nature of that problem broadly felt throughout much of Japanese culture. Involved was the reappraisal of the status of culture and the more pressing question concerning its Japanese form. Even the most rabid putschist and admirer of fascism agreed on the importance of this intellectual issue of reconceptualizing the nature of Japanese culture in the industrialized context of the twentieth century. In much of this, an earlier cosmopolitanism evolved into an appreciation of Japanese culture distinct from Western, capitalist, and "modern" society. Thus, although such thinking did not necessarily require an overt revolt against the West, it informed a good deal of the Japanese vision of itself as an alternative model of culture superior to the achievements of the West.

Watsuji Tetsurō

One of the most influential theorists of this cultural problem was the philosopher Watsuji Tetsurō, who taught at Kyoto University between 1925 and 1934 and then at Tokyo University until 1949. As a young scholar, Watsuji, like many of his contemporaries, immersed himself in the culture of cosmopolitanism exemplified by a deep fascination with Western philosophy and literature and in particular with the problem of the self in modern society. His graduate thesis focused on Nietzsche. Even though he rejected the Neo-Kantian explanation, which had tried to derive consciousness of the entire world from the immediate life experience, Watsuji was nonetheless concerned with its conception of a "philosophy of life." Nietzsche's philosophy offered Watsuji a powerful critique of capitalist civilization and concentrated on the contradiction between social constraints of inequalities and individual expressibility. He also was attracted to Nietzsche's idea of the heroic and creative individual. Watsuji promoted the superiority of spiritual over material civilization and thus prized the creative elite over the general populace, whose lives were determined by the relative abundance or deprivation of material things. It was within this frame of reference that he opposed universal manhood suffrage, the labor movement, and the social mass parties of the late 1920s. Nietzsche also made precisely the same criticism of the socialist movement in Germany in the 1880s. As applied by Watsuji, the Nietzschean thesis also denounced rationalism, technological culture, and utilitarianism, all of which were representations used to mask the materialistic and inauthentic life-style of the newly emergent industrial bourgeoisie. In much the same manner that Nietzsche had sought an authentic and creative moment in ancient Greece, untainted by modern bourgeois rationalism, which had appropriated much from the Judeo-Christian heritage, Watsuji similarly sought in ancient Japan a comparable manifestation of an essential creative spirit. Watsuji's quest was reminiscent of Tachibana's search for an original utopian movement at the beginning of history. But unlike him, Watsuji was more concerned with the creative spirit than with the communal ties of brotherhood that Tachibana had emphasized. However, their search for an unalloyed existence, free from materialistic impulses, suggests a close resemblance. In the environment of the 1920s, Watsuji recommended a "spirit of opposition" that would lead individuals to free themselves from the material realities of the present. Such a liberation could be realized through an identification with the genuine creativity in the indigenous culture. Watsuji was specifically interested in showing how Buddhist art and architecture represented, after the Middle Ages, the purest expression of the Japanese creative spirit. In a series of works – "Pilgrimages to Ancient Temples" (*Koji junrai*, 1919), "The Culture of Ancient Japan" (*Nihon kodai bunka*, 1920), and "Studies of the Japanese Spirit" (*Nihon seishinshi kenkyū*, 1926) – Watsuji reminded his contemporaries of the pure expression of the Japanese creative power that was manifested in the past but neglected in the present. It should be noted that this path to a tradition of aesthetic purity had already been charted at the turn of the century by the art historian and Pan-Asianist Okakura Tenshin.

Watsuji's plea on behalf of Japan's creative past was reminiscent of Nietzsche's efforts to restore some of the great monuments of ancient Greece. His valorization of the creative spirit in ancient and medieval times was grounded in the conviction that he had discovered the essential creative form of the Japanese people. Here Watsuji idealized this creative tradition and even believed that the early Japanese Yamato court embodied it over time. In that ancient culture, the communitarian society resolved the contradictions between spirit and physicality, nature and person, sovereign and subject. Just as the spirit of ancient Greek culture was destroyed by Roman "materialism," so Watsuji feared that Western civilization, exemplified by Anglo-American self-centered individualism, now threatened to eliminate Japan's spiritual legacy. Americans, Watsuji once wrote, were especially afflicted by the plague of materialism. Relentlessly pursuing material things, they had lost their souls, discarded their philosophy, neglected their arts, and returned to the life of the "birds and beasts." Americans, he noted, had exchanged "capital" for the blood and iron of the ancient Romans. But it came to the same thing. With it, they had enslaved the world to the demands of materialistic civilization. Thus in Watsuji, we see what earlier German politicians had referred to as the necessary "cultural struggle" (*Kultur Kampf*) that provided some of the ideological arguments for war stated in cultural terms. The thought of Watsuji, as it derived from Nietzsche, synthesized the idea of a "spiritual community" (*seishinteki kyōdōtai*) and the "personalism" of the philosophy of existence (*iki no tetsugaku*) and resulted in a powerful resistance to modern bourgeois culture, its rationalism, and the civilization that spawned it.

It was within this frame of reference that Watsuji embarked on a scholarly project to uncover the historical roots of Japanese ethics. In doing so, like Ōkawa, he expanded his understanding of the area of authenticity to include all of Asia. He justified this inclusion by using Buddhism as the integrative spiritual force. This "cultural struggle" also included a contest between Asian spirituality and Western materialism. The crucial element in Watsuji's grasp of Buddhism was the category of "nothingness" (*mu*), which Nishida Kitarō had already articulated in broad philosophical terms. To Watsuji, the transition from "nothingness," as the detachment from existing material conditions, to the pure life was the identification of that

Buddhist category with universal "nature" itself. This elision of "nothingness" with "nature" was aimed at transcending the rationalist proposition that nature was an "object" to dominate or manipulate for human ends, however they might be defined. This ethic of nothingness thus opposed the rational characterization of the self as being "outside" nature rather than within its embrace. Watsuji sought, therefore, to clarify the source of this Asian view and the reasons for its superiority over the Western dialectic between humans and nature. To do so, he believed that it was necessary to begin by considering human society within nature and to explore its customs, habits, and mores in their essential and pure setting. Watsuji saw in the world of thought two basic but different ways of thinking, logical reasoning and intuition. Although the former obviously belonged to the traditional Western mode of thinking, and the latter to the East, it was important to explain the consequences of these two divergent epistemologies. It was this problem that prompted Watsuji to compose his well-known essay entitled "Climate and Culture" (Fūdo, 1935).

When Watsuji was a student in Germany in 1927, he had devoted much attention to Heidegger's classic work "Being and Time" (Sein und Zeit, 1926), which juxtaposed the relationship between existence and the dimension of historical time. In his own work, Watsuji clarified his relationship to Heidegger: Although "timefulness" was extremely important to Heidegger, especially in his exposition of a subjective and existential structure, Watsuji wondered why at the same time he had not seen "spacefulness" in a comparable philosophical light. The central problem for him, he admitted in the preface of "Climate and Culture," was to consider in detail the significance of climate and environment as they related to historical culture. In his words: "The activity of man's self-apprehension, man, that is, in his dual character of individual and social being, is at the same time of a historical nature. Therefore, climate does not exist apart from history, nor history apart from climate."[14] If Heidegger had seen time as distinct from nature and thus remained within the dialectic that he had inherited from Hegel, Watsuji aimed instead to introduce existentialism into nature, thus earning Tosaka Jun's criticism that he had "subjectivized" nature.

By concentrating on "climate and space," Watsuji was able to identify the essential features of the two major climatic divisions –

14 From Watsuji Tetsurō, Climate, translation of Fūdo by Geoffrey Bownas (Tokyo: Hokuseido Press, 1961), p. 8.

monsoon and mediterranean – that accounted for the basic differences between Europeans and Asians. The theory resembled the prevailing geopolitical discussions on the geographical determination of culture, political relations, and racial differences. In Watsuji's analysis, the mediterranean zone was characterized as temperate, semiarid, and essentially pastoral, requiring relatively nonintensive agricultural labor. Grains could be planted with ease without the arduous construction of terraced farms to ward off severe climatic conditions. Nature, therefore, was seen in this area as benign and also subservient, as evoked in the female image of "mother nature." Nature was also predictable, geometrical, steady, and hence calculable. It represented orderliness and stood for "reason." "In other words," Watsuji wrote, "where nature shows no violence she is manifested in logical and rational forms. . . . There is a link between lenience and the rationality of nature, for where she is lenient man readily discovers order in nature. . . . Thus Europe's natural science was clearly the product of Europe's meadow climate."[15]

In monsoon Asia, however, Watsuji saw a unique seasonal relationship between the Asian continent and the Indian Ocean. During the summer months, the monsoon blew across the land from the southwest when the sun crossed the equator, and in the winter, the winds reversed direction. The result was intense humidity and heat in the longer summer months, punctuated by torrential rains. In Watsuji's view, the combination of moisture and heat had produced countries that were rich in plants and an epistemology that saw the world as a place teeming with plant and animal life. "For nature is not death but life, for death stands instead by the side of man. Hence, the relation between man and his world is not that of resistance, but that of resignation."[16] Watsuji also noted that the violent rainstorms, savage winds, floods, and droughts persuaded the inhabitants of this area to abandon all resistance to the elemental forces of nature. Here, he believed, he had found the source of Asia's characteristic resignation to the inclemency of nature that was often reflected in the religions of Asia. Even more fundamental, however, nature was not bound by regularity and order but, on the contrary, was harsh and irregular, producing cultures that did not view the space around them in terms of geometric reason. Whereas the Mediterranean climate encouraged the human domination of nature as a benign and passive object, thus allowing for a view of progressive

15   Ibid., p. 74.   16   Ibid., p. 19.

and predictable historical time, the monsoon climate produced a different kind of culture. Human life was wholly engulfed by nature and hence resided outside progressive historical time, as it was not governed by logical sequence but was subordinate to nature and its eternal presence. It is important to recall that Hegel earlier had proposed, in his recounting of the migration of "liberty" from monsoon cultures to the West, that Asia did not possess "history" and thus had not developed a concept of "progressive" time. Watsuji may be seen in this regard as trying to recast the Hegelian scheme in terms of the relative strengths of East and West and as avoiding the characterization of world history according to the movement of the absolute spirit from one world area to another. To Watsuji, therefore, the Western spirit had led to an individualism that separated humans not only from nature but also from the society around them. Although in Asia, nature and the community superseded the individual, in the West, humans constantly struggled to dominate nature and to claim a separate life meaning from society. Here Watsuji complemented Heidegger's conception of "human intentionality," *ex-sistere*, which is temporal and bounded by history, with his idea of "relationality," *aidagara*, which calls for humans' unique relationship to a specific "spatial" environment.

Central to Watsuji's theory of relationality was the characterization of Japan within monsoon Asia and, in turn, its position in the world. Watsuji argued that although Japan faced conditions similar to those of the great continental civilizations such as India's and China's, it also possessed features quite unlike the rest of Asia because it encountered climatic conditions that ranged from cold to temperate, marked by abrupt and predictable seasonal changes. In short, Japan was at the eastern extremity of the monsoon zone and thus had a "dual" weather system. The rhythms between monsoon and nonmonsoon, cold and temperate, produced a society in which the emotional vitality and passionate swings that followed the shifting season were distinct from those of the continental Asian cultures. This observation led to Watsuji's principal argument, that owing to its particular climatic conditions, Japan had created a distinctive culture based on spacial "relationality." In particular, Watsuji pointed to the organizational structure of the "household" (*ie*) and the emotionality fostered within that space. In the household, its several members were not merely a gathering of individuals but a cooperative group of selfless human beings engaged in fundamental roles of nourishing life. However, in the household, its members were not totally resigned to the massive and unpredictable forces of nature, as on the Asian continent, but also nurtured a tense and active relationship with nature. Watsuji commented, therefore, "that passivity in Japan indicated a distinctive form of selfless action," that disciplined action served not the advancement of self-interest but the good of others in the communal whole.[17] Though admitting that this communal conception of action was no longer as prevalent as it was in the Tokugawa era, he nonetheless was convinced that it distinguished the Japanese mode of action from the individualism shaped by Western history and especially European capitalism. Hence Japanese capitalism resembles Western capitalism only in external and superficial ways. It is grounded in the climatic and spatial foundations of Japanese civilization and is thus not influenced by Western individualism.

Watsuji claimed to have gained many of his insights into the uniqueness of Japan after his "return" from an extended tour of Europe. For the first time, he acknowledged, he realized the inappropriateness of Western uses of space, as manifested in imported buildings and trams in the Japanese setting. He likened the tram, for example, to a "wild boar" rampaging through the fields, out of step with traditional civilized society. Although he did not go as far as to urge the eradication of these objects from Japan, at the same time, he clearly viewed them as "foreign." Watsuji thus despaired of the urban sprawl that had come to dominate the Tokyo landscape, viewing Western objects as an intrusion into the established order of things. He emphasized that the Japanese house was constructed so as to minimize privacy or to create it with only minimal separations and without the need of locks and bolts. Its security relied only on the language of trust. Despite his concern that Western architecture might steadily erode the value of community on which the small Japanese house was constructed, he also felt deeply that the people would neither relinquish their attachment to domestic architecture nor give up the integrity of that space, even as industrial capitalism persisted. Because of this attachment, true parliamentary democracy or proletarian movements, as had developed in the West, would not (and should not in his view) establish firm roots in Japan. Although there could be leaders of such movements in Japan, the people would remain confined to their architectural "space" and to the natural history that produced it. What Watsuji meant was that Japan,

17   Ibid., pp. 136–7.

owing to its unique sense of space, was unlikely ever to assimilate the conception of the "public" that so much Western political practice required.

Although Watsuji did not advocate an open revolt against the West, as he expressed his thought in terms of an aesthetic protest, it is obvious that much of what he had to say could easily be worked into a programmatic ideology advocating a frontal rejection of the Western presence in Asia. His extended treatise on climate, in short, may be summed up as an indictment of Western individualism, materialism, and rationalism. His judgment against both parliamentary democracy and Marxist proletarian movements as inappropriate to Japan was also a principal condition for an overall rejection of Western civilization as a hegemonic force over Japan.

Yanagida Kunio

Watsuji's ideas on community and aesthetic space interconnected with two other influential themes also current in his day, the ethnographic folklorism (minzokugaku) of the cultural anthropologist Yanagida Kunio and the aesthetic nostalgia of the novelist Tanizaki Junichirō. Compared with Watsuji, Yanagida proceeded from a deep distrust for the expansive power of the Meiji state. Reflecting his upbringing in a family of devout believers in local Shinto, as well as his scholarly training under Matsuura Shūhei, a well-known poet and scholar of national studies in the Meiji era, Yanagida was especially influenced by the critical attitude toward the bureaucracy and its ideology, such as the Confucianism of the Tokugawa era, that had been shaped in the popular national studies. It is hardly surprising that Yanagida revered Hirata Atsutane (d. 1843), one of the major thinkers of this antibureaucratic intellectual tradition in the Tokugawa who functioned as the unspoken inspiration for his own effort to formulate a Japanese science of folklore. Yanagida viewed with intense foreboding the bureaucratic penetration into the regional and local countryside. He feared its disruption of the Japanese communal life that was rooted in indigenous and customary beliefs.

Even before Yanagida resigned from his post in the Ministry of Agriculture in 1919, he had already been actively interested in Japanese folklore and popular customs. He published his first major collection of folktales, called "Tales of Tono" (Tōno monogatari, 1910), based on extensive travels particularly in the northwest regions of the country. In recounting these tales, Yanagida was able to show the vast disparity of customs and beliefs in these regions. More importantly, he was able to use these tales to support the idea that commoners in Japan were unimpressed with the official order or with a powerful emperor and, in turn, with the claims of state Shinto. Through this approach, Yanagida stated his opposition to the government's policy of coordinating Shinto shrines throughout the country within a unified bureaucratic system.

In turning his focus to the preservation of indigenous communal culture, Yanagida set out also to formulate a distinctive Japanese social science. Here he rejected the historical method that emphasized written documents and political events as constituting the central experience of the past. By avoiding this authoritative reconstruction of history, Yanagida envisioned the reunderstanding of the culture of the people as it was lived in villages and towns. Essential to his analysis were unwritten oral traditions, folktales, local dialects, regional religious practices, rituals and beliefs, and seasonal festivals. Although an assiduous collector of data concerning folk customs, Yanagida was not simply an antiquarian but believed that knowledge should be socially useful. This conviction stemmed from an earlier concern for agricultural economics that would enhance the well-being of the country populace in concrete ways. Therefore, the construction of a science of folk culture meant that it should help solve problems of rural poverty and distress caused by modern technology. He believed that his method promoted the cause of "social reconstruction" (*shakai kaizō*) and also that people learning about themselves without superficial adornments might lead to self-knowledge and self-renovation. A new society based on indigenous culture would thereby be created from within that culture itself, without relying on the bureaucratic and technological instruments being fashioned above by the central government. In order to achieve these goals, Yanagida revealed a pragmatic eclecticism so that the data could include a wide variety of materials and strategies. The ethnographic method of British anthropology, for example, though drawn from without, was considered appropriate to the task of organizing and ordering local data derived from the Japanese experience.

Yanagida's project was informed by an identification with the "abiding folk" (*jōmin*). Before being a functional individual of society as a farmer, laborer, or white-collar worker, all were first and foremost members of the *jōmin*. What this meant was that one of the most divisive aspects of modern Western capitalism was its relocation of the people according to a functional division of labor based on presumed rational premises that in fact had come to be manifested in contending classes. Although most evident in Western industrial society, comparable conflict could be observed in the context of industrial expansion in Japan. To call attention to the abiding folk and their customs was to also discuss the peculiar form of community to which they had given expression through a life-style actually lived in the countryside. Yanagida identified its distinctive feature as communitarianism, which referred to the horizontal social relations held together by a system of mutual assistance and confirmed by a territorial tutelary shrine deity. Moreover, he was confident that the communitarian life in the villages characterized Asian society and was in imminent danger of disintegrating before the relentless penetration of Western capitalism and central bureaucracies. Yanagida thus counterposed an Asian gemeinschaft against these modern intrusions. It was for this reason that he strongly resisted the policy of the Meiji state to organize the local shrines according to a systematic bureaucratic scheme.

Yanagida promoted the movement to preserve local folktales and beliefs as a means to oppose the reorganization, in late Meiji, of shrines throughout the country within the framework of state Shinto. He believed state Shinto to be a dishonest and artificial representation of popular religious practices. In folk Shinto, he emphasized, there were no professional priests or formalized doctrines. Its beliefs had sprung from the experiences of the collectivity and had been transmitted as an oral tradition since ancient times by ordinary laypersons. Moreover, these beliefs were centered on respect for communal deities wherever they were enshrined. These deities, accordingly, represented the spirit of human ancestors, both men and women equally. No deity was to be seen as hierarchically superior to another, as proposed in state Shinto. Also important, the collective beliefs of folk Shinto were rooted in a worship of nature in which trees, creatures, and all other natural objects were endowed with a spirit comparable to that of human beings. Finally, Yanagida repeated that the central purpose of folk beliefs was to offer respect for the spirits of the departed ancestors. Often, this form of worship was associated with fertility deities of agricultural production. In all of this, he emphasized that folk Shinto exemplified the continuing reality of an agrarian community worshiping itself and celebrating its own communal unity and solidarity between human beings and nature. In place of the state that was responsible for the bureaucratization of folk Shinto, Yanagida envisaged an expanded tutelary shrine. In short, popular community would assume greater importance than the hierarchic state.

Although Yanagida was certainly not an exponent of militant revolt against the West, his emphasis on popular, agrarian community suggested a powerful alternative to the claims of the modern industrial and technological state, which he saw as a Western import. In this regard, his ideas may be seen as dovetailing with those of the more militant variety of agrarian fundamentalists. Even though Yanagida did not become involved in programmatic political action, as did some of these fundamentalists, such as Inoue and Tachibana, he did share a kinship with their ideas.

Tanizaki Junichirō

Yanagida's protest against modern rationalism, based on the "natural culture" of one's native place, can also be related to a similar criticism from the point of view of indigenous aesthetic theory. In this theory, the "native place" is identified with aesthetic space. The Heideggerian perspective that Watsuji used in his essay on climate and character, in which he emphasized the importance of geography and, in turn, living space, is shared by a number of writers who called attention to the determinant relationship between "geography" and indigenous "aesthetic style." Perhaps the most elegant representative of this view was the novelist Tanizaki Junichirō. In his essay "In Praise of Shadows" (*In'ei raisan*, 1934), Tanizaki redefined space in terms of nuances that were grounded in indigenous culture and that he as a Japanese chose not necessarily because they were superior to the aesthetics of other societies but because they were Japanese and he preferred them.[18] The trend toward Western industrialism was irreversible. At the same time, he felt that for this reason the aesthetic choice of "shadows" must be made in order to preserve Japan's distinctive creative soul. In an ironic gesture, Tanizaki explained the reason for his choice:

But I know as well as anyone that these are the empty dreams of a novelist, and that having come this far we cannot turn back. . . . If my complaints are taken for what they are, however, there can be no harm in considering how unlucky we have been, what losses we have suffered, in comparison with the

18 Tanizaki Junichirō, *In Praise of Shadows*, translation of *In'ei raisan* by Edward Seidensticker and Thomas Harper (New Haven, Conn.: Leete's Island Books, 1977), p. 42.

Westerner . . . we have met a superior civilization and have had to surrender to it, and we have had to leave a road we have followed for thousands of years.[19]

The importance of Western technology, which Tanizaki called "borrowed gadgets," had resulted in inconvenience for the Japanese, the worst of these being the incandescent light bulb that had invaded the world of shadows. This powerful gadget had illuminated the fine distinctions in Japanese life and had erased the blurred and shadowy lines that were central to indigenous sensibility.

Tanizaki developed his argument by referring first to an example that would strike his audience as absurd, the interior space of the Japanese toilet in comparison with the well-lit Western version and then, building outward from that reference, to more elegant and exquisite examples, both visual and spatial. Along with spaces defined by Japanese architecture reminiscent of Watsuji, Tanizaki also focused on the shadowy coloring of foods, skin complexion, lacquer ware, pottery, and the No drama. These were elements in the world of shadows on which Japanese should self-consciously "meditate," precisely because of the unwanted glare of Western technology whose light demanded precision rather than subtlety. The shadows for Tanizaki signified silence and tranquility. The apparent mystery that Westerners saw in the Orient referred to the "uncanny silence of these dark places."[20] In these places were found the creative "magic" and "mystery" that had been vital to the cultural tradition of the Japanese, who had "cut off the brightness on the land from above and created a world of shadows. . . ."[21]

It is important to emphasize that for Tanizaki the world of shadows was no longer a dominant and realistic presence, as he saw the pull toward technology as relentless and unavoidable. The world of shadows was, therefore, for him an aesthetic and cultural choice that had to be articulated intellectually as an abstraction. Yet Tanizaki strained to express the ineffable, seeking to restore a tangible emotional identity that time and change threatened to banish. His melancholic meditation dramatized the contrast between Japanese and Western comprehensions of the world. Our way of thinking, he wrote, concentrates on finding "beauty not in the thing itself but in the patterns of shadows, the light and the darkness, that one thing against another creates."[22]

In the West, the restless quest for light has dominated aesthetic

19 Ibid., p. 8. 20 Ibid., p. 20. 21 Ibid., p. 33. 22 Ibid., p. 30.

sensitivity, as best characterized by the ever-increasing brightness exhibited in the candle, succeeded by the oil, gas, and electric lamps.

Although Tanizaki made no claim as to the superiority of Japanese aesthetics, it is also clear that his preference for it was absolute. Instead of arguing that it should be defended militantly, he asserted that perhaps through literature or the arts, something essential to the world of shadows might still be saved. "I do not ask," he concluded, "that this be done everywhere, but perhaps we may be allowed at least one mansion where we can turn off the electric lights and see what it is like without them."[23]

The Romanha writers

The cultural protest against Western technology that Tanizaki encapsulated with the metaphors of the "electric light" and the "toilet" was echoed by a school of contemporary aestheticians referred to as the "Japan romantic school" (Nihon romanha). These were writers such as Yasuda Yojūrō (1910–81), the acknowledged leader of the group, Hayashi Fusao (1903–75), Kamei Katsuichirō (1907–66), Satō Haruo (1892–1964), Hagiwara Sakutarō (1886–1942), and, for brief periods in their young careers, the well-known novelists of the postwar era, Dazai Osamu (1909–48) and Mishima Yukio (1925–70), and were associated with a literary journal called *Nihon romanha*, which was first published in 1935.[24] These writers rallied around the intellectual position in a statement written by Yasuda Yojūrō that came to be seen as the "manifesto" of the entire group. This manifesto marked their collective break with Marxism and literary modernism, best summed up in Hayashi Fusao's words as a "farewell to realism."

Although the intellectuals in this group concentrated their criticism on the status of modern civilization, their opposition was expressed in a general condemnation of literary modernism. In the manifesto itself, they specifically identified naturalism and realism as the literary forms of rational Western society. They further called attention to the literature of vulgar and popular customs that de-

23 Ibid., p. 42.
24 See Takeuchi Yoshimi and Kawakami Tetsutarō, eds., *Kindai no chōkoku* (Tokyo: Fūzambō, 1979); and also Takeuchi's essay, "Kindai no chōkoku," in Kamei Katsuichirō and Takeuchi Yoshimi, eds., *Kindai Nihon shisōshi kōza*, vol. 7: *Kindaika to dentō* (Tokyo: Chikuma shobō, 1959), pp. 227–81. Also, Hiromatsu Wataru, *Kindai no chōkoku ron* (Tokyo: Asahi shuppansha, 1980).

picted in exhaustive detail the petty trivia of everyday life. The purpose of the Japan romantic school, they announced, was "to wage war" with the pernicious trend of literary naturalism. They feared above all that the requirements of rational society had eroded the artistic sensibility of indigenous Japanese culture, expressed most recently by Tanizaki. Naturalism had vulgarized the "voice of the people," mechanized artistic talents, and made a fetish of the popular spirit. The creative self had lost all autonomy before the incessant demands of mass markets.

The romantics called upon their contemporaries, therefore, to return to the authentic literary tradition. It was time, they announced, to celebrate openly the Japanese songs of all the ages since the nation's ancient beginning and to call these the songs of youthfulness (*seishun*). In this context, these men outlined the creation of a new literary movement that would eliminate the influences of Western-oriented writings. Identifying their movement as the "main way" (*hondō*), they denounced the prevailing subordination among their contemporaries to what they termed vulgar and mediocre Western aesthetic forms. And again reminiscent of Tanizaki on "shadows," they described their effort to restore a native aesthetic sensibility and recommended the rejection of the present as "self-conscious irony." It was therefore their journal's stated aim to represent the condition of traditional aesthetics that had been diminished by the impact of Western technology and to provide a new forum for its resuscitation.

The sense of loss that the romantics felt was often articulated with the metaphor of the "return" (*kaiki*). It was a theme already in evidence in activists such as Ōkawa Shūmei as well as in writers such as Watsuji and Tanizaki. For the romantics, the return was also accompanied by an awareness that it could not be fully realized. It was clearly expressed by writers such as Kamei Katsuichirō who thus identified the return with the "dream" (*yume*). The longing and yearning for return coupled with the acknowledgment that the journey's end would never be reached went far toward defining the special character of these writers as romantics. The idea of the return was perhaps best captured by the poet Hagiwara Sakutarō in his poem entitled "The Return to Japan" (*Nihon e no kaiki*, 1938).

In this poem, Hagiwara lamented that although the Japanese had not been deprived of material things, they had surrendered their spiritual selves. "We have not lost things," he thus wrote, "but we have exhausted our all."[25] He admitted that he too had been attracted to Western culture at an earlier time, enjoying the creature comforts that it had provided, such as beds, sofas, and foods. Now, however, these things no longer satisfied him. He would thus seek a quiet home with a small tearoom and locate it in an out-of-the-way area of Kyoto and strum gently on the ancient *biwa* in the presence of a traditionally kimonoed Japanese woman. This extremely influential poem provided the romantics with a coherent metaphor to express their vague yearnings for a return to Japan. It also conveyed the return to a true aesthetic self, a sense of "wholeness," an attachment to the native land as a pristine manifestation of nature, and the identification with an indigenous historical time distinct from the Western chronological scheme of human history. These themes can be found in such writings as Yasuda Yojūrō's "The Japanese Bridge" (*Nihon no hashi*, 1936), which called for a "return" to the Japanese classics and the ancient aesthetic sensibility. The return to a concrete and familiar geographical "place" was also evident in Yokomitsu Riichi's novel, *The Lonely Journey Home* (*Ryoshū*, 1946). This novel describes an exchange student in Paris contemplating his slow journey across the Siberian tundra, becoming increasingly aware of the profoundness of the "return" to his spiritual home. And finally, it was at this time that Tanizaki himself translated the *Tale of Genji* (1938) into elegant modern Japanese, hoping thereby to preserve the spirit of that ancient classic for his contemporaries who had strayed too far from the "Japanese thing" (*Nihonteki na mono*).

Even more important, the return also contained the concept of a reidentification with indigenous time. Hayashi Fusao's "farewell to realism" referred to a rejection of the Western rational description of the past and the narrative of material progress. Just as the Western portrayal of human experience in literary form was said to be inappropriate to Japan, so too was its mode of conveying the meaning of history. Rational description was seen as a facade for the presentation of the West's supremacy. Along with this, the dialectical mode of representing history was also discarded as misleading and inapplicable to any understanding of Japanese history. In its crudest ideological guise, the romantics claimed that history did not begin with the Christian era; rather, in the case of Japan, it should be measured according to the origins of the nation,

25 Hagiwara Sakutarō, *Nihon e no kaiki* (Tokyo: Hakusuisha, 1938).

calculated as being roughly 660 B.C. The main issue, however, was not so much when the rational sequence began. For the romantics, the crucial point was to find a creative origin, or an authentic "moment" in which a whole was revealed for which Western modes of calculating time could not account. The return to an original aesthetic moment and to Japan's natural homeland also meant the avoidance of the Western evolutionary scheme of history. In short, the yearning for "wholeness," "nature," "native place," true and enduring aesthetic "spirit," and the culture of the indigenous folk all called attention to the dimension of "timelessness" that signified the abandonment of historicism and the discounting of progressive historical time itself.

The return to true origins and the belief in the timelessness of a cultural uniqueness distinct from the West also inaugurated a quest to create a new future that would go beyond the limitations of the present. Much of this assessment was already implicit in the meditations of Yasuda Yojūrō and the romantics. In an essay written in 1937 entitled "On the End of a Theory of Civilization and Enlightenment" (*Bunmei kaika no ronri no shūen ni tsuite*), Yasuda complained that modern literature expressed or concretized Western knowledge so that literary movements had merely become the thoughtless pursuit of rationalism. In this essay, he also anticipated the deterioration of the self without ever specifying what this actually meant. Yet it was true that for Yasuda, intelligence in modern Japan referred to a theory of civilization and enlightenment, which he identified with the new Meiji bureaucratism and the men who founded it. In its speculative form, it was transmitted downward as Marxism and proletarian literature. Despite the power of this modernist tradition, in Yasuda's view, there had been a number of courageous people who had self-consciously opposed the modern state and its ideology. Among those he favored most were Kumoi Tatsuo (d. 1869) and Saigō Takamori (1827–77). Beyond these rebels, Yasuda also cited, from the late Meiji era, the Japanist group, such as Miyake Setsurei (1860–1945) and the cultural essentialist Okakura Tenshin. In a sense, Yasuda saw the romantics as inheritors of this tradition of critical idealism directed against rationalistic modernism and the tyranny of the self. In proposing the end of a theory of civilization and enlightenment, Yasuda and the romantics were also suggesting the possibility of transcending or overcoming the modern, *kindai no chōkoku*, as this effort came to be called. "The last stage of civilization and enlightenment was the development of Marxian literature and art," Yasuda announced.[26] To him, Marxism was also the last stage in the civilization and enlightenment movement that began in the early Meiji era. And he therefore saw the special mission of the Japanese romantic school as ending this last phase of history and starting a new one or, as he put it, to span "a bridge in the night reaching toward a new dawn." The metaphoric phrase "bridge in the night" was used to attract many intellectuals and writers to take part in the famous debates of July 1942 in Kyoto on the theme of overcoming modernity. All believed that the debates would mark the end of modern civilization in Japan and disclose the character of the glorious new age.[27]

THE DEBATE ON MODERNITY

In particular, the participants in the debate on modernity represented two major intellectual groups, the literary society (*bungakukai*) and the romantic school. Included were literary and film critics, poets, novelists, composers, philosophers, scientists, psychologists, and historians. Among the better-known figures were Kobayashi Hideo, Nishitani Keiji, Kamei Katsuichirō, Hayashi Fusao, Miyoshi Tatsuji, Kawakami Tetsutarō, and Nakamura Mitsuo. The debate took place shortly after the outbreak of the Pacific War and had as its central purpose a discussion of the larger "world-historical" meaning of the event itself as it might relate to the vision of the uncertain future that these intellectuals sought to envisage. Kawakami Tetsutarō, one of the organizers of the sessions, best stated this overall concern in his concluding remarks. Aside from the deliberations' success of failure, he observed, it was an indisputable fact of immense importance that such intellectual debates had taken place within the first year of the outbreak of the war. Moreover, he saw the discussions as reflecting a struggle between "the blood of the Japanese that truly motivates our intellectual life" and "Western knowledge that has been superimposed on Japan in modern times." Unavoidably, therefore, the conflict must be a desperate and bloody one.

Using the analysis of Takeuchi Yoshimi (1910–77), an eminent scholar close to the antimodernist temperament of the romantic

---

26 Yasuda Yojūrō, "Bunmei kaika no ronri no shūen," quoted in Takeuchi and Kawakami, *Kindai no chōkoku*, p. iii.
27 Ibid., p. iv.

movement, the details of the discussions may be separated into the following broad themes: Takeuchi emphasized the commonly shared assumption that the outbreak of the Pacific War had convinced the participants that the conflict was both intellectual and military. The intellectual confrontation was between "Western intelligence" and the "blood of the Japanese."[28] The struggle was analogized to "war" as "peace" was to cultural submission. In Kamei's terms, "more to be feared than war was peace. . . . Rather a war among kings than the peace of slaves."[29] The idea of "overcoming" was also a criticism of evolutionary as well as dialectical historicism. According to Takeuchi, this included the denial of the Meiji movement for "civilization and enlightenment" (bummei kaika), a view that had been advanced by members of the romantic school. The participants were also disappointed with the insensitivity of the population at large regarding the meaning of that confrontation, often resorting, in their view, to the mere recitation of slogans. And connected with this, the discussants expressed the hope that the symposium would help overcome the fragmentation of culture into specialized fields and eliminate the widespread feelings of alienation in society, by reconstituting a sense of cultural wholeness. All the participants felt immersed in the problem of "Japan's modern intellectual fate" (gendai Nihon no chiteki unmei) and the peculiar tragedy in which they were compelled to live out their lives, a view expressed most eloquently for the entire symposium by Kamei Katsuichirō in his perception of the "modern" as being an unyielding illness or malaise.

Although some used the metaphor of disease to refer specifically to the actual outbreak of the "glorious" war, Kamei used his phrases as a general proposition in the intellectual struggle against modernity. But in either case, the analogy to actual events could hardly be separated from the war, suggesting therefore that the war's larger purpose was to accomplish the final conquest of the modern. In retrospect, this view cast a cloak of intellectual deception on the proceedings themselves. Takeuchi went through some pain to argue that the deliberations at the end remained entirely unresolved and to point out that this was due to the many differences in viewpoints among the participants regarding the meaning of the future order. Yet the sentiments expressed by certain intellectual luminaries such as Miyoshi Tatsuo (1902–64), Kawakami, Kamei, and others clearly

---

28 Ibid., p. 166. 29 Ibid., p. 298.

suggest an intellectual convergence beneath the metaphoric umbrella of "overcoming modernity."

Among many, the celebration of the "glorious war" contributed to their willingness to abandon all desire to "resist" the course of events that the government had taken. Although this desire had remained strong even after Japan's invasion of China, it dissipated rapidly after the outbreak of the Pacific War. In its new meaning, the war was interpreted as a revolt against the "modern" West and its hegemony over Asia, a view that was not unattractive by any means to Marxists and former Marxists as well. By contrast, the earlier attack on China was seen differently, not as the uncontrolled expansion of Japanese imperialism, but as part of the liberation of Asia, not yet under the domination of the West, and its subsequent modernization under Japanese tutelage.

For most, "modern" was invariably associated closely with rational "science." Much of the discussion concentrated, therefore, on showing how modern science had developed in a historically specific context, namely, the Renaissance and its aftermath in Western Europe. Recalling the thinking of Watsuji in his "Climate and Culture," the debaters traced the spirit of the European Renaissance to its roots in ancient Greece where the philosophy of science was first articulated. As expressed by Hayashi Fusao, the subsequent development of science in the West differed substantially from the Japanese experience. In the myths of the West, he noted, men were always in a state of "struggle" with the gods. But in Japan, gods and men did not contend with each other, as conflict occurred among the gods alone. This reference to mythology was aimed at showing that Western science was fundamentally inappropriate to the spirit of the Japanese people. Kamei went even further to argue that because the Japanese spirit had been alienated from the gods (*kami*), in overcoming modernity the Japanese must reintegrate themselves with the spirit of these *kami*. Here, Kamei employed *kami* as a metaphor representing the spirit of the entire Japanese people. He defined the ways of achieving this reunion as the central problem of contemporary Japanese philosophy. In the end, the wish to overcome the West became a revolt against reason itself.

On closer examination, the basic culturalist premise appears to militate against the idea of a progressive "overcoming" of modernity. Kobayashi Hideo recognized best the problem it inspired and underscored most clearly the inescapable ambivalence resulting from any attempt to overcome the modern. The real enemy were ideas of change and advancement, which unfailingly mislead modern people to create false intellectual expectations. The "burden" of history had now come to presuppose the demonstration of progressive modernization. Among the accounts written by modern historians of Japan covering the various ages, Kobayashi claimed to have found all of them to be merely reviews or narrative summations of the past and hence shallow representations of human actualities. This was especially true of those discussions of aesthetic forms embedded in the past. Beauty, Kobayashi insisted, did not "evolve" in a progressive manner leading to modernity. It could not, therefore, be understood from the perspective of the modern experience. Yet to him, it was this subject of beauty in history in specific places and contexts that had to be perceived and grasped. However one understood history from the modern point of view, such a stance actually prevented the mind from encountering the structure of beauty in history because of the presupposition of historical evolution that concealed beauty as beauty. In short, beauty was closed off from the historian's view. The discerning eye, however, must disengage itself from the existentialist dimension of history and penetrate the underlying structure that goes beyond that immediate moment. Kobayashi exemplified this argument by explaining that the essence of Kamakura religious art contained a deep and abiding form that outlived its immediate history and the moment that had given expression to it. The art objects of the Kamakura period are before our eyes, he explained, but they contain a beauty that is independent and possesses an abiding "life" that transcends modern scholarly interpretations. Because such objects contain a passion and an elegance unbound by the specific constraints of the historical era, beauty may indeed be said to be universal. In the debates themselves, Kobayashi readily admitted that his view pointed to a universalistic conception of aesthetic form, which, as his critics acknowledged, indeed differed from modernistic historicism. Ironically, Kobayashi's ideas about beauty appeared to coincide with Western Platonic idealism, which the debaters were quick to point out. On this point, Kobayashi agreed that the distinction between existence and eternal form should be kept separate in order to grasp the fundamental aesthetic in history. Here, he acknowledged his sympathy for the spirit of Plato's idealism and, among recent philosophers, Henri Bergson's conception of creativity.[30]

30 Ibid., p. 229.

To Kobayashi, then, "overcoming" the West meant essentially reidentifying with the Platonic idea of eternal forms of truth and beauty that had fallen beyond the purview of modern interpretations based on the idea of progressive evolution. Rejecting the use of such terms as *ancient, medieval, modern*, and the like, Kobayashi refused to see the "overcoming" of modernity as an "advancement" to a new and glorious era. Rather, he thought of it as "transcending" the limitations of Western modernism and as readdressing the question of eternal and enduring forms of beauty. Kobayashi's idea of lasting beauty, however, simultaneously coincided with prevailing opinions regarding the adverse effects of Western civilization in modern Japan and the need to be liberated from that unhappy legacy. Although the advocates of "overcoming" modernity spoke of a vague future better than the present – and Kobayashi did not indulge in such thinking, as he remained skeptical of this mode of conceptualizing time – they agreed on the imperative to reidentify with indigenous cultural ideals and to allow them enough space and time that they might serve as sources of renewal and creative inspiration within a continuing history.

What troubled Kobayashi most was the fear that Japan would become a pale replica of Western societies. He dramatized his concerns on this issue by drawing on the ironic lines from Marx's *Eighteenth Brumaire*. He thus referred to the modernization of the West as a "tragedy" and the second manifestation of it in Japan as a "comedy." The quintessential comedians in Japan, he observed, had not yet captured the stage, but they inevitably would.[31] The central issue for him was the proposition that history was constant change, whereas in his view, change in fact was basically unimportant to the creative act of producing art and literature. Convinced that aesthetic creations were "unhistorical" and eternal, as they were expressed in terms of form and order and not of history, Kobayashi was equally convinced that modern persons (including the Japanese) had abandoned the life-giving energy of art. Yet it was the engagement with this aesthetic, Kobayashi asserted, that generated the dynamic and balancing "tension" undergirding the flow of history itself and that could not be grasped from the perspective of linear change in which one thing was shown to be different and somehow better than what came before. For this reason, then, Kobayashi expressed profound pessimism about the ideas of "change" and "progress," claiming to

31   Ibid., p. 219.

feel "sick" and "nauseous" about them. In expressing these views, Kobayashi had assumed a position close to one already occupied by Tanizaki.

What Kobayashi hoped to overcome was the conception of linear time that Japanese had imported from the West during the Meiji era. Many of his colleagues at the debates were also deeply concerned with the general question of evolutionary time and, more specifically, the meaning of "civilization," *bummei*, that had captured the attention of early Meiji intellectuals. To Kamei Katsuichirō, for example, the civilization of enlightenment in Meiji Japan had introduced the Western idea of the specialization and compartmentalization of knowledge. This epistemological import, he claimed, resulted in the loss of a sense of "wholeness" in life among the Japanese. An identifiable event, the incorporation of Western ideas of functional specialization, was thus a major disruptive force in the spiritual life of Japan. Those who contested this disruptive impact sought solutions in nonconformist modes of thinking. Kamei cited as an outstanding example in this regard the Christian leader Uchimura Kanzō (1861–1930). To Kamei, Uchimura's greatness was his refusal to conform to the pattern of specialization that had increasingly come to dominate the world around him. Although an expert in marine biology, Uchimura saw his work as part of a unified system of knowledge in which all things were informed by an intrinsic and divine spirit (*kami*), and he retained his identification with this view of the universe. His "churchless Christianity" (*mukyōkai*) was nothing other than a sophisticated rendition of this deeper ontological commitment to a unified view of the universe.

The process of specialization, however, proceeded into the twentieth century. The cause of this disquieting trend was the adoption of Western utilitarianism accompanying the assimilation of the idea of progress in the Meiji enlightenment. In the process, the "philosopher of real life" (*tetsujin*) was destroyed. Central to Kamei's antimodernist vision was the restoration of the philosophy of "wholeness" and the "unity of knowledge" as it related to all beings, creatures, and things evident in the folk Shinto of these wise men. The resemblance here to the ideas of Yanagida Kunio is apparent, except that Kamei focused on literate culture rather than on country villages and oral tradition. Kamei and his colleagues had also shaped a cultural position analogous to that held by some of the political activists who had turned against Meiji history as a "betrayal" of the spirit of the Meiji Restoration, by manifestly constructing the bureaucratic and technological state. Even though Kamei was silent on the particular problem of state formation, unlike Kita Ikki and Nakano Seigō, he did see in the Meiji movement for civilization the unrelieved inundation of Western utilitarian and functional philosophies that, in the twentieth century, promised to destroy the theory of knowledge founded on the unity of all things that had informed the spirit of Japanese civilization before the modern era. In Kamei's harsh terms, Meiji civilization and enlightenment had introduced "deformed specialists" into contemporary Japanese culture.

This critique of Meiji bureaucratic culture was taken a step further by another leading participant in the debates, Hayashi Fusao, a novelist, cultural critic, and former Marxist who had turned his intellectual allegiance to the pure cultural ideals of Japan as advocated by the Romantic school. "I believe," he stated, "that civilization and enlightenment meant the adoption of European culture after the Meiji Restoration and resulted in the submission of Japan to the West." From an external perspective, the Meiji Restoration represented the last opposition of the East against the West. Although at one level, it may be seen to have been a victory – as India was overwhelmed and China dismembered, and only Japan managed to withstand the Western wave – yet at another level, in order to maintain opposition to Europe, it was also necessary to incorporate Western utilitarian civilization. Civilization and enlightenment were thus a utilitarian culture devoid of fundamental substance.[32] Hayashi believed that the Japanese dissatisfaction with this utilitarian culture emerged in the late 1880s, at which time a number of reflective intellectuals began to call for a return to cultural fundamentals. Among these prescient critics were again the Christian idealist Uchimura Kanzō, the art historian Okakura Tenshin, and such heroic figures as Saigō Takamori and General Nogi Maresuke (1849–1912). Hayashi also contended that all the men who drew attention to this critique of utilitarian civilization were defeated by the Westernizing trends of the time. Until recently, he concluded, the European conception of civilization had persisted as the dominant force over the skeptical view of progress found in the native tradition. It was in this context that Hayashi discussed the East Asian War as the final chance to turn back the tide of utilitarianism in Asia. Those in Japan who still held to this Western epistemology must also be defeated and transformed according to true native sensibilities.

32   Ibid., pp. 239–40.

Hayashi believed that the bureaucratic culture and elitism spawned by utilitarianism in the Meiji period had been resisted by the Movement for Popular Rights. Although some of the discussants disagreed with his view, seeing the movement as a product of the very ideals he had criticized, Hayashi clung to the belief that it was an indigenous movement directed against the acquisition of absolutist power by bureaucratic cliques bent on constructing a utilitarian state. In this manner, Hayashi reinterpreted the Meiji Restoration by denying its revolutionary impulse, rejecting the French or American models of such transformation, and emphasizing instead the emergence of the Japanese people as a "classless" community unified with the emperor.

Consistent with this position, Hayashi and his colleagues singled out "Americanism" as the primary force behind the global expansion of utilitarianism. Increasingly in the twentieth century, Europe had come to be replaced by the United States as the leader of the Western world. The debaters specifically cited the importation, following World War I, of crass, hedonistic materialism among Japan's urban youth, exemplified among faddish groups who called themselves "modern boys" (*mobo*) and "modern girls" (*moga*). American movies, especially, had spread the cult of "fast living" (*supīdo*) and "eroticism," seducing young Japanese minds and leading them away from their cultural roots. These cultural invasions were the result of the power of mass-production strategies developed in the United States. However impressive these strategies might seem in a certain quantitative sense, they also undermined Japan's cultural virtues and the society's faith in itself. They were especially visible in the marketing of a mass culture that reflected the absence of a deeply rooted sense of cultural purpose in the United States itself. Because the United States was a relatively new nation, these men reasoned, its cultural traditions in art and morals were perilously shallow. Their products, therefore, were accessible to everyone, owing to their simplicity and lack of philosophical depth. But here indeed was the deceptive nature of utilitarian mass-production culture that undermined societies with long cultural traditions. The danger of this Americanism was its capacity to spread a "universalistic" culture of simple materialism. Thus, from a land of immigrants characterized as a "frontier" nation, the United States had acquired a new and negative image in world history.

Implicit in the comments on the mass production of movies and other American "gadgets" was the view that the ready acceptance of this materialistic culture by the youth of the early twentieth century was due to the insidious influences of Meiji utilitarianism. This harsh reading of Meiji intellectual and political history was closely linked to the deep concern that the twentieth century had witnessed the emergence of a consumer culture satisfied only with the possession of plenty rather than with the quality and beauty of scarcity and restraint. American democracy, therefore, had as its real substance the satisfaction of the masses with trivial goods produced in large quantities, a condition that had permeated Japanese life as well.

The repeatedly pessimistic appraisal of the Meiji enlightenment by the debaters points to a deep intellectual bifurcation in the intellectual history of the 1920s and 1930s. Their comments, though locked in the language of historical reassessment, were also directed against contemporaries who were quick to evaluate positively the Meiji movement for civilization and enlightenment as the starting point for a humane modern order. The representative figure of this position was the leading theorist of Taishō democracy, Yoshino Sakuzō. Under his direction, there was a collaborative effort to reconstruct Meiji intellectual history. The multivolume work on that subject, *Meiji bunka zenshū*, remains a monument to Yoshino's conviction that the Meiji achievement rescued Japan from a somnolent feudal order and backwardness and set society upon its civilizing course. Yoshino and his colleagues took a dim view of the bureaucratic elites that had come to dominate the Meiji state and that sought to redirect politics away from the democratic future as envisaged in the early Meiji enlightenment. But if the antimodernists and Yoshino found common cause in their condemnation of the bureaucratic order, they parted company over the more compelling question concerning the essence of modern Japanese culture. Hayashi Fusao and his group decried the emergence of utilitarian bureaucratism, functional specialization, and mass production and consumerism. To resist these forces, they demanded the restoration of "timeless" cultural values. Although the participants in the debate differed widely among themselves, they all subscribed to an "ahistorical" perception of culture and frequently expressed it in recurring criticisms of linear conceptions of time such as "progress." By contrast, Yoshino and those like him who prized the Meiji enlightenment denied the virtue of "timeless" culture and emphasized instead the "timefulness" of historical movement and the continuous human potential for achieving new creative and moral goals in the future.

The debate on "overcoming the modern" concluded with a general consideration of the possibilities for Japan in the context of the early 1940s. The problem in the final analysis was how might Japan retain its technological achievements yet preserve those irreducible cultural elements that made the Japanese distinctive. None of the participants, when faced with the choice, contemplated the unrealistic solution of turning back the clock of industrialization. To these men, however, the "machine" must be defined unequivocally as the mere servant of humans, and the human spirit the creator of technology. Spirit, therefore, was determined to be autonomous and separate from manufactured things and unaffected by such products. They denied in this regard the Marxist theory of "alienation" in which manufactured goods were objects that "dehumanized" the spirit. The true "potential" (*kanōsei*) for modern Japan, then, was in the creation and retention of a culture in which the human spirit would remain independent by being anchored to timeless and essential values, whereas manufactured goods would function simply as external objects divorced from aesthetic considerations. It was over the question of how best to resurrect and clarify this cultural essence that they emphasized the significance of the great literary texts from ancient history. The importance of the great scholars of the "national studies" of the Tokugawa period, such as Motoori Norinaga, was that, by "rediscovering" those classics in the eighteenth century, the classics themselves became manifestations of the spirit and highly esteemed artifacts.

The criticism of the harmful effects on Japanese culture by Meiji utilitarianism and the bureaucratic state was inseparable from the more general denunciation of the international order constructed and dominated by the Western powers. The criticism of domestic bureaucratism, therefore, also included the rejection of Western hegemony over Asia. To overcome the modern meant to many of these men the internal and external uprooting of Western materialism and power in Asia. Their reidentification with Japanese ideals thus led them to acknowledge the importance of reviving similar cultural ideas in other Asian countries and recognizing the necessity of Japan protecting them against colonialism. Liberating Japanese cultural idealism from Western materialism and separating Asia from Western hegemony were thus closely related sentiments, so much so that the attack on modernity provided the underlying intellectual justifications for the ideology enunciated by Prime Minister Konoe Fumimarō (1891–1945) in the declaration of 1938 calling for the establishment of an "East Asian Cooperative Union." It was in Konoe's conception of cultural communalism that the more pragmatic formulations of a "new order" were articulated. Japan's Asian neighbors, the declaration boasted, would live in friendship, defend the area in common, and cooperate economically. Although the Chinese in particular were invited to join with Japan in creating such a system of mutual cooperation, there was little doubt – despite language that strained to suppress Japan's own imperial ambitions – that the "new order" would in fact be directed primarily by Japan. Here, the rejection of the presence of Western bureaucratism was linked to Pan-Asianism in order to authorize Japan's own expansion as the hegemonic power in Asia and virtually paralleled the American claim to rope off the Western Hemisphere by the cordon sanitaire authorized by the Monroe Doctrine. It is inconceivable that the participants in the debates against modernity were not aware of the relationship between their criticism and the expansionist designs of those in the government. It may indeed be the case, as claimed by some later, that the debates did not produce a coherent and comprehensive ideology for the Pacific War and that it was hardly their aim to come up with one. Yet the fact remains that their negative reading of the Meiji legacy of the bureaucratic state had turned ironically to an endorsement of expansionism by that very order, or at least its successor, that they had so consistently vilified. In particular, the language demanding an East Asian war as the condition for Asia to reestablish control over its own cultural destinies indeed only underscores the unconsciously ironic deception in which the debaters were implicated.

EPILOGUE

In the 1930s, the Japanese romantic Yasuda Yojūrō called attention to Japan as irony. What he was referring to was the effort to preserve those elements in traditional life that attested to Japan's irreducible uniqueness while seeking to become a modern society. Yasuda recognized that the conditions for modernity necessitated eliminating those elements and forms from the past that he and his associates sought to preserve. What he failed to see was the possibility of other kinds of ironies that war and defeat eventually made certain. Indeed, more than one level of irony was already present in the debates against modernity and the strident call for a war against the West. The debaters could not have known that a total military defeat of Japan would, in fact, remove "war" itself as a central object in the discourse on culture that had dominated the 1930s. Without the militancy of the prewar years, however, much of the earlier discourse spilled over into the postwar period as issues of compelling and immediate concern. It was almost as if the earlier discourse had not quite yet completed an agenda that was interrupted by the war and that the cessation of hostilities then offered as an occasion to return to unfinished business. The implication was that nothing really had changed, yet the physical and social landscape everywhere announced ruin and tragedy. But just as ironic was that despite the criticism by the prewar writers and intellectuals against the modern state and its bureaucratic excesses, what would eventually emerge in the rubble was an even more rational bureaucratic arrangement of power, dedicated not to the pursuit of war but to industrial growth and supremacy. If, as Yasuda noted earlier, modern Japan could be understood only as a totally ironic experience, a double irony prevailed to characterize the postwar restoration, because the arguments of cultural exceptionalism that earlier had been used to criticize modern organizational forms were later harnessed to represent the spiritual basis for the installation and success of a large-scale technological order capable of unprecedented productive power. The new Japanese order succeeded in producing, on a scale and at a level of excellence never before reached by most industrial nations, those things that earlier cultural critics had denounced as Western and dangerously disruptive of traditional Japanese life.

The overarching irony was captured by Kamei Katsuichirō, a refugee from the prewar debate on modernity, in a self-reflective and plaintive confessional essay, "The Ideal Image of Twentieth Century Japan" (*Nijūseiki Nihon no risō*, 1954). Even as postwar Japan prepared itself for massive industrial expansion, Kamei was calling for a return to Asia. The summons evoked the echo of earlier declarations for a Japanese return to the cultural homeland:

One of the problems with which the Japanese have been burdened since the Meiji Era has been the necessity of examining Japan's place in Asia and our special fate as Asians. Japan, as everyone knows, was the first country in Asia to "modernize," but it is not yet clear what meaning this modernization had for Asia. It is also a question whether Asian thought, which possesses strong traditions despite repeated taste of defeat and a sense of inferiority before Western science, is doomed to perish without further struggle, or if it is capable of reviving in the twentieth century something which will enable us to surmount the present crisis. . . . [T]o study it [Asia] has become since the defeat the greatest responsibility incumbent on us.[33]

Kamei continued an earlier critique by stating his open displeasure with Meiji rationalism and enlightenment and sought to return to the vision of Asian unity announced by Okakura Tenshin when he opened his *Ideals of the East* with a rousing call to brotherhood, "Asia is One!" Japan had abdicated its place in Asia, Kamei noted, by slavishly miming Western civilization, only to win for itself the status of a poor "stepchild." Worse still, it ended by using foreign technological instruments to wage war against Asian brothers. Japan must now return to Asia and, directed by a sense of genuine guilt and humility, secure its place as the "stepchild of the Eastern world." The need for cultural resistance against the West, he pleaded, was far from over and would continue throughout the rest of the twentieth century to complete the work begun by Gandhi, Tagore, Lu Hsun, and Okakura.

Kamei's reminder to "return to Asia" heightens our awareness that although the harsh language of the earlier "revolt against the West" had been removed because of the war, Japan's proper cultural place had remained as the central intellectual issue for the postwar period. Japan's real roots, in short, were to be found only in Asia, closer to the native land and not within the remote confines of Western civilization. This sense of cultural kinship by propinquity was reinforced by the elegant meditations of Takeuchi Yoshimi, a scholar of considerable stature who disclosed an affinity for leading cultural critics such as Okakura and Ōkawa Shūmei. Takeuchi, an authoritative interpreter of Chinese literature and culture, the translator of Lu Hsun's complete works, proposed to his generation the construction of a new science of knowledge which he described as "Asia as method" (*hōhō to shite no Ajia*). Acknowledging that this method, inspired by Asians' diverse experiences, had not yet been fully formulated, Takeuchi was certain that a sympathetic understanding of how Chinese, Japanese, and other Asian peoples had comprehended the challenge of modernity would offer instructive models for the task ahead.

In this essay, in which Takeuchi introduced the possibility of finding an alternative method to understand the Asian experience,

33 Tsunoda Ryusaku, Theodore de Bary, et al., *Sources of Japanese Tradition* (New York: Columbia University Press, 1958), pp. 392–3.

he confessed how he, as a student before the war, had studied China and Chinese literature as if neither the language nor its considerable literature any longer existed. Even more, he noted, he was not certain that China was anything more than an abstraction. "When we studied Chinese history and geography we never studied the fact that there were humans there."[34] Only on his first trip to China did he recognize how remote and abstract his training had been from the real thing and how ill prepared he was to cope with the enormity of a living experience. He admitted that he could not even communicate with the Chinese because his training had been principally in the classical language and had omitted the spoken tongue. It was as if, he mused, nobody really spoke Chinese. Yet Takeuchi apparently felt real empathy with the Chinese he encountered, recognizing that they, like the Koreans, were Japan's closest neighbors, indeed friends and brothers, yet made to appear remote by virtue of his education. To redress this great failing, he began a study of the spoken language and ultimately discovered a living literature embodied in the writings of Lu Hsun. This discovery that people did live in China, which hitherto had been prevented because of the dead hand of sinology, inspired Takeuchi to devote his own life to seeking the traces of what he called the "heart" (*kokoro*) of living Chinese.

The recognition of geographic immediacy and an authentic Chinese experience revealed to Takeuchi that Japan's own efforts to direct China's modernization were based on the same method that led him and his contemporaries to overlook the human presence and the possibility of vast differences. His own subsequent research showed him that the Chinese, the Koreans, the Indians, and other Asians had, owing to their own cultural experiences, forged different responses to the challenge of Western modernity. But what all Asians shared, apart from geography, was the quest to make sense of modernism without forfeiting their own cultural endowments. This, he observed, was not only the message of Tagore, as seen in his several trips to China and Japan, but also of Tenshin. Ironically, it was confirmed by Westerners like John Dewey and Bertrand Russell when they also visited Japan and China. Yet the Japanese, owing to their propensity to identify with Western techniques and methods, were blinded by their own experience of grappling with the problem and sought to impose on the rest of China a method of modernity alien to their own impulse. To return to Asia meant, therefore, to

34 Takeuchi Yoshimi, *Hōhō shite no Ajia: Waga senzen, senchū, sengo* (Tokyo: Sōkisha, 1978).

account for the diverse approaches enabled by living experiences and to develop an authentic method stressing differences, not abstract sameness. "There are severe limits to Western power," Takeuchi wrote:

I believe that Asians have always recognized them. Oriental poets have intuitively known this. Whether it is Tagore or Lu Hsun, they have accomplished the ideal of a general humanity in their own personal examples. The West has invaded the East; there has been opposition to this. Some, like Toynbee, have proposed to homogenize the world, but many contemporary Asians have not seen this as merely a Western limitation. In order to realize superior Western cultural values, the West has to be entrapped once more by Asia, as a means of revolutionizing Westerners themselves; it has to create universalism according to this cultural rewinding of values. The strength of the East is in revolutionizing the West in order to elevate the universal values that the West produced.

This, Takeuchi concluded, was the problem for the contemporary East and West and should be the "model for Japan, as well."[35]

A central corollary to this new "return to Asia" was the renewed emphasis on the communitarian ideal of folk culture that the Meiji state had unthinkingly suppressed in order to satisfy bureaucratic expediency. The older form of communalism celebrated by the ethnographer Yanagida Kunio was, in postwar Japan, the clarion cry of all those who believed that the state had intruded too far into the daily lives of ordinary people. Hence it is not surprising that writers and movements would derive identity and forms of enablement by summoning the ideal of the *jōmin*, the abiding people, in their several efforts to contest and even reverse state intervention. In a sense, Yanagida himself became something of a folk hero in the postwar era, and the so-called Yanagida boom that swept the country in the 1960s and early 1970s attests to the veracity of this alternative. Yet like its prewar progenitor, the new communalism was linked to all those sentiments that called for a return to Asia. The boom and its consequences for the restitution of folk culture did not mean simply a revival of the great anthropologist's writings nor a fad popularized by intellectuals and scholars. Rather, it was a countrywide movement to save folk arts and crafts, to emphasize the diversity and difference of regional and local culture against the inexorable demands of bureaucratic sameness. Because of Yanagida's emphasis on the structureless communitarianism of indigenous folk life, scholars, writers, and intellectuals began to explore the utility of this ideal

---

35 Ibid., vol. 3, p. 420.

for the new postwar social order. The appeal escalated as the rationalistic momentum of Japan's "phoenixlike" industrial recovery quickened. In the 1960s, intellectuals and activists like Yoshimoto Ryūmei or Takaaki (1924–) and Irokawa Daikichi (1925–) appropriated Yanagida to anticipate the state and became leaders of local protest movements demanding bureaucratic accountability in such vital issues as ecological pollution and the apparent elimination of regional self-governance. Yoshimoto, perhaps the most powerful theorist of this resuscitated ideal of community, hoped to transmute the state into a structureless entity occupied by a folk held together by mutual respect and affection. Yet this concentration on the community opened the way for a renewed emphasis on particularism and cultural exceptionalism. The discourse on cultural exceptionalism was transformed into a social science or "sociology" focused on explaining Japan's uniqueness. But it should be recalled that Yanagida and his generation of researchers had already called attention to the possibility of establishing a social science in Japan as the necessary methodology to grasp *difference*. Where the new interest in social science departed from this prewar precedent was in its insistence that normative conceptions and methods could be used to explain what was unique about Japan. Many of its most strident students were Japanese who had been trained in the West. Books too numerous to mention that appeared in the 1960s and 1970s pledged to performing a "scientific" analysis of Japan's uniqueness, why Japan was fundamentally unlike and hence superior to other societies.

The withdrawal from a universalistic understanding of the world to the familiar confines of a culturally unique homeland was most pronounced among ultranationalistic critics such as Hayashi Fusao, another survivor of the prewar debates on modernity. His own celebration of the native land was expressed in a work called "Japan, the Green Archipelago" (*Midori no Nihon rettō*, 1966) and in an influential dialogue with Mishima Yukio on the meaning of Japanism. Mishima also made his own statement in the "defense of culture" (*Bunka bōeiron*, 1969). It is hardly surprising that both attempted to reconfirm the martial spirit of the prewar restorationist radicals who had sacrificed their own lives to dramatize the urgency of the cultural problem. Whereas Mishima extolled the revolutionary idealism of Ōshio Heihachirō, recalling the prewar idealization of this late Tokugawa radical, Hayashi provided an historical interpretation of the Pacific War. In his "Thesis Affirming the Great East

Asia War" (*Dai Tōa sensō kōteiron*, 1964), Hayashi saw Japan's revolt against the West as the culmination of the "first one-hundred-year war in Asia" that began with the Opium War in 1840 and reached its climax with the bombing of Pearl Harbor. War was now over for Japan, but a second one-hundred-year war had already started in other places in Asia, such as Southeast Asia and the Chinese mainland. Thus Hayashi read these signs as an affirmation of Japan's own revolt against the West and a justification for its decision to go to war despite the overwhelming odds favoring defeat and destruction. And as recent events showed, he concluded, the contest was still far from over.

Both the range of articulations concerning what it means to be Japanese (*Nihonjinron*) and the concomitant impulse to "return to Asia" were represented by the Nobel laureate Kawabata Yasunari (1899–1972). Although he reached back to the idea of enduring aesthetic forms marking Japan's exceptionalism – as proposed earlier by Tanizaki, Kobayashi, and the Romantics – in his Nobel Prize acceptance speech, "Japan, the Beautiful," Kawabata called attention to this "unique" inheritance of the beautiful that distinguished the Japanese from others. Yet some years earlier in an eloquent poetic eulogy that he delivered to his departed friend Yokomitsu Riichi, he acknowledged this tradition of beauty as part of a larger Asian whole. His language applied to an entire generation of prewar and, later, postwar intellectuals and writers of whom Yokomitsu was perhaps the archetype because of his own tortuous odyssey from West to East. Kawabata lamented:

> Sufferer of the New Asia that fought the West,
> Pioneer of the New Tragedy in the Asian Tradition,
> You shouldered such a destiny.
> And you left the world sending a smile to Heaven.[36]

36   Quoted in Yuasa Yasuo, *Watsuji Tetsurō* (Tokyo: Minerva shobō, 1981), dedication page.

CHAPTER 6

POSTWAR SOCIAL AND POLITICAL THOUGHT, 1945–90
ANDREW E. BARSHAY

THE POSTWAR MOMENT:
"COLLECTIVE REPENTANCE" AND BEYOND

On August 30, 1945, Prime Minister Higashikuni Naruhiko held a press conference. Higashikuni, appointed to office in order to preside over Japan's transition from a vanquished empire to occupied dependent, was asked how his government proposed to explain Japan's defeat to the nation, particularly "those segments of the country still in a state of anxiety and agitation." Higashikuni counted chief among the causes "the rapid destruction of our fighting capacity," followed by "the truly horrific extent of the war damages we have suffered" due particularly to the appearance of the atomic bomb and the advance of Soviet forces. Turning to domestic conditions, Higashikuni arraigned "the reckless and excessive issuance of regulations and laws, and the application of controls that . . . were ill-suited to Japan" for rendering the population "hamstrung and unable to act." Both civil and military officials, Higashikuni charged, had "unknowingly led the country toward defeat." Though in their own minds they were acting for the benefit of the country, "the actual situation was just the same as if, with its arteries hardened, the nation had become completely unable to move, and had dropped dead of a cerebral hemorrhage." A further cause of our defeat, Higashikuni stated,

lies in the decline of the nation's moral fiber [*kokumin dōgi*]. That is, the military and civilian officials were, half openly, and general population more covertly, engaging in black market commerce. That matters have reached this point, of course, is the fault of the government's policies, but again the decay of the people's morality is also one of the causes. And so on this occasion I think the armed forces, government officials, and the population as a whole must search their hearts thoroughly, and repent. Nationwide, collective repentance [*ichioku sō-zange*] is, I believe, the first step on our road to reconstruction, and the first step toward national unity.[1]

Higashikuni's call for repentance is deeply important for the intellectual history of postwar Japan, in ways far beyond what he himself could have imagined. Higashikuni places the responsibility for Japan's defeat on the nation as a whole. It would not be enough for the military or the government to acknowledge their roles. Ultimately, the people themselves must repent, for they had lost their "moral fiber" and so helped bring about Japan's defeat. Its aftermath was not a time for vituperation but for "repentance" over collective failure to sacrifice life, limb, and material necessities to the war effort. The first official response to defeat was to mobilize the population in a final act of contrition for having survived.

Higashikuni was not alone in calling for collective repentance. The philosopher Tanabe Hajime (1885–1962), successor to Nishida Kitarō at Kyoto Imperial, had already, in the late fall of 1944, delivered his valedictory lectures on the theme of "metanoesis" (the same *zange* as in *sō-zange*) and in October 1945 set his signature to the long preface to the book, *Philosophy as Metanoetics* (Zangedō toshite no tetsugaku, 1946), which emerged from the lectures. Agonized by indecision over whether to criticize the wartime government at the risk of "causing divisions and conflicts among our people," Tanabe had "let go and surrendered himself humbly to [his] own inability." This act of self-surrender led Tanabe, "through metanoia, or the way of *zange*, to a *philosophy that is not a philosophy*: philosophy seen as the self-realization of *metanoetic consciousness*" (l).[2]

In giving himself up to a "philosophy to be practiced by Other-power (*tariki*)," Tanabe found the capacity to perform the intellectual service that he believed proper to a philosopher in time of war. "In the last analysis," Tanabe argues, "everyone is responsible, collectively, for social affairs. Once one assumes this standpoint of social responsibility, there can be no doubt that metanoetics is indispensable for each person at each moment. Therefore metanoetics, like morality, can provide the way to a universal phi-

1 "Nihon saiken no shishin – Higashikuni shushō kisha kaiken," as transcr. in *Sengo shisō no shuppatsu*, ed. Hidaka Rokurō (Chikuma Shobō, 1968), p. 54.
2 Tanabe Hajime, *Philosophy as Metanoetics*, tr. Takeuchi Yoshinori (University of California Press, 1986), pp. xlix–lxii. Original in *Tanabe Hajime zenshū* (Chikuma Shobō, 1963), 9:3–15. All emphases in original.

losophy" (liv–lv). As Japan itself came under attack, Tanabe "was transformed, converted, by the absolute and elevated to a spirit of detachment. . . . [M]etanoetics is as strong as we are weak." As Japan "met the unhappy fate of unconditional surrender," Tanabe urged his fellow Japanese "to perform metanoesis when we reflect on how this catastrophe came to be. Looking back, I have come to realize that my own metanoesis of a year earlier was destined to prepare the future for my country. The thought of this coincidence brought me great sorrow and pain." In remarks that might have been directed at Higashikuni's government, Tanabe adds:

Of course, I despise the leaders primarily responsible for the defeat who are now urging the entire nation to repentance only in order to conceal their own complicity. Metanoesis is not something to be urged on others before one has performed it for oneself. Still, it is clear that we the nation of Japan, having fallen into these tragic and appalling circumstances, should practice metanoesis (*zange*) together as a people. . . . I feel compelled to conclude that metanoetics is not only my private philosophy but a philosophical path the entire nation should follow. (lix–lx)

Tanabe reaches, finally, for a prophetic tone:

One step in the wrong direction, even one day's delay, may be enough to spell the total ruin of our land. Unless we all undertake the new way of *zange*, free ourselves from the evil institutions of the past, and collaborate in carrying out whatever changes are necessary in the social system, there is no possibility of reconstruction. The only course open to us at present is metanoetics. . . . Does not the Old Testament prophet Jeremiah show us the way? (lxi)

Tanabe, then, sought to lend moral and philosophical dignity to the experience of defeat by casting it as the opening of the way to self- and national transformation and to a "universal philosophy."[3]

For Tanabe, the ethic of responsibility weighed heavily indeed. "Naturally," he says, "I was indignant at the militarists and the government for having duped the people and suppressed criticism among them, for having had the audacity to pursue the most irrational policies in violation of international law, causing our nation to be stripped of its honor before the rest of the world." "But in the strict sense," he argues, "we Japanese are all responsible for the failure and disgrace since we were unable to restrain the reckless ways of the government and the militarists. After those who are

3 This conceptual structure, in which collective repentance by the "nation of Japan" occupies the center of a philosophical project of personal transformation and the realization of universality, replicates the "logic of species" (*shu no ronri*) that had formed the crux of Tanabe's social and historical thought since the early 1930s.

directly to be blamed for the disasters that befell Japan, the leaders in the world of social and political thought are most responsible. There is no excusing the standpoint of the innocent bystander so often adopted by members of the intelligentsia" (liv). Tanabe's language here is revealing. Whether a more activist and critical stance by the intelligentsia would have prevented the war from occurring cannot be known, but Tanabe clearly charges it with a grave sin of omission.

No doubt Tanabe's self-criticism was sincerely meant: It was tragic that "the government and the militarists" could not be restrained. But Tanabe's moral system itself placed the notion of service above that of recusal. It does not seem to have occurred to Tanabe that "contributionism," the willing provision by the intelligentsia of ideological resources to the state, might be a problem, or that refusal to serve might be a noble act and not merely the irresponsibility of the "bystander." It seems no less problematic that Tanabe continued to press for a single path for all Japanese. In the end, Tanabe remained locked in a world in which "the compassion of Other-power" might be underwritten by state coercion.

If Tanabe's response to defeat demonstrates both the peculiar power and constraints of his moral imagination, for other intellectuals defeat was a more explicitly political problem: Faced with the demand to disavow Japan's war effort and their own role in it, they sought a way to refuse. A case in point is the political scientist Yabe Teiji (1902–67), a member of the Law Faculty at Tokyo Imperial and of Prince Konoe's brain trust. Yabe, who had resigned his university post in preference to being purged from it, left a day-to-day record of the birth of "postwar" Japan and his reactions to the shifting situation.

On August 10, 1945, Yabe began to chronicle Japan's final collapse: "At Hiroshima on the sixth, two enemy planes using a new type of bomb – called 'atomic bomb' [the English words are transcribed], causing a tremendous number of deaths and casualties. A kind of thrill [*hitotsu no suriru da*]." The Soviet declaration of war and invasion of Manchuria left Yabe "stunned and shocked, bereft of words."

Now at last, the worst of all possible situations is upon us, we have no room to choose, no room to negotiate. Everything we've worked for up to now has been rendered meaningless . . . the Greater East Asia Ministry, the government of Greater East Asia, the bringing down of the Tōjō cabinet, the ideological war [*shisōsen*] and so much else. Who could have imagined that we would have to set to work on the domestic arrangements to accompany unconditional surrender?

August 15, the day of Japan's capitulation, Yabe wrote, was

a historic day, one without precedent in the history of the Empire. At 12:01, in His Majesty's sonorous voice, [came] the rescript announcing the end of the war. In the garden with its flourishing sweet potatoes and cucumber and tomatoes, and in the full light of the summer sun, I bow in reverence toward the Palace, lowering my head as His Majesty's extraordinary Rescript is broadcast, unable to stop the flood of bitter tears. Though mortifying in the extreme, the Potsdam Declaration has been accepted, and with it unconditional surrender. The time for endurance begins today. What fate awaits us I do not know, but I am determined to live as a righteous patriot [*shishi jinjin*], leading the way to Japan's revival . . .

On August 16: "More now coming out re the true character of the atomic bomb used at Hiroshima. This is a revolution in science." A few weeks later, on September 3: "People like Ozaki Yukio and Hatoyama Ichirō are now being lionized in the papers. Unpleasant, somehow. It's disgusting to see these spectators, who contributed nothing to the war, carrying on as if they had risen up to meet the challenge of the times." On September 12: "Yesterday afternoon, General Tōjō attempted suicide with a pistol, keeping the American soldiers who had come to take him into custody waiting while he did so. But he was unsuccessful, and is being treated by a U.S. Army doctor. A shameful spectacle."

On December 2:

After dinner I had a smoke and read Kasai Zenzō's "Confessions of a Wild Drunk" [*Kyōsuisha no kokuhaku*]. It reached me. Only someone who has made it through the sufferings of life could grasp the mad drunkenness of such a squalid and miserable person. Thinking of the defeat and suffering that oppress my spirit these days, and even more of the shameful conduct of the stupid Japanese, I could only sympathize with this unhappy writer.

On December 8, Yabe's mood was one of mordant self-reflection:

Lessons I have learned from the present situation: (1) If one intends to make university teaching one's life work, one must confine one's study to books on one's office shelves, and have no ties to actual politics. (2) If one wishes to live as a teacher and scholar, one must not have a practical view of life. One must adopt an indifferent, escapist attitude. (3) One must not write books in the midst of war or social upheaval. (4) One must not allow oneself to be compelled to offer opinions when free speech is not permitted. (5) One who wishes to be influential in the academy must not become active in the wider society.

Some months later, on June 4, 1946:

On the train, read [Joseph] Grew's *Report from Tokyo*. Since Grew was supposed to be a pro-Japanese American, I was favorably disposed. But to the contrary, on reading it I had a feeling of loathing. All he says is that there are splendid people in Japan, but concerning this war he offers nothing more than the usual self-righteous twaddle that Japan was 100% the aggressor, the U.S. 100% in favor of peace.

The release of the Nuremberg Trial records occasioned the following (December 12):

Learning of these [German crimes] alone is enough to show how evil a thing war is. But the problem is, have the Russians, English, and Americans who sit in judgment over the German forces absolutely never previously committed such acts themselves? And what of the world-historical reasons [*kongen*] why the war had to happen in the first place? Are we to believe that the English, Americans, and Russians have no responsibility? Nonsense!

Finally, let us note this brief passage, dated May 3, 1947: "Today marks the day the new Constitution goes into effect, with downpour continuing from last night, and cold. No doubt a rain of tears sympathizing with the Japanese people."[4]

Yabe was clearly unwilling to accept as legitimate a political system imposed by Occupation fiat on Japan. But one suspects that his substantial exclusion from it – had he not contributed to the war effort? – also rankled deeply. For him, state service, particularly in a time of crisis, remained of paramount value. Hence his contempt for those who had been "bystanders" during the war, and for "intellectuals" who now built "democratic" castles in the air.[5] Yabe's attitude, which combines a more or less passive rejection of significant aspects of the postwar order with an ethic of "contributionism," is significant for two reasons: first, as a contrast with thinkers who, while belonging to different generations, professions, and social milieux, positively embraced the "postwar" as a moment of new moral and political possibilities, and in so doing inaugurated "postwar" intellectual history as such; and second, because the attitude of rejection and "contributionism" has in fact endured and continued to interact in one form or another, and in varying degrees of strength, self- and mutual awareness, with that of postwar-as-possibility.

4 *Yabe Teiji nikki* (*YTN*) (Yomiuri Shinbunsha, 1974), 1:830–2, 837, 865, 868–9, 871; 2:44, 101, 107, 146.
5 See *YTN*, 2:120.

THE DEMOCRATIC ENLIGHTENMENT, 1945–60

In his oral autobiography, the Marxian economist Uno Kōzō describes the reaction to the emperor's announcement of the war's end at the Mitsubishi Economic Research Institute. Uno had joined Mitsubishi in 1944; he had earlier lost his university position despite being acquitted – twice – of charges, dating from 1938, of violating the Peace Preservation Law.

> At Mitsubishi we had learned quickly . . . about the Imperial Conference held on whatever day it was in August. So when we heard the [surrender] broadcast we weren't in the least surprised. At the house next door to mine they all cried and so forth, but I only thought: finally, perhaps liberation is at hand. Now I should add that at Mitsubishi, as we were rejoicing over our liberation, Inoki Masamichi, who was working in the next office, grew angry. Finally, our noisy celebration was just too much; "shut up!" he finally shouted. "Better close the door," we said, and so we did.[6]

In Uno's reaction – one far removed, emotionally and intellectually, from those of Higashikuni, Tanabe, Yabe, and of his colleague, the political scientist Inoki Masamichi – "postwar" carried the most positive possible connotation. For Uno, as for Japan's Communists, and for the left across the board, Japan's defeat and occupation meant liberation from domestic repression that had lasted (for some) nearly twenty years: On the orders of SCAP, some 3,000 political prisoners were freed in early October 1945, and the Peace Preservation Law of 1925 was repealed.

Liberation was as much historical as personal. Thus the Communist Party, newly and unexpectedly legalized, "expressed its profound gratitude for the fact that, through the occupation of Japan by the Allied forces that have liberated the world from fascism and militarism, the way has been opened for the democratic revolution in Japan."[7] It is important, however, to specify more precisely *from* what Japan was supposed to have been liberated, and to delineate, further, the relation between the "liberated *from*" and the "liberated *for*" implied in the rather schematic formulation of the Communist Party's official welcome to Occupation forces.

"Postwar" thought is postimperial thought, in a dual sense. Externally, its point of departure was determined by the rapid dissolution

---

6 Uno Kōzō, *Shihonron gojūnen* (Hōsei Daigaku Shuppankyoku, 1981), p. 589. Uno's work is discussed later in the section entitled "Science and Culture after Anpo."
7 Tokuda Kyūichi et al., "Jinmin ni uttau" (October 10, 1945), as repr. in Hidaka, *Sengo shisō*, p. 245.

of the Japanese empire and by a dramatic contraction of perspective to what the economist Ishibashi Tanzan had once called "little Japan"; control over Japan's destiny now lay with the occupying power. Internally, "postwar" was defined by the unprecedented release, under Occupation aegis, of currents of thought and opinion that regarded the war itself as a product of the "imperial system" (*tennōsei*), and that took the dissection and dismantling, the negation, of that system as the chief task facing Japan.

To be sure, the "trial of the *tennōsei*" was contemporaneous with, and substantially enabled by, SCAP's proclaimed assault on Japan's "irresponsible militarism" in all its forms. Maruyama Masao, for example, opened his famous essay on "ultranationalism" with an echo of SCAP's "Five Reforms" Directive to Shidehara Kijūrō of October 1945: "What was the main ideological factor that kept the Japanese people in slavery for so long and that finally drove them to embark on a war against the rest of the world?"[8] And probably all parties used the intellectual currency of attacks on "feudalism" to draw the line between the "old" and "new" Japan. But the public scrutiny of the *tennōsei* by Japanese intellectuals was more than a matter of political expedience. Though Maruyama framed his question in terms used by the victors, his answer was one that they could not possibly have produced. Maruyama had direct experience of both the elite intellectual and military milieux of the empire in its last phase, which he used to brilliant descriptive effect. For Maruyama, "ultranationalism" was marked by the "interfusion of ethics and power. . . . National sovereignty was the ultimate source of both ethics and power, and constituted their intrinsic unity." Under such circumstances, "Japanese morality never underwent the process of interiorization that we have seen in the case of the West, and accordingly it always had the impulse to transform itself into power. Morality is not summoned up from the depths of the individual and does not hesitate to assert itself in the form of energetic outward movement."[9]

In thus arraigning a state that arrogated to itself all the functions of private conscience, Maruyama worked from assumptions concerning the state and the individual that were drawn not so much from the Anglo-American liberal or pragmatic traditions as from a

8 Maruyama, "Theory and Psychology of Ultranationalism" (1946), in ibid., *Thought and Behaviour in Modern Japanese Politics*, pbk. ed. (Oxford, 1969), p. 1. Cf. Japanese text of directive in appendix to *Kyōdō kenkyū: Nihon senryō*, ed. Shisō no Kagaku Kenkyūkai (Tokuma Shoten, 1972), p. 541.
9 Maruyama, "Theory and Psychology," p. 9.

combination of Kantian moralism and "left-Hegelian" historicism. His philosophical culture and that of his readership were far removed from that of Japan's American occupiers; in the early postwar period, moreover, it was a popularized version of that culture, rather than American "whiggishness," that entered school textbooks.[10]

Intellectuals like Maruyama and the members of the many groups that began to form immediately after the formal surrender had no illusions about being able to influence Occupation policy directly. "Politics," like citizenship, would henceforth have to be a matter of mass action – but also informed and guided action: Here was the *raison d'être* of groups of "enlighteners" such as the Youth Culture Conference (Seinen Bunka Kaigi), Association for Free Discussion (Jiyū Konwakai), People's Culture League (Jinmiu Bunka Dōmei), and the League of Japanese Men of Culture (Nihon Bunkajin Renmei), which are largely forgotten today. Others, such as the Twentieth-Century Research Institute (Nijusseiki Kenkyūjo), Institute for the Science of Thought (Shisō no Kagaku Kenkyūkai), and the more explicitly political Peace Problems Symposium (Heiwa Mondai Danwakai) and Association of Democratic Scientists (Minshushugi Kagakusha Kyōkai, or Minka) stood at the forefront of intellectual life after the war, along with a revived Association for Historical Study (Rekishigaku Kenkyūkai) and other formerly suppressed bodies, and remain better known. It is true that with the decision to leave emperor Hirohito on the throne, permit the return of purged politicians and officials to public life and carry out what was termed the "Red Purge" in 1950, and finally to push through a peace treaty that excluded both the Soviet Union and the People's Republic of China, American policies would seem to have regressed badly. But the "enlighteners" were determined to impart as much substance as possible to the initial promise that "August 15" would mark a genuine liberation: from an oppressive system that in their judgment had been in existence since the 1890s, and indeed from a society whose "backwardness" and "irrationality" had driven it to follow its leaders into a total war against powers they could not hope to defeat.

The account of defeat as liberation is deceptive on one important point. Uno himself merely felt vindicated by Japan's defeat. He moved into the postwar era with his world view intact, convinced that he had been "right" all along, and untroubled by any sense of a

10 Cf. R. P. Dore, *Shinohata: Portrait of a Japanese Village* (Pantheon, 1978), p. 56.

moral burden that was both personal and historical.[11] But in understanding "postwar" thought, we must be attentive to just such a
sense of moral burden. Indeed, Uno and those like him, especially
newly released or returned Communists, appeared as "mirrors
which in their brilliance shed glaring light on the weakness that
haunted the innermost hearts" of Japanese intellectuals.[12] The issue
of "repentance," in other words, was not so easily dispensed with.

The felt need for national repentance in Higashikuni's sense was
not to survive the signing of the surrender instrument aboard the
Missouri. With the Allied decrees calling for the "strengthening of
democratic tendencies among the people" and "the elimination for
all time" of militarism and ultranationalism, the original sense of
failure vis-à-vis the emperor was transmuted to a more abstract sense
of guilt vis-à-vis history itself, for having failed to prevent the war;
along with this, albeit less consistently, came expressions of guilt vis-
à-vis "the people" and Japan's former colonial subjects for having
fought the war as it had been fought. It was on this basis, Maruyama
Masao has argued, that Japanese intellectuals formed a "community
of contrition" (*kaikon kyōdōtai*). This, he claims, was the most
recent of – only – three moments in modern Japan's intellectual
history when the country's prematurely sectionalized and overspe-
cialized intellectuals were able to reach beyond the confines of their
organizational functions and styles of discourse to address genuinely
"universal" issues: reason, science, progress, freedom, democracy,
peace – and "universality" itself.

Intellectuals had resolved that in order for "rationed freedom" [under the
Occupation] to be transformed into a self-generating force, they themselves
as intellectuals, just as the Japanese nation itself, had to make a new start.
At the core of this resolution flowed a difficult-to-distinguish blend of
hopeful joy for the future and contrition for the past. . . . In other words, in
the immediate postwar years, *all intellectuals, from their varying standpoints
and in their varying spheres of concern, experienced a shared emotion: self-
criticism.* A sense of questioning – whether their mode of being as intellectuals up to then was acceptable, whether perhaps a new departure, based on
a fundamental reappraisal, was not necessary – such questions began to
spread over the ashes.[13]

11 See Wada Haruki, "Sengo Nihon ni okeru Shakai Kagaku Kenkyūjo no shuppatsu,"
    Shakai kagaku kenkyū 32, no. 2 (August 1980): 216–32.
12 Maruyama, Masao, "Kindai Nihon no chishikijin," in ibid. *Kōei no ichi kara* (Miraisha,
    1982), p. 118.
13 Maruyama, "Kindai Nihon no chishikijin," pp. 114–15, with emphasis added. The two
    other moments of intellectual community, according to Maruyama, were the early Meiji
    decades, through 1889, and the 1920s, which coincided with the virtual hegemony of
    Marxism over Japanese intellectual life.

This transmutation of "repentance" (or "contrition") marks the inauguration of "postwar" historical consciousness. In this sense, Higashikuni's remarks do not yet belong to postwar Japanese thought and intellectual history but rather to the liminal period that came between the acceptance of the Potsdam Declaration and the beginning of the Occupation. At the same time, they provide a near-perfect crystallization of the consciousness *against and through which* "postwar" Japanese thought sought to define itself. If the assignment of responsibility for defeat belongs to the prehistory of postwar thought, the assignment of responsibility for war marks its beginning. Among intellectuals, this sense of responsibility included contrition for having been unable to prevent the war from occurring. But this was more abstract, perhaps less personally painful than public self-condemnation for having given one's intellectual energy to it. This latter stance entailed a *tenkō* or "reorientation" to the collective task of rooting out discredited mentalities and of making a commitment to a morally healthy, politically progressive, historically just cause. In this respect, the economist Ōkuma Nobuyuki (1892–1977) is conspicuous for the extraordinary thoroughness with which he revealed his wartime activities and writings; he examined in public the consequences of his having failed to realize that it was "not only capitalism that controlled one's destiny" and led to alienation. Intellectuals, Ōkuma insisted, had to look squarely at their personal moral culpability in having adopted the language of "loyalty" and having rationalized their service to the "advanced national defense state" as a means of combating capitalism. He pledged to devote his postwar life to exposing what he called "the evils of the state."[14]

More common than Ōkuma's self-abnegation was the rapid embrace of those who had been "right," abstracting, as it were, a concrete historical object vis-à-vis which guilt was to be felt or expressed. The result, Wada Haruki has argued, has been a continued "ethnocentrism" in Japanese thinking about the meaning of August 15 as liberation: from the *tennōsei*, certainly, but also from the necessity to confront the real history of empire. But the empire's disappearance from the map, Wada insists, did not justify its disappearance from the mind; it should have remained as a historical problem of the first order.[15]

---

14   See Arase Yutaka, "Sengo shisō to sono tenkai," in *Kindai Nihon shisōshi kōza*, ed. Ienaga Saburō et al. (Chikuma Shobō, 1959), 1:352–3; and Matsumoto Sannosuke, "Ōkuma Nobuyuki ni okeru kokka no mondai," *Shisō*, no. 837 (March 1994): 4–39.
15   See Wada Haruki, "Sengo Nihon ni okeru Shakai Kagaku Kenkyūjo no shuppatsu."

It is easy now to attack such absence, as it is to criticize the notion that embracing those who had been "right" was a sufficient response to the question of war responsibility. It was at the least credulous, if not politically expedient. But the implosion of values attending Japan's defeat was real. Given such a total failure after years of effort and the waste of millions of lives, it was not strange to wonder whether the cause itself was not fatally flawed or to turn to those who could claim (rightfully or not) to have had a prior understanding of the deeper causes of those flaws. Ōkuma's key point, however, was that as long as the organizational logic of subjection to a single cause remained untouched, intellectually nothing would be gained. That indeed turned out to be a persistent problem, only exacerbated by avoidance, credulity, and expedience.

In any case, the perspective of a war that was not inevitable, leading to a defeat that was, formed the prism through which Japan's entire modern experience was to be viewed and judged: Such was the defining condition of "postwar" thought. To it, however, must be added the complicating element of a diffuse, "free-floating" sense of victimization (*higaisha ishiki*). This was present, Maruyama notes, among intellectuals in their thirties vis-à-vis their elders,[16] and more broadly among younger people vis-à-vis the state that had fed them in the millions to the bloody engine of war. At the same time, as the first and only target of – American – atomic weapons, Japan assumed the status of victim that virtually transcended history. In a more narrowly political sense, finally, the stance of victim was also assumed by those for whom defeat had meant the loss of recent prestige or status – and could also, in the long run, serve the purposes of ruling strata in their attempts to resist Occupation policy, as a replacement for the now politically untenable call for collective repentance. To quote (albeit out of context) the critic Takeuchi Yoshimi: "National [*minzokuteki*] consciousness arises through oppression."[17]

Whatever the psychological complexities marking the conscience and consciousness of Japan's intellectuals, these did not, and could not, determine the specific social and political content of the "not-yet" that Japan had now become. The first step in that definition was

16 Maruyama, postscript to "Kindaiteki shi'i" (1945), in ibid., *Senchū to sengo no aida* (Misuzu Shobō, 1976), p. 190.
17 Takeuchi, "Kindaishugi to minzoku no mondai" (1951), in ibid., *Kindai no chōkoku* (Chikuma Shobō, 1983), p. 266.

the collective negation of the past – and also of the present to the extent that it perpetuated the past. Thus the fall of 1945 brought a flood of criticism of the emperor system, with a debate over war responsibility following the next spring. Much of this was localized, even inchoate, as denunciations of "collaborators" (for example, by *Yomiuri* employees of the paper's owner), student strikes calling for the ouster of "reactionary teachers," and exposé-style articles and books on the extent of the imperial family's land and stock ownership all emerged alongside serious examinations of the inner workings and mentalities of Japan's prewar and wartime elites and discussions of the legal and political prospects for Japan's becoming a republic.[18]

Such negation was "not the opposite of construction – it [was] only the opposite of affirming existing conditions."[19] For a postwar consciousness, Japan was a "not-yet" to be struggled for; as a national society, Japan had, through war, defeat, and Occupation, assumed a kind of historical "plasticity" and was therefore the proper object of a reenergized, liberated imagination. It was not so much to be "reconstructed," as Watsuji Tetsurō, Abe Yoshishige, Amano Teiyū, Nanbara Shigeru, Hasegawa Nyozekan, and other intellectuals of mid- to late Meiji vintage would hold; nor could it be realized solely by the imitation, however intelligently undertaken, of an American or any other real-world model. Postwar Japan was to be imagined anew: It was in this sense not only "a nation lying in utopia" but one whose *reality* was now to be created. Historical plasticity and utopia were not the antitheses of reality but aspects of it.[20]

Beyond the sloganeering, advertisement, and political cant represented in the ubiquitous phrase "New Japan," the postimperial era was to be one, first and foremost, of democratization (*minshuka*) in all spheres. The Occupation and its policies – such as the encouragement of the labor movement, elimination of agrarian tenancy, constitutional and other legal reforms – could be regarded as legitimate insofar as they promoted democratization, not as defined *by* the Occupation or Japanese government but by self-described "demo-

---

18 For relevant texts, see "*Tennōsei*" *ronshū*, ed. Kuno Osamu and Kamishima Jirō (San'ichi Shobō, 1975), Toda Shintarō, *Tennōsei no keizaiteki kiso bunseki* (San'ichi Shobō, 1947), and the references in Carol Gluck, *Japan's Modern Myths* (Princeton University Press, 1985), pp. 314–15, n. 9.

19 Leszek Kolakowski, "The Concept of the Left," in ibid., *Toward a Marxist Humanism* (Grove Press, 1968), p. 68.

20 See Maruyama Masao, "'Genjitsu'shugi no kansei" (1952), in ibid., *Gendai seiji no shisō to kōdō*, exp. ed. (Miraisha, 1966), pp. 172–7.

cratic forces" (*minshu seiryoku*) themselves. Workers and unions, agrarian tenants and smallholders, women, left-wing parties, younger academics, writers, journalists, students – these were to be the arbiters of democratization.

Two visions, or "idioms," of democratization are discussed here: first, the Marxist, class-based revolutionary version, which advanced rapidly to the forefront of public discourse owing to its integral, systematic character, teleological clarity, and newly elevated political stature; second, the "modernist" version, which in its social analysis drew substantially on Marxism but abjured the centrality of class in favor of a notion of praxis derived variously from the ego and its desires, personal ethics, or from objectivist models of adaptive behavior. In their shared insistence that consciousness be linked to social praxis, these idioms were similar enough to enable their adherents to cooperate on a range of political and educational projects, such as those organized under the umbrella of the Minshushugi Kagakusha Kyōkai. This united front, as it was called by the party, or "community of contrition" as Maruyama termed it, operated at some level for the duration of the Occupation and episodically through the Security Treaty crisis of 1960. But its constituent visions were also sufficiently different to produce deep and lasting disagreements that emerged through the very process of trying to sustain that "community."

For the newly released or returned leaders of the Communist Party – Tokuda Kyūichi and Shiga Yoshio, then Nosaka Sanzō – and the adherents of Marxism, "democratization" meant, or should be made to mean, democratic revolution in preparation for a transition from capitalism to socialism. Such was the historic task now facing Japan – and the frame within which intellectual, cultural, or literary positions would have to be formulated – in the midst of a highly fluid political situation. Cultural concerns did not inhabit an autonomous sphere but were to be subordinated to instrumental criteria: whether or not they would advance the formation of a self-conscious proletariat. Depending on circumstances, proletarian consciousness might, of course, have to be mediated by the party, but how to enforce a judgment about this or that circumstance without using undemocratic means proved an exceedingly difficult problem. Nor was there any consensus on strategy – witness the disputes about the revolutionary value of short-lived attempts at "production control" (*seisan kanri*) by factory workers, and the supplanting of the Tokuda-Shiga line by Nosaka's "lovable Party" approach, its replacement in

1950 by a call for militance and illegal activity, and finally (by the mid-1950s) a local version of the "thaw."

Longer-running questions of historical interpretation (which supposedly underlie strategy) also remained to be resolved. Indeed, the history of postwar Marxism in Japan begins with the revival of the familiar prewar debates over the stage attained by Japanese capitalism, the nature of the Meiji Restoration, landlordism, feudal remnants, and so on.[21] At least in terms of the land reform, the longstanding Kōza-ha or "feudalist" position, which saw agrarian tenancy as the fundamental obstacle to the development both of capitalism and bourgeois democracy, was vindicated by Occupation policy.[22] But within a decade, the Kōza/Rōnō framework itself was beginning to erode. It could hardly survive the dissolution of tenancy, and indeed of the Japanese peasantry itself, once rapid industrial growth began to absorb the rural population. Instead, initially *within* that framework but gradually absorbing it and causing it to metamorphose, debates began that centered on the category and varieties of monopoly capital, especially the extent to which "state monopoly capital" had formed in Japan: It was by overcoming state monopoly, Marxists believed, that a capitalist Japan would give way to a socialist Japan.

This was far more than a theoretical issue. In desperate postwar conditions, economists were concerned with the revival of production and accumulation, and almost all analysts acknowledged that some degree of state planning would be essential for even a minimal recovery. The government's own 1946 report on prospects for reconstruction emphasized the need for rigorous data collection with a prefatory phrase that is unthinkable today: "No matter whether Japan adopts a capitalist or a socialist system in the future, . . ."[23] Given the often bitter experience by intellectuals of the imperial state's compulsory communitarianism, as well as the abysmal failure of wartime planning, the question of how the state could be made to act both democratically and "scientifically" was crucial. Such concerns were typical of the Marxian-influenced economists who served in official positions in this period. Arisawa

21 See Germaine Hoston, *Marxism and the Crisis of Development in Prewar Japan* (Princeton University Press, 1986), chap. 9.
22 See, for example, Yamada Moritarō, "Nihon nōgyō no tokushusei" (1945), "Nōchi kaikaku no igi" (1948), and "Nōchi kaikaku katei kiroku no hitsuyōsei" (1948), in *Yamada Moritarō chosakushū* (Iwanami Shoten, 1984) 3:169–87; Dore, *Shinohata*, p. 57.
23 Saburo Okita, comp., *Postwar Reconstruction of the Japanese Economy*, Ministry of Foreign Affairs (September 1946) (University of Tokyo Press, 1992), p. 96.

Hiromi (1896–1988) and Tsuru Shigeto (1912–) held short-term
positions of considerable responsibility for economic policy questions prior to turning more or less permanently to academic work.
The two men, while personally close, had quite different intellectual
formations. As a graduate of the first class of Tokyo Imperial's
faculty of economics, Arisawa's intellectual trajectory coincided
with the inauguration of Tōdai's lineage of Marxian economics. He
lived and studied in Germany in the middle years of the Weimar
republic and was deeply imbued with German notions of planned
economy that had arisen from that country's catastrophic experience
of total war between 1914 and 1918. He combined these notions
with that of state monopoly capital to form his basic approach to
research and policy work (concentrating especially on energy provision to industry) after 1945: The concept and analysis of both
"priority production" and later of the industrial "dual structure"
were substantially owed to him. For his part, Tsuru Shigeto received
his undergraduate and graduate degrees at Harvard; he worked
directly with Wassily Leontief and Paul Sweezy, knew Schumpeter's
work intimately, and his classmates included John Kenneth
Galbraith and Paul Samuelson. Among the permanent features of
Tsuru's thought is an internal dialogue between Marxism and
Keynesianism. Together, Arisawa and Tsuru attempted to work
out the "social economy," first of recovery, then of growth, by
addressing in the broadest sense the conditions under which "productive forces' could be enhanced through rational allocation of
resources, and working people and investment protected from the
ravages of inflation. Both belonged to a "bureaucratic left" that,
while in some ways was reminiscent of the "social bureaucrats" of
the 1920s, operated in a transformed political environment and was
far freer to make use of Marxist analyses; in this sense, it is distinct
to the early postwar era. Compared to Tsuru, Arisawa was the more
radical believer in central planning. Tsuru, no less an institutionalist,
was more democratic in temper and became an early critic of "GNP-
ism" and its massive social costs.[24]

24 For Arisawa, see (inter alia) *Gakumon to shisō to ningen to – wasurenu hitobito* (1957; Tokyo
    Daigaku Shuppankai, 1989); *Keizai seisaku nōto* (Gakufū Shoin, 1949); "Nihon
    shihonshugi no unmei," *Hyōron* (February 1950). For Tsuru, *The Economic Development
    of Japan* (*Selected Essays*, Vol. II) (Edward Elgar, 1995); *Japan's Capitalism: Creative
    Destruction and Beyond* (Cambridge University Press, 1993); *Taisei henkaku no seiji
    keizaigaku* (Shin Hyōron, 1983); "Kōdo seichō ron e no hansei," in *Tsuru Shigeto
    chosakushū*, vol. 4 (Kōdansha, 1975). Recent secondary treatments include Bai Gao,
    "Arisawa Hiromi and His Theory for a Managed Economy," *Journal of Japanese Studies*
    20, no. 1 (Winter 1994): 115–53, Laura Hein, "In Search of Peace and Democracy:

The influence of Marxism – likened by Shimizu Ikutarō to coming into contact with a live electric cable – was felt far beyond the realm of economics.[25] Its characteristic concerns, with change in the mode of production and with grasping the "totality" of the social process, were being taken up by party intellectuals, anxious to speak persuasively to non-Marxists, and by many more outside party ranks and not subject to its discipline. For the first time – as a corollary to this more open discursive situation – serious attention was being directed to issues of ideology and consciousness. These had been badly neglected (or avoided as taboo) under the combined impact of "national polity" orthodoxy and the defensive marginalization by the prewar party of "anthropological" or "humanist" approaches to Marxism, such as that of Miki Kiyoshi, which tended to be dismissed as petty bourgeois deviations. But the postwar condition itself, of the need to survive amidst the stupefying ruins of empire, of reflection on recent history and the exposing of personal wartime conduct in all its forms, ensured that the political, philosophical, and moral problems of action would be raised among intellectuals with unprecedented force and urgency.

It is here that the "modernist" idiom of democratization found its entry and that the central philosophical debate of the early postwar decades was joined. The debate over subjectivity (*shutaisei ronsō*) was played out between 1946 and 1948. Although left off unresolved, it formed a touchstone for all subsequent attempts to develop a nonnationalist system of ethics for action in the public sphere. At its heart was this question: Granted that democratization, or democratic revolution, was the desideratum – granted, too, that reliance on Occupation authorities, to say nothing of Japanese ruling circles, was likely to bring disappointment or frustration – what was to be the historical *agency* involved in bringing it about? *Who*, to use J. Victor Koschmann's terms, was to be the "subject of action" in a democratic revolution?[26]

The subjectivity debate began among literary critics and writers. With the founding of the journal *Shin Nihon bungaku* in December

Postwar Japanese Economic Thought in Political Context," *Journal of Asian Studies* 53, no. 3 (August 1994): 752–78, and Tessa Morris-Suzuki, *A History of Japanese Economic Thought* (Routledge, 1989), chaps. 4 & 5.

25 Shimizu's comment in "Zadankai: Yuibutsu shikan to shutaisei" (*Sekai*, February 1948); repr. in *Kindaishugi*, ed. Hidaka Rokurō (Chikuma Shobō, 1964).

26 See J. Victor Koschmann, "The Debate on Subjectivity in Postwar Japan: Foundations of Modernism as a Political Critique," *Pacific Affairs* 54, no. 4 (Winter 1981–2): 609–31, and his longer study, *Revolution and Subjectivity in Postwar Japan* (University of Chicago Press,

1945, party writers called for an "'objective' form of literature that could revive the earlier efforts of proletarian writers to portray faithfully the 'true life of the masses.'" Kurahara Korehito, Nakano Shigeharu, and Miyamoto Yuriko, writers whose political bona fides included time in prison, insisted that the party establish a strong, even militant, cultural policy. In doing so, they were following the Tokuda-Shiga political line: Like "political struggle," literature had more than a reflective role to play in society. As the *conscious* (and self-proclaimed) expression of the objective "life" of the proletariat, party-guided literary production was to be positively constructive of culture.

A challenge to mandatory "objectivism" (and to the "politicism" that underwrote it) came almost immediately from within the community of Marxist writers but soon extended far beyond it. The journal *Kindai bungaku*, which began to publish in January 1946, brought out a stream of essays – by Honda Shūgo, Ara Masato, Hirano Ken, Odagiri Hideo – that in one way or another gave primacy to the individual ego, rather than to class, as the focus of literary effort. There was a predictable exchange of charges: The affirmation of ego or self would insinuate petty bourgeois interests and attitudes into the revolutionary movement, thus diluting its class consciousness, weakening its political resolve, and dissipating its effectiveness. "Objectively," the petty bourgeoisie could not lead the revolution but could at best serve in a supporting role, if not promote reaction. The countercharge decried the subordination of art to politics as damaging to culture but also politically counterproductive. Inauthenticity was impossible to conceal; didacticism would smother creativity. Novels, stories, essays, and poems did not write themselves as an unmediated reflection of class consciousness but required the active intervention of a writer. An "ego"- or "self"-less writer was an empty vessel and could produce nothing.

The writers who published in *Kindai bungaku* did not reject the notion of realism or of objectivity but insisted that such qualities "reflect" intentionality, which in turn required an autonomous perceiving "self." More to the point, the "real" to be depicted was one of physical and moral collapse, of a "gut-level" existentialism. In the midst of near-starvation and the reduction of personal life to its

1996); also Sakuta Keiichi, "*Kyōdōtai to shutaisei*" (1971), trans. as "The Controversy over Community and Autonomy," in *Authority and the Individual in Japan: Citizen Protest in Historical Perspective*, ed. J. Victor Koschmann (University of Tokyo Press, 1974), pp. 220–49; Hidaka Rokurō's introductory essay to *Kindaishugi* (Chikuma Shobō, 1964), pp. 7–52; Nakajima Makoto, *Sengo shisōshi nyūmon* (Ushio, 1968), esp. pp. 113–43.

rawest processes, was it not too soon, perhaps even immoral in some way, to draw one's gaze away from that reality in favor of an edifying but confining moral-political vision defined by (and as) "the party"? Tamura Taijirō wrote famously of the "gate of the flesh," a normless reality of impulse, desire, and subjugation. Honda Shūgo pressed for a "realism of depth rather than breadth"; Ara Masato, looking back at a "first youth" – spent as a rightist – that brought him the "sublime experience of negativity," called now for a "second youth" to be lived outward from the ego and subject to its demands. Thus Ara could write: "Who are the masses? I, I am the masses. There are no masses apart from me. Cast away doubt, hesitation, and fear, and walk the path illumined by your own candle!"[27]

But there were also ethical and political stakes to the affirmation of the ego. For Ara, the ego was the only sure guarantee against the worship of authority that had destroyed his first youth, and the only basis for "revolution" – Ara in fact joined the party in March 1946. The private realm of the self had to be established before that self could (re)turn to a reconstituted social world, one in which individuals would be bound together by "horizontal ties" (*yoko no tsunagari*) of equality and mutual respect. Picking up a similar theme, Takami Jun's "In Process" ("Kateiteki") addressed the moral costs of rationalized self-sacrifice for a "great cause" that one is forbidden to question. In the words of his character, Shimojima: "As he read Schweitzer, Shimojima was brought again to reflect that nothing had poisoned his life so much as a way of thinking in which that life was no more than a process toward some *thing*, a 'processual' way of thinking – that had taken hold of him."[28]

The controversy over subjectivity, then, was about the conditions and consequences of commitment; thinkers representing various points of view – Marxists (both orthodox and eclectic), Christians, Kantians, behaviorists – raised questions about the sufficiency of "ego" as a basis for a philosophy of action or praxis. The shift from a literary to philosophical focus was set in motion when party intellectuals – led by Matsumura Kazuto – used the Minka journal *Riron*, and later the party periodical *Zen'ei*, to attack assertions made by followers of the Kyoto philosophical school of the salience of their ethico-religious ideas to the "metanarrative" (as Koschmann terms

27 Ara Masato, "Dai ni no seishun" and "Minshū to wa tare ka" (both 1946), repr. in *Ara Masato chosakushū* (San'ichi Shobō, 1983), 1:10–67. Quote from concluding lines of "Minshū to wa tare ka."
28 Takami Jun, "Kateiteki" (1950), in *Takami Jun zenshū* (Keisō Shobō, 1971), 10:507.

it) of democratic revolution. Tanabe Hajime, whose "metanoetics" were discussed earlier, argued that only the imperial institution, not the party, was capable of the radical self-transcendence necessary to lead Japan toward the realization of a new form of social democracy based on love and equality.[29] Matsumura, who was generally overmatched when he faced professional philosophers, sensibly dismissed these claims. Tanabe's case for the political role of a self-transcendent imperial institution was a sophisticated atavism. But it was succeeded by a far more developed attempt to enfold an ethics of personal revolutionary commitment based on radical indeterminacy within the teleological claims of Marxism. This version, or vision, of subjectivity was the work of Umemoto Katsumi (1912–74); the responses to it, from within and without the Marxist camp, gave the subjectivity debate a philosophical depth and intellectual appeal lacking in its earlier literary phase.[30]

Umemoto himself had come to Marxism after Japan's defeat (he joined the party in 1946 and left it in 1960). His intellectual formation was broadly phenomenological. In a way reminiscent of Kawakami Hajime thirty years earlier, Umemoto was driven to unify two – incommensurable – philosophical tendencies. The first, determinist, tendency derived from his acceptance of the Marxian "meta-" or "first narrative" concerning the direction of history, the centrality of revolution to historical change, and the derivation of social consciousness from social being. The second, as with Kawakami (though Kawakami did not speak in such terms), arose from his sense of a "lacuna" (kūgeki) or flaw in Marxism: its "lack of a theory of subjective intentionality." Where did the "ethical willingness to commit oneself to revolutionary action," or more broadly the "acceptance of Marxism as world view rather than merely as a science," come from?[31] Umemoto drew his answer from Nishida and Watsuji, from the "philosophy of nothingness" and the ethics of "relationality." For each individual, Umemoto argued, there subsisted moments of absolute discontinuity, of radical indeterminacy or "emptiness" that were prior to socially determined consciousness

29 See Tanabe, "Zettaimu no tachiba to yuibutsu benshōhō: Mori Kōichi shi ni kotau" (June 1946), Tanabe Hajime chosakushū, 8:399–409.
30 See Umemoto Katsumi, "Yuibutsuron to ningen" (1947), "Yuibutsu shikan to dōtoku" (1948), "Mu no ronri to tōhasei" (1948), "Yuibutsu benshōhō to mu no benshōhō" (1948), "Shutaisei to kaikyūsei" (1948); also the later essays "Shutaiseiron no gendankai" (1951) and "Shutaisei: Sengo yuibutsuron to shutaisei no mondai" (1960) and the interview transcript, "Sengo seishin no kiten" (1968). In Umemoto Katsumi chosakushū (San'ichi Shobō, 1977), vols. 1 & 2.
31 Koschmann, "Debate," p. 619.

and constituted the space/time of freedom in which individual subjects could commit themselves to revolutionary action.

Umemoto's stance was bound to displease the orthodox. But he also broke with the main line of Kyoto school thinking that identified the ethnic nation, or community, as the only collectivity for which the free decision of self-sacrifice can be made – and in being concerned with the freedom of the decision to begin with. And yet, in the structure of Umemoto's thought, the crucial question is: How can the choice for the proletariat be made? It is not for what collectivities a choice can be made, let alone what new collectivities, or solidarities, can be created. Umemoto's attempt to substitute class for ethnos was part of a continuous, Ping-Pong–like process of attempting to fix a single subject as the driving agent of history that had been going on in Japanese intellectual circles since the 1920s. The *meaning* of that continuity, however, was only vouchsafed by the massive discontinuity of defeat.

In February 1948, the monthly *Sekai* (which had published Maruyama's essay on ultranationalism in its first issue and remained the flagship of the nonparty left) carried a round-table discussion on *shutaisei* that rehearsed the various responses to the question of the philosophical – or scientific – status of the term. In August, the Communist Party journal, *Zen'ei*, published a special issue devoted to the "critique of modernism." This, in effect, ended the debate as far as the party was concerned, though it hardly removed the issue of personal autonomy and commitment from pubic discourse or from Japanese thinking about democracy. But what was this "modernism" that the party felt it necessary to critique? And what connection did it have to the issues of subjectivity raised in the wake of Umemoto's interventions?

By 1948, relations between the party and SCAP had grown noticeably more tense, though not as bad as they were to become. Although Japan, compared to Germany, was somewhat insulated from Cold War pressures, they were inescapably present. They certainly diminished the party's tolerance of eclecticism, however sympathetic. As the party, in the name of a "Democratic National Front" (*Minshu minzoku sensen*), began to attack "American imperialism," it also pressed for ideological orthodoxy. Bourgeois reformism, imperialism's sop to the proletariat, had its intellectual counterpart in elitist eclecticism, idealism, and "subjectivism." Some of this atmosphere can be discerned in an exchange between Matsumura Kazuto and Mashita Shin'ichi, himself a Marxist, who had argued that Marxism as a "world view" was even more fundamental than Marxism as a science: "Science," Mashita warned, could be abused as long as it failed to serve ends that only a "world view" can generate. He was confident that a revolutionary ethic of "partisanship" (*tōhasei*) could be nurtured through the incorporation into Marxism of a notion of subjectivity drawn (through Umemoto) from Nishida. Matsumura, however, would have none of this:

At the level fundamental principle, there is absolutely no necessity of incorporating existential philosophy, the philosophy of Nishida Kitarō, or other fashions. To do so would be a serious mistake. Mr. Mashita has said that the problems addressed by existential philosophy must be taken up by Marxists or else the young people will lose interest. . . . [I]nsofar as they did so primarily out of an attraction to existentialism or Nishida's philosophy, they would never become truly Marxist. In that sense, I think Mr. Mashita's interpretation of Marxism is dangerous.[32]

It was the ideas of Umemoto and Mashita that party intellectuals initially branded as "subjectivist" or "modernist." But once in circulation, the term came to be applied across party lines to points of view as disparate as that of Shimizu Ikutarō and Miyagi Otoya, who denied scientific status to the very notion of subjectivity, and that of Maruyama Masao and Ōtsuka Hisao, for whom subjectivity was a moral, practical, and historical issue of momentous importance. In time, "modernism" acquired its own substantial, and positive, connotations – what it did not acquire was uniformity of meaning. And yet perhaps because of its looser intellectual structure and lack of an institutional center for the dissemination of orthodoxy, "modernism," not Marxism, would – in the long run – be the driving spirit of postwar social science.

By broad consensus, Maruyama Masao belongs at the center of any discussion of modernism, perhaps of postwar thought.[33] His vision of "the modern," which he never defined in any systematic fashion but developed in the context of numerous "occasional" essays, and of

32 Quoted in Koschmann, "Debate," pp. 622–3; orig. in "Zadankai," an Hidaka, *Kindaishugi*, pp. 164–5.
33 See Nakajima, *Sengo shisōshi nyūmon*, pp. 40, 68; Ishida Takeshi, *Nihon no shakai kagaku* (Tokyo Daigaku Shuppankai, 1984), pp. 188ff.; Sasakura Hideo, *Maruyama Masao ron nōto* (Misuzu Shobō, 1988), *passim*. See also *Gendai shisō* (22, no. 1 [1994]) devoted to Maruyama; and Rikki Kersten, *Democracy in Postwar Japan: Maruyama Masao and the Search for Autonomy* (Routledge, 1996). For a bibliography, see Imai Juichirō and Kawaguchi Shigeo, comp., *Maruyama Masao chosaku nōto*, exp. ed. (Gendai no Rironsha, 1987). Maruyama's complete works are now being published by Iwanami.

concrete political and historical analysis, attracted public attention in Japan virtually from its first articulation.

In the round-table discussion on subjectivity, Maruyama emerges as most sympathetic to Mashita Shin'ichi (and to Umemoto, who was absent), sharing with them the conviction that Marxism had to be seen as a world view and philosophy – in other words, as a total intellectual orientation capable of enunciating *ends*, and judging the *means*, of praxis. At the same time, he rejected their arguments for an identity between "partisanship" – conscious commitment to the proletariat – and the full realization of subjectivity. One lengthy exchange captures Maruyama's basic intellectual and political stance – and its ambivalent relationship to Marxism as well:

MARUYAMA: For quite a while now in our discussion, every time the word "ethos" or "subject" has come up, my name gets trotted out. It's not that I attribute to myself any intention to develop a philosophy of subjectivity; I merely want to point out what it is in arguments I've heard so far from Marxists that I don't find persuasive. . . . Now, Mr. Mashita has said that class partisanship represents the most concrete determination of the subject. But I don't think that such a determination settles the problem of the subject. . . . When we analyze the relations of production as a given object, and specify them concretely, their class nature comes through very clearly. But thus far it is only a question of being, not of subjectivity.

HAYASHI [Kentarō]: But in this case, what's different is that "partisanship" already includes the element of practice. It's not just class being.

MARUYAMA: Well then, I'd like to ask whether the praxiological concern – the class consciousness – contained in partisanship, refers to an *existing* class consciousness. How about it?

MASHITA: By "existing," you mean

MARUYAMA: I mean "actually existing" [*gen ni aru*]. Whether it's a consciousness as Dasein. People talk of consciousness as "high" or "low," but talking in this manner presumes some sort of *value*, according to which an actually existing consciousness is set against a consciousness that *ought* to exist. Right? In this sort of discussion, I think values are assumed. And isn't it because this value consciousness isn't made plain that people . . . feel that there's something cold in Marxism that prevents them from sticking to it?[34]

Maruyama's position, then, rests on a classic Kantian distinction between *Sein* (what is) and *Sollen* (what ought to be). Central to a "determination" of the subject was the individual's capacity, and responsibility, to act according to values neither derivable from objective class position nor exhausted by class-oriented practice. It was a matter, he would repeatedly insist, of "ethos."

34 "Zadankai," in Hidaka, *Kindaishugi*, pp. 143–4.

Maruyama was also pressed to clarify his own stance vis-à-vis a set of "objectivist" arguments made by Shimizu Ikutarō and Miyagi Otoya, who, while differing between themselves, contested the notion of an autonomous "subject" as scientifically valid.[35] While sharing Maruyama's equation of the "modern" with individual self-determination in a society no longer enmeshed in the "omnifunctional diffuseness of premodern groups," Shimizu considered the postwar "thirst for philosophy" an abnormal reaction to "the ethical condition of Japan – one of the fragmentation of the human being brought on by the collapse of an authoritative system of values and the loss of a [source of] commands; of salvation in the form of authority; and of the omission of the roundabout ways of science." And he placed the "talismanic quest" for subjectivity right at the center of this unhealthy craze:

> The demand for subjectivity has grown increasingly strong among outstanding social scientists. As long as social science was understood to take the form of *Geisteswissenschaft*, with its connotation of German Romantic influence – in other words, a conflation of science with philosophy – such a demand was never given explicit expression. [But] as social science went beyond *Geisteswissenschaft* to adopt the objective methods of modern science, a desire that once could be satisfied with the vague formulations of the "spiritual sciences" has now been put forward anew as the demand for subjectivity.[36]

Ultimately, "subjectivity" had no metaphysical essence. It could be demonstrated "scientifically" to take one of two forms: either as "the faculty for resisting the impact of change in the external environment and instead maintaining a consistent pattern of action in conformity with internalized values," or a more adaptive capacity of "self-determination" that, when deemed necessary by the individual, might lead to the "abandonment of value commitment" for the sake of the "long-run satisfaction of . . . desires." Both forms of action – or better, of behavior – reflected individual judgment and power of decision; the issue was how much alienation one could stand.[37]

A final instance of the "objective" reduction of the subject comes by way of Miyagi Otoya, who worked within a Marxist framework but was similar in spirit to Shimizu. If anything, Miyagi was more the explicit behaviorist; for him, "praxis" was a matter of response, experimentation, and adjustment. Unlike Shimizu, and

---

35 See Shimizu Ikutarō, "Shutaisei no kyakkanteki kōsatsu" (1947); repr. in Hidaka, *Kindaishugi*, pp. 168–93; and Sakuta, "Controversy."
36 Shimizu, "Shutaisei," pp. 170–1.
37 Quotes in this paragraph from Sakuta, "Controversy," pp. 233–4.

unlike his Marxist confrères, Miyagi insisted that whatever was "lacking" in Marxism, in terms of its understanding of subjectivity, could be supplemented by Freudian personality theory. All intentionality, he claimed, "should be understood as arising from drives and desires grounded in biology and the material conditions of existence."[38] Science could cover both epistemology and practice. Marxism was the master science – psychology, presumably, its handmaid.

A rather comic exchange toward the end of the round-table discussion leads us back to Maruyama and to the summing up of the interrelation of modernism's constituent elements:

SHIMIZU: As I see it, in the end, for Marxism, the various new psychological approaches exist in the great beyond. But as we pursue the problems of the human person with full scientific accuracy, it will become possible to run a single path to link two mutually separated fields. Given that Marxism is something that develops, that development will be carried out by its coming into contact with this new psychology, and having a single path opened between them.

MIYAGI: To express it symbolically, it will be a matter of MARX AND FREUD, won't it?

MARUYAMA: You should say, MARX AND FREUD AND ETHOS.[39]

It is typical and significant that Maruyama should have added "ethos" to his formula for a unified social science. While recognizing the compelling power of historical structures over individuals, as revealed in Marx's analysis of capitalist production, and the equally powerful operations of the psyche in shaping behavior, Maruyama nevertheless held up the importance of the sphere of conscious action. The Weberian term *ethos* evoked a universal, transcendent value struggling to subsist amidst the concrete particularities of both historical and psychological processes. Class did not fully explain the ego; nor did the ego exhaust the subject. A revolutionary transition might be necessary, but it was not certain that class struggle (as defined by the party) leading to socialist revolution was possible or appropriate for Japan, or that that was the most important level at which revolution would have to be carried out. Did democracy ultimately have to derive its significance from its supporting role in a socialist revolution?

To be sure, Maruyama spoke of the need to "complete the democratic revolution," as in the following passage from 1947:

38   Koschmann, "Debate," p. 620; see "Zadankai," pp. 132–5.
39   "Zadankai," p. 166; the capitalized phrases were spoken in English.

It has now been made our task to accomplish what the Meiji Restoration was unable to carry through: that of completing the democratic revolution. We are being pressed to confront the problem of human freedom itself. The situation facing Japan, of course, is not such that it can be resolved simply by rejoining the orthodox lineage of modern freedom. The bearer of "freedom" is no longer the "citizen" as conceived by liberals since the time of Locke but must rather be the broad working masses with workers and farmers at the core. Even then the issue is not merely the sensual liberation (*kankakuteki kaihō*) of the masses, but rather how and how thoroughly the masses are to acquire a new normative consciousness.[40]

Clearly, Maruyama sought the creation of a new "normality." Revolution was essentially a metaphor for a change in consciousness toward full "modernity." In associating modernity with a society that recognized this normative subject and its struggles, and affirmed that modernity, Maruyama was indeed a modernist. For him, democracy was not merely a means; it was an end. The "human type" he envisioned was not the "new socialist man" but the *homo democraticus*.[41]

In developing this vision, Maruyama was strongly influenced by Ōtsuka Hisao (1907–96), an economic historian with whom he worked closely at Tokyo University. Perhaps because he was a Christian – a follower of Uchimura Kanzō's "Non-Church" – Ōtsuka's ideas did not, in the long run, have the impact of Maruyama's. But in the early postwar years, Ōtsuka, along with older figures such as Nanbara Shigeru and Yanaihara Tadao, did a great deal to raise the public image and stature of the Protestant intellectual. Ōtsuka's significance here lies in his focus on the *historical* process by which modernity had developed in the West, an effort perfectly paralleled by Maruyama's writings on Tokugawa Japan. Both had begun their work in the late 1930s as acts of covert protest against the suffocating orthodoxy of "national polity" thought. In the process, they jointly created the *historiographical* foundation of postwar modernism.[42]

In Ōtsuka's case, as in Maruyama's, immersion in the work of

40 From Maruyama, "Nihon ni okeru jiyū ishiki no keisei to tokushitsu" (August 1947), in *Senchū to sengo no aida*, p. 305.

41 For further discussion, see Andrew Barshay, "Imagining Democracy in Postwar Japan: Reflections on Maruyama Masao and Modernism," *Journal of Japanese Studies* 18, no. 2 (Summer 1992); and Koschmann, *Revolution and Subjectivity*.

42 Arase, "Sengo shisō," p. 358: "The realities of peoples' lives during wartime brought about the dissolution, willy-nilly, of the top–down order established by the former Constitution, and fostered feelings that caused the principles of the new Constitution to be regarded as natural and proper; in the same way, the result of wartime academic scholarship was to lay the groundwork for the viewpoint of people creating institutions [*seido o tsukuru ningen to iu shiten*]."

Max Weber was crucial, engendering in both a sense of the irreducible difference of fact from value, and therefore of the necessarily provisional character of social scientific knowledge. Ōtsuka, who followed Weber's own research trajectory more closely, came to be concerned with the "nonrational" wellsprings of human action, which he identified with the realm of faith. Thus, while drawing upon Kōza-ha scholarship in his own comparative work on the origins of capitalism, he retained an overriding concern with the historical sources – in the Reformation and "spirit of capitalism" itself – of individual human autonomy. Indeed, Ōtsuka's essentially religious zeal to foster a new human type – the ethical producer – in Japan came to form a leitmotiv in his professional work.

For Maruyama, "interiority" or self-possession formed the normative core of subjectivity (*shutaisei*). To be modern was to exercise a transcendent, universal critical faculty in a particular social/national totality. A modern or "open" society, in turn, was one where the free and untrammeled association of individuals sets the norm, where politics was the creative space in which conflict was confronted and resolved in an ongoing history of "progress [in] the consciousness of freedom." (Maruyama took the phrase from Hegel's *Philosophy of History*.) It was a history made by human beings for human purposes not always – indeed seldom – understood or intuited with lasting clarity. Human society and institutions, therefore, were neither "natural" nor metaphysically guaranteed. Rather, they were vital *fictions* worked out by actors with some degree of such self-consciousness: This Maruyama took as a key indicator of modernity. The modern consciousness did not contrast fiction to reality or truth but rather negated any "natural," metaphysically guaranteed order that comprehended both the cosmic and human spheres.[43]

But was Japan modern? Yes and no. Both Ōtsuka and Maruyama saw in Japan a society that had industrialized on the basis of a still premodern rural social base and consciousness, that of the "community." Japan, that is, had industrialized but was not yet fully modernized. Here lay its tragedy and its hope: The process could now be "completed," insofar as a revolution ever can be. For Ōtsuka, the "community" was a remaining problem to be solved; the "modern human type" could not otherwise be formed.[44] Maruyama saw the

---

43   Foregoing two paragraphs adapted from Barshay, "Imagining," pp. 379, 382–3.
44   See esp. Ōtsuka, "Kindaiteki ningen ruikei no sōshutsu" (1946); repr. in *Ōtsuka Hisao chosakushū* (Iwanami Shoten, 1970), 8:169–75, "Jan Karuvan [Jean Calvin]" (1947), repr. in ibid., pp. 404–20; and *Kyōdōtai no kiso riron* (1955; Iwanami, 1984).

great task of enlightenment in dissecting and transforming the thought, mentality, or psychology of the masses, who were until now, or even still, mired in "Asiatic" or (semi)-feudal backwardness. Its great antagonist and challenge was Japan's "tenacious familial [*dōzokudanteki*] social structure and its ideology, which is the hot-house of the old nationalism."[45]

Ōtsuka's approach to "overcoming community" was Weberian and twofold: a rigorous separation of a scholarly analysis, almost exclusively of European history, from apologetics, but a deep and frequently expressed belief in the need of Japanese society for a Christian-inspired ethic suffused with local – national – concerns. A modern society was ruled in the last analysis by the consciences of its individual members, who also recognized their duties to the whole.[46] For Maruyama, the methods of political science and history were to be brought to bear on the analysis of Japanese society; at the same time, especially after the treaty issue arose in 1950, and again in Weberian fashion, well-considered, rigorously determined political action would have to follow.

The party's condemnation of modernism could only create difficulties for leftists facing the polarizing pressures generated by the nascent Cold War. By 1950, "realist" intellectuals such as Hayashi Kentarō (a historian of Germany and original member of Minka) were challenging Maruyama and other independent figures to choose up sides.[47] The treaty arguments – for a bilateral versus comprehensive pact – extended and hardened these lines, although the ideal of a peaceful, nonaligned Japan was powerful enough to make politically credible Japan's participation in the Bandung Conference of 1955, which marked the arrival of the recently decolonized "Third World" on the political stage.

Intellectually, the critique of modernism solved nothing. One contemporary, Takakuwa Sumio, remarked that the issue of subjectivity was left as an "open construction site exposed to the rain." In his popular history of postwar thought (written in 1968), the critic Nakajima Makoto argued that "the real beginning of postwar intellectual history lies in the debate over subjectivity; and the twists and

45 Maruyama, "Nihon ni okeru nashonarizumu – sono shisōteki haikei to tenbō," in ibid. *Gendai seiji no shisō to kōdō*, p. 168.
46 See esp. Ōtsuka, "Jan Karuvan," pp. 415ff.; also Uchida Yoshiaki, *Vēbā to Marukusu: Nihon shakai kagaku no shisō kōzō* (Iwanami Shoten, 1972), part 2.
47 See Hayashi Kentarō, "Gendai chishikijin no ryōshiki: Maruyama Masao shi e no hi-hihanteki hihan," *Sekai*, no. 58 (October 1950): 97–103.

frustrations of postwar thought arose from our having left the problem of subjectivity behind us unresolved as we leapt over the deep
gulf to take up issues of modernization, the welfare state, and arguments over nationalism."[48]

Yet the unresolved debate over subjectivity left a quite definable
legacy, which can be thought of as a secular "protestantism." In the
form given it by Maruyama and Ōtsuka, modernity entailed a mental
transformation, one predicated on the reforms of the early Occupation period, but that did not place socialism as its end state.
Instead, as his later invocation of "permanent revolution" suggests,
Maruyama saw modernity (with democracy as its utopia) as a condition of ongoing struggle against the forces of a corrupt and oppressive tradition.[49] In this sense, as with the Christian Ōtsuka, he was a
protestant thinker.

As with Protestant Christianity, modernism could also be divested
of its radical character and turned into a bland apology for the status
quo. This happened in Japan. Sometime in the 1960s, the peaceful,
egalitarian, and ethical democratic utopia of the late 1940s was
coopted, its categories transvalued, though not without protest from
the original "protestants" themselves.

Marxists and modernists shared the belief that a "democratic"
consciousness, whether tending toward socialism or to a fully
realized "modern" personality or self, would initially have to be
mediated to the masses in a campaign of popular enlightenment.
Among the modernists, the "masses" were more often invoked
than trusted; modernists were clear in their intent to change popular
mentalities. Their pitfall was one of convenient despair brought
on by a "situation" beyond their power to influence. Marxists,
faced with the pressure of attempting to lead actual mass movements, tended to oscillate between a stance of "following after" or
"separating themselves from" the masses, losing sight – according
to Arase Yutaka – of the need to challenge the thinking of the
majority.[50]

Given the centrality of elite intellectuals such as Maruyama to the
enlightenment campaign, we may look first at its impact on the

48 Takakuwa is quoted by Umemoto Katsumi in "Shutaiseiron no gendankai" (1951),
   Umemoto Katsumi chosakushū, 1:463; also in Koschmann, *Revolution and Subjectivity*, p.
   203; Nakajima quote from Nakajima, *Sengo shisōshi nyūmon*, p. 116.
49 See Maruyama, *Gendai seiji no shisō to kōdō*, exp. ed., p. 574.
50 Arase, "Sengo shisō," pp. 385–6. The problem is reminiscent, of course, of the
   Yamakawa/Fukumoto debates of the 1920s.

upper reaches of the educational system itself. The Occupation's purge of undesirable academics, along with the more or less voluntary self-removal of figures like Yabe Teiji, opened the way for a renascence of Marxist scholarship and organizations. In a review of *Nihon shakai no shiteki kyūmei* (1949), a collection of eight public lectures delivered at Tokyo University in 1946, the historian John Whitney Hall wrote as follows:

In post-war Japan the Rekishigaku Kenkyūkai clearly dominates the historical scene. One reason for this is undoubtedly the rather marked ideological fervor of its most active members. It comes as no surprise that these men, whose interests were in history as a social science, should have been strongly influenced by materialist theory, for most of them were trained in the twenties and thirties when Marxism was making its impression on Japanese educational institutions. It is somewhat surprising, however, to see the vitality of this line of thinking in the post-war period and the unmistakable evidence it gives of long and vigorous continuity dating back to the thirties when non-conformist views were so extremely dangerous. . . . The strong Marxist slant of some of these writings may be repugnant to us, but they can hardly be dismissed, not only because of the very real contributions which they can make to our understanding of Japanese history but because of the outstanding position of the school which they represent in post-war Japan.[51]

Along with Rekken came the establishment of institutes of social science in a number of universities: significant precisely because "social science" *was* for many people no more than a synonym for Marxism. The erstwhile Communist leader Fukumoto Kazuo, for example, had presented his memoirs, *Kakumei wa tanoshikarazu ya*, as "the reminiscences of a social scientist" – "albeit one different from the general run of professors in these fields," due to his long years of illegal activity and confinement in prison. But "social science" it was.[52] Indeed, in seeking to establish its Institute of Social Science (Shakai Kagaku Kenkyūjo, or Shaken) at the University of Tokyo, the founding committee had to overcome just such assumptions among officials whose sanction would be required for their plans to be realized. Thus, in its statement of purpose (dated March 1946), the institute's founding committee stressed its potential contribution to scientific knowledge and, even more, to state policy:

Social science in the University will progress only if it possesses a firm foundation and a broad perspective, formed on the one hand by its being

51   Hall, *Far Eastern Quarterly*, vol. 11 (November 1951): 97–8.
52   Fukumoto Kazuo, *Kakumei wa tanoshikarazu ya* (Kyōiku Shorin, 1950), pp. 3–4.

based on the realities of Japan; while on the other observing these in the light of current tendencies in the laws, politics, and economies of various nations abroad. However, social research in Japan has hitherto either restricted itself to the simple exploration of abstract theories, or tended toward arbitrary inductive judgments based on defective and incomplete data. . . . Despite the fact that wide-ranging and accurate collection of data, and their constant and rigorous analysis, are indispensable to the achievement of the goals set forth above, facilities for this purpose are virtually nonexistent in Japan: such indeed is the reason for the persistence of the failings just described. Nor is the need for such facilities exhausted in the reasons just offered. They are also crucial to the drawing up and implementation of legislation and public policy . . . as we in Japan now turn to a renewal of our policies along lines proper to a democratic and peaceful state.[53]

Shaken's subsequent history provides a window on the problems of applying enlightenment. While striving to establish itself as a "national" resource, the Institute faced continued suspicion, voiced by the Education and Finance Ministries as well as the Cabinet Legislative Bureau, over its political complexion, and periodically had to fend off charges that its work was "unproductive" and "ineffective." This was despite its record of major surveys, for example, of the administrative reforms associated with democratization (1947–8), the labor movement (1950–5), village structure (1953–63), unemployment (1955–9), and the urbanization of the Tokyo–Chiba corridor (1961–3) – the latter project being among the earliest to combine social and natural science approaches to the study of industrial pollution. In part, the official animus was ideological; the Institute did lay great stress on the importance of democratic reforms and later called into question the virtues of breakneck economic development after the mid-1950s.

But Shaken also had internal difficulties. Despite its professed goal of creating a "research community," its attempts to foster a style of communal, institute-wide fieldwork, discussion, and mutual criticism, and to offer public lectures and publications aimed at a wide audience, proved unsustainable.[54] Ideological and methodological antagonisms among members were part of the reason; persistent

53 "Shakai Kagaku Kenkyūjo setchi jiyū," repr. in *Shakai Kagaku Kenkyūjo no sanjūnen: Nenpyō, zadankai, shiryō* (Tokyo Daigaku Shakai Kagaku Kenkyūjo, 1977), p. 43. See also the institute history in "Shakai Kagaku Kenkyūjo," *Tokyo Daigaku hyakunenshi,* comp. Tokyo Daigaku Hyakunenshi Henshū I'inkai (Tokyo Daigaku Shuppankai, 1987), 8:373–476.
54 Takayanagi Shin'ichi, discussing Shaken as a *kyōdōtai,* stressed that it was to be a "community" – he uses the English word – not a gemeinschaft. *Shakai Kagaku Kenkyūjo no sanjūnen,* p. 67.

conflicts over status and hierarchy between professors and lower-ranking researchers and assistants were another. By 1952, amidst retrenchment and administrative recentralization in higher education, a ministry review recommended the institute's abolition. The report and its recommendation were attacked by Director Ukai Nobushige as "slovenly and thoughtless," and a concerted effort at joint resistance involving Shaken and the various other bodies similarly threatened seems to have brought a reprieve – at least the recommendation was shelved. But the showcase attempt to mount an institute-wide village survey (of Gōdo, Gumma Prefecture), meant to refute the charges themselves, ended in total failure, with senior researchers unable to agree on protocols and even bickering over housekeeping; this debacle was followed the next year by a strike among assistants, long frustrated over their limited chances for promotion and what they regarded as a coercive use of their labor in fieldwork such as the Gōdo survey. Beyond the compromise settlement of this particular strike (part of an upsurge of the student movement generally), the "clash between bureaucracy and democracy," as the issue was framed by Ōuchi Hyōe, led to an early return to individual and small-group specialization, the installation of a clear (and resented) hierarchy, and the institute's eventual eclipse by private institutes with a more pronounced orientation toward economic research. In the end, the institute does not seem to have made its hoped-for contribution to democratic culture in postwar Japan. Rather, bureaucratization – in part self-defensive in character – seems to have ensured its survival.

Beyond the academy, two other instances of applied enlightenment, both by organizations bearing the term "Science" in their names, are of some symbolic importance here. The Association of Democratic Scientists (Minshushugi Kagakusha Kyōkai, or Minka) drew a large and varied following and pursued an ambitious program of popular enlightenment on a range of science-related concerns – "science" being defined very broadly but with an emphasis on the criticism of the past and on the responsibility of scientists to advance the democratization of knowledge. However, Minka metamorphosed into a Communist Party front organization. Its campaigns in the early 1950s on behalf of a "science for the people," according to Nakayama Shigeru, manifested an "unreflective activism." While benefiting briefly from the rise in public esteem for critical scientists that followed exposés of the effects of fallout from the Bikini hydrogen bomb tests of 1954, Minka lost ground to "normal" science underwritten by corporate or state interest. And when the party itself in 1955 renounced its militancy, Minka cadres were left with little internal cohesion.[55] By contrast, the Institute for the Science of Thought (Shisō no Kagaku Kenkyūkai), whose leading figures included Tsurumi Shunsuke, Tsurumi Kazuko, and Minami Hiroshi – all wartime repatriates from the United States – did much to provide a critical introduction of postwar American social science, especially social psychology and its underlying pragmatic philosophy, to a Japanese audience.[56] The institute, however, was about practice, or application. Its ethos, as Ronald Dore described it, was that of "gadfly to the academic professions." Diverse as to discipline and method, members were "self-consciously intellectuals" with a shared sense of urgency to make the occupation reforms the foundation of a new society: "They judged that the opponents of the new society were temporarily in eclipse and the time given to make their reemergence impossible would be short."[57] The task at hand was to "codify" the philosophy of life of Japan's everyday people (hitobito) "and to increase the self-awareness of its possessors" – it being self-evident that "democratic change in Japanese society [would] never be finally accomplished" without a "change in the attitudes of the 'common man.'" Given the sense of urgency and the drive to exercise "influence," social science as the institute practiced it suffered from "the frequent failure to formulate specific problems, insufficient recognition of the need, at least to make the effort, to separate judgments of fact from judgments of value, and in the empirical work a lack of rigour in the collection of data and a certain naivety in the interpretation of statistics."

The striking feature of the institute's work was the catholicity of problems and phenomena that it considered worthy of investigation, and the attempt to allow "common" people to describe their ideas and culture in their own words. Interview-based studies (done in 1951), for example, treated "the philosophy" of geisha, doctors,

---

55 On Minka, see Ishida, *Nihon no shakai kagaku*, pp. 175–80, and Ishida's references (ibid., p. 274, n. 6); also Nakayama Shigeru et al., eds., *Science and Society in Modern Japan: Selected Historical Sources* (MIT Press, 1974), pp. 284–9. Ishida (1984, p. 180) reports membership figures as follows: 1946 (at founding), fewer than 200; 1947, approx. 1,000; 1948, 2,300; 1949, 6,800; 1950, approx. 10,000; 1951, 5,000; dropping thereafter until Minka ceased operations in 1957.
56 On Shisōken, see Lawrence Olson, *Ambivalent Moderns: Portraits of Japanese Cultural Identity* (Rowan and Littlefield, 1992), chap. 4; R. P. Dore, "The Tokyo Institute for the Science of Thought: A Survey Report," *Far Eastern Quarterly*, no. 13 (November 1953): 23–36.
57 Dore, "Institute," p. 23.

newspapermen, nurses, policemen, and firemen. Linguistic and content analysis of popular novels, songs, and films – as well as of academic writing – were typical of the group's ad hoc approach. Kawashima Takeyoshi's careful sociological analysis of *on* and *giri* – stimulated by, but critical of, Ruth Benedict's totalizing treatment of these notions – demonstrated the strength of the institute's attentiveness to real situations. This same feature characterizes the work for which the organization is probably best known: the compilation of large numbers of individual studies under a "joint research" rubric, most famously of the phenomenon of *tenkō*. Such works combine analysis of ideas with that of personal and social psychology. While revealing, this approach struck at least one conservative critic as intrusive and manipulative; "such social scientists," Etō Jun charged, "wished to judge without being judged."[58]

Etō may have been correct in pointing out the phenomenon of "upper-class intellectuals" seeking to "identify themselves with the common man whom they so often wish to love but cannot help despising."[59] The issue is not whether Etō himself cared to "love" the masses but, rather, whether, despite the inevitable intrusion of elitist feelings, a new relation between intellectuals and people formed during the period of the democratic enlightenment. I believe that it did, on both sides, and as a response to postwar conditions.

The Institute for the Science of Thought helped to establish a model of the "citizen-intellectual" that was at variance both with the dominant academic professionals of Shaken, who were compelled to bureaucratize or perish, and with the coopted, *parteilich* scientists of Minka. To be sure, self-criticism within Shaken was possible; Wada Haruki had attacked Shaken's failure to address the issue of Japanese imperialism in its own journal.[60] But in the long run, the role of Tsurumi and his colleagues in drawing both independent and academic intellectuals together as citizens, to act with other citizens, has been of greater significance. In its nondogmatic approach to thought, emphasis on shared themes and work, and organizational flexibility, it prepared the way for the "local residents" and antiwar movements of later decades; Tsurumi himself was a leading figure in Betonamu ni Heiwa o! Rengō (Beheiren), the determinedly antiinstitutional assemblage of popular groups at the center of Ja-

58 Other "joint research" projects have treated the Meiji Restoration, the Occupation, and the postwar "Circle Movement." For Etō's comments, see " 'Taiken' to 'sekinin' ni tsuite," in Etō, *Hizuke no aru bunshō* (Chikuma Shobō, 1960), p. 189.
59 Dore, "Institute," p. 24.
60 See Wada, "Sengo Nihon ni okeru Shakai Kagaku Kenkyūjo no shuppatsu," esp. p. 232.

pan's antiwar movement after the mid-1960s. The institute provided the prototype for an alternative style of intellectual work at a time when democratic enlightenment was being blunted by political reaction on the one hand, and was being fragmented internally by self-defensive bureaucratization on the other.

Nor was it alone in this role. Two final vignettes capture the possibilities and legacy of the enlightenment decades. The first concerns "People's University" (Shomin Daigaku) in Mishima (Shizuoka Prefecture). The brainchild of Kibe Tatsuji (b. 1915), a graduate of Tokyo Imperial and student of labor law under Suehiro Izutarō, it was the fulfillment of Kibe's hopes, nurtured throughout the war, of creating a means to provide workers with a practical – and political – education. Launched in early 1946, it drew nearly a hundred prominent academics and writers (such as Maruyama Masao, Nakamura Akira, and Nakano Yoshio) to lecture on democracy, labor and union organization and law, farmer cooperatives, and so on, relying on its broad membership (estimated at 5,000) to carry out its administrative and publications work. Kibe himself ran unsuccessfully for the Upper House of the Diet on the Communist ticket, remaining at the forefront of the prefectural labor movement until his untimely death (at age 34) in 1948, and left an organizational legacy in Mishima's reformist city administration, movement to block the growth of industrial complexes, and various cultural projects.

Among the best-selling books of the early postwar years was Muchaku Seikyō's *Yamabiko gakkō* (1951), a collection of compositions, both prose and poetry, and illustrated with woodcuts, by junior high-school students from the village of Yamamoto in Yamagata Prefecture. With its deliberate simplicity of style and combined evocations of the seasons, farm labor and life – in the midst, of course, of the land reform – and juvenile social naturalism, Muchaku's collection was a direct continuation of the prewar Life Composition Movement (Seikatsu tsuzurikata undō) that had been centered in Japan's northern prefectures and suppressed on charges that "Red" teachers were manipulating students to promote class tension.[61] Muchaku did have an "agenda." After having it "pounded into his head" as a child to emulate Ninomiya Sontoku, who "read books while hauling heavy loads of firewood on his back," Muchaku was determined to teach his charges that exhortations to "endur-

61 For a compelling and self-critical memoir of the prewar movement, see Kokubun Ichitarō, *Shōgaku kyōshi tachi no yūzai* (Misuzu Shobō, 1984).

ance" and "industriousness" were no more than a cloak for the acceptance of a fate of poverty: mechanization was the way out. When one of his students won the national prize, offered by the leftist Japan Teachers' Union (Nikkyōso) and the Textbook Study Association (Kyōkasho Kenkyū Kyōgikai) for best work in the junior high-school category for 1950, Muchaku accompanied the boy to Tokyo to accept the award, which was presented by the Minister of Education. He records two powerful memories of the ceremony. The first was that his student (by then 15), his shoulders already bent by the labor of hauling fertilizer over the years, was several inches shorter than the elementary school winner, a boy from Aichi. The second involved the keynote speech by Yanagida Kenjūrō, a popular philosopher who had recently declared his adherence to Marxism after years of affiliation with Nishida's school. "Modern morality," declared Yanagida to thunderous applause, "has nothing whatever to do with obedience or endurance. It is resistance! It is resistance!"[62]

CULTURE AND NATIONALITY IN
POST-OCCUPATION JAPAN

The standpoint of "resistance" as the task of "modern morality," with its clear parallels to the debate over subjectivity, had its objective correlative in the political struggles of the 1950s. Indeed, "for Japanese intellectuals," wrote Arase Yutaka, the years between the outbreak of war in Korea and the "thaw" represented "no less than a 'second war experience' [daini no sensō taiken], a period during which the task of defining their attitudes was pressed upon intellectuals with utmost urgency."[63]

For Japan, Arase argued, the Cold War meant first "the remilitarization policy adopted by the Occupation forces and the Japanese ruling class"; more broadly, it denoted "the impetus of the major intellectual events in both ideological camps" – McCarthyism on the one hand, and challenges to Soviet hegemony within the socialist camp on the other – in "forcing the Japanese intellectual world to undertake the self-examination of its own basic principles." At the same time, he notes,

because Japan did not take a direct part in the "war," attitudes taken by thinkers during this period allow no room for the evasion of responsibility

---

62 Muchaku Seikyō, *Yamabiko gakkō* (1951; Iwanami Bunko ed., 1995), pp. 323–4.
63 Quotes in this and following paragraph from Arase, "Sengo shisō," p. 377.

by appeal to "the situation." Although the tension that drove the process of attitude determination was as intense as during the [Pacific] War, suppression by state power was, in contrast to that period, never more than individual and local in its operation. With war and coercion no more than a partial possibility, the route of explaining action directly in terms of the situation was closed off. The attitude "chosen" by a thinking individual [shisō shutai] from amidst a diverse range of possibilities itself calls forth the direct inspection of the intellectual principles behind it.

The decade of the 1950s was one of highly polarized ideological politics, framed at either end by episodes that defined Japan's basic international posture, and marked by a succession of domestic struggles that repeatedly tested Japan's postwar democracy. Intellectuals organized as such were particularly active in the initial push for a comprehensive peace settlement, as they were to be in the end-of-decade anti–Security Treaty movement; the latter represented the apogee of intellectual activism and influence in postwar oppositional politics. But it was the former that compelled elite intellectuals to step beyond the role of enlightener to that of movement activist in the first place. In fact, it has been argued, without a consideration of the Peace Problems Symposium (Heiwa Mondai Danwakai), "it is hard to imagine how the '1960 Anpo' [movement] would have acted."[64]

The Peace Problems Symposium, formed in 1948, had a core membership of some fifty scholars, a Tokyo branch drawn from the "Iwanami Group" of academics and writers (some strongly tied to the journal Sekai), and a Kyoto-based, generally more radical group in Kansai. The symposium published three "Statements on Peace," the third of which was drafted within months of the outbreak of war in Korea and hence with particular urgency. (It appeared in December.) Interestingly, this statement, among the three, is the most academic in character, looking beyond the treaty issue itself to lay the theoretical grounds for Japanese neutralism and the broader notion of peaceful coexistence in a nuclear age. Prepared mainly by Maruyama Masao, Tsuru Shigeto, and Ukai Nobushige at the urging (among others) of Shimizu Ikutarō, who had recused himself on the grounds that the statement had to be written by someone "whose hands had not been soiled" by wartime work, the "Third Statement" is a model of utopian realism. "An atomic war," one of its propositions states, "teaches one the paradoxical truth that if one wishes to

64 See "San Furanshisuko kōwa; Chōsen sensō; 60-nen Anpo: Heiwa Mondai Danwakai kara Kenpō Mondai Kenkyūkai e," interview with Maruyama Masao in Sekai, no. 615 (November 1995): 36.

be most practical, one will have to be idealistic." And on this basis, the statement proceeds to examine the "method of thinking that accepts for its premises the aggravation of the opposition between [the Two Worlds] as a predestined and an unalterable fact." The thrust is clear enough from the propositions that head a number of its key sections: "A gap exists between the ideology and an actual state as an armed power" – a condition held to be true of both superpowers; "there are antagonisms operating in dimensions other than the schematic opposition of liberal democracy to communism" – in Asia in particular, the "antagonism between imperialism and nationalism"; "the powerful countries of the world are not necessarily opposed to one another to the same extent and depth as are the U.S. and Soviet Union." The position of the Third Statement, in short, was that survival depended on recognizing the "gaps" in apparently total views of the world. "Coexistence" would derive from the ideological adjustment by the superpowers themselves to the convergence in practice of their systems, and from the pressure for equilibrium caused by actual dispersal of political power outside the Two World framework, that is, among China, India, and perhaps among Western European states themselves.

What, however, of Japan? The statement evidences some of the Japan-as-victim motif. "In view of the pitiful experiences our Fatherland underwent, it is too plain just what was the outcome of justifying war and sacrificing peace for the value which was regarded as similar to God's justice." Although here the sense is of self-accusation – "Is it not at least the minimum responsibility of us Japanese toward the world to exercise self-discipline lest we should commit the same error twice?" – the statement fails to cross the line into an explicit reference to Japan's victims. Rather, it affirms a strict interpretation of the new Constitution's renunciation of war, and it offers a chastened Pan-Asianism, praising Nehru for articulating "the very essence of the Asian people's historic position and mission." Despite such parochialism and hints of a beneficent imperial consciousness, the arguments of the statement are essentially situational, and spring from the conviction that "in a third world war . . . what would emerge would not be one Rome, but two Carthages." The statement thus rejects any military role for Japan as a free (isolated) challenger to countries allied with either "side," along with that of mediator: That task should go to the United Nations. It warns against seeking to avoid the difficult, long-term task of internal reform by "stealing at fires" – taking economic advantage of conflicts among the powers – calling instead for "autonomous" efforts analogous to the New Deal.

Neither camp would be happy, with anti-Soviet interests seeing this neutralism as willful blindness to aggression, and anti-American forces attacking it for "turning the masses away" from Japan's own colonization. "Such contradictory criticisms," the statement concludes, "prove . . . that under existing conditions the claim for neutrality represents Japan's real position of self-reliance and independence."[65]

This was not to be. Despite widespread activism on behalf of a comprehensive, multilateral settlement, the peace treaty negotiated by Yoshida Shigeru with John Foster Dulles was bilateral, freezing out the socialist bloc. Yoshida famously dismissed proponents of a comprehensive settlement (Nanbara Shigeru in particular) as "academic sycophants"; his realist dictum that Japan had to "let the stronger have its way" (nagai mono ni makarero) took structural expression in Japan's "subordinate independence" under the treaty system. Under its aegis, Japan emerged from occupation, and the government undertook its announced and sometimes highly aggressive campaign to reconsider and (in certain cases) undo the reforms of the late 1940s in the name of recovered sovereignty, national amour propre, morality, and patriotism. No one would want to diminish the importance of the economic revival and subsequent growth that began by mid-decade, or to overlook its coincidence with the establishment of the so called "one-and-a-half party" system and subsequent long-term conservative dominance. Particularly because the scale and duration of that growth went far beyond what experts then considered possible, it has emerged as a genuine problem in intellectual history – all the more so as the transwar elements fueling that growth have been brought into scholarly view.

It is important, however, to avoid telescoping, attributing a false inevitability to, and providing retrospective justification for official policies. Instead, we recall the strikes, mass protests and sometimes violent demonstrations, the national petition campaigns and other forms of opposition to the Anti-Subversive Activities Law, passed by the Diet in 1952; the series of legislative attempts to recentralize control over education (aimed specifically at the highly ideologized

65 For text, see "Mitabi heiwa ni tsuite," Sekai, no. 60 (December 1950): 21–52, and translation (prepared at the time of issue), "On Peace for the Third Time," abridged in Japan Echo, no. 22 (1995): 21–31. See discussion in A. Gordon, ed., Postwar Japan as History, essays by Dower and Koschmann (esp. pp. 9–10, 402–3). Shimizu quote from "San Furanshisuko kōwa," p. 41.

teachers' union) of 1953, 1954, 1956, and 1957–9; and the Police
Duties Law (Keishokuhō) of 1958. In all of these struggles, intellectuals were actively, if not always centrally, engaged alongside Sōhyō
(the massive trade union federation established in 1950), the Japan
Teachers Union, and a large number of umbrella and ad hoc organizations. The ultimate issue was the power to define and shape the
development of Japan as a democratic society, in both its international and domestic aspects. By constraining Japan's relations with
the socialist world, the treaty system guaranteed the formation and
reproduction of *left-wing nationalism* in the postwar years. Directed
against "American imperialism" and the "Japanese ruling class," and
toward the empowerment, in Maruyama's phrase, of the "broad
working masses with workers and farmers at the core," it fused the
issue of Japan's international posture with that of domestic capitalism and its supersession by socialism. At the same time, this nationalism was highly disparate in form, depending on the interests of
the political parties, labor unions, professional, and – of great
importance – student organizations that espoused it. A united front,
therefore, was indispensable. Whether it would succeed was another
matter.

But what, for intellectuals on the left, was the "nation"? It was
kokumin; even more provocatively, it was *minzoku*. Ironically, in view
of the entrenched position of *minzoku* as the favored antagonist to
class in the historical visions of Kyoto school thinkers, the term
seems to have been reintroduced to public discourse in the early
postwar years by the left itself. As early as 1948, the Japan Communist Party was calling for a "people's democracy" and a "democratic
national front," echoing the rhetoric of Stalinist consolidation in
Eastern Europe. To this was added the antiimperialism that accompanied the party's turn to militant illegality following the Cominform
criticism and onset of the Korean war. But that *minzoku* was one still
divided into classes. As Takashima Zen'ya put it in 1950: "In the
sense that it is *class* that makes possible the carryover of a people
from one system to another, we should say that, at the same time as
it divides systems, it also links them together. . . . In order to eliminate the control or oppression of one people by another, it is necessary to remove class control or oppression *within* any single system or
nation."[66] In a similar vein, the medieval historian Ishimota Shō

66 Takashima Zen'ya, "Gendai shakai kagaku no ninmu," *Sekai* no. 58 (October 1950): 33–
    43.

argued prolifically for a "history-making movement" in which oppressed peoples and groups, including women, would literally unearth the materials of their own past – songs, tales, legends – thus empowering themselves and, inspired by the contemporary examples of the U.S.S.R., China, and liberation movements in Asia, create a new, *minzoku*-centered history that would "overcome" the biases and limitations of narratives concerned with "bourgeois modernization." Ishimota's two-volume *Rekishi to minzoku no hakken* (1952–3) won a wide readership.[67]

But Ishimota's vision of history as resistance did not fully convince or satisfy even the sympathetic. Uehara Senroku, like Ishimota a medieval historian, but one of Europe, and a postwar pioneer of "world history," stressed the task of "realizing world peace" as one never before faced by "any people, any nation." In Japan, the formation of national consciousness would have to incorporate, not dissolve, "individual consciousness" and "individual freedom," on the one hand, and a sense of belonging to the human race, on the other.[68] Uehara's position, of course, parallels that of Maruyama and that of the modernists. Appropriately, Maruyama's attacks on Japanese nationalism, along with Ishimota's construction of a history from below, provoked the most consequential articulation of left-nationalism in the early 1950s. It came from Takeuchi Yoshimi (1910–77), an influential interpreter of Lu Xun and commentator on postwar literature and politics, who used the term "modernism" to describe – and reject – both the party's definition of itself, including its claims concerning Marxism-Leninism as a "science," *and* modernism à la Maruyama. For Takeuchi, insofar as both orientations were essentially Western-derived, they represented no more than a language of intellectual "slavery," and in following them, Japan would merely be occupying the role of "top student"; in Gramscian terms, which fit well here, "modernism" fixed Japan's status as subaltern to the great powers.

It was not that modernism was to be condemned in its entirety. Its significance, Takeuchi argued, was transitional. In the wake of defeat, it helped Japanese intellectuals to "forget the nightmare of a blood-soaked ethnic nationalism" by conceiving of ethnos (*minzoku*)

67 Ishimota, *Rekishi to minzoku no hakken: Rekishigaku no kadai to hōhō* (Tokyo Daigaku Shuppankai, 1952); *Rekishi to minzoku no hakken: Ningen; teikō; gakufū* (Tokyo Daigaku Shuppankai, 1953); see also Arase, "Sengo shisō," pp. 372–3, Ishida, *Nihon no shakai kagaku*, pp. 170–1.
68 See Uehara, "Sokokuai to heiwa," *Dōtoku kyōiku* 52, no. 5; Uehara, "Minzoku ishiki no rekishiteki keitai," *Shisō*, no. 338 (August 1952).

in abstract terms. Now, however, modernism was holding back real *modernization*, which could only proceed on the Chinese model of revolutionary nationalism. This required a reconnection with and development of Japan's critical literary lineage formed by Futabatei Shimei, Kitamura Tōkoku, and Ishikawa Takuboku, and of the Japan Romantic School of the 1930s: "There can be no revolution," Takeuchi declared, "that is not rooted in national tradition." By focusing only on "self" or "class," and preventing the return of the "thrown-away" ethnos to literature – to public life – modernism blocked the people's capacity for self-transformation, perpetuating a *premodern* consciousness among them.[69]

From a present-day perspective, Takeuchi's call for Japan to emulate the revolutionary nationalism of China may seem farcical, but such dismissals assume a conservative recuperation of Japanese tradition driven by Japan's later economic success, which was still far off in 1951. Although Takeuchi did a great deal to deepen the idealization of China among Japanese intellectuals, their response to his call for a "people's literature" was decidedly mixed. Modernists (in Arase's words) were "largely negative and contemptuous"; Maruyama was abashed by his own former dismissal of China's revolutionary potential, but he saw no such future for Japan. Those with party ties were more sympathetic but rejected Takeuchi's argument for the "autonomy of literature," its freedom from subordination to politics; for him, genuineness was inherently as well as instrumentally important.

Takeuchi is read and quoted today for the same reason that he is dismissed: as an alternative, differently evaluated according to political stance, to the mainstream of conservative, traditionalist nationalism that formed late in the Occupation years and gained strength through the 1950s. By this point, left-nationalism in all its forms was compelled to place itself in opposition to a growing popular tendency to equate "peace" with "stability." In contrast to the early postwar years, it had become possible to speak of something like a "status quo" associated with continued economic recovery, the beginnings of growth, and the satisfaction of material demands. As Arase put it,

"Peace" has come to be felt as a part of everyday life. The political and economic standstill produced by the completion of Japan's postwar recov-

69 Takeuchi, "Kindaishugi to minzoku no mondai" (1951); Barshay, "Imagining Democracy," p. 403; Arase, "Sengo shisō," pp. 375–6.

ery and the emergence of a two-party system has generated a mood of "stability" amongst the majority of people who make up the middle stratum of society. In the past, the mass base of thought arose, in large part, of itself, from amidst the life and feelings of the people. But now, what is more strongly called for is the impetus to deny the "feelings springing from real life" [seikatsu jikkan]. Japanese thought has developed by responding subtly to a succession of critical political situations: Can it now make itself widely felt among the people in defiance of the mood of peace and stability? This is the arduous, but urgent task at hand.[70]

Arase, writing in 1959, captured well the shifting ground upon which the role of intellectuals had been configured. He sensed that "the mass line" had "turned into an ethos of 'following after' the masses," and he questioned whether any intellectual group on the left was prepared for a "collaboration of intellectuals and masses, albeit with a sense of tension arising from the differences in occupation between the two, and indeed on the basis of such recognized differences."

What had happened? The relative decline in mass support for the Communist Party allowed a more reformist or liberal left to emerge: the left of Sekai, and of a more professionally oriented interi and middle-class stratum for which the Socialist stance of "unarmed neutrality" (and shop-floor class struggle) was more appealing. Sekai, in fact, deserved credit – or blame, depending on one's politics – for the embrace of neutralism by the left wing of the Socialist Party.

Popular aspirations for stability – profoundly understandable aspirations – also heartened conservative nationalists who understood that while the aspects of the "old" society associated with war and mass death remained thoroughly discredited, other "cultural" orientations might indeed be reinvigorated and used to restore national self-respect, along with social and political discipline. After all, according to this view, it was unnatural for a nation to deny its identity, and for a people to be ashamed of their shared culture and past and to express patriotic sentiments. It was in this moment that the careers of eminent prewar figures such as Yanagita Kunio (1875–1962), Tsuda Sōkichi (1873–1961), and Watsuji Tetsurō (1889–1960) enjoyed a final flourish, while somewhat younger writers – Takeyama Michio (1903–84), for example – took center stage. Takeyma himself was spurred by what he saw as the injustice rendered at the Tokyo Tribunal to civilian officials (Hirota Kōki and

---

70 Arase, "Sengo shisō," p. 385.

Tōgō Shigenori, particularly). He even speculated, in his *Shōwa no seishinshi* (1956), that his conversations with Justice B.V.A. Röling might have provided the initial impetus for the latter's partial dissent from the trial verdicts.

The political purpose of *Shōwa no seishinshi* was to vindicate the prewar elite as honorable men, with limited power, struggling for the legitimate interests of Japan and against the "militarist" elements that sought to destroy them; its essential stance was a rejection of Marxist writings that sought to explain the war as an ineluctable outgrowth of Japan's incomplete modernization. Takeyama's avowed "old liberalism" dovetailed nicely with the bipolar "realism" against which *Sekai* had set itself; he joined with Watsuji Tetsurō, Fukuda Tsuneari, and others in writing for the journal *Kokoro* (and later for *Jiyū*) and was a member of the Japan Cultural Forum.

The emergence of a literature of vindication is not to be understood simply as the "real" Japan asserting itself. Sentiments that are labeled as "common sense" by their proponents are making an argument, not stating a fact. In the mid-1950s, there remained strong alternatives to this common sense. Yet we must recognize the significant intermingling of the tendencies at work in shaping postwar notions of culture and nationality. Any discourse in which nationalism plays a major part is bound to be especially protean and capable of political somersaults.

In Japan, the "postwar" era ended for the first time in 1956.[71] The historiographical markers of this first round may be termed "totemic": the literary critic Nakano Yoshio's article, "It is no longer 'postwar'"("Mohaya 'sengo' de wa nai"), which appeared in centrist journal *Bungei shunjū*, was soon matched by *Sekai*'s "farewell to postwar." That same year, the political scientist Matsushita Keiichi, in his first publication, raised the issue of "mass society" in a theoretical article concerned chiefly with the general process by which "the mass state, under the condition of the change in social forms during the stage of monopoly capitalism, emerges as the system

71 Other candidates for "the end" include 1968 (Nakajima Makoto, in *Sengo shisōshi nyūmon*, points to the "lost Pax Americana" in Vietnam and to the American debt crisis); 1972–3 (reversion of Okinawa plus oil crisis); 1989 (death of Hirohito and end of Cold War); and (on the grounds that the war responsibility issue still tends to be evaded) "not yet." See Carol Gluck, "The Past in the Present," in *Postwar Japan as History*, ed. A. Gordon, pp. 64–95; and "The 'Long Postwar': Japan and Germany in Comparison and Contrast," in *Legacies and Ambiguities: Postwar Fiction and Culture in West Germany and Japan*, ed. T. Rimer and E. Schlant (Woodrow Wilson Center Press, 1991), pp. 63–78.

transforms 'class' into 'mass.'" In his concluding paragraph, Matsushita notes: "In Japan too, incidentally, the general condition of the change in social forms in the stage of monopoly capital is advancing, albeit with peculiarities of its own. The problem, not only of 'feudal versus modern,' but even more acutely of 'the modern' itself, has to be raised."[72]

The placing of Japan, even if "incidentally," within the framework of advanced societies was of major moment. And the function of those "peculiarities of its own" in bringing about that (re)location was to be a central motif in assessments of Japan's modernization. In the mid- to late 1950s, the notion that Japan as a society was converging with those of the industrial West was strongly appealing. The issue was to determine which premodern values and social forms had proven to be functional in modernization, and which of these had not; which elements of tradition would most effectively put themselves out of business, or at least withdraw to specific, controllable areas as Japan moved toward mature modernity. The point is the modest reversal of Japan's status within the backward-advanced framework, the discovery that "tradition" was not a synonym for "backwardness" tout court.

Unquestionably, the positive reappraisal of Japanese modernization by Japanese scholars took certain cues from American writing by James Abegglen, Robert Bellah, Thomas Smith, and later Edwin Reischauer, among others. But among the most provocative affirmations of Japanese culture and civilization from this period were two "amateur" pieces that reveal intellectual predispositions and concerns rather different from, and a historical vision more sweeping than that of, American analyses of Japan's modernization.

Umesao Tadao (b. 1920), a young ethnologist, made the affirmative case for Japan as a civilization in a 1957 essay, "Preface to an ecological view of civilization." His basic view of Japan is easily summarized:

The truth is that Japan still possesses an advanced civilization regardless of its defeat. And some of its aspects are now more refined than they were in the prewar period. . . . Japan has enormous industrial power, highly developed transportation and communication networks, a well-rounded administrative organization, and a comprehensive educational system. Schooling has spread wide; goods are in abundant supply; and the standard of living is high. The average life expectancy is long, and the death rate is low. And science and arts have made great progress.

72 Matsushita Keiichi, "Taishū kokka no seiritsu to sono mondaisei" (1956) in ibid., *Sengo seiji no rekishi to shisō* (Chikuma Shobō, 1994), pp. 44, 60.

To be sure, Umesao recognized "shortcomings . . . and discontent," lags in technological development, and the poor condition of the many new universities. "Yet despite all the unevenness, there can be no doubt that from an overall perspective the way of life of the Japanese is that of an advanced civilization." "The foundation on which we stand," Umesao declared, "is, after all, our civilization, a tradition that deserves our protection." The "overall perspective" refers to the "ecological view of history" that was Umesao's theoretical apparatus. From this perspective, Japan, along with Western Europe, constituted a "first tier" of civilization whose two centers had developed in mutual independence at opposite ends of the Eurasian land mass. Via "autogenic succession," both had produced feudal societies and, in turn, revolutionary bourgeoisies. The "second tier" of great continental empires (China, Russia, India) had not done so. Contesting the East/West dichotomy in prose that was fresh and uninhibited, at times naïve, and self-consciously that of an amateur, Umesao's essay won a large and appreciative readership. In raising Japan to the status of an independent *bourgeois* – industrial – civilization, Umesao at once abandoned the Meiji-era equation of civilization with "power" and its troubling associations with the catastrophically failed militarism of the twentieth century.[73] At the same time, Umesao seemed to imply, though he did not say so openly, that "advanced" Japan ought to retain a role as exemplar in its own sphere.

Umesao's essay was easily criticized: Katō Shūichi, whose rejoinder raised his stature as a humanist critic-at-large, dismissed Umesao's argument that "Westernization" was little more than a late phase in a long process of autonomous development. To the contrary, it was the very essence of Japan's transformation. Umesao in fact was concerned entirely with the achievement of industrial capacity, and ignored not only Japanese society but the entire realm of culture and ideas: that – urban – realm in which Westernization was most profoundly felt. For Katō, the distortion and failures of the modern era resulted from the attempt to retain and use strategically the values and structures of rural society while pursuing national power. This was a project neither launched nor directed by the bourgeoisie. Indeed, Katō asserted, it was only the wartime "break-

---

73 Umesao Tadao, "Bummei no seitai shikan" (1957), repr. in *Bummei no seitai shikan* (Chūkō Bunko ed., 1974), pp. 73–111; abridged translation in *Japan Echo* 22 (1995): 42–50. Quote from translation, p. 44. See also Hiromatsu Wataru, *Seitai shikan to yuibutsu shikan* (Kōdansha Gakujutsu Bunko ed., 1991), esp. pp. 28–35, 78–88.

down in the collusion between the traditional family system and capital" – and the social leveling entailed in the state's sweeping ideological mobilization of "the Emperor's children" – that laid the basis for Japan's "independent development" as a democracy. Umesao, in effect, had written a "history" of the future. Now was the time for Japanese intellectuals to foster a "truly Japanese learning and Japanese art" by "identifying themselves more closely with the Japanese people" and with the "values and cultural tradition of the country."[74]

Katō's position is also notable as an indication of modernism on the cusp of its transition from a discourse of negation to one of affirmation. The emergence of a more positive, or tolerant, modernism should not be too surprising. Its core notion of subjectivity – of "self-mastery for the purpose of self-giving"[75] – did not intrinsically preclude receptiveness to Japan's aesthetic heritage or to the lifeways and implicit philosophies of everyday people. For Katō, the aesthetic was the medium through which he could come to value the "common people." Something similar may be said of Maruyama, though in his case, rather than the cultural *objects* made by the people, the medium of contact was Maruyama's appropriation of colloquial *language*; his juxtaposition of elite and mass in discourse itself. The sense of reconciliation with nationality is clear.

The key text in this regard, typical in its ambiguities, is Maruyama's *Nihon no shisō* (1961).[76] For Maruyama, the essence of Japanese thought is to have no essence. Japanese tradition has no "axis" analogous to Christianity in the West, or Confucianism in China. It is a "tradition without structure" in which "history" (Maruyama paraphrases Kobayashi Hideo) becomes the nostalgic "welling up" of national "memory," something "akin to the attachment felt by a mother toward a child she has lost." The intellectual landscape is far from empty, of course. Japanese thinkers have accumulated an extraordinary "stock" of discrete ideas to draw on for their own purposes. What is lacking is an "absolute being or a 'Way'

74 Katō Shūichi, "Kindai Nihon no bunmeishiteki ichi" (1957) trans. as "Modern Japanese Civilization in History," in *The Japan Interpreter* 1, no. 6 (Spring 1970): 29–44. Katō suggests that in prewar Japan, "labor as a class was accumulating a store of bitter experiences that caused some change in its collective value-consciousness, a change ... that partially accounts for the inherent strength of the post-war labor movement ... [and] that arose from within the developmental process of Japanese capitalism" (p. 35).

75 Quote from Jacques Maritain, *Existence and the Existent* (1948; Vintage ed., 1966), p. 82.

76 Maruyama, *Nihon no shisō* (Iwanami Shinsho ed., 1961).

that logically and normatively orders the world in its own characteristic manner."[77] In its absence, Maruyama argued, "Japanese
thought" formed a tenacious pattern by which "faith in felt reality"
(*jikkan shinkō*) and "faith in theory" (*riron shinkō*) operated as functional equivalents, cutting off the dialectic of mutual negation, test-
ing, or correction that Maruyama, from his transcendent position,
considered essential to the "normal" operations of the socialized
intellect.

Maruyama was not principally concerned with accounting for the
origins of Japan's nonaxiality. He begins *in medias res*, looking back
across the great but not far distant rupture of 1945. His argument has
to be understood in terms of the political function and consequences
of tradition as Maruyama experienced and perceived them. How did
"tradition," as mobilized under the modern emperor system, actually function? As of the late 1940s, Maruyama would have answered
that it functioned in a uniformly oppressive manner. By the time of
Nihon no shisō, he had softened considerably his attitude toward
"tradition," which he discusses in terms of an ethic of "being" as
opposed to "doing." Maruyama does not call for the elimination of
the ethic of "being," as he once seemed to, but for its incorporation
in a synthesis of traditional and modern styles of life and thought.
Echoing Max Weber, Maruyama finds that "being" is functional in
the sphere of art and culture: Indeed, it stands in immediate need of
protection from an obsessive "modern" concern with producing
results. (As he observed elsewhere, "*The Tale of Genji, Hamlet*, and
Faust cannot be shot off as rockets.")[78] At the same time, he finds
Japanese society lacking in a political ethic of "doing," where results
– the rationalization of means according to publicly determined ends
– do indeed matter. Thus Japan had become hypermodern in one
sphere, and insufficiently modern in another.

But how does this relate to "Japanese thought"? The answer lies in
the *totality* of elements, premodern, modern, and hypermodern, and
their particular distribution or valences within the social system; it is
in the whole, rather than in any of its parts, that the Japanese mode
of thought operates. And as Maruyama shows, there are definable
historical patterns to this operation. The ideology of *kokutai* – the
unbroken line of imperial rule over Japan – had legitimated rapid
institutional modernization in the name of the monarch. At the same

---

77   Maruyama, *Nihon no shisō*, p. 21. "Mother's nostalgia": Nakajima, *Sengo shisōshi nyūmon*,
     p. 84.
78   Maruyama, *Thought and Behavior* (1969 ed.), p. 310.

time, it claimed that the monarchy was the supreme embodiment and validator of the entire "system of patriarchal, factional, and personalistic human relationships that characterize village society" (p. 26). The *tennō* became the unassailable sign of a system of social/national givenness, and of a certain style of bureaucratically mandated change; the *tennōsei* was

purely pragmatic and opportunistic in that it avoided the attempt to establish itself on the basis of a fixed dogma such as is found in Christianity or Confucianism. At the same time, it took as its highest purpose the preservation of the system of authority with the emperor at the apex; and on this basis made it a taboo to question the legitimacy of its authority.[79]

The *tennōsei* in this sense was the most powerful and consequentially functional tradition of modern Japan. It provided the institutional and linguistic frame through which all other traditions received their official imprimatur. The task now was to *differentiate*, to overcome the deep-seated "need" for the all-encompassing legitimating frame that was at once so comforting and suffocating. Could Japanese people "comprehend their own fate" – and create their present and future – without recourse to a mental metaphor of *tennōsei*? Could they overcome "Japanese thought"?

Surveying the contemporary scene, Maruyama seems uncertain. He notes the tendency of modern organizations of all kinds in Japan to form themselves into "octopus pots" (*takotsubo*) in which the group's activities, ideas, and values become largely self-referential, the authority of the group self-justifying, and socially isolating. Parallel to this is the increasing sophistication, centralization, and uniformity of the mass media. The result of their interaction is a society in which lateral ties between groups of all kinds are weak; groups form images of themselves and the "world" that go unchallenged and "walk on their own." In the absence of such ties and of genuine feedback throughout society, critical and democratic consciousness is fragmented and blunted. It is precisely in this mix of hypermodernity in one sector with premodernity in another that Maruyama sees functional continuity with *tennōsei*, albeit sans *tennō* in the prewar mode. To it, Maruyama counterposes the ideal of a *sasara*-type society: Like a bamboo whisk, it has "a shared base" but is finely separated toward the tip. Owing to the wholesale importation of "systems" as whole packages during Japan's modernization, however, Japan had not developed in this way. *Nihon no shisō*, he

79 Maruyama, statement in Maruyama, Satō, and Umemoto, *Sengo Nihon no kakushin shisō* (1966; Gendai no Rironsha, 1983), pp. 48–9.

asserts, is also his own "self-criticism" from the point of view of "radical intellectual aristocratism linked interiorly with a radical democracy": He looks forward to a *sasara*-type society, one in which the image of "Karl Marx reading Hölderlin" would capture the intellectual life of its people.[80]

For all that it seems to set out an uncompromising task of mental revolution, and therefore remain true to modernism, *Nihon no shisō* is good natured and surprisingly upbeat in tone. "We (or you?) can do this!" is its chief message, and in this sense, it is rather far removed from Maruyama's writings of the early postwar years. It points to a modernism in process of differentiation, one making its peace, via the categories of aesthetics – including linguistic play – with nationality. Would modernism be drawn from that point into a discourse that valorized its moment as one of modernity achieved, pressing forward to the presentation of Japan as a new model of development? Would modernism retain the capacity for "utopian" resistance to the status quo, even at the risk of marginalization? Under what conditions, with what social allies? What, in short, would be the intellectual consequences of coming to terms with nationality?

THE *ANPO* WATERSHED

The issue was forced in the so-called "Anpo Struggle" of 1960. Linked strategically and ideologically to the long and bitter strike at the Mitsui Miike mine, it marks a watershed not only in the politics of the postwar period but also in its intellectual history, reminiscent in this sense of the popular agitation over the revision of the unequal treaties in the early 1880s and over the conclusion of the Portsmouth Treaty in 1905.

In the combined conduct of the "Anpo" and "Miike" struggles and in their results, we see at once the apogee of organized intellectual influence over mass political movements, and the direct cause of a "translation," brought about from the top down, in the very terms by which postwar Japan was to be defined. If the decade and a half that followed capitulation saw an attempt to realize a democratic utopia, the era that followed saw the rhetoric and some of the social substance of democratization coopted in the remaking of Japan as an industrial utopia. "Class" would no longer form the key category of

---

80 Maruyama, *Nihon no shisō*, parts III and IV, *passim*, and afterword.

social consciousness or the stuff of social conflict; the national past, as filtered through the discursive lens of "Japan the model modernizer," would be reclaimed in support of all the values needed for efficient, committed participation in capitalist enterprise. Democracy, in short, would be redefined as the maximizing of opportunities – accompanied by the relative narrowing of inequalities of status and reward – first for the greatest possible social participation in the generation of GNP, and second for its consumption.

Japanese across the board took democracy seriously. All political constituencies, including the government and ruling party, recognized this, if only in their rhetoric. The coming conflict was adumbrated in 1958, when the Liberal Democratic Party announced its bill to revise the Occupation-era Police Duties Law. Arguing that "the law currently in force lacks basic provisions for the security of society and the public and for the maintenance of order," the party asserted the need for a policy to deal with "violent incidents – the recent struggles over teacher certification and in opposition to moral education, as well as other incidents of collective illegal violence and bloodshed." While it would respect "individual freedoms and rights," the bill was "aimed at maintaining public safety and order, and is indispensable to the normal development of a democratic state."[81] The viability of Japan's "democratic" order rested on that of the Anpo system and vice versa. Legitimacy depended on the shared perception of consent. Herein lies the significance of Anpo: It was a struggle over consent.

Apart from its stated purpose, the Police bill, which had been prepared (in deep secrecy) within Prime Minister Kishi's inner circle, was a preemptive move against the mass opposition, which Kishi astutely foresaw, to continuation of the Anpo system. But instead of short-circuiting such opposition, the bill galvanized a wide social coalition in a dress rehearsal for the Anpo protests themselves: There was direct organizational continuity between the two movements. Though the Police bill was abandoned, it solidified the public's image of Kishi as the crystallization of political reaction and hostility to democracy. Kishi was not a relic of a discredited past but its living embodiment. He was particularly reviled by younger people, which further discredited his policies. More so than Socialist obstructionism, Kishi's rigid insistence on maintaining and deepening the U.S.–Japanese relationship as an anti-Communist military alliance,

81   See Masamura Kimihiro, *Sengo shi* (Chikuma Shobō, 1986), 2:100.

and the lengths to which he was prepared to go to see that happen, provoked genuine, widespread anger and a sense that Japanese democracy was in crisis. Indeed, Kishi seemed to make a point of sharpening every conflict: "Better decisive action in the short term," he once declared, "than long-term stability."[82] Kishi had no imagination for dialogue, let alone consensus. Yet as Masamura Kimihiro remarks, "It would not have been easy to amend America's world strategy, but it is inconceivable that Japan, as of the early 1960s, had no choice other than revision of the Security Treaty as pushed forward by the Kishi government."[83]

That revision removed provisions calling for United States intervention in a "domestic insurrection" in Japan, strengthened consultative mechanisms between Japan and the United States concerning the deployment of American forces, and fixed a term for the continuation of the agreement.[84] At the same time, by specifiying as a purpose of the pact "the security of Japan *and the maintenance of international peace and security in the Far East*," it widened the geographical scope of possible military "cooperation" that would involve Japan. The left had never accepted the original "realism" of a bilateral arrangement, and in the poisoned political atmosphere following Kishi's railroading of the treaty through the Diet, the objective basis for public acceptance of the new framework was severely threatened. On the other hand, by drawing on himself the waves of popular hostility, Kishi made his resignation the price for such acceptance, and acceptance the price of his resignation.

Such observations raise the question of the nature and purposes of the antitreaty movement itself. Why did it carry such emotional force? There was, of course, the ambient fear of nuclear conflict. Especially salient were the widespread anxieties about the stability and rationality of American military policies provoked by the "brinkmanship" of the late 1950s, at that point culminating in the U-2 incident. Such anxieties, aggravated by Japan's dependence on the United States (and resentment of that dependence), form a recurring theme, for example, in the sociologist David Riesman's extensive conversations, held in late 1961, with students and young

---

82 Kishi as quoted in Masamura, *Sengo shi*, 2:102.   83 Masamura, *Sengo shi*, 2:130.
84 In addition to Masamura, *Sengo shi* (2:103–36), see Usui Yoshimi, ed. *Anpo-1960* (Chikuma Shobō, 1969), Ide Busaburō, ed. *Anpo tōsō* (San'ichi Shobō, 1960), Tanigawa Gan et al., *Minshushugi no shinwa: Anpo tōsō no shisōteki sōkatsu*, 2nd ed. (Gendai Shichōsha, 1966), Masumi Junnosuke, *Contemporary Politics in Japan, 1955–1990*, tr. L. Carlile (University of California Press, 1995), and Jon Halliday, *A Political History of Japanese Capitalism* (Monthly Review Press, 1978), esp. chap. 9.

professionals in Japan.[85] Soviet proposals for peaceful coexistence and a nuclear-free zone in the Pacific, underlain by the general perception that de-Stalinization had allowed the U.S.S.R. to demonstrate the potential of socialism to "win" in a peaceful competition with capitalism, found a receptive audience in Japan.[86]

The movement, then, was "defensive" in that it sought to protect "peace," including the Constitution, from forces inimical to it. It operated ad hoc, with a spearhead consisting of the ex-Communist Party "mainstream" faction of Zengakuren, and the extremely active organizational role of younger academics and writers – the so-called "men of culture" – across the board; this is in contrast to the overall cautiousness of the Communist Party itself and to the split in Socialist ranks that occurred over treaty revision.[87] The mass protests, including the invasion of the Diet grounds, petition movements that collected multiple millions of signatures, organized small-business shutdowns, and so on, attained one of their major purposes when Kishi stepped down. It is no small thing to topple a government: This was a point that Riesman found himself repeating to those he met. But the treaty stood, and the movement could not escape the shroud of "failure." As Riesman noted, "the issue comes up in vitrually all serious conversations here and obviously had a traumatic impact on people."[88]

Apart from its record as a movement, the Anpo coalition occupies a central place in the intellectual history of Japanese democracy – one defined by the ties and tensions between its constituent groups. The nonparty *interi* such as Maruyama Masao, Shimizu Ikutarō, Takeuchi Yoshimi, and Tsurumi Shunsuke, and various organizations of like-minded academics and writers, provided the movement with prestige and with the mature "utopian realism" that we encountered earlier in connection with the original 1950–1 movement for a

85 Kennedy's recent election, if anything, seems to have made things worse. Riesman (b. 1909), the author of the influential study, *The Lonely Crowd* (1950) and of *Individualism Reconsidered* (1954), visited Japan for a "full exposure" series of lectures, meetings, tours, press conferences, etc. See David Riesman and Evelyn Thompson Riesman, *Conversations in Japan: Modernization, Politics, and Culture* (1967; Midway Reprint ed., University of Chicago Press, 1976), pp. 35, 39, 51, 55–7, 77, 133, 257, 307. Riesman was also struck by the virtual absence of any expressions of fearfulness toward China, and he wondered how that might change should China develop nuclear weapons (pp. 71, 77, 99, 103, 271, 324–5).

86 See Shuichi Kojima, "The Changing Japanese Perception of the Soviet Union as Seen in General Interest Magazines," *Konan Journal of Social Sciences*, vol. 2 (1988): 27ff.

87 At Miike, union strategy owed a great deal to the Rōnō Faction theorist Sakisaka Itsurō and his collaborators at Kyushu University, who were credited with heightening the strikers' class consciousness and militance. Masamura, *Sengo shi*, 2:114–5.

88 Riesman and Riesman, *Conversations in Japan*, p. 48.

multilateral peace treaty. The participation of figures like Maruyama and Shimizu was particularly important, since they had direct experience and memory of prewar repression; any comparisons they would draw between that experience and the present would not be drawn lightly. Similarly, Tsurumi, challenging Kishi's assertion that he represented the "voiceless" majority, was the catalyst in organizing the Society of the Voiceless Voices (Koe Naki Koe no Kai); the Institute for the Science of Thought as a whole was also active. Takeuchi, finally, attracted attention both for his dramatic framing of the political issue as a choice between "democracy or dictatorship" and for his resignation from his teaching post in protest of the treaty.

But what, conceptually, did such *interi* contribute? One indication comes from Maruyama's insistence that contrary to the widespread perception, and one reinforced by Kishi's conduct, "politics" was not inherently "dirty" and should not be permitted to become synonymous with the corruption of power. Beyond that, in a democracy, politics had to be more than "politics," more than institutions themselves. As he reminded his audience in a speech in May 1960, the wartime "Assistance" Diet had also met regularly. Democracy, therefore, was just as much a matter of the informing spirit of inconspicuous commitment as of "success" in manipulating institutions to some partisan purpose. One could fail, as Kishi had, even while succeeding.

How do we conceive of politics? . . . [I]t's a matter of habit, of seeing politics as activity that, even if it makes up only a small part of what we do, day in and day out, still occupies that place *consistently*, as part of carrying out the commonest of our social obligations. Moreso than any other ideology, however magnificent, or any system, however formally equipped it may be, democracy depends on this kind of thinking. This is its true foundation. Here in Japan we may have lacked the tradition of direct democracy practiced in the Greek city-states. But instead we have as our intellectual heritage the splendid concept of "homespun [lay] Buddhism." Put in contemporary terms, this means the political activity of nonprofessional politicians. You don't have to "take the political tonsure" in order to get involved in politics. When politics is left to politicians and Dietmen – people whose purpose is politics per se, or to groups such as parties who approach it in the same way – from that moment democracy begins to die.[89]

89 Maruyama, "Gendai ni okeru taido kettei," in ibid. *Gendai seiji no shisō to kōdō*, exp. ed. (Miraisha, 1966), pp. 446–61, quote from p. 458; orig. in *Sekai*, no. 175 (July 1960): 175–84.

For his part, Tsurumi Shunsuke offered a model of organizational creativity and ideological flexibility that complemented Maruyama's lay sermonizing: If the Peace Problems Symposium indirectly provided the guiding *ideas* of the Anpo protests, Tsurumi's organizational practice directly informed the anti–Vietnam War protests that began in Japan after 1965, and, equally significantly, the "local residents'" movements of the same era. The common theme was "democracy as the defense of everyday life" – one far more developed in Tsurumi's thinking than in Maruyama's.[90] The mode of political thinking represented by Maruyama and Tsurumi offered a not inconsiderable legacy of the "democratic enlightenment" as tested in the crucible of Cold War politics. The "new normative consciousness" that Maruyama had called for in 1947 had been formed.

Finally, the *interi* contributed the central "ideologeme" of the student movement itself: the call to revolutionary political action as the manifestation of subjecthood – *shutaisei*. One is struck in this respect by the contrast between the ideological *distance* separating the Shinjinkai of the 1920s from Yoshino Sakuzō, its mentor, and the substantial *continuities* across generational lines in the 1960 movement. To be sure, writers such as Yoshimoto Takaaki inserted themselves directly into Zengakuren circles, stressing that "Anpo" was all about exposing the "inner logic" of Japanese monopoly capital and working toward a revolutionary upsurge. Yoshimoto would quickly turn against Maruyama and the "men of culture" for having diverted the proper course of protest from blocking treaty revision at all costs toward the – meaningless? – goal of bringing down the cabinet, and within a few years criticize Maruyama and the modernist ethos for their fatal separation from the "masses."[91]

In a sense, Yoshimoto was right: Maruyama was *not* a revolutionary against capital, or a populist of any kind. But what of the claimed relationship between Zengakuren itself and the "masses"? It could

---

90 Riesman noted (Riesman and Riesman, 1976): "There is no touch of the ascetic in . . . Katō [Hidetoshi], who had written an article criticizing the asceticism of many Japanese Leftists who wanted to deprive the 'masses' of their baseball games and television on the ground that these leisure sports made them apathetic, whereas in fact protection of their right to these, Katō thought, made them politically active" (pp. 149–50).

91 See Yoshimoto Takaaki, "Maruyama Masao ron" (1962–3) in *Yoshimoto Takaaki zen chosakushū* (Keisō Shobō, 1969), 12:3–96; Kazuko Tsurumi, *Social Change and the Individual* (Princeton University Press, 1969), chap. 9; and Lawrence Olson, "Intellectuals and the 'People': On Yoshimoto Takaaki" (1978), chap. 3 of his *Ambivalent Moderns*.

not be other than imaginary, but the question is not to be dismissed. Rather, it calls attention to the odd symbiosis of Zengakuren and other radical student methods of protest with the decidedly milder, middle-class – or "mass" – elements of the movement, with the role of mediator between the two being played by the "men of culture." The student leadership had no use for the style and tactics of the old left and derided the nationwide petition movement, which was central to the activities of the National Congress to Block the Security Treaty Revision (Anpo Kaitei Soshi Kokumin Kaigi) as mere "incense offerings."[92] The student movement ethos was one of revolutionary subjectivity on the line, suggesting a sort of Luxemburgist spontaneity. But it seems obvious that student action against the treaty, by engaging that quintessentially "postwar" demand that praxis be grounded in a socialized consciousness, was living out a moral injunction received from an earlier generation, and on that basis tapping a deep reservoir or popular sympathy. This is what pushed the antitreaty movement forward. By the same token, violent civil disobedience, which was part of the student repertoire, was kept from isolation and protected from direct suppression by the larger scale of nonviolent protest that "surrounded" it. Just as important, student subjectivity-in-action was knowingly played out on a stage given national – indeed, international – visibility through the press and electronic media.

Here it is useful to recall Matsushita's remarks on the "change in social forms in the stage of monopoly capital . . . from 'class' to 'mass'." "Monopoly capital," even more than "American imperialism," was the stated target of student protests. The methods of protest and organization of the movement, particularly its eclipsing of the old left, remind us that "the Anpo protests . . . came at a time when the mixed economic system that had formed after the Second World War was entering a period of unprecedented prosperity. High economic growth was rapidly changing the lives of Japanese, and their consciousness as well. But the leading forces for reform [kakushin], including the reform parties and Sōhyō, failed to notice the fact."[93] In short, Yoshimoto was correct to have insisted that a mass line, so to speak, be followed; but even here he was picking up on the theme of "anonymous thought" articulated a decade earlier by Shimizu Ikutarō himself. Modernism had done its work and was

---

92 See articles by Kuroda Kan'ichi and Yoshimoto Takaaki in Tanigawa et al., *Minshushugi no shinwa*; on "incense offerings," see p. 176.
93 Masamura, *Sengo shi*, 2:136.

no longer, if it ever had been, a revolutionary force. The problem was that the actual masses were not revolutionary either. Rather, Anpo was the product of a perhaps unique confluence of ideas and social energies – those of enlightenment reformism plus revolutionary spontaneity, of class conflict localized in declining industries, as at Miike, plus a "mass" defense of everyday life. These were forced together in the crucible of Kishi's politics of intimidation, and though force did not entirely rule the day, neither could these disparate elements hold together once the central embodiment of that force had left the scene. Anpo, therefore, as Riesman put it, left a legacy of trauma. It also provided extremely useful object lessons in modes of political protest, and probably reinforced in the public mind the suspicion that, official rhetoric aside, democracy was either always a movement or to be realized in spheres other than the political.

SCIENCE AND CULTURE AFTER ANPO

In the wake of Anpo, the "postwar" utopianism that had marked Japanese thinking about democracy was definitively transvalued, literally "translated" from the political to the economic realm. The clearest symbol, a virtual cliché, of this transvaluation, is the so-called "Income Doubling Plan" announced by Ikeda Hayato, Kishi Nobusuke's successor as Prime Minister. Though received with skepticism and some fear in business circles (it seemed to threaten inflation), the plan did succeed; in fact, it exceeded expectations. Its intention was never hidden: to bring an end to the "season of politics" and to begin channelling Japan's industrial largesse to the long-neglected "regions." The result would be the "long-term stability" that Kishi had scorned. In political terms, the plan's success was doubly significant: first in that, along with serious government attention subsequently paid to maintaining employment levels, it seemed to compensate for the campaign of "industrial rationalization" that followed the union defeat at Miike, and for the incontrovertible fact that labor would never be a full partner in national-level policymaking. Second, as a delayed awareness of the environmental and social costs of rapid growth began to set in toward the end of the 1960s, fierce, sometimes violent discontent erupted among warehoused university students, while residents of Japan's smog-poisoned, space-starved megacities embraced a politics of environmental defense. Yet even as urbanites in considerable numbers elected reformist local governments, at the national level, the rural political base won for the LDP by Ikeda's policies remained relatively safe.

The "transvaluation" of democracy to the economic realm was paralleled by the emergence of a "model modernizer" discourse and announcement (in 1962) of the "Japanese miracle." The Japanese firm, and its capacity to mobilize and motivate labor, became a star in the social science literature; the "miracle" narrative disclosed the arrival of an industrial, or corporate, utopia. David Riesman provides a good example of one such birth tale. It took place at a "huge machine-tool and telephone combine" built by a pseudonymous "Mr. Otoyama," who had started from scratch after the war:[94]

This tour was memorable. I have worked at Sperry Gyroscope, and visited other plants, but this was an experience of a new sort. The plant was beautifully designed and spotless, spacious, and airy . . . and with not an item of sloppiness to be found anywhere. . . . The factory rooms and many aisles are decorated with the chrysanthemums and flower arrangements which are so omnipresent that we have almost come not to see them.

I've never seen such a pace of work: the young girls putting assemblies together, working with pincers or magnets under microscopes – it seemed to me that we were seeing the heart of Japanese productivity. Workers are trained in school for three months to do this sort of work. Girls work on the most detailed operations, while men do the slightly heavier work. There are balconies from which one can observe the plants, and the quiet is extraordinary. Workers don't talk to each other. . . . We watched the way in which the making of neon lights has been mechanized in the highest degree, the carefulness of inspection, the apparently easy and rational flow of work. Katō [Hidetoshi] told us that in white-collar offices in Tokyo there is consistent sabotage. People take two-hour "coffee breaks" without notice, disrupting work, but there is nothing like that here.

To be sure, there is nothing specifically "Japanese" – in the sense of traditional – about this hypermodern setting. Later in his diary, however, Riesman answers the question implicit in his description: What was Japanese about the process that had led to the creation of such enterprise, and "how in spite of cliques and in spite of 'feudalism' did so much get done?"

I was struck with the combination of "rationality" in Japanese industry with much traditionalism both in the corporate familism and the position of working women, and I suggested that the ability of Japanese traditions to

94   Riesman and Riesman, *Conversations*, pp. 74–6.

absorb and blend with modernization should not be underestimated. It seemed to me this was especially true because, as compared with other industrializing societies, Japan was a highly literate society where a certain amount of rationality already existed; it was also a fairly homogeneous society – unlike either the United States or the Soviet Union – again allowing for industrialization to be absorbed in a different way.[95]

It would be superfluous to pursue the theme of "model modernizer" at length. Two points do bear repeating here, however. First, the classics of this literature, such as Robert Bellah's *Tokugawa Religion* (1957) and Thomas Smith's *Agrarian Origins of Modern Japan* (1959), are hardly the sort of intellectual cardboard that the "modernization school" is sometimes held to have produced; their arguments are luminously intelligent and for this reason cannot but reveal a sense of the costs and ambiguities of Japan's modernization-through-tradition. Similarly, the theoretical discussions at the Hakone conference of 1960, upon which the "school's" reputation was ostensibly based, demonstrated repeatedly that Japanese participants, particularly Maruyama and the historian Tōyama Shigeki, were far from embracing any notion of modernization that did not place *democratization* at the center of its concerns. Maruyama remained within the sphere of modernism, which is a different intellectual project; Tōyama, as a Marxist, was unwilling to allow the category of "capitalism," including its implied transition to socialism, to be subsumed by "modernization." There was never any final meeting of minds. Riesman, who was no mean sociologist, serves here as an example of how that literature was read and its ideas combined with other notions in pursuit of a theory of comparative modernization. He also developed an assessment of Japanese "democracy" that confirms the cooptation of democracy into an ideology of service to enterprise:

One has to take care not to misinterpret what the Japanese mean by "democracy," a word they constantly use. It does not mean social equality; the consideration, for example, shown for one's equals and official superiors is not extended to those below. "Democracy" does seem to mean a way of doing business that combines commitment and high principle with lack of factionalism and internecine conflict. People refer to organizations as "undemocratic" if there is no harmony or consensus. Thus, democracy and politics would seem to be antithetical.[96]

Riesman's observations are typically acute but lack historical depth in one important respect: An ethos (or more cynically, a guise)

95   Riesman and Riesman, *Conversations*, pp. 304, 305.
96   Riesman and Riesman, *Conversations*, p. 202.

of equality was precisely the element of "postwar" social practice that legitimated the demands of corporate life, as that life was reworked into the modal form of Japanese democracy (and into the modal form of Japanese capitalism). That is, when compared to the prewar years, it is the narrowing of social distinctions and the abolition of the most invidious of them that is striking. It is true that Japan's industrial society was highly segmented and ridden with status distinctions ostensibly based on education and merit, with the important dividing line being that between employees of "the modal firm" and those who worked in less favored settings. But the overall narrowing of status differences relative to prewar society must be kept clearly in view, as Riesman here does not. It is a major achievement of postwar society.

Over the course of the 1960s, in the context of the strains created by rapid economic growth in Japan's relationship of "subordinate independence" to the United States, the "prism of historical judgment" that had formed in the wake of surrender was seriously challenged by other framing perspectives. The broader context of this reconfiguration was the rising tide of national pride and self-congratulation symbolized by the Tokyo Olympics of 1964. Amidst the genuine excitement and considerable naïveté that marked Japan's official rehabilitation (Tokyo, after all, was to have hosted the Olympics in 1940) came strong signals of historical revision. Claims were advanced by writers and critics such as Mishima Yukio and Etō Jun that "postwar" or "Occupation" democracy was a myth or fraud, since it rested on the evisceration of Japan's culture and tradition, or, in more modulated form, that the *early* postwar reforms had "gone too far," wounding the legitimate self-esteem of Japan's people in the name of an unrealistic, or utopian, vision of democracy that was also politically naïve.

Revision of "postwar," inevitably, brought the first attempts by publicists to "affirm" Japan's lost war effort. Rather than the resentful submission of the sort encountered in Yabe Teiji's reaction to his political isolation, or the muted and lofty "old liberalism" of Takeyama Michio, the affirmations of the Greater East Asia War were brought forward as a kind of militant nostalgia *and* a call to overdue national self-assertion. "The foreigner" could not be blamed any longer. Rather, it was the effete intellectuals of the left who had habituated Japanese public opinion to humiliation, cheap idealism, and the undeserved adulation paid to Marxism; also blameworthy were the "Americanizers" who idolized capitalism and "individualism" and vulgarized Japan's culture. The repudiation of "postwar" took a number of forms. Deliberately inflammatory historical arguments were made in connection with the indictment of the contemporary situation. Hayashi Fusao (1903–75), a member of the Shinjinkai, proletarian novelist, later an associate of the Japan Romantic School and postwar purge, rejected the "two wars" position of Takeuchi, who argued that Japan had engaged simultaneously in continental aggression and anticolonial struggle. Japan, Hayashi declared, had been engaged in a "single protracted war" since the opening of the country; the enemy had always been the West; Kido Takayoshi and Saigō Takamori were engaged in the same revolutionary struggle as Kita Ikki. Japan's "Hundred Years' War for East Asia" had "definitively ended" in 1945.[97] A younger philosopher, Ueyama Shunpei (b. 1921) – to whose work Hayashi's own was in fact a response – took a more reflective stance, writing on behalf of his own "wartime" generation so that their lives and deaths should not be meaningless. His tone bore a certain "remorse-fatigue," but he also had a political point:

The stipulations of Article 8 of the Atlantic Charter and Article 9 of the Japanese constitution rest on the self-righteous premise of the American government, which took the initiative in framing them both, that "we are a peace-loving people." To take what they propose at face value without a fundamental reconsideration of their shared premise is unacceptable.[98]

The "case" of Mishima Yukio (1925–70), whose Bunka bōei ron (On the Defense of Culture) appeared in the same year as the texts of Hayashi and Ueyama, is perhaps the best known, the most extreme, and most spectacular in its disposition. Its significance in the present context lies, perhaps, in the forceful attention it calls to the performative and fantastic element of the cultural "identity" that Mishima had set out to defend. Mishima's Buddhistic final works, his evocations of intuitionist rebels in the line of Wang Yangming thought (Ōshio, Saigō), his willingness to debate the ferociously anti-intellectual students of the radical left, his aestheticized militarism, combined with his rococo style of life and international literary stature and culminating in his "apotheosis" – all these carry a meaning. Far from defending a threatened culture, Mishima demonstrated its plasticity and lack of essence. He is the embodiment of a *surplus* of meaning that explodes into nonmeaning.

97 Hayashi Fusao, *Dai Tō-A sensō kōteiron* (Chūō Kōronsha, 1964), pp. 14, 23, 132.
98 Ueyama Shunpei, *Dai Tō-A sensō no imi* (Chūō Kōronsha, 1964), pp. 1, 29.

In Etō Jun (b. 1933), we have a case of personal nationalism and cultural conservatism ever more narrowed by historical monomania. In his early years, Etō's sensitive intelligence had produced empathetic readings of Natsume Sōseki and Kobayashi Hideo; his basic theme of cultural loss was already present. It has to compete, however, with a visceral reaction against the political disorder and violence of the 1960 demonstrations, which Etō combined with a sharp rejection of what he saw as the spurious and fraudulent "idealism" of the left. His post-Anpo experience in the United States led him to "reimagine" postwar Japan as a place analogous to the American South after 1865:

In short, the relationship between the federal government of the United States and the Confederacy formed the prototype for the relationship between America and the foreign nations it has vanquished. If we replace the federal government's "official" moral condemnation of racial discrimination with the moral condemnation by Americans of the Nanking Incident and attack on Pearl Harbor, we might even say that this relationship bears similarities to that between the United States and Japan. On December 7, there were as always television programs commemorating the surprise attack on Pearl Harbor, and my wife did not go out shopping on that day. I could not deny the existence within myself of emotions, different in quality to be sure, not a whit less intense than those experienced by whites in the south.[99]

On his return to Japan, Etō deepened his sense of living in a land once dominated by a now vanquished martial culture (Etō's forebears had occupied middling elite status in the Navy); his revulsion at the coarse materialism of his country became a quest for the classic moment of historical betrayal. Not that military victory had been possible; nor was Etō party to any romanticized Pan-Asianism. Rather, he felt that Japan's stature had been dishonestly stripped away by the surrender agreement. Instead of honor, Japan had been dealt bad faith. Thus his original sense of loss of meaning and "identity" was gradually focused on a single set of claims concerning the surrender and Occupation: that SCAP censorship stripped postwar Japan of the "truth" concerning its origins and of the possibilities for an organic culture. Moreover, it was not merely inept and stupid but malicious in operation, concealing the "fact" that Japan did not surrender unconditionally but merely concluded an agreement with the Allies; on this basis, he maintained that the 1946 Constitution was a self-violation of the Potsdam

99 Etō Jun, *Amerika to watakushi*, as repr. in *Etō Jun chosakushū* (Kōdansha, 1967), 4:52.

Declaration's requirement of free expression. Article 9 of that Constitution, needless to say, has been an object of particular revulsion. Etō's historical claims have not been widely accepted, but he has been a prolific writer, and one who is widely read.[100] As with many other intellects that find their imaginative range narrowing, Etō (like Shimizu Ikutarō) became a kind of atmospheric marker rather than an active thinker.

Appropriately, a final instance of the diffusion of post-Anpo nationalism comes from the official world. *Kitai sareru ningenzō* (1965), despite the evocation in its title of "humanity" at large, should be translated as "The Ideal Japanese": It offers in outline form an "image" of normal and normative Japaneseness. Prepared by the Kyoto School philosopher Kōsaka Masaaki (1900–69) for the Central Educational Commission in its study of middle school education, the text considers the question: "What should be the 'image of the ideal [Japanese] person' in the national society of the future?"[101] Its answer (befitting a commission report) is banal in many ways. But it is precisely for this reason that it registers the powerful shift in historical and political climate defined at its "outward" limit by figures such as Hayashi and Mishima.

Kitai sareru ningenzō recognizes that industrial society makes victims of those who live in it. Mechanization and "animalization" of human life are problems that beset every advanced nation. However, the report continues,

> It should be recognized that the Japanese of today also face circumstances particular to themselves. Defeat in the Second World War brought changes of grave importance to the received mode of existence of Japan as a state and society. Although new ideals have indeed been brought forward since the war, there has yet not been sufficient discussion of the concrete policies to be considered for their realization.

The text constantly reiterates the need for "discussion" of "concrete policies" but predictably, perhaps, is largely hortatory. Nevertheless, certain guidelines for normative behavior do come through. These are best grasped, however, in light of the text's basic stance on postwar history. In effect, Kōsaka was recommending that Japan's teenagers be taught that their society had suffered a grave cultural loss:

100 See Olson, *Ambivalent Moderns*, chap. 1.
101 Chūō Kyōiku Shingikai Dai-19 Tokubetsu I'inkai, *Kitai sareru ningenzō* (chūkan sōan zenbun); text from Kōsaka, *Shiken: Kitai sareru ningenzō* (Chikuma Shobō, 1965), pp. 202–32.

The miserable reality of defeat, especially, gave rise to the misperception that everything in the Japanese past and way of life was mistaken, with the result that Japan's history and the national character of the Japanese came to be ignored. For this reason, even though new ideals are held up, the spiritual climate in which they were to have taken hold has instead been laid waste. . . . If in the rush to point out and eliminate faults among the Japanese, we lack the willingness to cultivate our strengths, it will prove impossible to substantiate new ideals in a form consistent with the spiritual climate of our country. We must never forget that we are Japanese.

Remembering Japaneseness, moreover, has a specific meaning:

As symbols of Japan we have had our flag, sung the national anthem, and shown respect and affection for the emperor. For Japanese this was in no way separate from their loving Japan and paying respect to its mission. The emperor is a symbol of Japan, of the unity of the Japanese people. We must reflect deeply on the fact that to venerate [keiai suru] Japan as our ancestral land is identical with venerating the emperor.

Thus, postwar Japan began with "the miserable reality of defeat" – beyond this, historically, it was not necessary to go. Instead, the important thing was to reaffirm national identity through the symbols – flag, anthem, emperor – presumably neglected in the rush to find fault. But such self-humiliation was no longer needed. Rather, it was time to reawaken a sense of national mission. Only having done so, Kōsaka argues, will Japanese develop their "social intelligence" and spirit of "spontaneous service." Only then will they recover sufficiently to build a "healthy democracy" and address the more universal problems of industrial society: "The crisis of modern man stems from human beings having lost trust in one another."

What, however, was the nature of the "trust" now in need of restoration? "Postwar Japan," Kōsaka asserts, "has lost the positive features that derived from the Volksgemeinschaft [minzoku kyōdōtai], but has yet to attain to the firm awakening of the individual. To restore this buried self while at the same time carrying through with our shared responsibilities as a people [minzoku] is one of our most important tasks." Indeed, "the single greatest failing of Japanese society lies in the weakness of social norms. It lies in the lack of decorum [reigi] proper to members of society, in ignoring order. This is what gives rise to confusion, and makes society into something ugly." The national mission, then, is the restoration of order, the reclamation of Volksgemeinschaft. State, nation, society, and community are one. Kōsaka concludes: "The ideal human being, in short, means the model of the human being that Japanese expect each other to emulate."[102]

The ideal Japanese, for Kōsaka, would seem to live in a society unconcerned with rights, or in no need of them, in which the only norm was one of order/disorder or propriety/impropriety, and without significant class or social diversity, in a democracy without a sovereign people, and in which spontaneity led only to service. It was, as Ōe Kenzaburō wrote, a society without youth, daring, or enjoyment – a society with no reason to hope.[103] It is unlikely that Kōsaka Masaaki would ever have admitted to the epithet "conservative industrial utopian," but that, in essence, is what his ideas represented. As such, they constituted the mainstream of post-Anpo nationalism, and it was as such, in the name of personal self-determination and social diversity, that Ōe attacked them.

The realization of an industrial utopia had important implications for the function and status of science, initially by way of the challenge posed to science by the fact of growth itself. It had not been predicted, nor, once underway, had it been expected to continue. The difficulties were felt first and most acutely by Marxists, especially economists for whom the long-term viability of Japanese economy depended on overthrowing capitalism, or more realistically on its passing through a final, state monopoly stage. The years from the late 1940s to the mid-1960s had seen the heyday of such analyses, most importantly by followers of Uno Kōzō, such as Ōuchi Tsutomu, and others, like the Socialist leader Sakisaka Itsurō, who were more closely aligned with the Rōnō faction. Their hopes and convictions foundered, however, on the rocks of Stalinism and sectarianism on the old left, on the unexpectedly rapid economic growth of the late 1950s, and on mistaken prognostications that the recession of the mid-1960s signaled the end of high growth.[104] More tellingly, the traditional left proved unable to lead, either theoretically or practically, the social struggles that emerged in the wake of the environmental disaster of "unbundled" industrial development.

Marxism, it seemed, was facing supersession (not for the first time, of course) as a political and "scientific" orientation. As else-

---

102 Kōsaka, *Shiken: Kitai sareru ningenzō*, pp. 206, 208–9, 210, 215, 221, 229.
103 Ōe Kenzaburō, *"Kitai sareru ningenzō o hihan suru"* (1965), repr. in *Sōzōryoku to jōkyō: Ōe Kenzaburō dōjidai ronshū* (Iwanami Shoten, 1981), 3:60–72.
104 Nakamura Takafusa, *Shōwa shi* (Tōyō Keizai Shinpōsha, 1993), p. 543.

ANDREW E. BARSHAY

where, the most consequential response to this situation was a return to a set of avowed "first principles," and it is in this context that the work of Uno Kōzō (1899–1977) finally came into its own as perhaps the dominant indigenous tradition in Japanese Marxism.

Working in considerable isolation at Tōhoku Imperial University, Uno Kōzō had in the mid-1930s set about a reconstruction and elaboration of Marx's *Capital* that would restore the "inner logic" that connected it to its source in Hegel's dialectics. The result was successive versions of *Keizai genron* (1951, 1964), in which Uno developed his analysis of political economy in its pure state. The analysis, he insisted, must go back to the "commoditization of labor power," the essence of capitalism; for Uno, this starting point was the equivalent of the Pure Land Buddhist's *nenbutsu*.[105] Marx, Uno claimed, had confused the analysis of capitalism in the abstract with the "actually existing capitalism" of his day. Now, since capitalism had developed in ways clearly at variance with Marx's own expectations, the time had come to separate its "pure" (or ideal) form from the "stages" – mercantilist, liberal, and imperialist – that subsequent history had disclosed; this was the argument developed in *Keizai seisaku ron* (1936, 1971). The final goal of Marxism as economic science, Uno held, was "contemporary analysis," but he himself did virtually nothing along these lines, leaving that work to a large number of disciples.[106]

The Uno School is unmistakably scholastic in character, a feature that has led certain interpreters to liken Uno to the French Communist philosopher Louis Althusser. To be sure, neither Uno nor his many followers developed a theory of ideology. Rather, his school shares with Althusser the experience of having to theorize under conditions of capitalist surge and socialist decline. The domain of practice contracts visibly for both – hence, concomitantly, the preeminence of all-generative "structures" in their modes of thought. Uno's school is marked by a rigorous (and, for its critics, quietist) discrimination between economic science and ideological commitment. The parallels to Weberian social science – of which Uno was unconvincingly critical – are patent. Not sur-

---

105 Tamanoi Yoshirō, "Uno keizaigaku no kōseki to genkai" (1977) in ibid., *Ekonomī to ekorojī* (Misuzu Shobō, 1986), pp. 289–309.
106 Of Uno's writings, only his *Principles of Political Economy* has been translated (Humanities Press, 1980) – by Thomas [Tomohiko] Sekine, who has vigorously promoted Uno's system in a number of works. For a recent collection of articles by Japanese specialists, see Shimizu Masanori and Furihata Setsuo, eds., *Uno Kōzō no sekai: Marukusu riron no gendaiteki saisei* (Yūhikaku, 1983).

prisingly, Uno-school Marxism has in its turn produced both a "left" and "right" wing. It is said to have inspired the ferocious critiques of Japanese capitalism by the most radical elements of the postwar student movement; among Uno's academic descendants, there are clear ideological differences traceable to one or another aspect of Uno's own suggestive but unfulfilled call for contemporary analysis.

Uno's was not the only significant attempt within Japanese Marxism to "return to Marx" in order to face the problems posed by the capitalist surge of the 1960s. A school associated with Uchida Yoshihiko (1913–89) and Hirata Kiyoaki (1922–95) formulated critiques both of Japanese capitalism and Soviet-style socialism on the basis of their shared development as societies in which the "rights of the state" predominated over those of society or individuals. Japanese capitalism, Uchida had argued,

has developed . . . through the association of the supermodern with the premodern, and not with the modern or civil. It is precisely the survival of premodernity itself that has permitted such a rapid development of supermodernity in Japan. From which one may conclude, paradoxical though it may seem, that in Japan capitalism has developed thanks to the weakness of civil society.[107]

For his part, Hirata took up the task (long delayed in Japanese Marxist circles) of critically examining "actually existing socialism" from the point of view of Marx's own texts. Focusing on Marx's assertion that the "negation" of capitalist private property reestablishes "individual property on the basis of . . . cooperation and the possession in common . . . of the means of production produced by labor itself," Hirata argued that socialism meant nothing less than the reestablishment of individual property.[108] Together, Uchida and Hirata undertook to reconceptualize the notion of civil society, detaching it from capitalism and from the notion of private property. By restoring the unity between work and property, Marxists of the "civil society" school sought to provide the theoretical basis for an independent socialism.[109]

107 Toshio Yamada, "Les tendances du marxisme japonais contemporain," in Le marxisme au Japon, issue of Actuel Marx, no. 2 (1987): 40, emphasis added. See also Uchida, "Shihonron to gendai," Sekai, no. 262 (September 1967): 33–53, trans. as "Japan Today and Das Kapital," in Japan Interpreter 6, no. 1 (Spring 1970): 8–28; Uchida, Shihonron no sekai (1966); and Uchida, Nihon shihonshugi no shisōzō (1968).
108 Marx, Capital, vol. 1 (Penguin/NLR ed., 1990), p. 929.
109 Hirata Kiyoaki, "Shakaishugi to shimin shakai" (1968), repr. in "Sekai" shuyō ronbunsen, 1946–1995, pp. 495–521; see also Hirata, "La société civile japonaise contemporaine," in Le marxisme au Japon, pp. 65–71, and Yamada, "Tendances," pp. 38–41.

A final instance of the Marxist response to the threat of super-session came from the philosopher Hiromatsu Wataru (1933–94). As with Uno and the "civil society" theorists, Hiromatsu also proceeded by way of a return to Marx and an anticonventional interpretation. In Hiromatsu's case (and in common with Althusser), the Marx of the 1844 Manuscripts, the Marx of "alienation," is turned against the Marx of the *German Ideology*. Marx matures; alienation gives way to reification. But, Hiromatsu argued, what Marx really meant by reification has been misunderstood, in part owing to the lasting influence of Georg Lukács, who had subsumed the "logic of reification" under that of alienation. The result was an over-Hegelianized Marx, in whose thought the constitutive "modern" notion of a consciousness divided between subject and object is held to be operative. The spurious understanding of reification regards the phenomenon of objectification as one in which a particular subject is related without mediation to a particular object. Hiromatsu, however, insisted that for Marx, reification does not take place except through the intersubjective mediation of human beings themselves; it is these *relations* that are reified and appear to individuals as "things." For Hiromatsu, because its ontology contains this theme of intersubjectivity, with the primacy it accords to social connections, Marxism properly understood not only overcomes the conventional divisions between "Soviet" and "Western," or "ortho-dox" and "subjective" within Marxism. It takes Marxism beyond the "modern"; it "overcomes" the subject/object division that consti-tutes the modern itself.[110]

Along with his recovery of the intersubjective ontology within Marxism, in the late 1970s Hiromatsu also produced a philosophi-cally serious treatment of the notion of "Overcoming the Modern" that so dominated Japanese intellectual life in the opening years of the Asia-Pacific War. Differing from the highly influential approach taken by Takeuchi Yoshimi, which concentrated on the literary aspects of the "movement," Hiromatsu took up the philosophical claims of the Kyoto School and its allied thinkers concerning the "standpoint of world history" and Japan's creative role at its center. Hiromatsu agreed with Takeuchi that the call to "Overcome the Modern" did present, "in concentrated form the aporia [the irreduc-ible contradiction] of Japan's modern history." But while Takeuchi stressed that the two symposia convened to promote this "over-

---

110 See Hiromatsu Wataru, "La philosophie de Marx 'pour nous'," in *Le Marxisme au Japon*, pp. 72–84.

coming" had failed both to confront aporia – particularly the dual character of Japan's war effort – as such, and to develop a coherent ideology that could "move reality," Hiromatsu saw precisely the opposite. Ideology need not be "coherent," and if the behavior of Japan's intellectual world was in itself a "reality," it was indisputably true that the ideology of "overcoming the modern" had "worked."[111]

From a strictly intellectual and philosophical standpoint, however, there were problems. Despite their anticapitalist slogans, the "philosophers of world history" had failed to offer any real critique of monopoly capitalism in Japan. It was indeed "difficult to acknowledge" that the Kyoto School philosophers had developed "a means for the systematic transcendence of the horizon of modern knowledge." Still, Hiromatsu argued, the "notion of a unified world history beyond the dualistic East/West framework," the attempt to "grasp world history according to a multi-axial dynamic" – in general, the drive to overcome philosophical dualism – remained legitimate intellectual tasks.[112] By the end of his life, Hiromatsu saw those tasks being fulfilled. "[Build] a New System in East Asia along a Japan–China Axis!" he exhorted. "Let it become the premise for a New World Order! We have entered a period in which, *provided it includes a radical reexamination of Japanese capitalism itself*, this could very well serve as the slogan of the anti-establishment left."[113]

Whatever its future may hold, the prestige and authority of Marxism as an economic and social science were on the wane by the end of the 1960s. In its place, a cadre of sophisticated analysts, less concerned with grasping the dialectical "whole" of political economy than with the empirical and practical work of tracking macroeconomic trends, came to the fore. Ultimately, avowedly "value-free," empirical science of this kind was not, any more than Marxism was, to be spared both withering criticism *and* ideological cooptation.

The example of Shimomura Osamu (b. 1910), a government economist who has been called the "prophet of Japanese high growth," should suffice to indicate the importance of empirical

---

111 Hiromatsu Wataru, *"Kindai no chōkoku" ron: Shōwa shisōshi e no ichi dansō* (Asahi Shuppansha, 1980), pp. 148, 160–4, 172.

112 Hiromatsu, *"Kindai no chōkoku" ron*, pp. 224–50 *passim*; quotes from pp. 249–50.

113 Hiromatsu, "Tōhoku Ajia ga rekishi no shuyaku ni; Ōbei chūshin no sekaikan wa hōkai e" (*Asahi shinbun*, March 16, 1994), emphasis added. I am grateful to Yōsuke Nirei for this reference.

economics in its rising phase. In its proper Biblical sense, a prophet
was not so much one who unaccountably sees into the future but one
who sees through to the essence of his time, and therefore senses
why one of all possible futures is most likely to materialize. Such was
Shimomura. In October 1960, at the outset of the Ikeda administration, Shimomura argued forcefully that (at a time when predicted
American GNP growth was 5%, and the UK's 4%), the Japanese
economy could afford to grow at a 9% clip, and that such growth was
something to be pursued "positively, constructively, enthusiastically,
and creatively." The "Shimomura thesis" that underlay these exhortations asserted that "plainly put, the growth rate will more or
less parallel the size of private fixed investment as a percentage of
GNP." Shimomura thus argued (at first quite controversially) for
stimulatory policies that would allow the realization of the growth
potential he saw in the investment practices of Japanese firms. A
fervent supporter of Ikeda's income-doubling policy, Shimomura
was convinced, correctly, that as of the early 1960s, the Japanese
economy could afford to grow for some time (though not indefi-
nitely) without inflation or foreign exchange difficulties; his studies
showed the economy in a phase of excess capacity rather than excess
demand.[114]

As with other prophets or visionaries, Shimomura needed "do-
ers," particularly Ōkita Saburō, a cautious but committed believer in
indicative planning and the real architect of Ikeda's economic policy.
Nor was the "prophet" in control of his message once it had been
transmitted: There would be ideologists anxious to make use of it
to further their own interests, as well as professional critics,
counterprophets with a considerable intellectual investment in the
outcome of the original prophecy.

For the ruling party and government, business interests, and sections of the mass media and journalism, the economic argument for
the possibility of continued growth fed a political ideology that may
be termed "growthism." (To speak of "capitalism" always hinted at
disapproval, but "growth" was unambiguously good.) As an ideology, "growthism" combined two features that mark its period and
that would not easily remain together after the 1970s. The first was
the quantitative mania that was well-nigh universal in industrial
societies of that era; second, and particularly significant in the con-

114 Shimomura Osamu, *Nihon keizai seichō ron* (Kin'yū Zaisei Jijō Kenkyūkai, 1962),
     pp. 109–10. See also Morris-Suzuki, *History of Japanese Economic Thought*, esp. pp. 138–
     40.

text of this essay, was a celebratory nationalism. Some of this was humorous, as in the naming of successive economic booms after mythohistorical figures and events, moving backward in "time" from Jinmu through Iwato (the sun goddess's cave) to Izanami. In a similar vein, a group of three consumer durables were dubbed the "three sacred treasures" in echo of the imperial regalia. Such rhetoric points to the inversion of the early postwar perspective on the relation of Japan's culture to economic growth, indicating as well a spreading sense of middle-class attainment and recovery of national purpose. Japan was about growth through production and trade, quantifiable and increasing. It was not a dangerous but a normal country and one, moreover, that was beginning to be discussed as a model for other developing nations. To be sure, the reconsideration of the Tokugawa legacy of rurally based, "traditional" values and patterns of social organization to modernization after Meiji was well under way. But "growthism" as a whole preserved much of the earlier convergence theory of industrial development. We are not yet in the presence of the full-blown *nihonjin ron* of later decades. Japan was not held up as a model of an alternative modernity of a status equal, let alone superior, to that of the West.

Within the ideological framework of "growthism," there was serious debate as to how growth had occurred, and how it could be sustained and enhanced (that is, protected from inflation or rising wage demands, or from fluctuations in international trade). In her *History of Japanese Economic Thought*, Tessa Morris-Suzuki has recently provided an expert outline of these arguments, which need not be rehearsed in detail here. Given an intellectual (and social) universe in which so much was shared, however, certain points of contrast bear mentioning. We note the "positive" role ascribed by a modern (i.e., non-Marxian) economist such as Shinohara Miyohei to the great "macro" factors of "industrial dualism, technological adaptability, and increasing export competitiveness" in explaining the long-term causes of Japan's twentieth-century economic growth; for Shinohara, "postwar recovery" – "the greater the destruction, the faster the rate of recovery" – was only a phase in this longer history. Shinohara was appropriately sensitive to the operations of the so-called "Kuznets cycle" and was quick to see possible bottlenecks, particularly caused by rising labor wages as growth narrowed the gap between industrial strata. Under such circumstances, Shinohara forecast declining rates of growth by the 1960s – he was off by a decade – and argued that Japan's advantage of dualism would have

to be replaced with one derived from "rents" gained through technological innovation. What was missing from Shinohara's approach,
however, was an appreciation of the role, first, of the early postwar
reforms – *zaibatsu* dissolution, land reform, encouragement of unionism, elimination of military expenditure – in providing a basis for
growth, and second, of the role played by economic planners in
analyzing and guiding the macro processes generated by conditions
of "postwar recovery." In the early postwar years, it was precisely
this area in which Ōkita Saburō, along with Tsuru Shigeto, Arisawa
Hiromi, Ōuchi Hyōe, Shimomura Osamu, and many other economists including Uno Kōzō, had been involved. Recalling that period,
with its passionate and ideologically open arguments over Japan's
economic future, Ōkita later commented mordantly on the absence
of such "general debates" in the era of high "growthism."[115]

It cannot have been that there was nothing of substance to debate.
As Tsuru Shigeto, Miyamoto Ken'ichi, and Miyazaki Yoshikazu
began to insist, totemic GNP indicators concealed both dreadful
environmental effects along with steep social costs: the cooptation of
organized labor and its nullification as a national political force, a
social pigeonholing, via the educational system, of an oppressive
kind. "Growthism" also cast doubt on the integrity of social science,
indeed of science generally, which seemed to have abdicated any
critical, national role, becoming instead a business of expertise for
hire.[116] Economists – social scientists generally – became a set of
intellectual subalterns whose work was marked by the deepening
hold of quantitative methodology, and whose "overdetermined"
function seemed to be the further promotion of economic growth.
By the mid-1960s, for example, the practical applications of the
avowedly scientific study of human action were being given ever
greater stress. Behaviorism was firmly rooted in the world of Japanese social science. As Riesman noted in passing (in connection with
the University of Tokyo): "Generally speaking, the Departments of
Law, Economics, and Engineering are conservative, and so is Psychology (perhaps this is because many graduates go into industrial
psychology)."[117]

The overriding concern of behaviorism to discover the laws of
functional or optimal behavior in a given environment, or in re-

115 See Morris-Suzuki, *History*, chap. 5, *passim*.
116 See Ui Jun, "A basic theory of *kōgai*" (1972) in *Science and Society in Modern Japan*, ed.
     Nakayama et al., pp. 290–311; Ishida, *Nihon no shakai kagaku*, pp. 1–6, 207–12, 218–23,
     240–1.
117 Riesman and Riesman, *Conversations*, p. 347.

sponse to a given stimulus, and to determine how that behavior was to be analyzed, elicited, and corrected if necessary, clearly opened what was a strongly "structuralist" and interdisciplinary discourse to ideological critique. In his popular history of postwar thought, for example, Nakajima Makoto presented an overview of the relationship between structuralism and behaviorism, considering its particular implications for Japan: Given the enormous sway of corporate capital over the Japanese economy, Nakajima argued, the behaviorist method, by its ever more minute fragmentation of action, could not help but deepen the self-alienation of those "whole" human beings subject, as in the workplace, to pressures for ever greater efficiency.[118] Nakajima himself drew on Kitazawa Masakuni, whose theories of a "semi-automatic" management society dependent upon the manipulation and control of computerized information by elites were gaining considerable notoriety. The world now, Kitazawa asserted, is one where "we shed tears for aged peasant women in Vietnam while calmly participating in mechanisms of slaughter", a world where "syntax notwithstanding, in their deep structures there is no more than a hair-breadth's difference between 'monopoly capital,' with its intensified state controls, and 'socialism,' over which the people's capacity for democratic control has been lost." The task for the present, Nakajima holds, is to radicalize structuralism, to "insert its scalpel into the infinite number of combinations that operate in our unconscious thinking at the level of everyday life: that is, into the very structure of contemporary civilization."[119] In Nakajima's narrative, then, science and administration were bringing about the convergence of capitalism and socialism; the fate of advanced societies was a shared dehumanization.

Nakajima's strictures coincide with the resurgence of the student left, which had been building since mid-decade, and with the violence – the worst of it internecine and lacking real ideological justification – that racked Japan's universities at the end of the 1960s.[120] The differences between the so-called "Anpo 1970" pro-

118 See the special issue of *Shisō* (no. 509 [November 1966]) on behavioral science, particularly Yoshimura Tōru, "Kōdō kagaku no gendaiteki igi," and Minami Hiroshi, "Kōdō kagaku no seikaku to kadai"; also Nakajima, *Sengo shisōshi nyūmon*, pp. 112–19.

119 Kitazawa Masakuni, "Ningen – sono botsuraku to saisei; Kyūshinteki kōzōshugi no ningenkan," *Tenbō* no. 111 (March 1968): 20, 31; Nakajima quote from *Sengo shisōshi nyūmon*, p. 114.

120 On university protests, see Shakai Mondai Kenkyūkai, ed., *Zengakuren kakuha* (Futabasha, 1969), Tōdai Funsō Bunsho Kenkyūkai, ed., *Tōdai funsō no kiroku* (Nihon Hyōronsha, 1969), Nihon Daigaku Bunrigakubu Tōsō I'inkai Shokikyoku, ed., *Hangyaku no barikēdo* (San'ichi Shobō, 1969); Halliday, *Political History*, pp. 251–61.

tests and those of a decade earlier are many and profound. In raw numbers, the former were larger – despite the automatic renewal, rather than revision, of the treaty – since they coincided with the high tide of the antiwar movement. At the same time, the universities themselves became central sites of struggle, with sharpening generational and structural conflict; organizationally, the movement's most significant product was the National Union of Struggle Councils (Zenkyōtō), founded in 1969 and clearly reflective of the "anti-authoritarian, anti-bureaucratic, egalitarian camaraderie of the world behind the barricades in which it was conceived."[121] Thus while defeat in 1960 brought rapid dissipation of militancy on the student left, no such collapse came in 1970. Critics such as Kitazawa as well as movement theorists argued that "student power" would lead the necessarily "post-proletarian" revolution in an age of converging systems.

The movement was far less effective than it might have been. Revolutionary theory was too often used to legitimate organized vendettas amongst rival groupings. Urgent issues – the nexus of Japanese capital with American military power, the simultaneous corruption and centralization of authority in university administrations, and the merciless processing of youthful intelligence into corporate fodder along with the increasingly rigid segmentation of the working population – were all needlessly obscured in the mania for "struggle." One should distinguish, of course, between the sects involved with local farmers to obstruct the development of Narita Airport, which tended toward populism with a revolutionary rhetorical mantle, and the Japanese Red Army Faction, in which proxy terrorism and fratricide became the chief dynamic. There were real sociopathologies at work in the latter; no one familiar with their ghastly denouement at Mt. Asama and the Lod Airport can think otherwise.

"Anpo 1970" was unquestionably significant. It decisively weakened the authority of science and of the teachers, specialists, and officials who espoused it, exposing both the insidiousness and vacuousness of "growth" as a national ideal. But it also degraded the very notion of subjectivity, discrediting the utopianism and collective struggle that are the only justification for the existence of the left. Insofar as "postwar" thought was substantially synonymous with the career of the concept of democratic subjectivity,

121 Gavan McCormack, "The Student Left in Japan," as quoted in Halliday, *Political History*, p. 255.

"postwar" *as* thought reached its end along with the 1960s; the so-called "Zenkyōtō generation" has been left to pick up the pieces. One can therefore agree, though for reasons different from those he adduces, with Nakajima Makoto's argument for 1968 as "the end of postwar."

BEYOND "POSTWAR"

In this social and intellectual context – with scientific authority weakened and utopian struggles marginalized – "culture" emerged, seemingly by default, as the key category in public discourse. Under vastly different circumstances, "culture" in the sense of ethnic unity and affinity, rather than of personal cultivation, had been installed as a hegemonic idea in the late 1930s. No argument is being made here that the return of "culture," particularly during the 1970s, represents a simple replay of the earlier episode. The rupture of 1945 and the trends leading up to the 1960 Anpo protests had brought too many changes for such a thing to occur. Yet if the operative and interconnected ideals of the era culminating in the 1960 Anpo were those of subjectivity, democracy, and science, with the 1970s we see a category shift to a "new" set of ideals that were also "old."

Its beginnings were obscure; in Nakajima's 1968 account of postwar thought, for example, "culture" hardly appears on the horizon. It was underwritten initially by the local residents' and antipollution movements (extensions in some ways of the 1960 protests) in which politics meant both the "negative" mobilization of victim consciousness and the "positive" assertion of local ties and sentiments of belonging. And it is to be noted that late-stage "modernist" social scientists, such as Matsushita Keiichi and Takabatake Michitoshi, were deeply involved as theorists in such movements.

The end of high growth after the collapse of the Bretton Woods system and the 1973 Yom Kippur War, along with steep inflation, seems to have triggered a variety of social doubts and anxieties, generating concerns about national identity and purpose. It is useful to remember that the phenomenon of the so-called *nihonjin ron* (recently examined by Kosaku Yoshino) did not begin simply as an exercise in national self-celebration but was a product of "shock."[122] To be sure, in the overheated atmosphere of the "bubble" economy

122 See Kosaku Yoshino, *Cultural Nationalism in Contemporary Japan* (Routledge, 1994).

of the 1980s, *nihonjin ron* took on what E. H. Norman had once
described as a "garish luster," with panegyrics to Japan's ethnic –
even racial – superiority being trumpeted in the face of American
decline. Although the efforts and funds, both official and corporate,
that were poured into the culture industry during these years
succeeded in producing a sleek, slick international image of a
"postmodern" Japan still in touch with its ostensible roots, much of
this "discourse" was fluff at best. This is not to say that maintaining
an international role as financier and high-end exporter amidst growing Asian competition and American pressure for liberalization, and
with an economy driven by absurdly inflated land values and faced
with rising social-welfare costs, could have been unproblematic.
With the end of the Cold War and the collapse of the bubble, the
task of rethinking Japan's basic political arrangements domestically
and in foreign policy has become urgent. But this period, punctuated
by the death of Hirohito, the spate of less than welcome "fiftieth-
anniversary" observances, the Hanshin earthquake and Aum
Shinrikyō incident, has instead brought a classic malaise.

The shift to culture was already making a preliminary "run-up" by
the mid-1960s. Many historians writing in those years, for example,
had come to question both the elitism and eurocentrism of the
would-be democratic enlighteners – their teachers – and sought to
move the profession toward a new "people's history." *Minshūshi*,
while hardly a uniform approach, in fact embodied a triple reaction
against the elitism of the early postwar modernists such as
Maruyama and Ōtsuka, formulaic Marxism, and the triumphalist
version of modernization that emerged in the wake of the 1964
Olympics and Meiji Centenary celebrations of 1968. Also salient was
the sense that, with the ever deeper American involvement in Vietnam, and emerging signs of defeat, the modernization "paradigm"
had crashed and burned. Americans were now learning what Japanese of the Co-Prosperity Sphere generation already knew.[123]

Positively put, "people's history" was a manifestation, in part
romantic, of an intellectual quest for community. It attempted to
discover in the lifeways and "conventional morality" of the folk the

123 The strong desire to lessen Japan's implication in the Vietnam War certainly fed the
movement for the reversion of Okinawa to Japanese control. In a less than healthy sense,
however, the debacle in Vietnam also threw the onus of imperialism onto the United
States, relieving Japanese across the ideological spectrum of feelings of historical guilt
inherited from an earlier time. Nakajima (1968, p. 202) bluntly reminds his readers that
in China, Japan had perpetrated "the greatest slaughter in modern history."

roots of an indigenous democracy (or more broadly a decent society) in pre- and post-Restoration Japan. This quest led a number of major practitioners, such as Irokawa Daikichi, Kano Masanao, Yasumaru Yoshio, and Haga Noboru, to "unearth" a vast and rich body of historical material. Significantly – in another example of "return" – it also led to a reconnection with the work of prewar ethnographers, especially Yanagita Kunio. This was a methodological choice, in the sense that revolution generated by class struggle was no longer operative as a frame for historical interpretation. But it was more than that. Particularly in Irokawa's case, *minshūshi* was a passionate neonativism meant to redeem the past, and it was the engine of a "left-populist" campaign to reclaim for rural people the legacy of the Freedom and Popular Rights Movement as one belonging to a "Japan that might have been."[124]

The historiographical quest for community had clear literary and philosophical counterparts. Ōe Kenzaburō's *Dōjidai gēmu* (1979), has its archetypal setting in "Village–Nation–Microcosm," a "small village in a forest which fundamentally opposed the nation as a state"; it is based on Ōe's own "experience of village life in the mountains of rural Shikoku." To this, Ōe adds his version of the tragic history of Okinawa as a place that had refused both imperial Japanese and American hegemony. *Dōjidai gēmu* culminates in a fifty-day total war waged by the village's people against "the emperor's" forces, by whom they are annihilated.[125] Finally, we turn to the "models" of the folk community developed by Tanigawa Gan, concerning which Sakuta Keiichi has written a penetrating essay. For Tanigawa, as for Ōe, the "community" in modern Japan was radically precarious. Historically, the mode in which a community articulated with the nation and state reflected the variation between the economically advanced "Western Japan" type of village, which was characterized by multiple, pluralistic small communities, as opposed to a backward "Eastern" variety in which village social organization was "limited to unilinear subordination." Insofar as the Western type was associated with industrialization, it came to dominate Japanese society generally, reflecting as it did the de facto

124 See Kano Masanao, "The Changing Concept of Modernization: From a Historian's Viewpoint," *Japan Quarterly* 32, no. 1 (1976): 28–35; Irokawa Daikichi, *The Culture of the Meiji Period* (Princeton University Press, 1985); and Carol Gluck, "The People in History: Recent Trends in Japanese Historiography," *Journal of Asian Studies* 38, no. 1 (1978): 25–50.

125 See Ōe Kenzaburō, "From the Ranks of Postwar Literature" (unpublished conference paper, 1983), pp. 8–10.

pluralism of Japan's elites themselves. For Tanigawa, both types generated distinctive forms of psychological insecurity: one arising from "dual," or multiple, belonging in the former, and from "semi-belonging" in the latter. Functionally, however, the urge among advanced strata to reduce their insecurity through "purifying" their commitments was complemented by the "totalism of complete commitment" that would give the backward, "semi-belonging " strata relief from fears of complete loss of position. Both represent quests for autonomy that paradoxically yield the opposite, except at the largest collective level – that of the nation. "When these forces," Sakuta concludes, "are faced in the same direction and become mutually reinforcing, the energy they generate is awesome indeed."[126] Though the inflections differ, there seems to be a common understanding among those searching for community that though some "model" society of the village might once have provided, or might yet provide, the basis for an "embedded" personal autonomy, it might as easily replicate the bureaucratic oppressiveness of the "nation," now absorbed by the state itself.

Such visions implicitly raised a practical question. If the "nation" in which the community is physically situated is associated with corporate capital and a homogenizing culture industry, how can it serve as the springboard for personal autonomy? For Ōe and perhaps Tanigawa (who was writing on this theme as early as 1961), localism not only had to be critical; it had to be "microcosmic," as those individuals who made the *choice* for community simultaneously reached out beyond the nation for the world. That is, they did not act as "representatives" of an entity called "Japan" but did so rather as members of an imaginative community with a cultural identity that was only in part that of "Japan." If in some way this stance resembles that of a "world-writer" such as Tolstoy, in other ways it seems deeply tied, albeit resistant to, the highly organized world of Japanese capital, including its "internationalized" projection. Apart from peripheries like Okinawa, where local administrations regularly challenge central policies, the stance of political resistance in the age of culture comes to depend increasingly on personal symbolic practice.

Since the 1970s, and accelerating into the 1980s, industrial societies have experienced an accumulation of "post"-phenomena. *Industry,*

---

126 See Sakuta, "The Controversy over Community and Autonomy," pp. 242–6.

Europe, Marxism, communism, revolution, ideology, humanism, subjectivity – all these terms have seen "post" prefixed to them. The clumsy locution "post-postwar" reminds us that the shift to "post" is not a tidy one but also that "postwar" itself was the original condition – the temporal and institutional frame – for the emergence of all subsequent "post"-phenomena. If postwar made possible the postmodern, then the postmodern in turn enabled the "post-postwar."

Revealing instances of "post-postwar" thought come from the area of political economy. Tamanoi Yoshirō (1918–85) was an economist who began his career as a student of Uno Kōzō, was influenced by Karl Polanyi, and then set off on an intellectual journey that involved him in a broad collaborative critique of technological civilization.[127] This work in turn led Tamanoi toward a synthesis of "economic" and "ecological" perspectives and to close ties to Ivan Illich and the radical critique of developmentalism; Illich speaks of Tamanoi as his mentor. Illich and Tamanoi shared a concern with the proper mode of use for technologies: a matter of scale of deployment, and of the level and kind of political controls exercised over them – a matter, in sum, of things "being the right size."[128] In *Economy and Ecology* (*Ekonomī to ekorojī*, 1986), which collects many of his last articles, it is possible to trace Tamanoi's eclectic path. Seeking to develop his notion of "economy in the broad sense" – one that could bring together conceptions of economy both prior to and after the "commoditization of labor power" – Tamanoi had found a key in Polanyi's analysis of socially embedded markets and the consequences of their subsequent "alienation," following him into the examination of the family and other nonmarket systems of labor. At the same time, Tamanoi's concern for regional economics, springing from his deepening connections to Okinawa, led him to address issues of development and ultimately of the "life-world," including

127 See Tamanoi Yoshirō, ed., *Bummei toshite no keizai* (Ushio Shuppansha, 1973). Interestingly, Tamanoi was introduced to Polanyi's work by his student Kumon Shunpei, who has been among the most energetic propagators of the notion that Japan's "household" (*ie*) system has created in Japan a distinct form – and model – of industrial organization. See Nakamura Hisashi, "Nihon ni okeru seimeikei no keizaigaku: Tamanoi Yoshirō no shigoto ni manabu," in Imamura Hitoshi, ed., *Kakutō suru gendai shisō: Toransumodan e no kokoromi* (Kōdansha Gendai Shinsho, ed., 1991), pp. 119–33, esp. p. 124.

128 Neither for Illich nor for Tamanoi did the critique of developmentalism imply any kind of Luddism. As early as 1970, Illich was advocating a rudimentary form of computer networking in what he called a "deschooled" society. See Illich, *Deschooling Society* (Penguin ed., 1970), pp. 26–7; David Cayley, *Ivan Illich in Conversation* (Anansi Press, 1992); and Illich, "Disvalue," in ibid., *In the Mirror of the Past* (Marion Boyars, 1992).

the degradation, or entropy, of the physical matrix of the economy itself.

Tamanoi remained, as Uno had, an academic economist but also one who felt himself facing problems outside the scope of his early training. In confronting these problems, Tamanoi burst not only the confines of Uno School Marxism but also of national culture. In view of some of the blatantly ideological writing – by Umehara Takeshi, for example – claiming that the allegedly "holistic" and nondualistic attitude of Japanese toward the relation between human communities and the natural world promises to overcome the fatal divisions produced by the technological civilization of the West, Tamanoi's work is a salutary reminder that the path beyond Marxism, or beyond narrow economic science, did not have to end in the nation and its unitary culture.

More commonly, however, it has done just that. Two examples, one from the Uno School, and another tangentially related to it, will provide our final cases. Among the direct line of Uno-school adherents, Baba Hiroji (b. 1933) has shown the strongest inclination to "change the paradigm," as he has put it, of Marxian economics itself, away from orthodox assumptions of dearth and exploitation to those of "excess affluence" and increasing purification of the circulation process in the current stage of finance capital: Baba has gathered his writings on this theme in his recent *Mass Enrichment and Finance Capital* (*Fuyūka to kin'yū shihon*, 1986). For Baba, the impetus to make this shift – and here is the crux of the issue – comes from the sustained high growth rates achieved by the "Japanese system" itself. Focusing on the *habitus* of Japanese firms and their internal labor markets, Baba observes that under Japan's regime of "companyism" (*kaishashugi*), "an enormous pool of workers' services is available free of charge" to firms, so much so that he has come to doubt "that Japanese workers are really selling just their labor power as a commodity." "Frankly," he says, "I also doubt whether Japanese capitalism really merits the name of capitalism. My impression is that the Japanese system is capitalist at the macroscopic level but socialist at the microscopic level."[129] Thus Baba has introduced a degree of sociocultural specificity into Uno-school analyses. Although he repeatedly cautions against seeing the "Japanese system" as a model for other advanced societies, and indeed raises questions about its long-term fairness and sustainability, Baba's approach has

129 Baba Hiroji, "Changing the Paradigm of Japanese Marx Economics," *Annals of the Institute of Social Science*, no. 27 (1985): 26–53; quotes from pp. 40, 43.

opened his work, and retroactively the Uno school itself, to charges by some elements of the left that it has betrayed both the scientific and political ideals of Marxism. At the very least, the "back door" had been opened for the reentry of "culture" into economic science.[130]

If Baba had opened the "back door," the main gate was thrown open by a new generation of semiofficial analysts and publicists seeking to treat the "Japanese system" in terms of an immanent "science of Japanese culture": in effect, the mirror image of the scientific reformism of Arisawa Hiromi and Tsuru Shigeto. Among the many such texts, "*Ie*" Society as a Civilization (*Bunmei toshite no ie shakai*, 1979) is probably the most famous, owing to the academic credentials of its authors (Murakami Yasusuke, along with Kumon Shunpei and Satō Seizaburō) as well as the enormous, trans-civilizational scope of its historical claims. Its essential argument states that the household organization of eastern Japan's warrior society, in a consciously manipulated form, had enabled a Japanese industrialization marked by a collectivist, rather than individualist, instrumental rationality. The work of Murakami and his collaborators in effect appropriated the optimistic social science theories of convergence only to trump them. Japan emerges as a model *political economy*, that is, not merely as a type of economy alone, offering technical features for piecemeal adoption. This new norm of sociocultural achievement, moreover, was meant not for still developing societies but for the most advanced – increasingly those of Asia – as they moved beyond older modes of industrialism to more "relationally" organized, information-based production. For Murakami, as with Talcott Parsons, values were ultimately what gave this political economy its orientation and motivational force; Murakami's particular emphasis lay on the "post-class" character of Japan as a society occupied by a vast "middle mass."[131] Thus from within the industrialized capitalist world, Japan is held to have challenged the hegemony of the Atlantic Rim in

130 See John Lie, "Reactionary Marxism: The End of Ideology in Japan?" *Monthly Review* 38 (April 1987): 45–51, and Baba's reply, "Revolution and Counterrevolution in Marxian Economics," in *Monthly Review* 40 (June 1989): 52–8, and a longer version, "*Fuyūka to kin'yū shihon o megutte*," in *Shakai kagaku kenkyū* 40, no. 3 (September 1988): 51–62.

131 See Murakami, Kumon, and Satō, *Bummei toshite no ie shakai* (Chūō Kōronsha, 1979), and the shorter English version, Murakami, "Ie Society as a Pattern of Civilization," in *Journal of Japanese Studies* (Summer 1984): 279–363. Murakami, "The Japanese Model of Political Economy," in Yamamura and Yasuba, eds., *The Political Economy of Japan* (Stanford University Press, 1987); Murakami, *Shin chūkan taishū no jidai* (Chūō Kōronsha, 1984).

defining the constitution of so-called civil society, in particular contesting the centrality of the market as the master paradigm for social relations generally. The argument depends on treating Japan as a single historical actor. But it is by no means clear that this is a conceptual strength.

At first sight, Murakami's work would seem a fitting culmination to the process by which science and culture finally merge in Japanese public discourse. As such, it shared a moment with Ezra Vogel's anxiety-driven *Japan as Number One* (1979), and Chalmers Johnson's highly influential *MITI and the Japanese Miracle* (1981). These works, while considerably less grandiose than Murakami's and differing from each other in style and emphasis, clearly belong to the moment of merged perspectives. This is doubly ironic: Despite Johnson's claim to be resisting cultural explanations in favor of an institutional approach, the antecedents of MITI are products of the very period in which "culture" enjoyed hegemony over political economic thought; moreover, Murakami's work itself reads like a paean to "what was," as instrumental values, it is argued, give way to those of consumption. In other words, the owl of Minerva has flown in Japan as well.

But where? The answer, it would seem, is *urbi et orbi* – to the city and to the world. In place of the manipulated *rural* values that Murakami saw as having been coopted into the effective service of modern industrial production, Japanese postmodernism has been marked by the emphasis on ostensible continuity in traditional *urban* patterns of consumption, along with a rather naïve celebration of the unitive potential of information technology. In the wake of the Cold War and the collapse of the bubble economy, such celebration has seemed increasingly forced. But it reflects, inevitably, the overwhelmingly urban orientation of contemporary Japanese life and thought. Meanwhile, official collectivism à la Murakami and postmodern affirmations of consumption are both being challenged by harder-edged perspectives, critical of labor stratification, the "hollowing out" of industry, and the creation of a Japanese-dominated periphery in Asia. A transformation of Japanese academia – of the intelligentsia – may also occur as women and national minorities (Koreans especially, and those of Chinese origin) make their way, slowly and painfully, into positions of real authority in the scholarly world. The result may be a "difference model" of Japanese society, along with a reconceptualization of Japan's relation to the "world system," that does not yet exist. Indeed, a pluralization of views is already under way in Japan, but such diversity does not seem to be regarded as valuable in and of itself. Particularly in the area of political thought, the end of Japan's "postwar" – in the sense discussed earlier – has left a noticeable vacuum, with little in the way of contributions to democratic theory having emerged for decades. Thus the hegemony of "culture," which began by default and is now rather fissured, seems likely to continue. That would be unfortunate, since it would obscure the significance of the developments with which postwar Japanese thought has been concerned. Ideological deformations notwithstanding, Japan's postwar history provides overwhelming evidence that visions of alternative modes of industrial and postindustrial society, of modernity and postmodernity, can become problematic reality.

BIBLIOGRAPHY

Abe Isoo. "Meiji sanjūnen no shakai minshutō." *Nihon shakai undō* in *Shakai Kagaku* (February 1928).

Abe Isoo. "Shakaishugi shōshi." In Kishimoto Eitarō, ed. *Shakaishugi shiron*. Tokyo: Aoki shoten, 1955.

Abe Isoo. *Meiji Shakaishugiron*. Tokyo: Wabei kyokai, 1907.

Abe Isoo. *Shakaishugiron*. Tokyo: Heiminsha, 1903.

Adachi Gan. *Kokumin undō no saishuppatsu*. Tokyo: Kasumigaseki shobō, 1940.

Akita, George. *The Foundations of Constitutional Government in Modern Japan, 1868–1900*. Cambridge, Mass.: Harvard University Press, 1967.

Akuto Hiroshi, Tominaga Ken'ichi, and Sobue Takao, eds. *Hendōki no Nihon shakai*. Tokyo: Nihon hōsō kyōkai, 1972.

Ara Masato. "Dai ni no seishun" (1946) and "Minshū to wa tare ka" (1946). Repr. in *Ara Masato chosakushū*, vol. 1. Tokyo: San'ichi Shobō, 1983.

Aruhata Kanson "Kindai shisō to Shinshakai." *Shisō* 460 (October 1962): 115–25.

Arai Naoyuki. "Senryō seisaku to jānarizumu." In *Kyōdō kenkyū: Nihon senryō*, ed. Shisō no kagaku kenkyūkai. Tokyo: Tokuma shoten, 1972.

Arase Yutaka. "Sengo shisō to sono tenkai." In Ienaga Saburō et al., ed. *Kindai Nihon shisōshi kōza*, vol. 1. Tokyo: Chikuma Shobō, 1959.

Arisawa Hiromi. "Nihon shihonshugi no unmei." *Hyōron* (February 1950).

Arisawa Hiromi. *Gakumon to shisō to ningen to – wasurenu hitobito* (1957). Tokyo: Tokyo Daigaku Shuppankai, 1989.

Arisawa Hiromi. *Keizai seisaku nōto*. Tokyo: Gakufū Shoin, 1949.

Asahi shinbun Yamagata shikyoku, ed. *Kikigaki: Aru kenpei no kiroku*. Tokyo: Asahi shinbunsha, 1991.

Baba Hiroji. "Changing the Paradigm of Japanese Marx Economics." *Annals of the Institute of Social Science*, no. 27 (1985): 26–53.

Baba Hiroji. *Fuyūka to kin'yū shihon*. Kyōto: Mineruva Shobō, 1986.

Baba Hiroji. "*Fuyūka to kin'yū shihon* o megutte." *Shakai kagaku kenkyū* 40, no. 3 (September 1988): 51–62.

Baba Hiroji. "Revolution and Counterrevolution in Marxian Economics." *Monthly Review* 40 (June 1989): 52–8.

Baba Tatsui. "In a Japanese Cage." In Meiji bunka kenkyūkai, ed. *Meiji bunka zenshū: Jiyū minken hen (zoku) bessatsu.* Tokyo: Nihon Hyōronsha, 1968.

Barshay, Andrew E. *State and Intellectual in Imperial Japan: The Public Man in Crisis.* Berkeley and Los Angeles: University of California Press, 1989.

Barshay, Andrew E. "Imagining Democracy in Postwar Japan: Reflections on Maruyama Masao and Modernism." *Journal of Japanese Studies* 18, no. 2 (Summer 1992): 365–406.

Barshay, Andrew E. "Toward a History of the Social Sciences in Japan." *Positions: East Asia Cultures Critique* 4, no. 2 (Fall 1996): 1–35.

Beasley, W. G. *Select Documents on Japanese Foreign Policy 1853–1868.* London: Oxford University Press, 1955.

Beckmann, George M. *The Making of the Meiji Constitution: The Oligarchs and the Constitutional Development of Japan, 1868–1891.* Lawrence: University of Kansas Press, 1957.

Beckmann, George M., and Okubo, Genji. *The Japanese Communist Party, 1922–1945.* Stanford, Calif.: Stanford University Press, 1969.

Berger, Gordon Mark. *Parties Out of Power in Japan, 1931–1941.* Princeton, N.J.: Princeton University Press, 1977.

Blacker, Carmen. *The Japanese Enlightenment: A Study of the Writings of Fukuzawa Yukichi.* Cambridge, England: Cambridge University Press, 1964.

Bowen, Roger W. *Rebellion and Democracy in Meiji Japan.* Berkeley and Los Angeles: University of California Press, 1980.

Braisted, William R. *Meiroku zasshi: Journal of the Japanese Enlightenment.* Cambridge, Mass.: Harvard University Press, 1976.

Chubachi, Masayoshi, and Taira, Koji. "Poverty in Modern Japan: Perceptions and Realities." In Hugh T. Patrick, ed. *Japanese Industrialization and Its Social Consequences.* Berkeley and Los Angeles: University of California Press, 1976.

Craig, Albert M. "Fukuzawa Yukichi: The Philosophical Foundations of Meiji Nationalism." In Robert E. Ward, ed. *Political Development in Modern Japan.* Princeton, N.J.: Princeton University Press, 1968.

Crump, John. *The Origins of Socialist Thought in Japan.* New York: St. Martin's Press, 1983.

Davis, Sandra. *Intellectual Change and Political Development in Early Modern Japan.* London: Associated University Presses, 1980.

Dōshisha daigaku jinbunkagaku kenkyūjō, ed. *Rikugō zasshi* (microfilm). Tokyo: Nihon shiryō kankōkai, 1964.

Dore, Ronald P. "The Tokyo Institute for the Science of Thought: A Survey Report." *Far Eastern Quarterly,* no. 13 (November 1953): 23–36.

Dore, Ronald P. *Education in Tokugawa Japan.* Berkeley and Los Angeles: University of California Press, 1965.

Dore, Ronald P. *Shinohata: Portrait of a Japanese Village.* New York: Pantheon, 1978.

Dower, John W. *Empire and Aftermath: Yoshida Shigeru and the Japanese Experience, 1878–1954.* Cambridge, Mass.: Harvard University Press, 1979.

Duus Masayo. *Haisha no okurimono.* Tokyo: Kōdansha, 1995.

Duus, Peter. "Liberal Intellectuals and Social Conflict in Taisho Japan." In Tetsuo Najita and Victor Koschmann, eds. *Conflict in Modern Japanese History.* Princeton, N.J.: Princeton University Press, 1982.

Duus, Peter. "Whig History, Japanese Style: The Min'yūsha Historians and the Meiji Restoration." *Journal of Asian Studies* 33 (May 1974): 415–36.

Duus, Peter. "Yoshino Sakuzō: The Christian as Political Critic." *Journal of Japanese Studies* 4 (Spring 1978): 301–26.

Duus, Peter. *Party Rivalry and Political Change in Taishō Japan.* Cambridge, Mass.: Harvard University Press, 1968.

Eguchi Keiichi. "Manshū jihen to daishinbun." *Shisō* 583 (January 1973): 98–113.

Eguchi Keiichi. "Santō shuppei, 'Manshū jihen' o megutte." In Inoue Kiyoshi and Watanabe Tōru, eds. *Taishō-ki no kyūshinteki jiyūshugi.* Tokyo: Tōyō keizai shinpōsha, 1972.

Eguchi Keiichi. *Shinpan: Jūgonen sensō shōshi.* Tokyo: Aoki shoten, 1991.

Eguchi Keiichi. *Shōwa no rekishi 4: Jūgonen sensō no kaimaku.* Tokyo: Shōgakukan, 1988.

Eguchi Keiichi. *Taikei Nihon no rekishi 14: Futatsu no taisen.* Tokyo: Shōgakukan 1993.

Eizawa Kōji. *"Daitō-A hyōeiken" no shisō.* Tokyo: Kōdansha, 1995.

Eizawa Kōji. *Taishō demokurashii-ki no kenryoku no shiso.* Tokyo: Kenbun shuppan, 1992.

Eizawa Kōji. *Taishō demokurashii-ki no seiji shisō.* Tokyo: Kenbun shuppan, 1981.

Etō Jun. *Amerika to watakushi.* In *Etō Jun chosakushu,* vol. 4. Tokyo: Kōdansha, 1967.

Etō Jun. *Hizuke no aru bunshō.* Tokyo: Chikuma shobō, 1960.

Etō Shinkichi, and Marius B. Jansen, trans. *My Thirty-three Years' Dream: The Autobiography of Miyazaki Tōten.* Princeton, N.J.: Princeton University Press, 1982.

Fletcher, William Miles, III. *The Search for a New Order: Intellectuals and Fascism in Prewar Japan.* Chapel Hill: University of North Carolina Press, 1983.

Fogel, Joshua A. *Politics and Sinology: The Case of Naitō Kōnan (1866–1934).* Cambridge, Mass.: Harvard University Press, 1984.

French, Calvin L. *Shiba Kōkan: Artist, Innovator, and Pioneer in the Westernization of Japan.* New York: Weatherhill, 1974.

Fujita Shōzō. *Tennōsei kokka no shihai genri.* Tokyo: Miraisha, 1966.

Fujiwara Akira, Awaya Kentarō, and Yoshida Yutaka, eds. *Shōwa 20-nen, 1945-nen.* Tokyo: Shōgakukan, 1995.

Fujiwara Akira, Imai Seiichi, and Tōyama Shigeki. *Shōwa shi,* rev. ed. Tokyo: Iwanami shoten, 1959.

Fujiwara Akira. *Taiheiyō sensō ron.* Tokyo: Aoki shoten, 1982.

Fujiwara Akira. *Taikei Nihon no rekishi 15: Sekai no naka no Nihon.* Tokyo: Shōgakukan, 1993.

Fukawa Kiyoshi. "Nihonjin no hi-senryō kan." In Shisō no kagaku kenkyūkai, eds. *Kyōdō kenkyū: Nihon senryō.* Tokyo: Tokuma shoten, 1972.

Fukumoto Kazuo. *Kakumei wa tanoshikarazu ya.* Tokyo: Kyōiku shorin, 1950.

Fukushima Jūrō. "Senryōka ni okeru ken'etsu seisaku to sono jittai." In Nakamura Takafusa, ed. *Senryōki Nihon on keizai to seiji.* Tokyo: Tōkyō daigaku shuppankai, 1979.

Fukushima Masao, Kawashima Takeyoshi, Tsuji Kiyoaki, and Ukai Nobushige, eds. *Kōza: Nihon kindaihō hattatsu shi – shihonshugi to hō no hatten,* vol. 6. Tokyo: Keisō shobō, 1959.

Fukuzawa Yukichi. *An Encouragement of Learning,* trans. D. Dilworth and U. Hirano. Tokyo: Sophia University Press, 1969.

Fukuzawa Yukichi. *An Outline of a Theory of Civilization,* trans. David A. Dilworth and G. Cameron Hurst. Tokyo: Sophia University Press, 1973.

Fukuzawa Yukichi. *Fukuzawa Yukichi on Education: Selected Works,* trans. E. Kiyooka. Tokyo: University of Tokyo Press, 1985.

Fukuzawa Yukichi. *Fukuzawa Yukichi on Women: Selected Works,* trans. E. Kiyooka. Tokyo: University of Tokyo Press, 1988.

Funayama Shin'ichi. *Meiji tetsugakushi.* Kyoto: Minerva shobō, 1959.

Furuta Hikaru. *Kawakami Hajime.* Tokyo: Tōkyō daigaku shuppanbu, 1959.

Gao Bai. "Arisawa Hiromi and His Theory for a Managed Economy." *Journal of Japanese Studies* 20, no. 1 (Winter 1994): 115–53.

Gayn, Mark. *Japan Diary.* Tokyo: Tuttle, 1981.

Gendai shakai to kōdō kagaku. Special issue of *Shisō,* no. 509 (November 1966).

Gluck, Carol. "The 'Long Postwar': Japan and Germany in Comparison and Contrast." In Ernestine Schlant and Thomas Rimer, eds. *Legacies and Ambiguities: Postwar Fiction and Culture in West Germany and Japan.* Washington, D.C.: Woodrow Wilson Center Press, 1991.

Gluck, Carol. "The Past in the Present." In Andrew Gordon, ed. *Postwar Japan as History.* Berkeley and Los Angeles: University of California Press, 1993.

Gluck, Carol. "The People in History: Recent Trends in Japanese Historiography." *Journal of Asian Studies* 38, no. 1 (November 1978): 25–50.

Gluck, Carol. *Japan's Modern Myths: Ideology in the Late Meiji Period*. Princeton: Princeton University Press, 1985.

Gondō Seikei. "Jichi minsei ri." In Hashikawa Bunzō, ed. *Gendai Nihon shisō taikei*, vol. 31: *Chōkokkashugi*, 31: Tokyo: Chikuma shobō, 1964.

Goodman, Grant, "Dutch Studies in Japan Re-examined." In Josef Kreiner, ed. *Deutschland-Japan: Historische Kontakte*. Bonn: Grundmann, 1984.

Gordon, Andrew, ed. *Postwar Japan as History*. Berkeley and Los Angeles: University of California Press, 1993.

Gotō Yasushi, ed. *Tennōsei to minshū*. Tokyo: Tōkyō daigaku shuppankai, 1976.

Gotō Yasushi. *Jiyū minken: Meiji no kakumei to hankakumei*. Tokyo: Chūō kōronsha, 1972.

Government Section, Supreme Commander for the Allied Powers. *Political Reorientation of Japan, September 1945 to September 1948*, 2 vols., reprint ed. Grosse Pointe, Mich.: Scholarly Press, 1968.

Grappard, Alan. "Japan's Neglected Cultural Revolution: The Separation of Shinto and Buddhist Deities in Meiji (*Shinbutsu bunri*) and a Case Study: Tonomine." *History of Religions* 23 (February 1984): 240–65.

Haga Tōru, ed. *Nihon no meicho: Sugita Gempaku, Hiraga Gennai, Shiba Kōkan*. Tokyo: Chūō kōronsha, 1971.

Haga Tōru. *Taikun no shisetsu*. Tokyo: Chūōkōronsha, 1968.

Hagiwara Sakutarō. *Nihon e no kaiki*. Tokyo: Hakusuisha, 1938.

Hall, Ivan Parker. *Mori Arinori*. Cambridge, Mass.: Harvard University Press, 1973.

Hall, John W. "Changing Conceptions of the Modernization of Japan." In Marius B. Jansen, ed. *Changing Japanese Attitudes Toward Modernization*. Princeton, N.J.: Princeton University Press, 1965.

Hall, John W. "Review of *Nihon shakai no shiteki kyumei*." *Far Eastern Quarterly*, vol. 11 (November 1951): 97–104.

Halliday, Jon. *A Political History of Japanese Capitalism*. New York: Monthly Review Press, 1978.

Hane, Mikiso. *Peasants, Rebels, and Outcastes: The Underside of Modern Japan*. New York: Pantheon, 1982.

Hanzawa Hiroshi. *Ajia e no yume*, vol. 6 of *Meiji no gunzō*. Tokyo: San'ichi shobō, 1970.

Hardacre, Helen. "Creating State Shintō: The Great Promulgation Campaign and the New Religions." *Journal of Japanese Studies* 12 (Winter 1986): 29–63.

Hardy, A. S. *Life and Letters of Joseph Hardy Neesima*. Boston: Houghton Mifflin, 1892.

Harootunian, H. D. "Ideology as Conflict." In Tetsuo Najita and J. Victor Koschmann, eds. *Conflict in Modern Japanese History*. Princeton, N.J.: Princeton University Press, 1982.

Harootunian, H. D. *Toward Restoration*. Berkeley and Los Angeles: University of California Press, 1970.

Hashikawa Bunzō. *Kindai Nihon seiji shisō no shosō*. Tokyo: Miraisha, 1968.

Hata Ikuhiko. "Onnenshikan kara no dakkyaku." *Keizai ōrai* (February 1979).

Hatada Takashi. "Nihonjin no Chōsenkan." In *Nihon to Chōsen*, vol. 3 of *Ajia-Afurika Kōza*. Tokyo: Keisō shobō, 1965.

Havens, Thomas R. H. *Farm and Nation in Modern Japan*. Princeton, N.J.: Princeton University Press, 1974.

Havens, Thomas R. H. *Nishi Amane and Modern Japanese Thought*. Princeton, N.J.: Princeton University Press, 1970.

Havens, Thomas R. H. *Valley of Darkness: The Japanese People and World War Two*. New York: Norton, 1978.

Hayashi Chikio. "Nihonjin no ishiki wa seitōshijibetsu ni dō chigau ka." In Nihonjin kenkyūkai, ed. *Nihonjin kenkyū* No. 2 (*Tokushū: Shijiseitōbetsu nihonjin shūdan*). Tokyo: Shiseidō, 1975.

Hayashi Chikio. "Sengo no seiji ishiki." *Jiyū* (January 1964): 57–65.

Hayashi Fusao. *Dai Tō-A sensō kōteiron*. Tokyo: Chūōkōronsha, 1964.

Hayashi Fusao. *Dai Tōa sensō kōteiron*, 2 vols. Tokyo: Banchō shobō, 1964, 1966.

Hayashi Kentarō. "Gendai chishikijin no ryōshiki: Maruyama Masao shi e no hi-hihanteki hihan," *Sekai*, no. 58 (October 1950): 97–103.

Hayashi Shigeru et al., eds. *Heimin shinbun ronsetsushū*. Tokyo: Iwanami shoten, 1961.

Hayashi Shigeru, *Taiheiyō sensō. Nihon no rekishi*, vol. 25. Tokyo: Chūō kōronsha, 1967.

Hearn, Lafcadio. *Out of the East and Kokoro*, vol. 7 of *The Writings of Lafcadio Hearn*. New York: Houghton Mifflin, 1922.

Hein, Laura. "In Search of Peace and Democracy: Postwar Japanese Economic Thought in Political Context." *Journal of Asian Studies* 53, no. 3 (August 1994): 752–78.

Henderson, Dan F., ed. *The Constitution of Japan: Its First Twenty Years, 1947–67*. Seattle: University of Washington Press, 1968.

Hidaka Rokurō, ed. *Sengo shisō no shuppatsu*. Tokyo: Chikuma shobō, 1968.

Hidaka Rokurō. *Sengoshi o kangaeru*. Tokyo: Iwanami shoten, 1980.

Higashikuni Naruhiko. "Nihon saiken no shishin – Higashikuni shushō kisha kaiken" (August 30, 1945). Transcribed in Hidaka Rokurō, ed. *Sengo shisō no shuppatsu*. Tokyo: Chikuma shobō, 1968.

Higashikuni Naruhiko. *Ichi kōzoku no sensō nikki*. Tokyo: Nihon shūhōsha, 1959.

Hirakawa Sukehiro. "Furankurin to Meiji Kōgō." In Hirakawa Sukehiro. *Higashi no tachibana, nishi no orenji*. Tokyo: Bungei shunjūsha, 1981.

Hirakawa Sukehiro. "Nihon kaiki no kiseki – uzumoreta shisōka, Amenomori Nobushige." *Shinchō* (April 1986): 6–106.

Hirano Yoshitarō, ed. *Kōtoku Shūsui senshū*, 3 vols. Tokyo: Sekai hyōronsha, 1948–50.

Hirata Kiyoaki. "La société civile japonaise contemporaine." In *Le marxisme au Japon*, special issue of *Actuel Marx*, no. 2 (1987): 65–71.

Hirata Kiyoaki. "Shakaishugi to shimin shakai" (1968). Repr. in *"Sekai" shuyō ronbunsen, 1946–1995*. Tokyo: Iwanami shoten, 1995.

Hiromatsu Wataru. *"Kindai no chōkoku" ron: Shōwa shisōshi e no ichi dansō*. Tokyo: Asahi shuppansha, 1980.

Hiromatsu Wataru. "La philosophie de Marx 'pour nous.'" In *Le Marxisme au Japon*, special issue of *Actuel Marx*, no. 2 (1987): 72–84.

Hiromatsu Wataru. "Tōhoku Ajia ga rekishi no shuyaku ni; Ōbei chūshin no sekaikan wa hōkai e." *Asahi shinbun*, March 16, 1994.

Hiromatsu Wataru. *Seitai shikan to yuibutsu shikan*. Tokyo: Kōdansha, 1991.

Hoare, J. E. "The Japanese Treaty Ports, 1868–1899: A Study of the Foreign Settlements." Ph.D. diss., University of London, 1971.

Honda Itsuo. *Kokumin, jiyū, kensei: Kuga Katsunan no seiji shisō*. Tokyo: Bokutakusha, 1994.

Hosoi Wakizō. *Jokō aishi*. Tokyo: Kaizōsha, 1925.

Hoston, Germaine A. *Marxism and the Crisis of Development in Prewar Japan*. Princeton, N.J.: Princeton University Press, 1986.

Howes, John F. "Japanese Christians and American Missionaries." In Marius B. Jansen, ed. *Changing Japanese Attitudes Toward Modernization*. Princeton, N.J.: Princeton University Press, 1965.

Howes, John F. "Uchimura Kanzō: Japanese Prophet." In Dankwart A. Rustow, ed. *Philosophers and Kings: Studies in Leadership*. New York: Braziller, 1970.

Hozumi Yatsuka. "Mimpō idete, chūkō horobu." *Hōgaku shimpo* 5 (August 1891).

Hozumi Yatsuka. *Kenpō teiyō*. Tokyo: Yūhikaku, 1935.

Huber, Thomas M. *The Revolutionary Origins of Modern Japan*. Stanford, Calif.: Stanford University Press, 1981.

Huffman, James L. *Fukuchi Gen'ichirō*. Honolulu: University of Hawaii Press, 1979.

Hunt, Frazier. *The Untold Story of Douglas MacArthur*. New York: Devin-Adair, 1954.

Ide Takesaburō, ed. *Anpo tōsō*. Tokyo: San'ichi shobō, 1960.

Ienaga Saburō, ed. *Ueki Emori senshū*. Tokyo: Iwanami shoten, 1974.

Ienaga Saburō. "Nihon ni okeru kyōwashugi no dentō." In Kuno Osamu and Kamishima Jirō, eds. *Tennōsei ronshū*. Tokyo: San'ichi shobō, 1974.

Ienaga Saburō. *Kakumei shisō no senkusha*. Tokyo: Iwanami shoten, 1955.

Ienaga Saburō. *Kenryokuaku to no tatakai*. Tokyo: Kōbundō, 1964.

Ienaga Saburō. *Kindai seishin to sono genkai*. Tokyo: Kadokawa shoten, 1950.

Ienaga Saburō. *Rekishi no naka no kenpō, jō*. Tokyo: Tokyo daigaku shuppankai, 1977.

Ienaga Saburō. *Sensō sekinin*. Tokyo: Iwanami shoten, 1985.

Ienaga Saburō. *Taiheiyō sensō*. Tokyo: Iwanami shoten, 1968.

Ienaga Saburō. *Ueki Emori kenkyū*. Tokyo: Iwanami shoten, 1960.

Igarashi Akio. *Meiji ishin no shisō*. Tokyo: Seori shobō, 1996.

Ike Nobutaka. *Japan's Decision for War*. Stanford, Calif.: Stanford University Press, 1967.

Ike Nobutaka. *The Beginnings of Political Democracy in Japan*. Baltimore: Johns Hopkins University Press, 1950.

Imai Juichirō and Kawaguchi Shigeo, comp. *Maruyama Masao chosaku nōto*, exp. ed. Tokyo: Gendai no rironsha, 1987.

Inoue Kiyoshi. "Nihon teikokushugi hihanron." In Inoue Kiyoshi and Watanabe Tōru, eds. *Taishō-ki no kyūshinteki jiyūshugi*. Tokyo: Tōyō keizai shinpōsha, 1972.

Inoue Kiyoshi. *Nihon no rekishi 20: Meiji ishin*. Tokyo: Chūōkōronsha, 1966.

Inoue Kōji. *Chichibu jiken*. Tokyo: Chūōkōronsha, 1968.

Inumaru Giichi. *Kōza: Gendai no ideorogii II, Nihon no marukusushugi, sono 2*, Tokyo: San'ichi shobō, 1961.

Iriye Akira. *Pacific Estrangement: Japanese and American Expansion, 1897–1911*. Cambridge, Mass.: Harvard University Press, 1972.

Irokawa Daikichi, Ei Hideo, and Arai Katsuhiro, eds. *Minshū kenpō no sōzō*. Tokyo: Hyōronsha, 1970.

Irokawa Daikichi. *Jiyū minken*. Tokyo: Iwanami shoten, 1981.

Irokawa Daikichi. *Kindai kokka no shuppatsu*. vol. 25 of *Nihon no rekishi*. Tokyo: Chūōkōronsha, 1966.

Irokawa Daikichi. *The Culture of the Meiji Period*. Princeton, N.J.: Princeton University Press, 1985.

Ishida Takeshi. "Movements to Protect Constitutional Government – A Structural Functional Analysis." In George O. Totten, ed. *Democracy in Prewar Japan: Groundwork or Façade?* Lexington, Mass.: Heath, 1965.

Ishida Takeshi. *Meiji seiji shisōshi kenkyū*. Tokyo: Miraisha, 1954.

Ishida Takeshi. *Nihon no shakai kagaku*. Tokyo: Tokyo daigaku shuppankai, 1984.

Ishii Ryōsuke. *Japanese Legislation in the Meiji Era*. Translated by William J. Chambliss. Tokyo: Pan-Pacific Press, 1958.

Ishikawa Tatsuzo. "Kokoro no naka no sensō." *Chūōkōron* (March 1963): 201–7.

Ishimoda Shō. *Rekishi to minzoku no hakken: Rekishigaku no kadai to hōhō*. Tokyo: Tokyo daigaku shuppankai, 1952.

Ishimoda Shō. *Rekishi to minzoku no hakken: Ningen; teikō; gakufū*. Tokyo: Tokyo daigaku shuppankai, 1953.

Itō Hirobumi. "Some Reminiscences on the Grant of the New Constitution." In S. Ōkuma, ed. *Fifty Years of New Japan*. vol. 1. London: Smith, Elders, 1909.

Itō Hirobumi. "The Constitution of the Empire of Japan." In A. Stead, ed. *Japan by the Japanese*. London: Heinemann, 1904.

Ito Hirobumi. *Commentaries on the Constitution of Empire of Japan*, trans. Miyoji Ito. Tokyo: Chūō daigaku, 1906.

Itoh Makoto. *The Basic Theory of Capitalism: The Forms and Substance of the Capitalist Economy*. Totowa, N.J.: Barnes and Noble, 1988.

Itoh Makoto. *Value and Crisis: Essays on Marxian Economics in Japan*. New York: Monthly Review Press, 1980.

Itoya Toshio. *Kōtoku Shūsui kenkyū*. Tokyo: Aoki shoten, 1967.

Iwasaki Chikatsugu. *Nihon marukusushugi tetsugakushi josetsu*. Tokyo: Miraisha, 1971.

Jansen, Marius B. "Modernization and Foreign Policy in Meiji Japan." In Robert E. Ward, ed. *Political Development in Modern Japan*. Princeton, N.J.: Princeton University Press, 1968.

Jansen, Marius B. "Monarchy and Modernization in Japan." *Journal of Asian Studies* 36 (August 1977): 611–22.

Jansen, Marius B. "Oi Kentarō: Radicalism and Chauvinism." *Far Eastern Quarterly* 11 (May 1952): 305–16.

Jansen, Marius B. "Rangaku and Westernization." *Modern Asian Studies* 18 (October 1984): 541–53.

Jansen, Marius B. *Japan and Its World: Two Centuries of Change*. Princeton, N.J.: Princeton University Press, 1980.

Jansen, Marius B. *The Japanese and Sun Yat-sen*. Cambridge, Mass.: Harvard University Press, 1954.

Kaigo Tokiomi. *Kyōiku chokugo seiritsushi no kenkyū*. Tokyo: Tokyo daigaku shuppankai, 1965.

Kamei Katsuichirō and Takeuchi Yoshimi, eds. *Kindai Nihon shisoshi koza*, vol. 7: *Kindaika to dentō*, 7. Tokyo: Chikuma shobō, 1959.

Kamishima Jirō, ed. *Kenryoku no shisō*, vol. 10 of *Gendai Nihon shisō taikei*. Tokyo: Chikuma shobō, 1965.

Kanda Fuhito. *Shōwa no rekishi 8: Senryō to minshushugi*. Tokyo: Shōgakukan, 1989.

Kano Masanao. "The Changing Concept of Modernization: From a Historian's Viewpoint." *Japan Quarterly* 32, no. 1 (1976): 28–35.

Kano Masanao. "Yonaoshi no shisō to bummei kaika." In Kano Masanao and Takagi Shunsuke, eds. *Ishin henkaku ni okeru zaisonteki shochōryū*. Tokyo: San'ichi shobō, 1972.

Kano Masanao. *Meiji no shisō*. Tokyo: Chikuma shobō, 1964.

Kano Masanao. *Shihonshugi keiseiki no chitsujō ishiki*. Tokyo: Chikuma shobō, 1969.

Kanō Masanao. "Meiji kōki ni okeru kokumin soshikika no katei." *Shikan*, no. 69 (March 1964): 18–46.

Kanō Masanao. *Taishō demokurashii no teiryū.* Tokyo: Nihon hōsō shuppan kyōkai, 1973.

Karasawa Tomitarō. *Kyōkasho no rekishi.* Tokyo: Sōbunsha, 1960.

Kata Kōji. "Gunsei jidai no fūzoku." In Shisō no kagaku kenkyūkai, ed. *Kyōdō kenkyū: Nihon senryō.* Tokyo: Tokuma shoten, 1972.

Katayama Sen. "Waga shakaishugi." In Kishimoto Eitarō, ed. *Katayama Sen, Tazoe Tetsuji shū.* Tokyo: Aoki shoten, 1955.

Katō Shūichi. "Modern Japanese Civilization in History." *The Japan Interpreter* 1, no. 6 (Spring 1970): 29–44.

Katō Hiroyuki. "Kokutai shinron." In Yoshino Sakuzō, ed. *Meiji bunka zenshū: Jiyū minken hen.* Tokyo: Nihon hyōronsha, 1927.

Katsura Tarō. "Katsura Tarō jiden III". Unpublished material in the Kokuritsu kokkai toshokan, Kensei shiryōshitsu.

Kawai Eijirō. *Meiji shisōshi no ichi dammen: Kanai Noboru o chūshin toshite.* vol. 8. Reprinted in *Kawai Eijirō zenshū.* Tokyo: Shakai shisōsha, 1969.

Kawai Ichirō et al., eds. *Kōza: Nihon shihonshugi hattatsu shiron,* vol. 3: *Kyōkō kara sensō e.* Tokyo: Nihon hyōronsha, 1968.

Kawai Kazuo. *Japan's American Interlude.* Chicago: University of Chicago Press, 1960.

Kawakami Hajime. "Minponshugi to wa nanzoya." *Tōhō jiron* (October 1917).

Keene, Donald. "The Sino-Japanese War of 1894–95 and Its Cultural Effects in Japan." In Donald H. Shively, ed. *Tradition and Modernization in Japanese Culture.* Princeton, N.J.: Princeton University Press, 1971.

Keene, Donald. *The Japanese Discovery of Europe, 1720–1820.* Stanford, Calif.: Stanford University Press, 1969.

Keiō Gijuku, ed. *Fukuzawa Yukichi zenshū.* 21 vols. Tokyo: Iwanami shoten, 1962.

Kenpō chōsakai. *Kenpō seitei no keika ni kansuru shōiinkai hōkokusho.* (*Kenpō chōsakai hōkokusho fuzoku bunsho,* no. 2). Tokyo: Kenpō chōsakai, July 1964.

Kersten, Rikki. *Democracy in Postwar Japan: Maruyama Masao and the Search for Autonomy.* London and New York: Routledge, 1996.

Kinoshita Hanji. "Kokuminshugi undō no gendankai." *Chūōkōron* 615 (December 1938): 216–23.

Kisaka Jun'ichirō. *Shōwa no rekishi 7: Taiheiyō sensō.* Tokyo: Shōgakukan, 1989.

Kishimoto Eitarō and Koyama Hirotake, eds. *Nihon kindai shakai shisōshi.* Tokyo: Aoki shoten, 1959.

Kishimoto Eitarō and Koyama Hirotake. *Nihon no hikyōsantō marukusushugisha.* Tokyo: San'ichi shobō, 1962.

Kita Ikki. "Nihon kaizō hōan taikō." In *Gendai Nihon shisō taikei,* vol. 31: *Chōkokka shugi,* ed. Hashikawa Bunzō. Tokyo: Chikuma shobō, 1964.

Kitazawa Masakuni. "Ningen – sono botsuraku to saisei: Kyūshinteki kōzōshugi no ningenkan." *Tenbō*, no. 111 (March 1968): 16–36.

Kiyooka, Eiichi, trans. *The Autobiography of Fukuzawa Yukichi*. Tokyo: Hokuseidō Press, 1948.

Kojima Shuichi. "The Changing Japanese Perception of the Soviet Union as Seen in General Interest Magazines," *Konan Journal of Social Sciences*, vol. 2 (1988): 21–49.

Kōsaka Masaaki. *Shiken: Kitai sareru ningenzō*. Tokyo: Chikuma shobō, 1965.

Kōtoku Shūsui. *Hyōron to zuisō*. Tokyo: Jiyūhyōronsha, 1950.

Kōtoku Shūsui. "Shakaishugi no taisei." *Nihonjin*, August 20, 1900.

Kōtoku Shūsui. *Shakaishugi shinzui*. Tokyo: Iwanami shoten, 1955.

Kōtoku Shūsui. *Teikokushugi: Nijūseiki no kaibutsu*. Tokyo: Iwanami shoten, 1954.

Kokubun Ichitarō. *Shōgaku kyōshi no yūzai*. Tokyo: Misuzu shobō, 1984.

Konoe Fumimaro. "Against a Pacifism Centered on England and America." *Japan Echo* 22 (1995): 12–14.

Konoe Fumimaro. "Ei-Bei hon'i no heiwashugi o haisu." In Kitaoka Shin'ichi, ed. *Sengo Nihon gaikō ronshū*. Tokyo: Chūōkōronsha, 1995.

Konoe Fumimaro. *Sengo Ō-Bei kenbunroku*. Tokyo: Chūōkōronsha, 1981.

Koschmann, J. Victor. "The Debate on Subjectivity in Postwar Japan: Foundations of Modernism as a Political Critique." *Pacific Affairs* 54, no. 4 (Winter 1981–2): 609–31.

Koschmann, J. Victor. *Revolution and Subjectivity in Postwar Japan*. Chicago: University of Chicago Press, 1996.

Koyama Hirotake and Koyama Hitoshi. "Taishō shakaishugi no shisōteki bunka." *Shisō* 466 (April 1963): 119–30.

Koyama Hirotake and Sugimori Yasuji. "Rōnoha marukusushugi." In Sumiya Etsuji, ed. *Shōwa no hantaisei shisō*. Tokyo: Haga shobō, 1967.

Koyama Hirotake. "Nihon no marukusushugi no keisei." In Sumiya Etsuji, ed. *Shōwa no hantaisei shisō*. Tokyo: Haga shobō, 1967.

Koyama Hirotake. *Nihon marukusushugishi*. Tokyo: Aoki shoten, 1956.

Kublin, Hyman. *Asian Revolutionary: The Life of Sen Katayama*. Princeton, N.J.: Princeton University Press, 1964.

Kuki Shūzō. *"Iki" no kōzō*. Tokyo: Iwanami shoten, 1967.

Kume Kunitake, ed. *Bei-Ō kairan jikki*. 5 vols. Tokyo: Iwanami shoten, 1977.

Large, Stephen S. "Perspectives on the Failure of the Labour Movement in Prewar Japan." *Labour History* 37 (November 1979).

Large, Stephen S. *Organized Workers and Socialist Politics in Interwar Japan*. Cambridge, England: Cambridge University Press, 1981.

Lie, John. "Reactionary Marxism: The End of Ideology in Japan?" *Monthly Review* 38 (April 1987): 45–51.

Makise Kikue. "Kichi no mawari de no kikigaki." In Shisō no kagaku kenkyukai, ed. *Kyōdō kenkyū: Nihon senryō*. Tokyo: Tokuma shoten, 1972.

Maritain, Jacques. *Existence and the Existent* (1948). New York: Vintage, 1966.

Marshall, Byron K. *Capitalism and Nationalism in Prewar Japan: The Ideology of the Business Elite, 1868–1941*. Stanford, Calif.: Stanford University Press, 1967.

Marshall, Byron. *Academic Freedom and the Japanese Imperial University, 1868–1939*. Berkeley: University of California Press, 1992.

Maruyama Kanji. "Minshuteki keikō to seitō." *Nihon oyobi Nihonjin* (January 1913).

Maruyama Masao, Satō Noboru, and Umemoto Katsumi. *Sengo Nihon no kakushin shisō* (1966). Tokyo: Gendai no rironsha, 1983.

Maruyama Masao. "Chūsei to hangyaku." In *Kindai Nihon shisōshi kōza*. 8 vols. Tokyo: Chikuma shobō, 1960.

Maruyama Masao. "Fukuzawa Yukichi ni okeru 'jitsugaku' no tenkai." In Ishida Takeshi, ed. *Kindai Nihon shisō taikei 2: Fukuzawa Yukichi shū*. Tokyo: Chikuma shobō, 1975.

Maruyama Masao. "Fukuzawa Yukichi ni okeru chitsujo to ningen." "Fukuzawa Yukichi no tetsugaku." In Hidaka Rokurō, ed. *Gendai Nihon shisō taikei 34: Kindaishugi*. Tokyo: Chikuma shobō, 1964.

Maruyama Masao. "Kaidai." In Fukuzawa Yukichi chosaku hensankai, ed. *Fukuzawa Yukichi senshū*. Tokyo: Iwanami shoten, 1952.

Maruyama Masao. "Kindai Nihon no chishikijin." In *Kōei no ichi kara*. Tokyo: Miraisha, 1982.

Maruyama Masao. *Gendai seiji no shisō to kōdō*, exp. ed. Tokyo: Miraisha, 1966.

Maruyama Masao. *Nihon no shisō*, Iwanami Shinsho ed. Tokyo: Iwanami Shoten, 1961.

Maruyama Masao. *Nihon seiji shisōshi kenkyū*. Tokyo: Tokyo daigaku shuppankai, 1953.

Maruyama Masao. *Senchū to sengo no aida*. Tokyo: Misuzu shobō, 1976.

Maruyama Masao. "Patterns of Individuation and the Case of Japan: A Conceptual Scheme." In Marius B. Jansen, ed. *Changing Japanese Attitudes Toward Modernization*. Princeton, N.J.: Princeton University Press, 1965.

Maruyama Masao. *Studies in the Intellectual History of Tokugawa Japan*. Translated by Mikiso Hane. Princeton, N.J.: Princeton University Press, 1974.

Maruyama Masao. *Thought and Behaviour in Modern Japanese Politics*, expanded ed., ed. Ivan Morris. London: Oxford University Press, 1969.

Masaki Hiroshi. *Chikaki yori 5: Teikoku Nihon hōkai*. Tokyo: Shakai shisō sha, 1991.

Masamura Kimihiro. *Sengo shi*, vol. 2 Tokyo: Chikuma shobō, 1986.

Matsumoto Sannosuke. "Meiji zempanki hoshushugi shisō no ichi dammen." In Sakata Yoshio, ed. *Meiji zempanki no nashonarizumu.* Tokyo: Miraisha, 1958.

Matsumoto Sannosuke. "Ōkuma Nobuyuki ni okeru kokka no mondai." *Shisō,* no. 837 (March 1994): 4–39.

Matsumoto Sannosuke. *Kindai Nihon no chiteki jōkyō.* Tokyo: Chūōkōronsha, 1974.

Matsumoto Sannosuke. *Meiji seishin no kōzō.* Tokyo: Nihon hōsō kyōkai shuppankai, 1981.

Matsumoto Sannosuke. *Meiji shisō ni okeru kindai to dentō.* Tokyo: Tokyo daigaku shuppankai, 1996.

Matsumoto Sannosuke. *Meiji shisōshi.* Tokyo: Shin'yōsha, 1996.

Matsumoto Sannosuke. *Nihon seiji shisōshi gairon.* Tokyo: Keisō shobō, 1975.

Matsumoto Sannosuke. *Tennōsei kokka to seiji shisō.* Tokyo: Miraisha, 1969.

Matsunaga Shōzō. "Jiyūminken-ha ni mirareru shōkokushugi shisō." *Shichō* 89 (October 1964): 56–65.

Matsunaga Shōzō. *Nakae Chōmin no shisō.* Tokyo: Aoki shoten, 1970.

Matsunaga Shōzō. *Nakae Chōmin.* Tokyo: Kashiwa shobō, 1967.

Matsuo Takayoshi. "Katayama Sen, Miura Tetsutarō, Ishibashi Tanzan." In Takeuchi Yoshimi and Hashikawa Bunzō, eds. *Kindai Nihon to Chūgoku – ge.* Tokyo: Asahi shimbunsha, 1974.

Matsuo Takayoshi. *Taishō demokurashii no kenkyū.* Tokyo: Aoki shoten, 1966.

Matsushita Keiichi. "Taishū kokka no seiritsu to sono mondaisei" (1956). *Sengo seiji no rekishi to shisō,* Tokyo: Chikuma Shobō, 1994.

Matsushita Yoshio. *Meiji Taishō hansensō undōshi.* Tokyo: Sōbisha, 1949.

Matsuzawa Hiroaki. "Meiji shakaishugi no shisō." In Nihon seiji gakkai, ed. *Nihon no shakaishugi.* Tokyo: Iwanami shoten, 1968.

Matsuzawa Hiroaki. *Nihon shakaishugi no shisō.* Tokyo: Chikuma shobō, 1973.

Mayo, Marlene. "The Western Education of Kume Kunitake 1871–1876." *Monumenta Nipponica* 28 (1973): 3–68.

McKean, Margaret A. "Political Socialization Through Citizen's Movement." In Kurt Steiner, Ellis S. Krauss, and Scott Flanagan, eds. *Political Opposition and Local Politics in Japan.* Princeton, N.J.: Princeton University Press, 1980.

Meiji bunka zenshū. 24 vols. Tokyo: Nihon hyōronsha, 1927–30.

Meiji hennenshi hensankai, ed. *Shimbun shūsei: Meiji hennenshi.* 15 vols. Tokyo: Tōkyō zaisei keizai gakkai, 1934–6.

Meiroku zasshi: Journal of the Japanese Enlightenment. Translated by William R. Braisted. Cambridge, Mass.: Harvard University Press, 1976.

Miki Kiyoshi. "Kaishakugakuteki genshōgaku no kisogainen." In: Sumiya

Kazuhiko, ed. *Kindai Nihon shisō taikei*, vol. 27: *Miki Kiyoshi shū*. Tokyo: Chikuma shobō, 1975.

Miki Kiyoshi. Ōuchi Hyōe. ed. *Miki Kiyoshi zenshū*. vol. 3, Tokyo: Iwanami shoten, 1966–8.

Miller, Frank O. *Minobe Tatsukichi, Interpreter of Constitutionalism in Japan*. Berkeley and Los Angeles: University of California Press, 1965.

Minami Hiroshi. "Kōdō kagaku no seikaku to kadai." *Shisō*, no. 509 (November 1966): 28–41.

Minami Hiroshi. *Nihonjinron: Meiji kara konnichi made*. Tokyo: Iwanami shoten, 1994.

Minear, Richard H. *Japanese Tradition and Western Law: Emperor, State, and Law in the Thought of Hozumi Yatsuka*. Cambridge, Mass.: Harvard University Press, 1970.

Minobe Tatsukichi. "Waga gikai seido no zento." *Chūōkōron* 553 (January 1934): 2–14.

Minobe Tatsukichi. *Chikujō kenpō seigi*. Tokyo: Yuhikaku, 1927.

Minobe Tatsukichi. *Kenpō satsuyō*. Tokyo: Yuhikaku, 1926.

Mishima Yukio. "Bunka bōeiron." In Saeki Shōichi, ed. *Mishima Yukio zenshū*, vol. 33. Tokyo: Shinchōsha, 1973–6.

Mita Munesuke. *Gendai nihon no shinjō to ronri*. Tokyo: Chikuma shobō, 1971.

Mita Munesuke. *Social Psychology of Modern Japan*. London and New York: Kengan Paul International, 1992.

"Mitabi heiwa ni tsuite." *Sekai*, no. 60 (December 1950): 21–52. Abridged translation, "On Peace for the Third Time." Repr. in *Japan Echo*, no. 22 (1995): 21–31.

Mitani Ta'ichirō. "Shisōka toshite no Yoshino Sakuzō." In Mitani Ta'ichirō, ed. *Nihon no meicho 48: Yoshino Sakuzō*. Tokyo: Chūōkōronsha, 1972.

Mitani Ta'ichirō. "Taishō shakaishugisha no 'seiji' kan – 'seiji no hitei' kara 'seijiteki taikō' e." In Nihon seiji gakkai, ed. *Nihon no shakaishugi*. Tokyo: Iwanami shoten, 1968.

Mitani Ta'ichirō. *Taishō demokurashiiron*. Tokyo: Chūōkōronsha, 1974.

Mitchell, Richard H. *Thought Control in Prewar Japan*. Ithaca, N.Y.: Cornell University Press, 1976.

Mito-han shiryō. 5 vols. Tokyo: Yoshikawa kōbunkan, 1970.

Miwa Kimitada. *Matsuoka Yōsuke*. Tokyo: Chūōkōronsha, 1971.

Miyake Setsurei. *Dōjidaishi*. 6 vols. Tokyo: Iwanami shoten, 1949–54.

Miyazawa Toshiyoshi. "Meiji kempō no seiritsu to sono kokusai seijiteki haikei." In Miyazawa Toshiyoshi, ed. *Nihon kenseishi no kenkyū*. Tokyo: Iwanami shoten, 1968.

Miyazawa Toshiyoshi. *Tennō kikansetsu jiken*, 2 vols. Tokyo: Yūhikaku, 1970.

Miyoshi Masao. *As We Saw Them*. Berkeley and Los Angeles: University of California Press, 1979.

Monbushō. *Monbushō chosaku kyōkasho: Minshushugi.* Tokyo: Komichi shobō, 1995.

Moore, Barrington. *Social Origins of Dictatorship and Democracy: Lord and Peasant in the Making of the Modern World.* Boston: Beacon Press, 1967.

Morinaka Akimitsu, ed. *Niijima Jō sensei shokanshū zokuhen.* Kyoto: Dōshisha kōyūkai, 1960.

Morinaka Akimitsu, ed. *Niijima sensei shokanshū.* Kyoto: Dōshisha kōyūkai, 1942.

Morris-Suzuki, Tessa. *A History of Japanese Economic Thought.* London and New York: Routledge, 1989.

Muchaku Seikyō. *Yamabiko gakkō* (1951). Tokyo: Iwanami shoten, 1995.

Muragaki (Awaji no kami) Norimasa. *Kōkai nikki.* Tokyo: Jiji tsūshinsha, 1959.

Murakami Yasusuke, Kumon Shunpei, and Satō Seizaburō. *Bummei toshite no ie shakai.* Tokyo: Chūōkōronsha, 1979.

Murakami Yasusuke. "Ie Society as a Pattern of Civilization." *Journal of Japanese Studies* 10, no. 2 (Summer 1984): 279–363.

Murakami Yasusuke. "The Japanese Model of Political Economy." In Kozo Yamamura and Yasukichi Yasuba, eds. *The Political Economy of Japan.* Stanford, Calif.: Stanford University Press, 1987.

Murakami Yasusuke. *Shin chūkan taishū no jidai.* Tokyo: Chūōkōronsha, 1984.

Nagai Hideo. *Jiyū minken.* vol. 25 of *Nihon no rekishi.* Tokyo: Shogakkan, 1976.

Nagai Michio. "Mori Arinori." *Japan Quarterly* 11 (1964): 98–105.

Nagai Ryūtarō. *Kaizō no risō.* Tokyo, 1920.

Najita Tetsuo. "Nakano Seigō and the Spirit of the Meiji Restoration in Twentieth Century Japan." In James W. Morley, ed. *Dilemmas of Growth in Prewar Japan.* Princeton, N.J.: Princeton University Press, 1971.

Nakajima Makoto. *Sengo shisōshi nyūmon.* Tokyo: Ushio, 1968.

Nakamura Katsunori. *Meiji shakaishugi kenkyū.* Tokyo: Sekai shoin, 1966.

Nakamura Takafusa. *Shōwa shi,* vol. 2 Tokyo: Tōyō Keizai shinpōsha, 1993.

Nakayama Shigeru, David Swain, and Eri Yagi, eds. *Science and Society in Modern Japan: Selected Historical Sources.* Cambridge: MIT Press, 1974.

Naoi Michiko. "Kaisō ishiki to kaikyū ishiki." In Tominaga Ken'ichi, ed. *Nihon no kaisō kōzō.* Tokyo: Tōkyō daigaku shuppankai, 1979.

Nezu Masashi. *Tennō to Shōwashi, jō.* Tokyo: San'ichi shobō, 1976.

NHK hōsō yoron chōsajo, ed. *Gendai Nihonjin no ishiki kōzō.* (*NHK Books,* 344) NHK. Tokyo: Nihon hōsō shuppankai, 1979.

Nihon Daigaku Bunrigakubu Tōsō I'inkai Shokikyoku, ed. *Hangyaku no barikēdo.* Tokyo: San'ichi shobō, 1969.

Nishida Kitarō. *Zen no kenkyū.* Tokyo: Iwanami shoten, 1946.

Nishimura Kumao. *San Furanshisuko heiwa jōyaku*, vol. 27 of Kajima heiwa kenkyūjo, ed. *Nihon gaiko shi*. Tokyo: Kajima kenkyūjo shuppankai, 1971.

Nishio Yōtarō. *Kōtoku Shūsui*. Tokyo: Yoshikawa kōbunkan, 1959.

Nitobe Inazō. *Zenshū*, 16 vols. Tokyo: Kyōbunkan, 1969–70.

Norman, E. H. *Japan's Emergence as a Modern State: Political and Economic Problems of the Meiji Period*. New York: Institute of Pacific Relations, 1940 and later printings.

Norman, E. H. *Soldier and Peasant in Japan: The Origins of Conscription*. New York: Institute of Pacific Relations, 1943.

Notehelfer, F. G. *American Samurai: Captain L. L. Janes and Japan*. Princeton, N.J.: Princeton University Press, 1985.

Notehelfer, F. G. *Kōtoku Shūsui: Portrait of a Japanese Radical*. Cambridge, England: Cambridge University Press, 1971.

Nozoe Kenji. *Kikigaki: Hanaoka jiken*. Tokyo: Ocanomizu shobō, 1992.

Numata Jiro. "Shigeno Yasutsugu and the Modern Tokyo Tradition of Historical Writing." In W. G. Beasley and E. G. Pulleybank, eds. *Historians of China and Japan*. London: Oxford University Press, 1961.

Ōe Kenzaburō. "From the Ranks of Postwar Literature." Unpublished paper, presented at symposium, "1950–1983: The End of the Postwar Period?" University of California, Berkeley, 1983.

Ōe Kenzaburō. "*Kitai sareru ningenzō o hihan suru*" (1965). In *Sōzōryoku to jōkyō: Ōe Kenzaburō dōjidai ronshū*, vol. 3. Tokyo: Iwanami shoten, 1981. Orig. in *Bungei shunjū* (March 1965).

Ōe Kenzaburō. *Dōjidai gēmu*. Tokyo: Shinchōsha, 1979.

Ōkawa Shūmei. "Anraku no mon." "Kakumei Europpa to fukkō Ajia." In *Gendai Nihon shisō taikei*, vol. 9: *Ajia Shugi*, ed. Takeuchi Yoshimi. Tokyo: Chikuma shobō, 1964.

Ōkawa Shūmei. "Nihon seishin kenkyu." In *Gendai Nihon shisō taikei*, vol. 31: *Chōkokka shugi*, ed. Hashikawa Bunzō. Tokyo: Chikuma shobō, 1964.

Ōsawa Masamichi. *Ōsugi Sakae kenkyū*. Tokyo: Dōseisha, 1968.

Ōsugi Kazuo. *Nit-Chū jūgonen sensōshi*. Tokyo: Chūōkōronsha, 1996.

Ōtsuka Hisao. "Jan Karuvan [Jean Calvin]" (1947) and "Kindaiteki ningen ruikei no sōshutsu" (1946). Repr. in *Ōtsuka Hisao chosakushū*, vol. 8. Tokyo: Iwanami shoten, 1970.

Ōtsuka Hisao. *Kyōdōtai no kiso riron* (1955). Tokyo: Iwanami shoten, 1984.

Ōyama Ikuo. "Kokka seikatsu to kyōdō rigai kannen". *Shin shosetsu* (February 1917).

Ōyama Ikuo. "Rokoku kagekiha no jisseiryoku ni taisuru kashōshi to sono seiji shisō no kachi ni taisuru kadaishi." *Chūōkōron* 33 (May 1917).

Ōyama Ikuo. *Ōyama Ikuo zenshū*, vol. 1. Tokyo: Chūōkōronsha, 1947.

Odaka Toshirō and Matsumura Akira, eds. *Taionki, Ōritakushiba no ki, Rantō kotohajime*. vol. 95 of *Nihon koten bungaku taikei*. Tokyo: Iwanami shoten, 1964.

Oka Toshirō. "Kindai Nihon ni okeru shakai seisaku shisō no keisei to tenkai." *Shisō* 558 (December 1970): 69–88.

Oka, Yoshitake. "Generational Conflict after the Russo-Japanese War." In Tetsuo Najita and Victor Koschmann, eds. *Conflict in Modern Japanese History.* Princeton, N.J.: Princeton University Press, 1982.

Okakura Kakuzō. *Ideals of the East, with Special Reference to the Art of Japan.* Rutland, Vt.: Tuttle, 1970.

Ōkita Saburō, comp. *Postwar Reconstruction of the Japanese Economy* (September 1946). Tokyo: University of Tokyo Press, 1992.

Okumura Kiwao. "Henkaku-ki Nihon no seiji keizai." In *Kenryoku no shisō,* ed. Kamishima Jirō, vol. 10 of *Gendai Nihon shisō taikei.* Tokyo: Chikuma shobō, 1965, pp. 274–90.

Olson, Lawrence. *Ambivalent Moderns: Portraits of Japanese Cultural Identity.* Savage, Md.: Rowman and Littlefield, 1992.

Packard, George R., III. *Protest in Tokyo: The Security Crisis of 1960.* Princeton, N.J.: Princeton University Press, 1966.

Passin, Herbert. *Society and Education in Japan.* New York: Columbia University Press, 1965.

Peattie, Mark R. *Ishiwara Kanji and Japan's Confrontation with the West.* Princeton, N.J.: Princeton University Press, 1975.

Pierson, John D. *Tokutomi Sohō 1863–1957: A Journalist for Modern Japan.* Princeton, N.J.: Princeton University Press, 1980.

Pittau, Joseph. *Political Thought in Early Meiji Japan: 1868–1889.* Cambridge, Mass.: Harvard University Press, 1967.

Pyle, Kenneth B. "Advantages of Followership: German Economics and Japanese Bureaucrats, 1890–1925." *Journal of Japanese Studies* 1 (Autumn 1974): 127–64.

Pyle, Kenneth B. "The Ashio Copper Mine Pollution Case." *Journal of Japanese Studies* 1 (Spring 1975): 347–50.

Pyle, Kenneth B. "The Technology of Japanese Nationalism: The Local Improvement Movement, 1900–1918." *Journal of Japanese Studies* 33 (1973): 51–65.

Pyle, Kenneth B. *The New Generation in Meiji Japan: Problems of Cultural Identity, 1885–1895.* Stanford, Calif.: Stanford University Press, 1969.

Riesman, David, and Evelyn Thompson Riesman. *Conversations in Japan: Modernization, Politics, and Culture* (1967), Midway Reprint ed. Chicago: University of Chicago Press, 1976.

Ryan, Marleigh G. *Japan's First Modern Novel: Ukigumo of Futabatei Shimei.* New York: Columbia University Press, 1967.

Saigusa Hiroto. *Nihon no yuibutsuronsha.* Tokyo: Eihōsha, 1956.

Saitō Takao. *Saitō Takao seiji ronshū.* Izushi-machi, Izushi-gun, Hyōgo-ken: Saitō Takao sensei kenshōkai, 1961.

Sakata Yoshio. *Tennō shinsei.* Kyoto: shibunkaku, 1984.

Sakata Yoshio, and John W. Hall. "The Motivation of Political Leadership in the Meiji Restoration." *Journal of Asian Studies* 16 (November 1956): 31–50.

Sakuta Keiichi. "The Controversy over Community and Autonomy." In J. Victor Koschmann, ed. *Authority and the Individual in Japan: Citizen Protest in Historical Perspective.* Tokyo: University of Tokyo Press, 1974.

"San Furanshisuko kōwa; Chōsen sensō; 60-nen Anpo: Heiwa Mondai Danwakai kara Kenpō Mondai Kenkyūkai e." Interview with Maruyama Masao in *Sekai*, no. 615 (November 1995): 35–48.

Sansom, G. B. *The Western World and Japan.* New York: Knopf, 1950.

Sasakura Hideo. *Maruyama Masao ron nōto.* Tokyo: Misuzu shobō, 1988.

Satō Tatsuo. *Nihonkoku kenpō seiritsu shi,* 2 vols. Tokyo: Yūhikaku, 1962, 1964.

Scalapino, Robert A. "Ideology and Modernization: The Japanese Case." In David E. Apter, ed. *Ideology and Discontent.* New York: Free Press, 1964.

Scalapino, Robert A. *Democracy and the Party Movement in Prewar Japan: The Failure of the First Attempt.* Berkeley and Los Angeles: University of California Press, 1962.

Scalapino, Robert A. *The Japanese Communist Movement, 1920–1966.* Berkeley and Los Angeles: University of California Press, 1967.

Schwartz, Benjamin I. "Notes on Conservatism in General and on China in Particular." In Charlotte Furth, ed. *The Limits of Change: Essays on Conservative Alternatives in Republican China.* Cambridge, Mass.: Harvard University Press, 1976.

Senda Kakō, ed. *Tennō to chokugo no shōwashi.* Tokyo: Sekibunsha, 1983.

Shakai Kagaku Kenkyūjo no sanjūnen: Nenpyō, zadankai, shiryō. Tokyo: Tokyo daigaku shakai kagaku kenkyūjo, 1977.

"Shakai Kagaku Kenkyūjo." In Tokyo Daigaku Hyakunenshi Henshū I'inkai, comp., *Tokyo Daigaku hyakunenshi,* vol. 8. Tokyo: Tokyo daigaku shuppankai, 1987.

Shakai Mondai Kenkyūkai, ed. *Zengakuren kakuha.* Tokyo: Futabasha, 1969.

Shibagaki Kazuo. *Shōwa no rekishi 9: Kōwa kara kōdo seichō e.* Tokyo: Shōgakukan, 1989.

Shillony, Ben-Ami. *Politics and Culture in Wartime Japan.* Oxford, England: Clarendon Press, 1980.

Shimizu Ikutarō. "Shutaisei no kyakkanteki kōsatsu" (1947). Repr. in Hidaka Rokurō, ed. *Kindaishugi.* Tokyo: Chikuma shobō, 1964.

Shimizu Ikutarō. *Aikokushin.* Tokyo: Iwanami shoten, 1950.

Shimizu Masanori and Furihata Setsuo, eds. *Uno Kōzō no sekai: Marukusu riron no gendaiteki saisei.* Tokyo: Yūhikaku, 1983.

Shimomura Osamu. *Nihon keizai seichō ron.* Tokyo: Kin'yū Zaisei Jijō Kenkyūkai, 1962.

Shinano Kyōikukai, ed. *Shōzan zenshū.* Tokyo: Meiji bunken, 1975.

Shinobu Seizaburō, ed. *Nihon gaikō shi: 1853–1972.* 2 vols. Tokyo: Mainichi shimbunsha, 1974.

Shinohara Hajime and Miyazaki Ryūji. "Sengo kaikaku to seiji karuchā." In Tōkyō daigaku shakaikagaku kenkyūjo, ed. *Kadai to shikaku,* vol. 1: *Sengo kaikaku.* Tokyo: Tokyo daigaku shappankai, 1974–5.

Shinohara Hajime. *Gendai Nihon no bunka henyō: Sono seijigakuteki kōsatsu.* Tokyo: Renga shobō, 1971.

Shisō no Kagaku Kenkyūkai, ed. *Kyōdō kenkyū: Nihon senryō.* Tokyo: Tokuma shoten, 1972.

Shively, Donald H. "Motoda Eifu: Confucian Lecturer to the Meiji Emperor." In D. S. Nivison and A. F. Wright, eds. *Confucianism in Action.* Stanford, Calif.: Stanford University Press, 1959.

Shively, Donald H. "Nishimura Shigeki: A Confucian View of Modernization." In Marius B. Jansen, ed. *Changing Japanese Attitudes Toward Modernization.* Princeton, N.J.: Princeton University Press, 1965.

Shively, Donald H. "The Japanization of Middle Meiji." In Donald H. Shively, ed. *Tradition and Modernization in Japanese Culture.* Princeton, N.J.: Princeton University Press, 1971.

Shively, Donald H., ed. *Tradition and Modernization in Japanese Culture.* Princeton, N.J.: Princeton University Press, 1971.

Siemes, Johannes. *Hermann Roesler and the Making of the Meiji State.* Tokyo: Sophia University Press, 1966.

Sievers, Sharon Lee. "Kōtoku Shūsui, The Essence of Socialism: A Translation and Biographical Essay." Ph.D diss., Stanford University, 1969.

Silberman, Bernard, and Harootunian, H. D., eds. *Japan in Crisis: Essays on Taishō Democracy.* Princeton, N.J.: Princeton University Press, 1974.

Smethurst, Richard J. "The Military Reserve Association and the Minobe Crisis in 1935." In George M. Wilson, ed. *Crisis Politics in Prewar Japan: Institutional and Ideological Problems of the 1930s.* Tokyo: Sophia University Press, 1970.

Smethurst, Richard J. *A Social Basis for Prewar Japanese Militarism: The Army and the Rural Community.* Berkeley and Los Angeles: University of California Press, 1974.

Smith, Henry D., II. *Japan's First Student Radicals.* Cambridge, Mass.: Harvard University Press, 1972.

Smith, Thomas C. "Japan's Aristocratic Revolution." *Yale Review* 50 (March 1961): 370–83.

Smith, Thomas C. *Political Change and Industrial Development in Japan: Government Enterprise, 1868–1880.* Stanford, Calif.: Stanford University Press, 1955.

Sōseki zenshū. 34 vols. Tokyo: Iwanami shoten, 1956–7.

Spaulding, Robert. *Imperial Japan's Higher Civil Service Examinations.* Princeton, N.J.: Princeton University Press, 1967.

Stanley, Thomas A. *Ōsugi Sakae: Anarchist in Taishō Japan.* Cambridge, Mass.: Harvard University Press, 1982.

Storry, G. Richard. *Japan and the Decline of the West in Asia, 1894-1943.* New York: St. Martin's Press, 1979.

Storry, G. Richard. *The Double Patriots: A Study of Japanese Nationalism.* Boston: Houghton Mifflin, 1957.

Sugiyama Mitsunobu. *Shisō to sono sōchi,* 1: *Sengo keimō to shakai kagaku no shisō.* Shin'yōsha, 1983.

Sumiya Mikio. *Dai Nihon teikoku no shiren.* vol. 22 of *Nihon no rekishi,* Tokyo: Chūōkōronsha, 1965.

Sumiya Mikio. *Nihon no shakai shisō.* Tokyo: Tokyo daigaku shuppankai, 1968.

Tachibana Kōsaburō. "Nihon aikoku kakushin hongi." In *Gendai Nihon shiso taikei,* vol. 31: *Chōkokka shugi,* 32, ed. Hashikawa Bunzō. Tokyo: Chikuma shobō, 1964.

Takahashi Hisashi. "Tōa kyōdōtai ron." In Miwa Kimitada, ed. *Nihon no 1930 nendai.* Tokyo: Sōryūsha, 1980.

Takami Jun. "Kateiteki" (1950). In *Takami Jun zenshū,* vol. 10. Tokyo: Keisō shobō, 1971.

Takami Jun. *Haisen nikki.* Tokyo: Bungeishunjūsha, 1991.

Takashima Zen'ya. "Gendai shakai kagaku no ninmu." *Sekai,* no. 58 (October 1950): 33–43.

Takeuchi Yoshimi, and Kawakami Tetsutarō, eds. *Kindai no chōkoku.* Tokyo: Fūzambo, 1979.

Takeuchi Yoshimi. "Kindai no chōkoku" (1959) and "Kindaishugi to minzoku no mondai" (1951). In *Kindai no chōkoku.* Tokyo: Chikuma shobō, 1983.

Takeuchi Yoshimi. *Hōhō to shite no Ajia: Waga senzen, senchū, sengo.* Tokyo: Sōkisha, 1978.

Takeuchi Yoshitomo and Suzuki Tadashi. " '*Shinkō kagaku no hata no moto ni*' to '*Yuibutsuron kenkyū.*' " *Shisō* 465 (March 1963): 108–19.

Takeuchi Yoshitomo. *Shōwa shisōshi.* Tokyo: Minerva shobō, 1958.

Tamanoi Yoshirō, ed. *Bummei toshite no keizai.* Tokyo: Ushio shuppansha, 1973.

Tamanoi Yoshirō. "Uno keizaigaku no kōseki to genkai" (1977). In *Ekonomī to ekorojī: Kōgi no keizaigaku e no michi.* Tokyo: Misuzu shobō, 1986.

Tanabe Hajime. "Zettaimu no tachiba to yuibutsu benshōhō: Mori Kōichi-shi ni kotau" (1946). In *Tanabe Hajime chosakushū,* vol. 8. Tokyo: Chikuma shobō, 1963.

Tanabe Hajime. *Philosophy as Metanoetics,* trans. Takeuchi Yoshinori. Berkeley and Los Angeles: University of California Press, 1986.

Tanaka Akira. *Iwakura shisetsu dan.* Tokyo: Kōdansha, 1977.

Tanaka Nobumasa. *Dokyumento Shōwa tennō 4: Haisen, jō.* Tokyo: Rokufū shoten, 1987.

Tanaka Stefan. *Japan's Orient*. Berkeley: University of California Press, 1993.

Tanigawa Gan et al., eds., *Minshushugi no shinwa: Anpo tōsō no shisōteki sōkatsu*, 2nd ed. Tokyo: Gendai shichōsha, 1966.

Tanizaki Junichirō. *In Praise of Shadows*, trans. Edward Seidensticker and Thomas Harper. New Haven, Conn.: Leete's Island Books, 1977.

Teters, Barbara Joan. "A Liberal Nationalist and the Meiji Constitution." In Robert K. Sakai, ed. *Studies on Asia*. vol. 6. Lincoln: University of Nebraska Press, 1965.

Teters, Barbara Joan. "The Conservative Opposition in Japanese Politics, 1877–1894." Ph.D. diss., University of Washington, 1955.

Teters, Barbara Joan. "The Genro-In and the National Essence Movement." *Pacific Historical Review* 31 (1962): 359–78.

Tōa remmei dōshikai. "Shōwa ishin ron." In *Gendai Nihon shisō taikei*, vol. 31: *Chōkokka shugi*, ed. Hashikawa Bunzō. Tokyo: Chikuma shobō, 1964.

Tōdai Funsō Bunsho Kenkyūkai, ed. *Tōdai funsō no kiroku*. Tokyo: Nihon Hyōronsha, 1969.

Tōyama Shigeki. *Meiji ishin to gendai*. Tokyo: Iwanami shoten, 1968.

Tōyama Shigeki. "Mimpōten ronsō no seijishiteki kōsatsu." In Meiji shiryō kenkyū renrakukai, ed. *Minkenron kara nashonarizumu e*. Tokyo: Ochanomizu shobō, 1957.

Toda Shintarō. *Tennōsei no keizaiteki kiso bunseki*. Tokyo: San'ichi shobō, 1947.

Tokuda Kyūichi et al. "Jinmin ni uttau" (1945). Repr. in Hidaka Rokurō, ed. *Sengo shisō no shuppatsu*. Tokyo: Chikuma shobō, 1968.

Tokushū: Maruyama Masao. Gendai shisō 22, no. 1 (1994).

Tokyo nichinichi shinbunsha and Osaka nichinichi shinbunsha, eds. *Kaisetsu: Senjinkun*. Tokyo: Tokyo nichinichi shinbunsha, 1941.

Totten, George O., III, ed. *Democracy in Prewar Japan: Groundwork of Façade?* Lexington, Mass.: Heath, 1965.

Totten, George O., III. *The Social Democratic Movement in Prewar Japan*. New Haven, Conn.: Yale University Press, 1966.

Treat, P. J. *The Early Diplomatic Relations Between the United States and Japan, 1853 1868*. Baltimore: Johns Hopkins University Press, 1917.

Tsuda Sōkichi. *Bungaku ni arawaretaru waga kokumin no shisō*. Tokyo: Rakuyōdō, 1918–21.

Tsunoda, R., and de Bary, W. T., eds. *Sources of Japanese Tradition*. New York: Columbia University Press, 1958.

Tsuru Shigeto. "Kōdo seichō ron e no hansei." In *Tsuru Shigeto chosakushū*, vol. 4. Tokyo: Kōdansha, 1975.

Tsuru Shigeto. *Japan's Capitalism: Creative Destruction and Beyond*. Cambridge: Cambridge University Press, 1993.

Tsuru Shigeto. *Taisei henkaku no seiji keizaigaku*. Tokyo: Shin hyōron, 1983.

Tsuru Shigeto. *The Economic Development of Japan (Selected Essays,* Vol. II). New York: Edward Elgar, 1995.

Tsurumi Kazuko. *Social Change and the Individual.* Princeton: Princeton University Press, 1969.

Tsurumi Shunsuke. *A Cultural History of Postwar Japan, 1945–1980.* London and New York: Kegan Paul International, 1987.

Uchida Yoshiaki. *Vēbā to Marukusu: Nihon shakai kagaku no shisō kōzō.* Tokyo: Iwanami shoten, 1972.

Uchida Yoshihiko. "Japan Today and *Das Kapital.*" *Japan Interpreter* 6, no. 1 (Spring 1970): 8–28.

Uehara Senroku. "Minzoku ishiki no rekishiteki keitai." *Shisō,* no. 338 (August 1952).

Uehara Senroku. "Sokokuai to heiwa." *Dōtoku kyōiku* 52, no. 5.

Uesugi Shinkichi. *Teikoku kenpō chikujō kōgi.* Tokyo: Nihon hyōronsha, 1935.

Uete Michiari. *Nihon kindai shisō no keisei.* Tokyo: Iwanami shoten, 1974.

Ueyama Shunpei. *Dai Tōa sensō no imi.* Tokyo: Chūōkōronsha, 1964.

Ui Jun. "A basic theory of *kōgai*" (1972). Repr. in Nakayama Shigeru et al., ed. *Science and Society in Modern Japan: Selected Historical Sources.* Cambridge, Mass.: MIT Press, 1974.

Umegaki Michio. *After the Restoration: The Beginnings of Japan's Modern State.* New York: New York University Press, 1988.

Umemoto Katsumi. "Mu no ronri to tōhasei" (1948), 'Sengo seishin no kiten" (1968), "Shutaisei: Sengo yuibutsuron to shutaisei no mondai" (1960), "Shutaisei to kaiyūsei" (1948), "Shutaiseiron no gendankai" (1951), "Yuibutsu benshōhō to mu no benshōhō" (1948), "Yuibutsu shikan to dōtoku" (1948), and "Yuibutsuron to ningen" (1947). In *Umemoto Katsumi chosakushū,* vols. 1 & 2. Tokyo: San'ichi shobō, 1977.

Umesao Tadao. "Bummei no seitai shikan" (1957). Repr. in *Bummei no seitai shikan,* Tokyo: Chūōkōronsha, 1974. Abridged translation published as "Introduction to an Ecological View of History." *Japan Echo* 22 (1995): 42–50.

Umetani Noboru. *Oyatoi gaikokujin: Meiji Nihon no wakiyakutachi.* Tokyo: Nihon keizai shimbunsha, 1965.

Uno Kōzō. *Principles of Political Economy.* Atlantic Highlands, N.J.: Humanities Press, 1980.

Uno Kōzō. *Shihonron gojūnen.* Tokyo: Hōsei daigaku shuppankyoku, 1981.

Uno, Helen. *Kokai Nikki: The Diary of the First Japanese Embassy to the United States of America.* Tokyo: Foreign Affairs Association of Japan, 1958.

Usui Yoshimi, ed. *Anpo–1960.* Tokyo: Chikuma shobō, 1969.

Utsumi Aiko. *Chōsenjin B-C kyū senpan no kiroku.* Tokyo: Keisō shobō, 1982.

Wada Haruki. "Sengo Nihon ni okeru Shakai Kagaku Kenkyūjo no shuppatsu." *Shakai kagaku kenkyū* 32, no. 2 (August 1980): 216–32.

Wagner, Jeffrey Paul. "Sano Manabu and the Japanese Adaptation of Socialism." Ph.D. diss., University of Arizona, 1978.

Watanabe Haruo. *Nihon marukusushugi undō no reimei*. Tokyo: Aoki shoten, 1957.

Watanabe Hiroshi. "'Shinpo' to 'Chūka:' Nihon no bawai." In Mizoguchi Yūzō et al., eds. *Ajia kara kangaeru 5: Kindaika zō*. Tokyo: Tokyo daigaku shuppankai, 1994.

Watanabe Hiroshi. "'They Are Almost the Same as the Ancient Three Dynasties:' The West as Seen Through Confucian Eyes in Nineteenth-Century Japan." In Tu Wei-ming, ed. *Confucian Traditions in East Asian Modernity*. Cambridge, Mass.: Harvard University Press, 1996.

Watanabe Osamu. *Nihonkoku kenpō "kaisei" shi*. Tokyo: Nihon hyōronsha, 1987.

Watanabe Toru. "Nihon no marukusushugi undō ron." In *Kōza marukusushugi*, vol. 12. Tokyo: Nihon hyōronsha, 1974.

Watanabe Akio. "Japanese Public Opinion and Foreign Policy, 1964–1973." In Robert A. Scalapino, ed. *The Foreign Policy of Modern Japan*. Berkeley and Los Angeles: University of California Press, 1977.

Watanabe Hisamaru. "Shōchō tennōsei no seijiteki yakuwari." In Gotō Yasushi, ed. *Tennōsei to minshū*. Tokyo: Tōkyō daigaku shuppankai, 1976.

Watsuji Tetsurō. *Koji junrei*. Tokyo: Iwanami shoten, 1947.

Watsuji Tetsurō. *Nihon kodai bunka*. Tokyo: Iwanami shoten, 1920.

Watsuji Tetsurō. *Nihon seishinshi kenkyū*. Tokyo: Iwanami shoten, 1970.

Watsuji Tetsurō. *Climate*, trans. Geoffrey Bownas. Tokyo: Hokuseido Press, 1961.

Wilson, George M. *Radical Nationalist in Japan: Kita Ikki, 1883–1937*. Cambridge, Mass.: Harvard University Press, 1969.

Wilson, George M., ed. *Crisis Politics in Prewar Japan: Institutional and Ideological Problems of the 1930s*. Tokyo: Sophia University Press, 1970.

Yabe Teiji. *Yabe Teiji nikki*, vols. 1 & 2. Tokyo: Yomiuri shinbunsha, 1974.

Yamada Moritarō. "Nihon nōgyō no tokushusei" (1945), "Nōchi kaikaku no igi" (1948), and "Nōchi kaikaku katei kiroku no hitsuyōsei" (1948). In *Yamada Moritarō chosakushū*, vol. 3. Tokyo: Iwanami shoten, 1984.

Yamada Toshio. "Les tendances du marxisme japonais contemporain." In *Le marxisme au Japon*, special issue of *Actuel Marx*, no. 2 (1987): 34–44.

Yamaguchi-ken kyōikukai, ed. *Yoshida Shōin zenshū*. 11 vols. Tokyo: Iwanami shoten, 1934–6.

Yamaji Aizan. "Genji no shakai mondai oyobi shakaishugisha." In Kishimoto Eitarō, ed. *Shakaishugi shiron*. Tokyo: Aoki shoten, 1955.

Yamaji Aizan. "Niijima Jō ron." In Yamaji Aizan, *Kirisutokyō hyōron, Nihon jimminshi*. Tokyo: Iwanami shoten, 1966.

Yamakawa Hitoshi, "Tami o moto to sezaru Yoshino hakase to Ōyama Ikuo Shi no minponshugi" (1966), "Rōdō undō no shakaiteki igi" (1966),

"Rōdō undō ni taisuru chishiki kaikyū no chii" (1967), "Musan Kaikyū undō no hōkō tenkan" (1967), "'Kaizō Nihon' to musan kaikyū undō" (1968). In *Yamakawa Hitoshi zenshū*, ed. Yamakawa Kikue and Yamakawa Shinsaku, vols. 2–5. Tokyo: Keisō shobō.

Yamazumi Masumi. "Textbook Revision: The Swing to the Right." *Japan Quarterly* (October–December 1981): 472–8.

Yanagida Izumi. *Kinoshita Naoe*. Tokyo: Rironsha, 1955.

Yanagida Kunio. *Tōno monogatari*. Tokyo: Kyōdo kenkyūsha, 1938.

Yasuba Yasukichi. "Anatomy of the Debate on Japanese Capitalism." *Journal of Japanese Studies* 2 (Autumn 1975): 63–82.

Yasuda Tsuneo. *Nihon fuashizumu to minshū undō*. Tokyo: Renga shobō shinsha, 1979.

Yasuda Yojūrō. "Bunmei kaika no ronri no shūen." In Takeuchi Yoshimi and Kawakami Tetsutarō, eds. *Kindai no chōkoku*. Tokyo: Fūzanbō, 1979.

Yasuda Yojūrō. "Nihon no hashi." *Bungakukai* (October 1936).

Yasumaru Yoshio. *Nihon kindaika to minshū shisō*. Tokyo: Aoki shoten, 1974.

Yayama Taro. "The Newspapers Conduct a Mad Rhapsody over the Textbook Issue." *Journal of Japanese Studies* 9 (Summer 1983): 301–16.

Yoda Seiichi. "Sengo kazoku seido kaikaku to shinkazokukan no seiritsu." In *Kadai to shikaku*, vol. 1 of *Sengo kaikaku*, ed. Tōkyō daigaku shakaikagaku kenkyūjo. Tokyo: Tōkyō daigaku shuppankai, 1974–5.

Yoda Seiichi. "Senryō seisaku ni okeru fujin kaihō." In Nakamura Takafusa, ed. *Senryōki Nihon no keizai to seiji*. Tokyo: Tōkyō daigaku shuppankai, 1979.

Yokota Kisaburō. "Sensō hanzai to kokusaihō no kakumei." *Chūōkōron* (Janurary 1946): 31–40.

Yokota Kisaburō. *Sensō hanzai ron*. Tokyo: Yuhikaku, 1947.

Yokoyama Gen'nosuke. *Nihon no kasō shakai*. Tokyo: Kyōbunkan, 1899.

Yonehara Ken. *Ueki Emori*. Tokyo: Chūōkōronsha, 1992.

Yoshida Shigeru. *Kaisō jūnen*, 4 vols. Tokyo: Shinchōsha, 1957.

Yoshida Shigeru. *The Yoshida Memoirs*. New York: Houghton Mifflin, 1962.

Yoshimi Yoshiaki. *Jūgun ianfu*. Tokyo: Iwanami shoten, 1995.

Yoshimoto Takaaki (Ryūmei). "Maruyama Masao ron" (1962–3). In *Yoshimoto Takaaki zen chosakushū*, vol. 12. Tokyo: Keisō shobō, 1969.

Yoshimura Tōru. "Kōdō kagaku no gendaiteki igi." *Shisō*, no. 509 (November 1966): 1–17.

Yoshino Sakuzō. "Minponshugi, shakaishugi, kagekishugi." *Chūōkōron*. (June 1919).

Yoshino Kosaku. *Cultural Nationalism in Contemporary Japan*. London and New York: Routledge, 1994.

Yoshizawa Minami. *Betonamu sensō to Nihon*. Tokyo: Iwanami shoten, 1988.

Yuasa Yasuo. *Watsuji Tetsurō*. Kyoto: Minerva shobō, 1981.
Yui Masaomi. "Gunbu to kokumin tōgō." In *Fuashizumuki no kokka to shakai*, vol. 1 of *Shōwa kyōkō*, ed. Tōkyō daigaku shakaikagaku kenkyūjo. Tokyo: Tōkyō daigaku shuppankai, 1978.
"Zadankai: Yuibutsu shikan to shutaisei" (1948). Repr. in Hidaka Rokurō, ed. *Kindaishugi*. Tokyo: Chikuma shobō, 1964.

INDEX